DENG XIAOPING'S LONG WAR

THE NEW COLD WAR HISTORY
Odd Arne Westad, editor

This series focuses on new interpretations of the Cold War era made possible by the opening of Soviet, Eastern European, Chinese, and other archives. Books in the series based on multilingual and multiarchival research incorporate interdisciplinary insights and new conceptual frameworks that place historical scholarship in a broad, international context.

DENG XIAOPING'S
LONG WAR

The Military Conflict between China and
Vietnam, 1979–1991

XIAOMING ZHANG

The University of North Carolina Press CHAPEL HILL

Designed and set in Minion and Gotham types by Rebecca Evans
Manufactured in the United States of America
The paper in this book meets the guidelines for permanence and durability
of the Committee on Production Guidelines for Book Longevity of the
Council on Library Resources. The University of North Carolina Press
has been a member of the Green Press Initiative since 2003.

Jacket illustrations: Deng Xiaoping, as the new chair of the CMC,
reviewing the PLA forces after they completed a joint war exercise, June
1981 (cpc.people's.com.cn); PLA artillery positions on the Guangxi front,
1979 (Courtesy Xiaobing Li); background paper © depositphotos.com /
robynmac

Library of Congress Cataloging-in-Publication Data
Zhang, Xiaoming, 1951–
Deng Xiaoping's long war : the military conflict between China and
Vietnam, 1979–1991 / Xiaoming Zhang.
pages cm. — (The New Cold War History)
Includes bibliographical references and index.
ISBN 978-1-4696-2124-1 (cloth : alk. paper)
ISBN 978-1-4696-2125-8 (ebook)
1. Sino-Vietnamese Conflict, 1979. 2. Deng, Xiaoping, 1904–1997—
Military leadership. I. Title.
DS559.916.Z48 2015   959.704'4—dc23
2014037021

Portions of this work have appeared previously, in somewhat different
form, as "China's War with Vietnam: A Reassessment," *China Quarterly*
184 (December 2005), © 2005 *China Quarterly*, reprinted by permission
of Cambridge University Press, and "Deng Xiaoping and China's Decision
to Go to War with Vietnam," *Journal of Cold War Studies* 12, no. 3
(Summer 2010).

For Shengli Fang and Connie H. Zhang

Contents

Maps and Illustrations

Maps

Illustrations

Acknowledgments

I could not have completed this book without the institutional and financial support I have received. In particular, I thank the Air University Foundation for a grant that enabled me to do research in China in the summer of 2007 and the Air War College for a 2010–11 sabbatical that allowed me to finish an initial draft of the book.

Richard Hallion, Robert Ross, and two anonymous readers read the entire manuscript, while Andrew Scobell and Odd Arne Westad read an earlier vision of the manuscript and provided with critical comments and suggestions. In addition, Hallion, a mentor and friend, also did extensive editorial work on the manuscript. I am forever in his debt. Numerous individuals have helped me develop the Vietnamese side of my story. In particular, Merle Pribbenow provided translations of many Vietnamese-language materials and shared his knowledge and insights on the Vietnamese records. Li Danhui and Shen Zihua never tired of sharing newly available Chinese documents from their research.

I also thank the friends, colleagues, and fellow scholars who either have read and commented on parts of the manuscript at various stages or have supported me in other valuable ways: Cai Pengcen, Chao Lihua, Dai Chaowu, David Graff, Amid Gupta, Liu Lei, Martin Loicano, Lü Zhaoyi, Tao Liang, Arthur Waldron, Yu Weimin, and Zhai Qiang. My special thanks go to Shao Xiao, a history PhD student at East China Normal University and now a faculty member at Lingnan University, who patiently and efficiently helped me collect numerous Chinese publications. I also thank Wang Huazhang, a war veteran, for allowing me to use photos from his personal collections.

The staffs of several libraries offered essential assistance: the Jimmy Carter Presidential Library and Museum; the Yunnan Provincial Archives; the Shanghai Library; and the libraries of the Air University, East China Normal University, and Yunnan University. Members of the University of North Carolina Press editorial staff deserve great credit for their assistance in publishing this book. Cecelia Cancellaro, a freelance copy editor, did a superlative job, saving me from more mistakes than I can enumerate.

I owe a great deal to my wife, Shengli Fang, and daughter, Connie, who have tolerated my absence and inattention while I was researching and writing this study. I could not have completed it without their support and understanding of how much this book means to me.

A word on orthography: I employed the Pinyin form of romanizing the names of all Chinese persons and places, with the exception of Chiang Kai-shek. Apostrophes are used occasionally to help with pronunciation. The spelling of Vietnamese personal and place names follows the commonly accepted forms used in English-language literature on Vietnam (e.g., Ho Chi Minh, Le Duan, Ngo Dien Diem, Hanoi, Cao Bang, and Lang Son). Uncommon Vietnamese place names are taken from Vietnamese maps, with the assistance of the *Tu Dien Han-Viet Hien Dai* (Modern Chinese-Vietnamese Dictionary).

Abbreviations

AAA	antiaircraft artillery
ASEAN	Association of Southeast Asian Nations
CCP	Chinese Communist Party
CIA	Central Intelligence Agency
CMC	Central Military Commission
DRV	Democratic Republic of Vietnam
GLD	General Logistics Department
GPD	General Political Department
NATO	North Atlantic Treaty Organization
NLF	National Liberation Front
PAVN	People's Army of Vietnam
PLA	People's Liberation Army
PLAAF	People's Liberation Army Air Force
PLAN	People's Liberation Army Navy
POW	prisoner of war
PRC	People's Republic of China
SALT	Strategic Arms Limitation Talks
SAM	surface-to-air missile
SRV	Socialist Republic of Vietnam
UN	United Nations
USSR	Union of Soviet Socialist Republics
VCP	Vietnamese Communist Party

DENG XIAOPING'S LONG WAR

MAP 1 China

Introduction

In mid-February 1979, the world was shocked when military forces from the People's Republic of China (PRC) suddenly invaded the Socialist Republic of Vietnam (SRV). To many outsiders, the two nations seemed firm allies, and the invasion was all the more surprising because, in the words of the Chinese leadership in Beijing, the PRC had gone to war to "teach Vietnam a lesson" it would not soon forget. For the next twenty-nine days, China's People's Liberation Army (PLA) fought fiercely against Vietnam's army and militia. Though the Vietnamese fought doggedly, slowing the PLA's advance and inflicting heavy casualties, the Chinese army steadily ground down its opposition, breaking through Vietnam's hastily established defensive lines. The border region was devastated as the military rampage destroyed civilian infrastructure and leveled three provincial capitals. The invasion ended with Beijing claiming victory. The two communist nations, once called "brother plus comrade," then entered a more-than-decade-long enmity with further bloodshed along their borders.

Background of a Border War

Since the founding of the People's Republic in 1949, China has been involved in two large-scale wars—one in Korea against the United States, South Korea, and its United Nations allies, and the other against Vietnam in 1979. Beginning in the late 1980s, much was written about the PRC's involvement in the Korean War thanks to a more relaxed political atmosphere in the era of Deng Xiaoping and his successors and the release of many important documents. Coincidentally, in the early 1990s, many documents from the former Soviet Union also became available, casting new light on that nation's role in the Korean conflict.[1]

Regrettably, however, the war with Vietnam has become forgotten history in China as a result of the government's ongoing sensitivity regarding the subject. Current public knowledge and understanding about why China attacked Vietnam differs little from that at the time of the invasion—that is, the war against Vietnam was a self-defense counterattack conducted by PLA border defense forces in response to Vietnamese "hegemonic ambitions and provocations" along the border.[2]

Cold War historians have largely overlooked the fact that the war between China and Vietnam fractured the intimate relationship between the two countries that had existed for more than two decades. Instead, scholars have focused on the rivalry between the two superpowers—the United States and the Soviet Union—from the late 1940s to the early 1970s. Indeed, the last decade of the Cold War witnessed several conflicts involving communist countries, including the Vietnamese invasion of Democratic Kampuchea (Cambodia), the PRC invasion of the SRV, and the Soviet invasion of Afghanistan. But China's attack on Vietnam most shocked the international community. In particular, it roiled ideologues in the communist world who had traditionally argued (according to Marxist ideology) that war was invariably the product of imperialism and, therefore, that socialist countries would not fight each other.[3] Perhaps even more shocking was the idea that, as with China's border wars with India in 1962 and with the Soviet Union in 1969, China, not its opponents, had chosen to escalate the crisis and resort to the use of force.

Why did China attack Vietnam in 1979? Beijing's immediate answer to this question was that a variety of provocations had forced the PRC to take action against Hanoi's hegemonistic "imperial dreams" in Southeast Asia: SRV violations of China's borders and incursions into Chinese territory; the mistreatment of ethnic Chinese living in Vietnam; and Vietnam's increasing intimacy with the Soviet Union, which at the time was extending its sphere of influence into Southeast Asia.[4]

The official rationale gave no satisfactory answer to historians and analysts looking for deeper explanations. Existing studies offer a variety of arguments—Beijing's true objectives involved diverting Hanoi's military pressure away from Cambodia and tying down its forces on a second front; Beijing sought to discredit the Soviet Union as a reliable ally in response to a new Vietnamese-Soviet treaty relationship.[5] However, all of these interpretations suffered from a lack of documentation from both the PRC and the SRV.

Previous Scholarship on the War

Existing scholarship on the Sino-Vietnamese conflict can be categorized into two groups: scholarly works written prior to the end of the Cold War, and those that have emerged since 2000. Attempting to rationalize China's invasion of Vietnam, Gerald Segal's *Defending China* (1985) questioned the new Chinese leadership's intelligence in light of its seemingly rash and arrogant decisions regarding Vietnam's "superior military power."[6] King C. Chen's *China's War with Vietnam* (1987) posited a contrary view, arguing that Deng Xiaoping made a reasonable and sophisticated decision after lengthy consideration and repeated debates within the PRC leadership over domestic and international problems.[7] Robert Ross's *The Indochina Tangle* (1988) identified the foremost concern in China's decision to attack Vietnam as the potential Soviet threat rather than a border dispute or any other differences.[8] William Duiker's *China and Vietnam* (1986) depicted the Sino-Vietnamese conflict as stemming from the troubled relationship between the two communist countries during the First and Second Indochina Wars, which prompted Vietnam to ally with the Soviet Union against China in 1978.[9]

After the turn of the century, a resurgence of interest in China's strategic outlook and the logic behind its use of force has yielded several new and important studies about the war with Vietnam. The most representative are Andrew Scobell's *China's Use of Military Force* (2003), John Wilson Lewis and Xue Litai's *Imagined Enemies* (2006), and Li Xiaobing's *A History of the Chinese Modern Army* (2007).[10] A common feature of these studies is their treatment of this subject within a much broader analysis of Chinese strategic culture, China's national approach to war, and military modernization efforts. The only book devoted exclusively to the study of the Sino-Vietnamese conflict is Edward C. O'Dowd's *Chinese Military Strategy in the Third Indochina War* (2007), which argues that the PLA's poor and ineffective performance precluded China from achieving the strategic objective of evicting Vietnam from Cambodia.[11]

Three other notable scholarly efforts studying the Sino-Vietnamese conflict are Brantly Womack's *China and Vietnam* (2006), Sophie Richardson's *China, Cambodia, and the Five Principles of Peaceful Coexistence* (2009), and Nicholas Khoo's *Collateral Damage* (2011).[12] While stressing that "misperceptions in asymmetric relations" contributed to "implacable enmity" between China and Vietnam for twenty-five years, Womack argues that the Sino-Vietnamese conflict eventually ended because of Vietnam's "persistent and imaginative small country diplomacy."[13] Richardson contends that since 1979, the post-Mao Chinese leadership placed Cambodia at the center of China's foreign relations, resulting in Beijing not only delaying normalization of the PRC-USSR and PRC-SRV relations but also "actually compromising both economic development and territorial security."[14] Khoo presents an analytical explanation of the emergence of Sino-Vietnamese conflict in the 1970s, treating animosity between these two former allies as "collateral damage" caused by deteriorating Sino-Soviet relations since the early 1960s.

Issues, Inquiries, and Contentions

This book addresses many of the questions that other scholars of modern Chinese studies and international security have asked but adds insights from new and previously unavailable documentation and evidence from China. These questions include: Why did the PRC attack the SRV in 1979? What were Beijing's objectives in the 1979 invasion and in its border conflict with the SRV during the 1980s? What factors eventually contributed to the conclusion of the Cold War between the two communist countries in Asia? It retraces the thirteen years of hostility between China and Vietnam, arguing that two countries' previously intimate relationship was far more fragile than it appeared. The Chinese and Vietnamese had expressed ethnic bitterness and hatred toward each other for centuries. The Sino-Vietnamese alliance was formed largely because at the time they shared a common enemy: the United States. The alliance was doomed to collapse beginning in the late 1960s, when Beijing came to regard the Soviet Union, not the United States, as the greatest enemy.

The 1978 USSR-SRV alliance prompted Beijing to perceive Hanoi as a convenient proxy for Soviet expansionism in Southeast Asia. More important, such a change in the geopolitical landscape convinced Beijing's leaders that China's physical security was in jeopardy, which also meant that China's newly adopted national priority—economic reform—would likewise be threatened by the increasingly unfavorable security environment. Chinese leaders inevitably attached domestic considerations to the nation's external policies and foreign relations, rationalizing that going to war against Vietnam would help the PRC forge a new anti-Soviet strategic relationship with Western countries. In return for buttressing the West's anti-Soviet position, Beijing would receive a dividend in the form of technological and financial support for Deng Xiaoping's modernization program.

The conflict between China and Vietnam resulted in the largest military operation conducted by the PLA outside China's borders. This study also examines questions about the PLA's role and performance in the conflict to understand how Beijing resorted to force to achieve these international and domestic objectives. It includes a discussion of Chinese military strategy and preparations for the attack as well as the PLA's views of military operations. In addition, the study explores the conflict's political and military repercussions and the lessons learned by the Chinese themselves. Though roughly handled by the Vietnamese in the border conflicts, the PLA accomplished Beijing's strategic goals by diverting Vietnam's attention to the new military pressure on its northern border, which in turn undercut Vietnam's adventurism in Southeast Asia.

Yet the war also exposed many shortcomings and weaknesses within the PLA, revealing it as an anachronistic force with outdated combat experience; poorly trained soldiers; an obsolete air force and navy; and a bloated, over-staffed, and cumbersome command and control system.[15] Addressing questions about what happened on the battlefield not only helps us understand the PRC's way of fighting a war but also reveals the Chinese leaders' proclivity for using force against foreign threats for domestic purposes. Overall, the 1979 war with Vietnam greatly increased Deng Xiaoping's leverage to rally both civilian and military support for his economic development programs. This study thus weaves the discourse of the Sino-Vietnamese military conflict and its consequences into the larger history of China over the dramatic years since 1978. In short, while the war with Vietnam affected Sino-Vietnamese relations, it dramatically influenced the domestic balance of power between civil and military institutions within China in favor of economic development.

Last but far from least, from an international security perspective, the Sino-Vietnamese conflict shaped the Cold War by decisively tilting the balance against the Soviet Union in the 1980s. The end of the Vietnam War meant that the United States was no longer a major presence in Southeast Asia. However, in the wake of the growing hostility between China and the Soviet Union—as well as the latter's ally, Vietnam—Beijing's new strategic relationship with Washington enabled the United States to reenter the region, resulting in the emergence of a new structure of international relations that maintained a de facto regional balance of power. Fearing Vietnam's growing regional hege-mony, few countries in Southeast Asia protested China's invasion or its support of the ousted (and notorious) Pol Pot regime. In Cambodia, China's military conflict with Vietnam not only enabled the Khmer Rouge to survive but also prevented Western-oriented Thailand from falling into the Vietnamese sphere of influence. As China and the United States faced the same enemy—the So-viet Union—relations between Beijing and Washington steadily improved after 1979, with the United States providing China with advanced technology and even weapons systems. Although the two countries never formed an official alliance, they worked together against Soviet nuclear programs (for example, setting up joint electronic listening stations in northwestern China) and the Soviet invasion of Afghanistan. Geopolitical and security concerns no doubt provided the primary raison d'être for China's February–March 1979 invasion of Vietnam and the continuing border clashes throughout the 1980s. However, domestic economic reform and the need to reform the PLA also justified the decision to use force against Vietnam. Beijing's quest for economic reform, requiring a policy of openness to the outside world, improved China's international strategic position, ensuring that the Chinese leadership maintained an uncompromising stance against the Soviet Union, which, in turn, ensured that they remained uncompromising regarding Vietnam's hegemonic desires. Although the PLA's performance on the battlefield generated mixed outcomes, the war produced the kind of strategic outcomes Deng had desired and anticipated, including the most critical long-term benefit he sought—that is, Beijing's hostility toward both Hanoi and Moscow so altered the nature of the Cold War superpower rivalry that it facilitated the ultimate defeat of the Soviet Union, eliminating what had been a serious threat to the PRC's security.

Deng Xiaoping and the Sino-Vietnamese Conflict

China waged its war against Vietnam in the midst of a new round of power struggles in Beijing, as the recently reinstated Deng Xiaoping ascended to the top of the Chinese Communist Party (CCP). For the first time in PRC history, the PLA went to war not under its founding father, Mao Zedong, but under Deng Xiaoping, a longtime protégé of the deceased chairman. Unlike Mao, Deng served only as vice chair of the CCP and the Central Military Commission (CMC), the highest military command organ for the PLA. Deng, however, had the final word on national security issues, while other leaders who served with him acted more like his assistants than decision makers. But what roles did Deng play in China's war against Vietnam, and to what extent did his wisdom match—or fail to match—that of his predecessors? Was the Sino-Vietnamese military conflict inevitable no matter who was leading China during the last stage of the Cold War? The existing literature on Deng Xiaoping focuses primarily on his role in China's economic reform and opening-up policy, overlooking his role in China's attack on Vietnam and its consequences.[16]

In the CCP's bureaucratic tradition, the Politburo and its Standing Committee have the sovereign and ultimate command of going to war, while the CMC exerts authority over the Chinese military only after the Politburo and its Standing Committee have made their decision. But Deng's senior status and long military career within the CCP enabled him to act above these institutions. With support from both party oligarchs and the PLA's veteran generals, he emerged in the latter part of 1978 as the true architect of China's domestic and foreign policies. Deng's foreign policy continued on in Mao's footsteps, with the Soviet Union designated as China's primary enemy. Deng went further, however, by associating Vietnam's anti-China policies and acts—such as the new alliance between Moscow and Hanoi and the SRV's invasion of Cambodia—with the Soviet Union's increasing menace to China's national security. At the time, Deng believed that Soviet hegemony posed a very real and increasing danger to the world and that the United States was not responding with sufficient firmness. He believed that China's attack on Vietnam would constitute Beijing's major contribution to promoting an international united front against hegemony.

Deng also felt that China was being pinched between a Soviet threat from the north and a Vietnamese threat from the south, thereby endangering China's "Four Modernizations" (of industry, agriculture, science, and national defense). Facing a dire economic situation at home, Deng replaced Mao's radical policies with "reform and opening-up" (*gaige kaifang*). He believed that if China did not take military action against Vietnam (the self-proclaimed "world's third-strongest military power"), both Moscow and Hanoi would become increasingly aggressive along China's border, creating an undesirable disturbance and distraction that would negatively affect Chinese economic development. Moreover, Deng saw a corollary that could be used to justify China's military action against Vietnam: Beijing's use of force against Vietnam, an old enemy of Washington and a close ally of Moscow, would convince Western countries that China was a reliable and responsible country with strategic value, worthy of being an ally in their struggle against Soviet hegemonic expansion. He concluded that the West, especially the United States, would surely reward China with the financial and technological assistance that was critical to Beijing's economic development programs. The attractiveness of this rationale ensured that any negative repercussions—such as Beijing's support of the genocidal Khmer Rouge—were of little consequence to Deng.

Since Mao's death in 1976, intense factionalism and power struggles had riven the PRC's leadership, taking attention away from the nation's other challenges, particularly economic reform. The party and government bureaucracy, which was unwieldy and overstaffed with many who rose up during the Cultural Revolution, was perceived as a major obstruction to economic reform. Deng understood that the war with Vietnam provided him with the best means to mobilize the whole nation. He especially needed the PLA, the backbone of the CCP's power, to go along with his economic reform program.

However, by the late 1970s, the PLA was not the same army that had brought the CCP into power in 1949; it was overextended, obsolescent, ill-trained, and poorly equipped. And as a result of its participation in the Cultural Revolution, it had lost the respect and affection of the Chinese people and gained notoriety for abusing power. Deng mulled over two additional considerations: military action would help reinstate the PLA's legendary fame and glory and enable the PLA to regain lost combat skills and expertise, which he perceived as vital for the war with the Soviet Union that he expected to erupt by the mid-1980s. The PLA's poor performance on the battlefield in Vietnam validated his concerns and allowed him to reorganize the army immediately after the war, resulting in a major shift in power in Beijing.

Deng's solid control of the party, the government, and the PLA allowed him to curb disruptive and factional infighting and bring the army around to his way of thinking regarding matters such as modernization and strategy. With the PLA's support for his domestic programs and opening-up policy, Deng led the nation in the quest to achieve the Four Modernizations and economic development. In 1985, when the country needed to spend more funds on economic development, Deng convinced the PLA to accept a drastic decrease in military spending.[17]

Deng's strength of personality played a major role in shaping China's foreign policy. According to Mao, Deng had a character of "steel," making him unwilling to compromise and difficult to get along or even work with.[18] China's decision to go to war with Vietnam was certainly affected by his perception of the Soviet threat, which was both genuine and perilous, as well as his perception that the United States was too soft in its dealings with the Soviet Union. Deng always possessed and exhibited an underlying toughness in pursuing China's national interests. He was intransigent about China's Vietnam policy because he believed that the hostile relationship between the two countries resulted solely from Hanoi's anti-China policies. Consequently, after the 1979 war and throughout the 1980s, China maintained a rigid and tough position toward Vietnam, making no policy changes until Hanoi acknowledged its mistakes and accepted Deng's regional security model/framework—a neutral Southeast Asia—considered critical to China's national interests.

A political realist, he believed, "It doesn't matter whether a cat is white or black, as long as it catches mice." Consequently, he shaped China's foreign policy on the basis of shrewd pragmatism, not blind ideology. Underscoring economic reform as the nation's top priority, Deng was interested in improving and strengthening relations with countries from which China's economy could benefit. Beijing's hostile relations with Moscow, especially Hanoi, did not matter very much in China's domestic development programs. What mattered more to the Chinese leadership were the principles of sovereignty and territorial integrity with respect to Cambodia, the Sino-Soviet border, and Afghanistan. Deng would end China's animosity toward the Soviet Union and Vietnam only if Moscow and Hanoi capitulated to these principles—that is, if Vietnam withdrew from Cambodia and the Soviets pulled their military away from the Chinese border and out of Afghanistan.

Deng neither ordered the PLA to cease military operations on Vietnam's northern border nor approved the Vietnamese leadership's visit to China (to negotiate the resumption of a relationship between the two countries) until after the collapse of the Eastern European communist bloc in 1990. The winding down of the Cold War in Europe placed Hanoi in an awkward position, and it became increasingly concerned about the survival of communism in Vietnam itself. Hanoi's acceptance of Beijing's position on Cambodia—a prerequisite for the return of normalcy between the two countries—was inevitable. Given Deng's overwhelming commanding power within PRC leadership circles, war with Vietnam in 1978–79 became unavoidable once Deng had ascended to the PRC's supreme leadership position. Thus, the Sino-Vietnamese conflict can rightly be called Deng Xiaoping's War, and it became one of the longest conflicts fought during the Cold War.

Structure, Focus, and Implications

This eight-chapter book begins with an overview (chapter 1) of the PRC's involvement in Vietnam to lay a foundation for a further analysis of the Sino-Vietnamese conflict in a historical context. Focusing on the 1960s and 1970s, the chapter discusses the distrust and suspicion between the Chinese and the Vietnamese that may have been a reflection of an undercurrent of tension between Beijing and Hanoi during the wars against France and the United States. After many years of committing China's resources to Hanoi's war effort, the Chinese had created for themselves a new enemy, as the two countries later engaged in a conflict lasting more than a decade. The second chapter examines Beijing's management of its deteriorating relationship with Vietnam in 1978, focusing on how the decision to go to war was based on strategic thinking that perceived a Soviet-Vietnamese partnership as a threat to Chinese security and Sino-American cooperation as a means to improve the PRC's strategic position and facilitate economic reform with U.S. support. Because China's war decision was based on the belief that a Chinese attack on a Soviet ally served China's vital domestic and international interests, there was little possibility that the Sino-Vietnamese armed conflict could have been averted.

Chapters 3 and 4 examine how the PLA planned for battle against Vietnam, including Chinese military strategy, preparations for the attack, and the PLA's views of military operations. Chapter 5 reviews the conflict's political and military repercussions and the lessons learned according to the Chinese themselves. Chapter 6 provides an account of the border conflicts in the 1980s, analyzing how China pursued a policy of "bleeding Vietnam white" through international isolation and threats of military force while using these conflicts to provide combat training for more PLA troops. Chapter 7 scrutinizes how the border conflicts affected the social and economic development of two border provinces, Guangxi and Yunnan, and how the PLA used the conflicts to stimulate military modernization and to rebuild its reputation. This chapter also discusses how Chinese media, including literature, movies, and music, covered the conflict and how these cultural artifacts of war influenced Chinese society in the 1980s. The last chapter covers the events leading to the cessation of hostilities and the restoration of normality between China and Vietnam from the late 1980s through early 1990s. It illustrates how Deng still played hardball with the new Vietnamese leadership (which sought to improve Vietnam's relationship with China), forcing Hanoi to acknowledge its policy mistakes and to accept Beijing's terms for the resumption of their relations at the same time the communist world was collapsing.

Overall, this book bridges the gap between studies that focus too narrowly on the 1979 war and studies that look too broadly at Sino-Vietnamese relations. Based on research in recently declassified Chinese materials and memoirs by Chinese political and military leaders and veterans, this book adds a new dimension to the literature of modern Chinese foreign policy and military and international security. It addresses issues such as policy behavior; decision making; military planning; command and control; fighting and politics; combat tactics and performance; the role of the Beijing leadership, particularly Deng Xiaoping; scale and typologies of fighting; and the influences and legacies of the conflict. China's war with Vietnam not only remains relevant to the Chinese military institution and to our understanding of China's use of military force but also sheds light on contemporary discussions of China's role in the Asian-Pacific region and beyond as the PLA's military potential has grown significantly. Important continuities in PLA strategy and tactics and in China's approach to warfare began in the 1979 war with Vietnam and remain true in the twenty-first century. The PLA, for example, still uses Mao's and Deng's military thoughts as guidance for their current strategy and tactics, and the Chinese military remains an armed force under the party's control based on political propaganda and indoctrination. The unique characteristics of China's approach to warfare were apparent in 1979 and remain central today.

A Note on Chinese Sources Relevant to This Work

Although research on the Sino-Vietnamese conflict in Chinese archives remains impossible as of this writing, many internally circulated documents (including speeches given by the leadership and classified after-action reports by PLA units participating in the invasion and the ensuing border conflicts) have become available for examination by scholars from outside China. Like almost all military institutions, the PLA devoted its efforts to summarizing its combat experience, including its methods of operation, troop morale, and problems during combat operations. One major source is a two-volume anthology published by the General Political Department that collects reports from different units about the role of the PLA's political work in combat and troops' reaction to political work on battlefields. Another is an anthology of documents *Sources* compiled by the Guangzhou Military Region Forward Command Political Department Cadre Section. It provides insights into the problems the cadre system faced in the 1979 campaign along the border. Others are after-action reports on military operations by individual armies and different branches of the armed forces. For example, selected summaries have been anthologized by the 43rd and 55th Armies, and selected materials on the special subject of artillery have been published by the headquarters of the Kunming Military Region Artillery.[19] Some of these items are available in *Dui Yue ziwei huanji zuozhan ruogan zhuanti jingyan huibian* (*A Collection of Selected Materials on the Special Subject of the Counterattack in Self-Defense against Vietnam*).[20] An anthology of reports by the 1st Army affords insights on military strategy and tactics employed by the PLA as well as problems that occurred during the conflicts with Vietnam along the Yunnan border in the mid-1980s.[21]

In addition, memoirs by high-ranking military officers as well as by war veterans have now become available. The most prominent ones are Zhou Deli's memoirs, *Yige gaoji canmouzhang de zishu* (*Personal Recollections of a High-Ranking Chief of Staff*), and his recollections of General Xu Shiyou, commander of the Guangzhou Military Region, in the war with Vietnam, *Xu Shiyou de zuihou yizhan* (*The Last Battle of Xu Shiyou*). As the chief of staff of the Guangzhou Military Region at the time of the incursion, Zhou was in a unique position to observe how the General Staff assisted the CCP leadership in making decisions that shaped military strategy as well as to plan and direct the operations from Guangxi.[22] Zhang Zhen, one of Deng Xiaoping's top military lieutenants as director of the General Logistics Department (GLD) and then as deputy chief of the General Staff from 1979 to 1985, published his insightful memoirs in 2003.[23] Other useful sources are Yang Yong's and Wang Shangrong's biographies. Both men were deputy chiefs of the General Staff, assisting Deng in planning and organizing military actions in 1978 and 1979.[24]

From 1978 to 1991, Deng Xiaoping was the undisputed leader of China's party, state, and military, making every single important decision. The publications of his military works (*Deng Xiaoping junshi wenji*) and a chronicle of his life (*Deng Xiaoping nianpu*) containing his writings, speeches, and talks are fundamental for the study of the Chinese military. These documents provide valuable insight into Deng's thinking on the Sino-Vietnamese conflict, allowing correlations to be made between his decision to go to war with Vietnam and his domestic and foreign policies. The chronicles of Ye Jianying's, Chen Yun's, Li Xiannian's, and Nie Rongzhen's life also provide information about the timing of events and their roles in China's decision making about war.[25] Many of these documents are excerpts and only available in edited versions. Some full texts are available from Chinese websites, the most useful of which was *ZhongYue zhanzheng beiwanglu* (Memorandums of the Sino-Vietnam War), though it has been inaccessible since 2011.[26]

Since we lack full access to the PLA's records, validation of the objectivity of Chinese accounts is problematic. Evidence from government-controlled sources is always self-serving, intended to shape history in their favor. It is especially a challenge for those who study military-related subjects. During my earlier study of China's involvement in the Korean War, I came to realize that Chinese military records were largely built on reports given after combat. Because of the tension, fatigue, and excitement of combat, the memory of an event can be seriously affected by participants' psychological, physical, and intellectual capacity. The records of complex events always contain errors and inconsistencies, even though those writing the accounts endeavor to produce a narrative that makes sense based on their interpretations. The situation is worsened by the involvement of personal glory and success as well as the desire to create a positive image for propaganda purposes. (During recent research in the provincial archives of Yunnan, I swiftly recognized that the available published information is only a drop in the bucket compared to what I saw there.)[27] A deeply ingrained tradition of military secrecy and suspicion of anyone living in the West meant that I had little access to archival sources. Thus, I feel obliged to take extra caution about the Chinese account of the events while keeping my interpretation open-ended pending new information.

1 The Roots of the Sino-Vietnamese Conflict

Shared causes and conflicts hardly render nations and peoples immune from rivalries and differences that can lead to subsequent discord. In 1754, American colonists joined in common cause with the forces of the British Empire, fighting steadfastly over the next nine years against the French and their allies. But by 1776, the pronounced differences between those colonists and their ostensible mother country erupted into an open revolt in which the American revolutionaries triumphed in no small measure thanks to the assistance of the same French they had so recently fought. Fast-forward to the Second World War, during which Britain, America, and the Soviet Union spent four years—from the summer of 1941 through Hitler's suicide in his Berlin bunker in 1945—joined in common cause against Nazi Germany. Just three years later, however, wartime good feelings had given way to the uneasiness of a growing superpower rivalry that would last for the better part of five decades. Nor were matters different in the Pacific: America furnished aid and moral support to China from 1937 to the end of 1941. Then, after Pearl Harbor, America and China became allies in the battle against Japanese militarism. Yet after the war and the collapse of Chiang Kai-shek's government, American-Chinese relations began to become estranged; just five years later, American and Chinese forces fought bitterly, even savagely, in Korea while America received active support from Japan.

China and Vietnam had a similar relationship in the three decades following Mao Zedong's 1949 triumphal ascension to power. Ostensibly an ally and even mentor (a PRC term that is often resented by others as Chinese condescension) of a fellow communist partner dedicated to spreading Marxist-Leninist thought and society (and popularly perceived as such in the simplistic Cold War shorthand of both the East and West), Beijing's relations with Hanoi were far more complex and nuanced, reflecting centuries of Chinese-Vietnamese interaction. Allied in common cause against the anticommunist South and its Western (and Asian) supporters, the two fell out after 1973, their parting so volatile and acrimonious that it broke into open warfare in 1979.

China's conflict with Vietnam constituted an outgrowth (if not seemingly logical conclusion) of its twenty-five-year involvement in the latter's struggles against the French and the Americans. China certainly had been a major supporter of Vietnam, supplying men, material, and military expertise to its southern neighbor. Thus, many in the West were surprised when the SRV's foreign ministry issued a 1979 white paper offering a skeptical, even acerbic, interpretation of the Chinese-Vietnamese relationship. The review of Vietnamese-Chinese relations over the previous thirty years offered surprising revelations about the contentious interactions between the two countries. The document accused China of betraying Hanoi's unification hopes at Geneva in 1954 and of preventing Vietnamese communists from stepping up their armed struggle against the Saigon regime, allegedly effectively giving a green light for America's subsequent intervention in Vietnam, with all the attendant misery that endeavor entailed.[1] Beijing authorities repudiated all these allegations through their official media, vehemently condemning what they saw as Hanoi's deliberate distortion of China's assistance to Vietnam. Problems between China and Vietnam at the time can be described by an ancient Chinese proverb: "It takes more than one cold day for the river to freeze three feet deep" (*bingdong sanchi fei yiri zhihan*). To outside observers, these allegations and repudiations clearly indicated that serious problems had existed in the oft-touted "comrades in arms" relations between China and Vietnam from the very beginning.

Historian William Duiker notes that conflict between nations "is often motivated by a complex amalgam of emotions, assumptions, and expectations, many of them are the product of experience."[2] Studies since the end of the Cold War generally argue that the military confrontation between China and Vietnam was not merely a response to contemporary events, as people initially thought. Instead, China's involvement in Vietnam had been complicated since the 1950s, filled with frustrations, dissatisfactions, disappointments, and long-standing ill will—even hatred—between the two countries.[3] Faced with one common enemy (the United States), two not-always-friendly neighboring nations (China and Vietnam) formed an alliance during the early years of the Cold War. Beijing's ideological disagreement with the Soviet Union and ensuing anti-Soviet positions not only pulled the two ostensible allies further apart but also set a course for conflict between the two countries.

An overview and analysis of China's involvement in Vietnam following the founding of the PRC in 1949 provides a useful background for understanding how and why China and Vietnam became mutual adversaries by the late 1970s. Three contributing issues served as root causes for the unavoidable direct conflict between Beijing and Hanoi: (1) the inherent unequal characteristics of

Sino-Vietnamese relations, (2) the influence of Mao's radicalism on China's foreign and security policy, and (3) growing concern about the Soviet threat after Beijing's split with Moscow in the early 1960s. "The seeds for the destruction of the Asian communist alliance" were sowed throughout the years of China's involvement in Vietnam. They were not planted in a particular year by a particular event.[4]

Cracks in the Early Sino-Vietnamese Alliance

The development of the Beijing-Hanoi relationship must be considered within a much larger context than simply the post-1949 period. Indeed, it reflected centuries of a complex and contentious relationship of the Chinese and Vietnamese people. Over more than a millennium, Vietnam had grappled with China over cultural and political influence. While the Vietnamese embraced the advances and advantages offered by Chinese civilization, they also—and not surprisingly—sought to retain their own cultural and national identity. Further complicating the relationship were the inequalities inherent within the international communist movement, which effectively dictated a top-down centralized control and management system relegating the lower-level newer communist powers to a subordinate status in which they had to accept authoritative guidance from the higher-level older ones.[5] "Ideological cohesion on the basis of Marxism-Leninism," Stephen Walt notes, "is the foundation of [communist] international cohesion."[6] Thus, since their foundation in the earliest days of the prewar Comintern, both the CCP and the Indochinese Communist Party had been subordinated under the leadership of the Communist Party of the Soviet Union and had almost no direct interactions with one another until the 1949 creation of the PRC. Shortly thereafter, a new relationship among the three parties emerged. The Stalin regime's focus on Western Europe (fresh from the Big Power crisis of the Berlin Airlift) and concerns regarding military modernization (particularly moving into the atomic era) promoted a general indifference toward Southeast Asia. As a result, the CCP achieved elevated status as the regional leader of the Asian communist movement, both working to bring the Vietnamese (and other Asian communist movements) into closer contact with Beijing and gradually reducing the regional influence of the Soviet regime (with which, of course, the PRC would eventually come to blows).

In early 1950, when Mao Zedong and Ho Chi Minh visited Moscow, Soviet leader Joseph Stalin advised the Vietnamese Communist Party (VCP) leader that his party's request for assistance should be fulfilled by China. According to Thomas Christensen, the Soviet leader "did so for reasons that had more to do with his desire not to be bothered with such revolution than it did with his desire to see Mao play an active leadership role in the region."[7] Indochina, however, traditionally held great importance for China's national security. Moscow's lack of geopolitical interest in Indochina created a leadership vacuum that the new Chinese regime was more than happy to fill. The PRC's assumption of the mantle of Asian communist leadership elevated China's political and strategic status on the world stage. More important, it allowed China to continue its historical role as the guardian and protector of smaller and weaker neighboring states.[8] But with this position came significant challenges for the Chinese leadership. In its relationship with the VCP (as well as with the post-1954 government of North Vietnam and with the Vietnamese government as a whole after the forcible unification of North and South in 1975), China would manage not only a normal state-to-state relationship but also an ideologically committed party-to-party relationship, which, in China's view, meant Vietnamese obedience to a single authoritative Beijing-centered leadership. Given the history of Chinese-Vietnamese relations and Vietnam's historical tendencies toward independence (buttressed after 1973 by the popular perception that it had confounded the United States, the world's greatest superpower), conflict between the two countries and two parties became inevitable.

No documentation has surfaced about how Vietnamese leader Ho perceived Chinese involvement in Vietnam. Asian communists certainly seemed to have had doubts about and even a little scorn for China's assumption of regional communist leadership despite the fact that both Vietnam and Korea had historically looked to China for models of and inspirations for coping with and adapting to Chinese systems while striving to maintain national identity and independence. Vo Nguyen Giap, the well-known People's Army of Vietnam (PAVN) general, recollected after the Vietnamese revolution that the Vietnamese did not think China would be able to provide all they wanted at the time.[9] Giap's view might have been suggestive of a broader feeling within the Ho inner circle. In any case, his response was more polite than that of North Korea's Kim Il Sung. When the Chinese leadership asked him what he needed for his invasion of South Korea in the spring of 1950, the North Korean leader "arrogantly" responded that he had already secured what he needed—from the Soviet Union.[10]

Although Ho shared the ideology of the Chinese communist leadership, he, like many other Vietnamese, never gave up on the idea that China posed a potential threat to Vietnam's independence and freedom. A traditional Chinese (and more broadly Asian) strategic philosophy advocated maintaining friendly relations with distant nations and attacking (or maintaining vigilance against) those nearby (*yuanjiao jingong*). A longtime admirer of the Soviet system, Ho would have preferred direct Soviet intervention. But with his country so distant from Soviet security interests, the Viet Minh leader had no choice but to rely on China to support his revolutionary cause. The need for Chinese assistance placed him in the delicate and influential role of managing the special relationship between his emerging country and its giant neighbor to the north.[11]

Chinese support was certainly crucial to the Viet Minh's rejection of the French colonialism. But China's involvement in the Viet Minh's struggle against the French created a difficult relationship—by no means easy and trusting—between the two sides.[12] Chinese leaders were sensitive to the appearance of displaying big-state chauvinism toward their neighbors, repeatedly exhorting PLA troops serving in Vietnam during the First Indochina War to maintain "respect" for their Vietnamese counterparts and avoid being "complacent and arrogant."[13] Nevertheless, General Chen Geng, the top Chinese military leader in Vietnam, confided to his diary his abhorrence of Giap, describing the Viet Minh military leader as "slippery and not very upright and honest." Chen further observed that "the greatest shortcoming of the Vietnamese communists was their fear of letting other people know their weaknesses," which, he judged, made the Vietnamese leadership not truly "Bolshevik."[14] In his memoirs published in 2004, Giap, in turn, makes no mention of General Chen's significant contribution to the Viet Minh's earlier military victories in the First Indochina War. This absence may well have reflected lingering Vietnamese dissatisfaction with what Giap perceived as the Chinese general's prejudice and arrogance.[15]

The rift between the Chinese and Vietnamese communists started as early as the 1954 Geneva Conference, when participants had reached an agreement to divide Vietnam temporarily along the 17th Parallel. In 1979, Le Duan, secretary-general of the VCP, revealed that Vietnamese leaders bitterly resented how Zhou Enlai, China's premier and foreign minister and chief negotiator, pressured them to accept a comprised agreement at Geneva.[16] (Le Duan perhaps ignored the fact that although China, the Soviet Union, and the Viet Minh had been allies, all of them could certainly be expected to proceed to negotiations based on how they calculated their own interests). The Viet Minh leadership had fought the French with the goal of unifying the country under communist rule; after the hard-won military victory at Dien Bien Phu, these leaders believed they were in an advantageous position to liberate the whole country from Western rule and influence. For its part, China saw the conflict in Vietnam as another chance to stand up to Western imperialism and assert leadership in the region's revolution. Nevertheless, Beijing's leaders did not want China's involvement in Vietnamese affairs to jeopardize domestic rebuilding programs. Having just come out of the bitter and costly war in Korea, Chinese leaders were increasingly concerned about continuing conflict with the United States, which, in their calculation, loomed ever-larger after the Korean armistice in late July 1953. Moscow's absence of interest in Indochina, made greater still by the death of Stalin in early 1953, increased markedly following the withdrawal of Soviet airmen from Korea; by the time of the Geneva talks, the new Soviet leadership was seeking a détente with the West and was distracted by the need to consolidate power in the emerging post-Stalin era. Overall, the Soviet leadership was generally inclined to support the Chinese, since what China advocated usually accorded with Soviet interests. Thus, the clash between the mutual interests of the larger powers (as expressed by the Chinese and Russians) and the "parochial" interests of the smaller power (the Vietnamese) worked to bring China's and the Viet Minh's positions into conflict at the negotiation table in Geneva.

Neither Chinese nor Vietnamese leaders appeared to understand that their revolutionary ideologies might not remain congruent (and thus consistent) with their national security interests. Le Duan, who had served as secretary of the Southern Region Party Committee during the First Indochina War, was one of the Vietnamese leaders who most resented the role played by Chinese leaders, especially Zhou, at Geneva. In 1979, a quarter century after the Geneva settlement, he argued that China's willing division of Vietnam in 1954 caused great pain and suffering to the Vietnamese in the south, followed by what he termed an American "massacre [of the Vietnamese] in a terrible war."[17] Vietnamese sources alleged that Mao Zedong himself subsequently regretted China's role at Geneva, reportedly engaging in "self-criticism" before the Vietnamese leadership and admitting that China had made a serious mistake by urging the Viet Minh to make concessions at Geneva.[18]

In the late 1950s, Le Duan played a major role in urging North Vietnam's resumption of armed struggle in the South. His criticism of China at Geneva extended to a broader criticism of China's participation in the Korean War—the argument that Mao's intercession on Kim's side was intended only to protect China's "northern flank" rather than to assist the North Korean people.[19] After Korea, Chinese leaders were increasingly apprehensive about Washington's intention to intervene in Indochina, especially when American policymakers advocated use of nuclear weapons to stop the Viet Minh from achieving a victory at Dien Bien Phu.[20] At the Geneva Conference, Vietnam faced Chinese pressure to accept the new geopolitical-strategic circumstances, with Zhou Enlai pointedly stating that "if the Vietnamese continued to fight they would have to fend for themselves." He apparently threatened to terminate assistance. When North Vietnam began preparations to wage guerrilla warfare in the south after Geneva, Le Duan reported in March 1959 that Mao Zedong urged that Vietnam instead "lie in wait for a protracted period of time."[21]

Vietnamese leaders opposed this advice, secretly developing their own forces in the south and then ordering them to engage in mass uprisings to seize power from the Ngo Dien Diem's increasingly unpopular regime. In the fall of 1959, the first armed rebellion broke out at Tra Bong in South Vietnam.[22] Recognizing that it could not stop the Vietnamese from conducting guerrilla warfare, the Chinese leadership recommended in May 1960 that the Vietnamese not fight with any force bigger than a platoon (between thirty and thirty-five soldiers). China's attitude at Geneva and into the early 1960s convinced Le Duan that China did not support Hanoi's drive for unification through armed struggle.[23]

China's leaders wanted Hanoi to carefully husband its military strength, monitoring and maintaining close contact with the people to assess when opportunities might present themselves for successful local uprisings. When Hanoi's leaders consulted with their Chinese counterparts, the Chinese leadership argued that action in the South was premature and dangerous, given Hanoi's military weaknesses.[24] Beijing's concern about Hanoi's insurgency strategy in South Vietnam also reflected its (greater) concerns about China's national interests. The pressing Chinese domestic agenda for social and economic development following the Korean War and the ongoing prospect of cross-strait conflict with Taiwan (and perhaps its allies) forced Beijing's leaders to seek peaceful coexistence and political circumspection in foreign affairs. China's foreign policy at the time focused on wooing international support to break the U.S. policy of isolation against China so the country could focus on domestic reconstruction.[25] In 1958, Mao launched the Great Leap Forward movement, hoping to "surpass England and to catch up with America" (*ganYing chaoMei*). He may also have believed on some level that he could bypass the Soviet Union and become the foremost global communist society.[26] In the meantime, the Chinese leader was dissatisfied with the Kremlin's détente policy toward Western imperialism and demonstrated more enthusiasm for national independence movements than the Soviet Union did. Beijing's and Moscow's approaches toward opposing imperialism and promoting revolution diverged. Mao, however, did not want to provoke "U.S. retaliation closer to home."[27] In 1958, even though he ordered the shelling of Jinmen and Mazu Islands in response to Anglo-American interventions in the Middle East, the Chinese leader prohibited the PLA from initiating engagements with American ships and aircraft.[28]

Beijing needed a stable security environment and therefore adopted a policy that would neither hinder nor encourage Hanoi's efforts to liberate the South by military means. This policy approach frustrated the Vietnamese, making them suspicious of the sincerity of China's support for Vietnamese national liberation. During her reevaluation of Beijing's policy toward Vietnam in the 1950s, noted Chinese scholar Li Danhui points out that the Chinese leadership's failure to align China's national interests with its ideological commitment to support revolutions in other countries presaged troubles for the future of Sino-Vietnamese relations, troubles that would eventually burst into open cross-border conflict.[29]

Ideological Rivalry and China's Involvement in Vietnam

Despite Hanoi's complaints about China's insufficient support for national unification of the Democratic Republic of Vietnam (DRV), on the surface nothing appeared abnormal in their alliance from the late Stalinist era through Geneva and into the Khrushchev era.[30] Serious challenges and discontents with China's role in Vietnam came only after ideological quarrels erupted between Beijing and Moscow in the late 1950s—the differences that led to the well-publicized Sino-Soviet "split." Stalin's vision of China's role in Indochina legitimized Beijing's claim to be first and foremost in the Asian communist revolutionary movement. Vietnam's emergence as a communist nation offered an opportunity for the CCP leadership to carry out this "mandate." The Chinese leadership became increasingly concerned about their country's role in Vietnam following Khrushchev's pursuit of détente with the United States after 1959, which they perceived as a threat to China's support of Asian revolutionary programs. Vietnam thus served not only as a cockpit for East-West conflict but also as a theater for the growing showdown between China and the Soviet Union over their interpretations of Marxist-Leninist ideologies and respective policies toward the West.

In the early 1960s, revolutionary prospects in South Vietnam looked good. The Diem regime was increasingly unpopular (even with its foreign supporters, including the United States), and rising discontent among South Vietnam's noncommunist Buddhist population would culminate in the attention-getting 1963 public immolations by Buddhist monks. These events presaged the downfall (with the complicity of the Kennedy administration) and murder of Diem himself.

Given increasing evidence of the growing multiparty unrest in the South, Chinese leaders began to change their views, admitting among themselves that they had failed to fully appreciate the special circumstances in South Vietnam and thus had wrongly concluded the use of armed struggle against Diem's regime was premature.[31] In December 1960, China became the first foreign government to recognize the National Liberation Front (the Viet Cong) in South Vietnam. A few months later, in a meeting with Pham Van Dong, prime minister of the DRV, Mao spoke enthusiastically about the armed struggles launched by Hanoi, confidently predicting that Americans could not stop the Vietnamese from taking revolution into the South.[32]

Beijing had various reasons for supporting Hanoi's new strategy to liberate South Vietnam. The PRC regime had increasingly turned toward political radicalism, beginning with Mao's condemnation of those insiders who advocated peace and reconciliation in China's foreign affairs as well as restraining aid to the national liberation movements of other countries, given China's own economic difficulties. Mao denigrated what he saw as counterrevolutionary "revisionist" activities that promoted "three appeasements and one reduction"—that is, appeasements of imperialism, revisionism, and international reactionaries and reduction in assistance to national liberation movements.[33] To Mao, these ideas brought back bad memories: Khrushchev's lukewarm support of North Vietnam and Ho's difficulties in the struggle for Vietnam's national liberation reminded him of his own frustrating experience with Stalin's on-again, off-again support during China's revolution. At the Tenth Plenary Session of the Eighth CCP Congress (held in September 1962), the Chinese leader declared that China must "uphold the anti-imperialist banner" to support the armed struggles in South Vietnam and Laos as long as imperialism, reactionary, counterrevolutionary movements, and revisionism existed.[34] China's policy toward Vietnam began to take a radical turn in late 1962 and early 1963. Vigorous support for "wars of national liberation" in Indochina and elsewhere became the central focus of China's foreign policy. China's direct aid to North Vietnam ramped up accordingly.

Beijing's growing militancy became entangled with its own security concerns following the expansion of U.S. involvement in Vietnam. China envisioned itself in a continuing military confrontation with the United States, one that dated back to Korea and extended through the Taiwan Strait confrontations of the later 1950s. However, as much as the United States perceived itself as victorious in those conflicts, China believed that the United States had failed to achieve its strategic goals. Now, the Chinese leadership saw America as expanding its historical animus against the Chinese communist regime into Vietnam. From the Chinese perspective, Beijing's support for Hanoi's war of national liberation would break the "ring of encirclement" by U.S. imperialists and their allies and thus increase China's security.[35] The 1964 Tonkin Gulf incident convinced Chinese leaders that Beijing needed to prepare for possible U.S. expansion of the war into North Vietnam. Two weeks later, at the CCP's Central Secretariat meeting, Mao stated that America was planning a new war of aggression against China and that China therefore needed to prepare for war. In October, Mao stated again that the Chinese must be prepared for a large and possibly nuclear war. China's leaders viewed U.S. escalation in Vietnam as the prelude to such an attack. "Preparing for war" became a prominent national theme, penetrating every cell of Chinese society.[36] The introduction of U.S. combat units into South Vietnam in February 1965 heightened the possibility of a U.S. ground attack on North Vietnam. While increasing military preparations in its southern provinces, China carried greater than ever burdens to support the Hanoi regime.

In April, a series of negotiations between Chinese and Vietnamese leaders took place in Beijing. Vietnamese leader Le Duan requested that China send "volunteer pilots, volunteer fighters," and "engineering units for constructing and repairing railroads, highways, and bridges." He noted that the Chinese forces would help defend Hanoi and areas as far north as the Chinese border from U.S. air bombardment and that China's support would also bolster the morale and increase the confidence of the Vietnamese people fighting against the United States and the South Vietnamese government.[37] In response, Chinese leader Liu Shaoqi reaffirmed Beijing's position that assisting Vietnam against the United States was "an unshakable duty of the Chinese people and the Communist Party." The Chinese, Liu continued, would make their best effort to furnish North Vietnam with anything Hanoi requested, even granting Vietnamese leaders the authority to decide what PLA units they wanted to come into Vietnam. Both sides later signed agreements regarding China's assistance to North Vietnam.[38]

As a consequence, between 1965 and 1969 (the entire period of the American Rolling Thunder air campaign), a total of 320,000 Chinese troops served in North Vietnam. The greatest number in country at any one time was 170,000, equivalent to more than ten divisions. More than 1,100 Chinese died and 4,300 were wounded in Vietnam, the vast majority by American air strikes. The Vietnamese were appropriately grateful and appreciative of the aid and sacrifice of PLA personnel, with Le Duan noting that even though a small number of Chinese perished, their sacrifice might have saved 2,000,000 or 3,000,000 Vietnamese lives.[39] But he apparently still feared China as a potential threat to Vietnam's independence and freedom: he explained in 1979 that he believed that the deployment of Chinese forces in North Vietnam was probably a Chinese scheme to assess the state of Vietnam's defenses so that China could invade and occupy Vietnam and then use it as a base for expansion across Southeast Asia.[40]

In retrospect, Chinese leaders, particularly Mao, were fully aware that the deployment of Chinese troops to Vietnam, no matter how urgently and sincerely Hanoi asked for them, could ultimately exacerbate traditional suspicions and hostility and thus be a source of destabilization between the two counties. In April 1966, aware that some in Vietnam were suspicious that a hidden agenda lay behind China's assistance, Deng Xiaoping (secretary-general of the CCP Central Committee) cautioned Le Duan and Nguyen Duy Trinh (foreign minister of the DRV) that such suspicions about China reminded him that Mao had criticized some Chinese leaders who had shown "too much enthusiasm" for Chinese intervention in Vietnam. Such criticism, he told the Vietnamese leaders, offered evidence of Mao's "farsighted" thought. He reminded them that at that moment, China had 130,000 troops in Vietnam, with tens of thousands more on the border with North Vietnam. He pointedly asked the Vietnamese leaders to confirm whether China's "overenthusiasm" had triggered fears that Chinese assistance really aimed at taking control of Vietnam. In addition, he assured them that China had no such intentions and offered to solve the problem by immediately withdrawing Chinese troops from Vietnam and redeploying them to the hinterland. In response (and perhaps alarmed lest Deng carry through on his suggestion), Le Duan denied that the Vietnamese perceived China's involvement in Vietnam as a potential threat, a sharp contrast to the sentiments he would express thirteen years later.[41]

In fact, Hanoi's concerns were not completely unfounded. The Vietnamese leadership realized that the division between China and the Soviet Union had a negative impact on each nation's support for Vietnam against the United States. According to Le Duan, if the Soviet Union and China had not been engaged in ideological disputes against each other, "America could not have struck Vietnam as fiercely as they did" because the Americans were "unhampered."[42] To Ho Chi Minh, who regarded the Soviet Union and China as Vietnam's "big brother and big sister," the Sino-Soviet quarrel was bewildering. Hoping for united Sino-Soviet support for the Vietnamese revolutionary cause, Hanoi sought a middle course, automatically placing it in conflict with Beijing's doctrinaire position that anyone who claimed to support China's anti-imperialist policy must also support its antirevisionist policy. The Vietnamese perceived such doctrinal purity as unnecessary since they had a critical need for assistance from both communist powers and believed that Beijing's engagement in a destructive ideological fight with Moscow undermined communism.[43]

Thus, Hanoi leaders wanted Beijing and Moscow to resolve their differences through air-clearing dialogue. But Chinese leaders, especially Mao, believed that the Sino-Soviet dispute could not be resolved so easily and that a decade or more would pass before they could achieve an outcome "favorable to revolution and to a true solidarity."[44] Further, they believed that Vietnam's leaders failed to differentiate who was right from who was wrong in the two-party struggle for control of the international communist movement, mistakenly stressing unity over principle and too-readily acquiescing to the Soviet view of the world generally and Sino-Soviet relations specifically. Beijing's first uneasiness about Hanoi's position occurred in 1963, particularly after a joint communiqué between Ho Chi Minh and Czechoslovakian president Antonin Novotny commended the correctness of the Soviet Union's "peaceful coexistence" policy. *Renmin ribao* (People's Daily) published several Vietnamese Labor Party documents that implicitly criticized Hanoi's attitude toward the Soviets.[45] Beijing's cautiously oblique response reflected China's desperate effort to avoid offending potential allies in its ideological quarrel with Moscow. From a Chinese perspective, any direct criticism could easily alienate the DRV's leadership, particularly with an internal power struggle intensifying in Hanoi between those who favored closer ties to Moscow and those who favored remaining close to Beijing.[46]

Sino-Vietnamese Discord over Soviet Involvement

Since early 1965, the DRV had received increasing amounts of Soviet assistance, including MiG fighter planes, radar-directed antiaircraft artillery and surface-to-air and surface-to-surface missile systems (including the SA-2 SAM and the Styx antishipping cruise missiles), and other military supplies. In June 1965, China informed Hanoi that the PLA stood ready to enter Vietnam in accordance with an agreement between the General Staffs of the two countries. But the Vietnamese military leadership became evasive, asking for more time to explore the various issues raised by Chinese intervention and then making an excuse that the final decision rested not with the Ministry of Defense but rather with the Ministry of Transportation. When PLA forces were allowed to move into Vietnam, Hanoi required that Chinese military personnel travel only via passenger train, not via truck or on foot, allegedly for the sake of secrecy. In response to this odd request, the chief of the PLA General Staff complained that the Vietnamese expected the Chinese to help yet feared the consequences of "imperialists and revisionists" learning of Chinese assistance.[47] A month later, China suggested that Hanoi turn to the Soviet Union and Eastern

European countries to provide equipment and 230 million yuan worth of supplies. Hanoi did not respond directly to this suggestion but instead insisted that China help with these requests. Beijing viewed this as further evidence that the DRV leadership sought to minimize potential problems in Vietnam's relations with the Soviet Union and in the struggle against revisionism, even if doing so came at the expense of China.[48]

As relations with the Soviet Union became increasingly strained, Beijing's leadership grew ever more concerned over the extent of Soviet aid to—and hence influence in—Vietnam, a traditional sphere of Chinese rather than Russian influence. China's leaders perceived the aid as both undercutting their country's self-promotion of the Mao regime as leader of the global struggle against U.S. imperialism and constituting an attempt to nudge the DRV out of China's orbit and into that of the Soviet Union. In his talks with Vietnamese leaders, Zhou expressed his increasing concern over Moscow's involvement in Vietnam, arguing that the Soviets had not been "wholehearted" in helping the Vietnamese and that China was "always afraid of the revisionists standing" between the two countries.[49] According to the Chinese premier, Soviet aid to Vietnam sought to (1) isolate China, (2) improve Soviet-U.S. relations, and (3) manage "subversive activities" as well as "acts of sabotage" (which would likely cause problems for both China and Vietnam).

In 1966, the Great Proletarian Cultural Revolution was launched to remove from Chinese society those revisionists who opposed Chairman Mao's revolutionary ideology. Beijing's foreign policy also turned even more radically ideological, and its language, once carefully veiled, became more open and critical of the Soviet Union's involvement in Vietnam. Chinese leaders now became convinced that Moscow was using its assistance to split their country from Vietnam. They thus urged Vietnamese leaders to reject Soviet assistance, arguing that opposing the United States should go hand in hand with opposing Soviet revisionism. With Hanoi daily confronting the might of the U.S. Air Force and U.S. Navy, this appeal was hardly likely to succeed.[50] Indeed, Hanoi's leaders did not think their Chinese counterparts were correct about Soviet aid to North Vietnam, with Le Duan contending that relations between socialist countries must always reflect the realities of their international circumstances, not extraneous factors.[51] Facing Hanoi's different views on Beijing's antirevisionist position, the Chinese leadership took an increasingly uncompromising attitude, not only complaining about Hanoi's "anti-Chinese" sentiments but also threatening to redeploy Chinese troops in Guangdong and Guangxi Provinces to the north, against the perceived Soviet menace.[52] Concerned about the daily bombing of their country and the supply routes into the South as well as the state of NLF operations in the South against the Americans and South Vietnamese, Vietnam's leaders denied yet again that they had concerns about China's control of Vietnam. However, they were in fact alienated by China's pronounced anti-Soviet policy and its repeated complaints about its relations with North Vietnam.

The passage of Soviet war materials via China to North Vietnam was another issue that complicated the triangular relationship among the communist countries. The Soviets repeatedly accused the Chinese of obstructing the transit of Soviet military equipment bound for North Vietnam. Beijing denied all Soviet charges while raising questions about why Moscow could not ship aid materials by sea to North Vietnam.[53] Chinese leaders saw a Soviet conspiracy to use the shipments to pressure the already overloaded Chinese rail system so that any delay could be interpreted as evidence of China's lack of sincerity in helping North Vietnam. The ongoing Cultural Revolution placed China in an ever more intractable position for handling Soviet materials. Normal rail transportation was frequently interrupted by civil violence between the rival factions of the "revolutionary rebel organizations" in Guangxi Province. Especially during the first half of 1967, Soviet military supplies destined for Vietnam were frequently looted or stolen from trains and military warehouses. The Chinese at the time thus found it increasingly difficult to defend themselves against Soviet accusations.[54]

The deteriorating Sino-Soviet relationship during the latter part of the 1960s eventually derailed Chinese-Vietnamese relations. While the Soviet Union did indeed use its support for North Vietnam in an attempt to win influence in Hanoi, China did so as well, hoping to coerce the Vietnamese into endorsing Beijing's hard-line anti-Soviet revisionist position. Especially after suffering significant military losses during the 1968 Tet Offensive, the Vietnamese, who needed help from both socialist nations, were greatly annoyed by China's increasing intractability, particularly the PRC's growing perception of the Soviet Union, not the United States, as the primary threat to China's national security in early 1969. Perhaps even worse, Beijing began to withdraw Chinese troops from Vietnam, although leaders promised that the forces would return if the Americans came back.[55]

The mounting Soviet involvement in North Vietnam thus drove a wedge between Beijing and Hanoi. China's ideological disagreement with the Soviet Union presented the PRC with a new security challenge: using its relationship with North Vietnam not only as a forum to vie for leadership of world revolution but also to prevent the Soviet Union from forming a bond with Vietnam that might eventually endanger China from the south.[56] Thus, as China's leaders intensified their rhetoric about the Soviets, Vietnam and the Soviet Union forged even closer ties, further increasing Chinese anxieties about long-term geopolitical interests. This process further heightened tensions between Beijing and Hanoi, adding to the historical legacy of ill feelings, territorial disputes, and ethnic bitterness that had long characterized Chinese-Vietnamese relations

Overall, the PRC's leadership was correct in perceiving that Moscow had an agenda going far beyond "merely" assisting its Vietnamese brothers in their struggle against the West. Russian historian Ilya Gaiduk has confirmed that the Kremlin pursued a conscious policy of using Soviet aid to gradually bring North Vietnam into the Soviet orbit.[57] Since the end of the Vietnam War, historians and policy analysts have generally assumed (as policy and security experts thought during the war itself) that most Soviet assistance consisted of heavy and sophisticated military equipment such as fighter planes, radar, and surface-to-air missiles, while China provided primarily light automatic infantry weapons and logistical supplies. In fact, recently uncovered Chinese sources indicate that the PRC's military aid to Hanoi was far more extensive and substantial.[58] As extensive as Soviet support was, China's backing arguably represented a greater measure of dedication to the Vietnamese cause, since China had much less industrial capability than the Soviet Union and was in a state of domestic chaos as a result of Mao's Cultural Revolution. Thus, China was in a disadvantageous position when competing with the Soviet Union for Hanoi's favor, and any analysis of China's role in Vietnam must consider these circumstances.

Indeed, to the Chinese, the most distressing aspect of the Soviet involvement in Vietnam was the effort to reach a political settlement of the Indochina conflict. Prior to 1966, Soviet leaders failed to persuade the North Vietnamese to negotiate with the Americans. But as Soviet involvement and influence within North Vietnam increased, Hanoi's leadership began to divide into pro-war (effectively pro-China) and pro-peace (pro-USSR) factions. Diehard revolutionary Le Duan and his supporters steadily got the upper hand, advertising that negotiations with the United States would allow Hanoi to "achieve a decisive victory within a short time."[59] Beijing was aware of this development, publicly equating Moscow's quest for peace with the infamous Munich agreement before the Second World War and privately admonishing Vietnam's leaders not to expect to achieve anything at the negotiation table without first winning victories on the battlefield.[60]

But China's position quickly unraveled, appearing both inconsistent and contradictory. In 1971, Beijing quietly opened its own negotiations with the

Americans. Aware of this covert effort, the Soviet Union became even more aggressive in its attempts to manipulate the Hanoi regime, contrasting for Vietnam's leaders the differences between the Soviet Union's "consistent" policy and China's increasingly inconsistent one, which, the Soviets argued (turning the tables on the Chinese), was crafted to serve primarily Beijing's interests and only incidentally those of Hanoi. Soviet diplomats in Hanoi stressed to their Vietnamese counterparts that China's foreign policy effectively constituted both a "betrayal" and an "abandonment" of Vietnam, encouraging the DRV's leaders to assume a more independent course toward Beijing and to rely on Soviet support to stand firm against China's pressure.[61]

The deterioration of Sino-Soviet relations steadily impaired Hanoi's attitude toward Beijing. Evidence suggests that Hanoi was closer to Moscow than to Beijing during the heyday of America's war against Vietnam. Hanoi initially made strenuous efforts to get troops from the two belligerent allies to cooperate during operations in North Vietnam. But the Chinese later discovered that Hanoi arranged for Soviet surface-to-air missile units to redeploy to avoid U.S. Wild Weasel and Iron Hand anti-SAM attacks but moved Chinese antiaircraft artillery units into the positions previously occupied by the Soviets. The Chinese, therefore, were disproportionately targeted by the often-deadly counter-SAM missile, bomb, and strafing attacks. Moreover, when various disputes arose between Chinese soldiers and Soviet military personnel, Vietnamese authorities generally sided with the Soviets, even characterizing Chinese soldiers' hostility toward the Soviets as somehow impinging "on Vietnam's sovereignty."[62]

At the same time, Hanoi's news media published a steady stream of articles reminding the Vietnamese that dynastic China had often invaded their country.[63] Although Hanoi's leaders wanted the PRC to support their efforts to unify the country, they also sought to maintain an independent relationship with China. The presence of Chinese troops in Vietnam threatened Vietnamese national pride and triggered strong resentments. The combination of suspicions regarding Beijing's intentions and resentments of the PLA's presence in Vietnam led the country's leaders to block Chinese troops' efforts to learn about Vietnam's military strength and operations and to restrict Chinese troops from establishing routine contacts with the local population. At the government-to-government level, Hanoi also did not share any information with Beijing about the state of its ongoing negotiations with the United States.[64] When Miyamoto Kenji, secretary-general of the Japanese Communist Party, asked Chairman Mao in 1966 why China did not send troops to South Vietnam, Mao pointed out that North Vietnam did not want Chinese troops there but insisted that the Vietnamese fight alone in the region without external help (in contrast, of course, to the South, which employed American, South Korean, Thai, Australian, and various other forces).[65]

The former justice minister of the Provisional Revolutionary Government of South Vietnam, Truong Nhu Tang, has argued that by the time of Ho Chi Minh's death in 1969, the DRV's leadership had decided to ally itself with Moscow, and his death eased the implementation of this plan, although Hanoi made no official announcement because it still needed Chinese support.[66] In 1971, China moved to exclude the Soviet Union from taking a hand in the Indochina problem, proposing a united front among China, North Korea, North Vietnam, Laos, and Cambodia. Hanoi's leaders did not buy the Chinese idea, which would have forced them to take sides. A year later, China expressed a desire to send two PLA divisions to help repair railroads and bridges against U.S. air bombardment during Operation Linebacker. Despite its urgent need for exactly such forces, Hanoi tactfully refused.[67] Hanoi had always maintained vigilance about China's involvement in Vietnam but by the early 1970s was more than ever on its guard against developing or implementing any sort of inappropriate relationship with the Chinese government.

The growing hostility between Beijing and Moscow and their increasingly open efforts to secure Hanoi's allegiance placed Vietnam in a dilemma. Vietnam's historical pride and cultural sensitivity in dealing with the Chinese made the Vietnamese adopt a distrustful and even deceitful attitude toward their northern neighbor. In due course, animosity between China and Vietnam mounted in response to their differences, especially after Beijing began secretly to negotiate with the United States in the early 1970s.

Readjustment of China's Security Strategy

While the North Vietnamese leaned toward the Soviet Union in the late 1960s, Chinese leaders pondered their own strategy and security. They had ample evidence of the Soviet military buildup in the Far East between 1965 and 1969. The signing of a twenty-year treaty of friendship between Moscow and Ulan Bator in 1966 brought Soviet troops to the Chinese-Mongolian border, only a few hundred miles from Beijing. Soviet forces in Russia's Far Eastern region grew by nearly 60 percent, from approximately seventeen divisions in 1965 to twenty-seven divisions by 1969. If it came to war, the Chinese calculated, Soviet mechanized units could reach Beijing in a ten- to fourteen-day blitz. In 1967, Moscow's deployment of nuclear-tipped missiles to Soviet Far Eastern military districts brought even more pressure on China's security. Moscow's

August 1968 invasion of Czechoslovakia provided the Beijing leadership with evidence that the "socialist imperialist" Soviet Union might be more dangerous than the United States to China's security, for the Brezhnev regime clearly had few qualms about deploying military forces outside its own borders.[68] The Chinese leadership thus began to urge the country to prepare for a war against Soviet socialist imperialism, anticipating possible invasions of China from Manchuria, Mongolia, and Xinjiang.[69] As Sino-Soviet tensions rose and rhetoric escalated, border incidents did as well, doubling from 1963 to 1969 and culminating in a March 1969 exchange of fire between Chinese and Soviet border patrol units at Zhenbao/Damansky Island, on the far reaches of China's northeastern frontier.

Chinese leaders found themselves in the unenviable position of needing to prepare their country to fight both superpowers in either a separate war or, as strange as it might seem, a joint war. President Lyndon B. Johnson's 1968 decision halting the Rolling Thunder bombing campaign over North Vietnam bought China's leaders only modest breathing space. In early 1969, although Washington embarked on a peace approach toward Asia, the Chinese perceived instead a more dangerous and threatening United States given that new president Richard Nixon had a well-deserved reputation as a conservative anticommunist hawk. In the spring of 1969, the Ninth CCP Congress adopted a war-preparedness platform confronting both the United States and the Soviet Union. It specified that China needed to be ready to fight a major and early war that could be conventional or even nuclear.[70]

Mao's bitter experience and ideological disputes with the Soviet leadership dominated China's strategic thinking and security concerns. The steady escalation of Soviet anti-China propaganda, buttressed by the Soviets' growing Far East military presence and manifested in bloody border clashes between the two countries, confirmed to the Chinese leadership that the Soviet Union posed the greatest threat to China's future. Beijing's strategic focus steadily shifted from the south and east to the north. In June 1969, Mao approved a new "Three North" national defense plan emphasizing defensive operations in North, Northeast, and Northwest China.[71] Chinese concerns about a possible Soviet nuclear strike grew, appearing daily in news reports at home and abroad at a time when China had not yet established its own robust nuclear deterrent. Sino-Soviet relations deteriorated so seriously that in October 1969, China placed itself on imminent war status with the Soviet Union, and Mao and senior Chinese leaders secretly left Beijing for southern China while the PLA's central command went underground on Beijing's western outskirts.[72] From this point on, Chinese leaders showed less interest in promoting world revolution than in protecting their country's security. One immediate consequence was a major effort by Beijing to restore and repair the diplomatic relationships with various foreign countries that had been suspended during the Cultural Revolution. This attempt to return to the international fold presaged a more profound switch in China's diplomatic strategy from the global struggle against imperialism and revisionism to a regional response to the perceived threat posed by the Soviet Union.

Without access to archives in Hanoi, it is difficult to assess the North Vietnamese response to China's strategic change.[73] Given that Hanoi continued to regard Washington as its most dangerous enemy, the Vietnamese may at last have realized that Chinese assistance to win the war was unreliable. If so, they were too late: according to Chinese sources, 1970 marked the beginning of a decline in China's military assistance to North Vietnam, with the last deployed PLA unit returning to China that July.[74] The DRV leaders now became concerned about China's dwindling support, and their fears were further aggravated by China's abrupt move toward rapprochement with the United States after Henry Kissinger's stunning 1971 visit to Beijing, which set the stage for a hitherto even more inconceivable event, a state visit to the PRC by none other than Richard Nixon himself. Alarmed, the DRV leadership made a direct request to the Chinese leadership to cancel Nixon's visit, a request that likely evoked some grim and cynical bemusement among Beijing leaders long annoyed by Hanoi's perceived perfidy.[75] Beijing ignored Hanoi's demand while offering somewhat disingenuous reassurances to the North Vietnamese that China remained interested in their war and would never let its transforming priorities work against Vietnam's national interests.[76] Le Duan nevertheless laid the blame on the Chinese leadership for U.S. air bombardments directed against North Vietnam—Operations Bullet Shot and Linebacker in April and May 1972, followed later in the year by Linebacker II, which brought the full fury of American air power into Hanoi itself. In reality, however, the U.S. attacks occurred in response to Hanoi's ill-considered and ultimately frustrated 1972 spring offensive against the South.[77]

China's détente policy with the United States in the early 1970s weakened Beijing's effort to depict itself as the champion of world Marxist-Leninist revolution, especially in Vietnam. Thus, the PRC leadership found itself trapped. After late 1971, Chinese leaders became more interested in urging Hanoi to negotiate with the South Vietnamese leadership to "make it easier for the United States to accept a peaceful resolution."[78] Beijing still found it had to acquiesce to Hanoi's request for additional military assistance, as President Nixon commenced still further rounds of air attacks over North Vietnam and aerial mining of its harbors. From 1971 to 1973, China urgently sought to defend itself from an expected Soviet invasion but spent nine billion yuan to provide assistance to North Vietnam.[79] Since many of Hanoi's demands exceeded China's production capability, Beijing transferred arms and equipment directly from the PLA to the North Vietnamese inventory, including fighter aircraft such as the Shenyang J-6 (the Chinese-manufactured version of the Soviet MiG-19 jet fighter).[80] At the time, even Beijing believed that Hanoi should have insisted on Soviet assistance against U.S. mining operations rather than cajoling China's leaders into committing their own poorly equipped navy to sweep Haiphong Harbor.[81] As much as they scorned North Vietnam's political leaders, the PRC's leaders recognized that too much had been promised for too long, and any reduction or hesitation in responding to Hanoi's request could have fatally undermined China's remaining credibility and prestige in Vietnam. Nevertheless, the DRV leadership remained ungrateful, regarding China's contact with the United States as "throwing a life buoy to Nixon, who had almost been drowned"[82] and, worse, holding the Beijing regime responsible for the massive U.S. air campaign against North Vietnam, which set the stage for the 1973 peace accords.[83]

For the last year of the war, China continued to support the North Vietnamese cause of national unity, providing substantial assistance. However, the context had completely changed. With the danger of U.S. presence in Vietnam dramatically reduced, the years of rivalry with the Soviet Union for dominance in Vietnam came to a halt. Chinese influence in Hanoi withered, for the North Vietnamese found Beijing's advice unhelpful: Hanoi should cease fighting in the South for at least five years.[84] Avoiding the mistakes made after the 1954 Geneva Conference, the North Vietnamese no longer consulted and discussed their strategy and policy issues with the Beijing leadership as they planned and prepared for the final military campaign against the Saigon regime in 1974–75. After the Vietnamese communists won their war of national unification in April 1975, the conflicts of interest between Hanoi and Beijing began eclipsing their common Marxist-Leninist bond, ended any remaining civility between them, and eventually gave rise to a series of new hostilities in Southeast Asia.

In retrospect, the shift of Beijing's security interests from the south to the north devastated Sino-Vietnamese relations. That the Chinese leadership perceived the Soviet menace as more dangerous than the American threat drove Hanoi closer toward the Soviet Union in the early 1970s.[85] For many years, China had used the leverage furnished by its enormous assistance to Hanoi in an ultimately vain effort to keep the DRV away from the USSR. From a Chinese perspective, Vietnam was a coveted ally, since its ongoing alliance with China would prevent the Soviet Union from encircling China from the south.[86] Thus, China's involvement in Vietnam must be seen as more a competition with the Soviet Union for influence over Hanoi than a genuine commitment to support world revolution. Vietnam, conversely, used the Soviet Union to gain leverage over China for more aid. The ironic tragedy was that as long as China's perception of the Soviet threat continued to dominate its national security calculations, Beijing would not only lose Vietnam as a friend and ally but also inevitably set both nations on a course toward eventual confrontation.

From the Era of Mao Zedong to the Era of Deng Xiaoping

For all his antagonistic views on America, Mao himself launched China's rapprochement with the United States. He did so in hopes that China and America together could prevent Soviet hegemony. This strategic vision did not come to reality until Deng Xiaoping rose to lead the CCP at the end of the 1970s. A reform-minded pragmatist who survived being purged during the Cultural Revolution and who outmaneuvered potential rivals to become China's supreme leader after Mao's death in 1976, Deng is best remembered for the reforms that he introduced and directed during the last twenty years of his life. Deng opened China to foreign trade and influence, normalizing its relations with the West and embarking on a remarkable program of governmental, societal, economic, and technological transformation. But Deng also ordered the use of force against Vietnam after so many years of "lips and teeth" solidarity between the two countries.

Unlike Mao and Zhou, Deng's lack of a strong personal "attachment" to Vietnam provided an explanation for "why he had no qualms about launching an attack in 1979 'to teach Vietnam a lesson.'"[87] He was also in fact a major player in Sino-Vietnamese relations during the mid-1960s and the mid-1970s, a period that witnessed both the heyday of cooperation between Beijing and Hanoi and the emergence of the tensions that finally broke the alliance. Deng's perceptions of Soviet threat and Vietnamese ingratitude might have derived from his early experience dealing with Moscow and Hanoi in the Mao era.

In retrospect, Deng most bluntly addressed the problems in the Sino-Vietnamese relationship with the Vietnamese leader. Deng and Le Duan became acquainted in the early 1960s, and Deng participated in several talks with him concerning China's assistance to North Vietnam before being purged in October 1966. Deng was the first CCP leader to openly convey to Vietnamese leaders the Chinese displeasure over Vietnam's treatment of China. In the late summer of 1975 (two years after his rehabilitation and return to power),

Deng again asked Le Duan why the Vietnamese were increasingly concerned about northern threats given that they had triumphed over South Vietnam just months earlier.[88]

Surprisingly, given the acrimony of their exchanges, Le Duan apparently had great respect for Deng. According to Le Duan, Deng Xiaoping was the only Chinese leader he had met "with great understanding" of Vietnam.[89] Stein Tonnesson argues that Le Duan's positive attitude toward Deng probably reflected Le's preference for the kind of "straight, hard talks" that were typical of the Chinese leader.[90] The Vietnamese leader was wrong to believe that Deng would not continue Mao's anti-Soviet policy and would favor "rapprochement with the Soviet Union."[91]

Deng Xiaoping had already earned his CCP credentials by fighting Soviet "revisionism." In 1963, as a head of the CCP delegation to Moscow for party-to-party talks, he eloquently and vigorously debated with Soviet leaders about the correctness of the CCP's opposition to Khrushchev's efforts at de-Stalinization. Even many years after Deng had been purged, Mao still remembered Deng's outstanding performance at that meeting, urging other Chinese leaders not to forget that "he did not yield to the pressure of Soviet revisionists." This became an important factor in his survival and reemergence as a national leader following the Cultural Revolution. According to Mao, while Deng's personality made some people fear him, his talent as a military leader reassured them should China ever have to fight a war (presumably with the Soviet Union).[92] As a testimony to his reputation, not long after his return to leadership, Deng was appointed chief of the PLA's General Staff, serving as a key leader in the CMC even though he had not held any military leadership positions since the founding of the PRC.[93] The first major military operation executed under his command was a naval clash with South Vietnam over the Xisha (Paracel) Islands in January 1974. The PLA navy sank one South Vietnamese warship, damaged three others, and subsequently took control of the islands.[94] Hanoi perceived the incident not as a Chinese action against its enemies in the south but rather as an aggression against Vietnam as a whole; thus, it constituted another disturbing indication that in the immediate aftermath of the Vietnam War, relations between the two communist states were rapidly deteriorating.[95]

Deng initially assisted the ailing Zhou Enlai on foreign policy issues, focusing on promoting Mao's new "Three Worlds" strategic outlook. Mao's theory placed China and other developing countries (the "Third World") in opposition to both the United States and the Soviet Union (the "First World").[96] In April 1974, Deng spoke before the Sixth Special Session of the United Nations General Assembly, proclaiming the fundamentals of China's foreign policy based on "the theory of the Three Worlds." The strategy focused on preventing further expansion of the Soviet Union's sphere of influence, and although it did not minimize America as a potential foe, the approach recognized—consistent with the unfolding policy of détente—that the United States could be a useful ally in the anti-Soviet struggle. (However, China's efforts to normalize its relationship with the United States did not go as far as the leaders had hoped following President Nixon's visit, though gains were still remarkable in light of the bitter hostility between the two through the Mao era.)[97]

Mao relied strongly on Deng's support for anti-Soviet policies, and Deng did not let Mao down.[98] While repeatedly echoing the chairman's perceptions of the increasing dangers of war, Deng vigorously argued that the major source of this peril came from the "treacherous" Soviet Union. During meetings with foreign leaders, he exhorted them to unite in a "tit-for-tat struggle" against the USSR.[99] At the time, Le Duan thought Deng was under pressure to affirm his pro-Mao credentials and thus "avoid the accusation of revisionism."[100] In fact, the frequent repetition of similar anti-Soviet rhetoric during his political career indicates the sincerity of his conviction that Soviet revisionism constituted a more dangerous threat to the PRC than did Western imperialism. Such a worldview, however inaccurate it may have been, readily coincided with an interpretation of Vietnam as forming an integral part of the Soviet threat to China.

Even before the end of the Vietnam War, the DRV had requested that Beijing resolve long-standing territorial disputes with Hanoi, demanding, for example, that the Gulf of Tonkin be demarcated in such a fashion that two-thirds of its water area belong to Vietnam. The negotiations began in August 1974 but soon halted amid mutual disagreement. On the eve of Saigon's liberation, Hanoi made an even more aggressive move, seeking to occupy six islands in the Spratlys. It boldly declared both the Paracels and Spratlys to be Vietnamese territories and again requested that Beijing recognize those claims, which flew in the face of Vietnamese Premier Pham Van Dong's 1958 support for Beijing's territorial claim over these islands.[101] Hanoi's claim shocked the PRC's leadership, though the Chinese government turned it down without stronger protest simply by claiming that fundamental disputes did not exist.[102] Worst of all, under Deng's custodianship of China's foreign and military affairs, border clashes increased precipitously between Chinese and Vietnamese troops. In 1975, 439 incidents occurred, and the number doubled to 986 the next year.[103] While each side still nominally professed friendship, Lien-Hang T. Nguyen has rightfully observed that "both Hanoi and Beijing had already acted as proverbial enemies" by this time.[104]

Even as conflict loomed, Hanoi continued to seek Chinese aid at a time when Beijing was facing serious domestic economic problems after years of agricultural and industrial stagnation. In August 1975, Zhou Enlai met with Le Thanh Nhgi, the vice premier of the DRV, rejecting requests for further aid and noting (with a shade of humor in his voice) that the defeated South Vietnamese government of Nguyen Van Thieu had left "large quantities of weaponry and ammunition" for Hanoi and thus "served" as a much-better supplier for the Vietnamese communists than Chiang Kai-shek had for the CCP during the Chinese Civil War.[105] Even more significantly, Mao took the same tone during his meeting with Le Duan the next month, saying pointedly, "Today, you are not the poorest under heaven. We are the poorest. We have a population of 800 million."[106]

Deng served as chief negotiator in these talks with the Vietnamese leadership, stressing to Le Duan that China both had to reduce its aid and resented Vietnamese newspapers' resurgent rhetoric about a "China threat." "For the last few years, such things have still occurred and they seem to be more frequent than before," Deng said, adding forcefully, "The threat from the North is the main theme, even in your textbooks. We are not at ease with this. We have not annexed a centimeter of your territory."[107] For his part, Le Duan categorically denied that any such stories were appearing.

Hanoi's decision to oust the Khmer Rouge regime in Cambodia became a flashpoint in Sino-Vietnamese military conflict.[108] Since the declaration of Mao's Three Worlds theory in 1974, the Chinese leadership became less and less interested in pursuing so-called Asian revolutionary internationalism. China had supported both ousted Prince Norodom Sihanouk and the Khmer Rouge, though with very little enthusiasm for Pol Pot's murderous "true" communist revolution in Southeast Asia.[109] But after normalizing its Southeast Asian relations—with Malaysia in 1974 and with the Philippines and Thailand in 1975—China turned to promoting a neutral Southeast Asia as an alternative to the Soviet Union's efforts to enfold Asia into Moscow's sphere of influence. (Throughout 1975, Deng stressed this thesis repeatedly during his meetings with leaders from Cambodia, the Philippines, and Thailand.)[110] But in 1976, Deng fell from power yet again. Ezra Vogel suggests that had Deng not been ousted from office at the time, "he might have been able to patch over the long history of Vietnamese hostility toward China" and the ongoing differences between the two countries.[111] Deng's role as principal architect of the Sino-Vietnamese military conflict would prove otherwise.

In 1977, though increasingly concerned about Hanoi's attempt to establish its own sphere of influence over neighboring Cambodia and Laos, Beijing maintained a more moderate attitude toward its deteriorating relationship with Hanoi and the tension between Hanoi and Phnom Penh. In a meeting with Pham Van Dong, Vice Premier Li Xiannian raised several issues that endangered Sino-Vietnamese relations, including Vietnam's anti-China speeches, territorial disputes along the border and in the South China Sea, and Hanoi's naturalization policy toward ethnic Chinese residing in Vietnam.[112] He urged Vietnamese leaders to take measures to prevent Sino-Vietnamese relations from deteriorating further. The Vietnamese premier promised to bring the minutes of their talk back to the Politburo for the Vietnamese leadership to discuss.[113]

But just a few months later, during Le Duan's last visit to Beijing in November 1977, the Vietnamese leader again stubbornly expressed interest in receiving additional Chinese aid while making no mention of the issues Li Xiannian had previously put forward. In short, Le Duan acted as if the previous meeting had never occurred and instead announced that the only major difference between the two countries was their attitudes toward the Soviet Union and the United States—an absolute denial of the reality of everyday life on the border between the two nations, to give just one example. He then attempted to placate his hosts by promising that Vietnam would always regard "China as its best friend" and "brother" and "would do nothing else" to undermine the relationship.[114]

As Beijing and Hanoi danced about, China was also trying to cool down the increasingly heated relations between Hanoi and the Pol Pot regime in Phnom Penh. During the Khmer Rouge leader's visit to Beijing in late September, Chinese leader Hua Guofeng praised the Khmer Rouge's efforts to improve its relationship with several Southeast Asian countries[115] while pointedly advising Pol Pot "not to exacerbate relations with the Vietnamese communists."[116] He urged conciliation, telling Pol Pot that China wanted Vietnam and Cambodia to "find a solution by diplomatic means in a spirit of mutual comprehension and concessions."[117] At a news conference a few weeks later, Deng Xiaoping again urged Phnom Penh and Hanoi to resolve their problems through negotiations rather than through military means.[118] Sophie Richardson imputes Beijing's stance to Deng's return to power, noting the yet-again-rehabilitated Chinese leader's advocacy of Mao's Three Worlds neutralist Southeast Asia and "uncomfortable" attitude toward the Khmer Rouge's merciless radicalism.[119] Nguyen Trong Vinh, Vietnam's ambassador in Beijing, also believed that Deng's pragmatic approach could improve relations between China and Vietnam.[120] It is thus ironic that a few months later, the "moderate" and "pragmatic" Deng would ponder using force against Vietnam, even before Hanoi had actually invaded Cambodia. What led Deng to make such a dramatic change in China's foreign policy toward Vietnam? The answer lay in Vietnam and Cambodia.

Conclusion

China's involvement in Vietnam encompassed multiple sources of contention that, taken together, worked to trigger the breakdown of Sino-Vietnamese relations from an uneasy alliance to outright belligerency. Like Beijing's relationship with Moscow, the relationship between China and Vietnam was from the beginning both characterized and overshadowed by a top-down, senior partner–junior partner, communist party–to–communist party relationship that required the subordination of the lower level (Vietnam's party) to the higher level (China's party) for doctrinal guidance and strategic leadership. This kind of relationship had long been a problem between the CCP and the Communist Party of the Soviet Union, as the latter had dominated the international communist movement during the Comintern era. This party-to-party relationship also established a "comrade plus brother" state-to-state relationship between China and the Soviet Union and between China and Vietnam. Under the terms of this unequal relationship, the bigger country was responsible for making policy and providing aid for the smaller nation. In return, the latter was required to subordinate its own national policy and strategic interests to the leadership of the former, even if doing so conflicted with the junior partner's national interests. In its own "mentoring" relationship with Vietnam, China did not seem to realize that Vietnam's leaders would regard relations with Beijing in much the same way that China's leaders had regarded their relations with Moscow.

Throughout the 1960s, the PRC leaders' sense of superiority over their southern counterparts also dominated their perception of China's relationship with Vietnam.[121] Although officials in Beijing publicly (and repeatedly) declared that Vietnam was an equal, such rhetoric reflected their strong belief that, as Chen Jian observed, they "occupied a position from which to dictate the values and codes of behavior that would dominate their relations with their neighbors."[122] Though the PRC denied having imposed political and economic conditions on its military aid to Hanoi over the previous two decades, it did so in one fundamental and all-important fashion: demanding that Hanoi recognize China's role as global leader of national liberation movements.[123] While criticizing the Soviet Union for its great-nation chauvinism, which Mao and the CCP's other leaders perceived as infringing on China's national interests and prerogatives, the CCP leadership simultaneously and hypocritically demanded that the Vietnamese communist leadership accord an equivalent obeisance to the PRC and adopt Beijing's anti-Soviet line. Beijing not only occasionally opposed Hanoi's efforts to obtain Soviet assistance but also consistently denigrated and criticized the Soviet Union's Vietnam policy. Thus, the Chinese leadership's own strategic behavior ultimately drove the DRV away from China's embrace.

The roots of China's policy were intrinsically bound within Mao's radical view of the PRC as the logical leader of world revolution. This approach led the Chinese to regard their own policies as entirely justified and the policies of the Soviet Union as heretical. Vietnam became a central focus of the Sino-Soviet dispute simply by being caught between the two communist powers. Mao's ideological vision thus effectively guaranteed that China's policy toward Vietnam, at least from a Vietnamese perspective, would be both incomprehensive and contradictory, as Le Duan's criticisms subsequently detailed. China's position was most troubling for Hanoi because the Vietnamese needed help from both socialist brother countries to confront South Vietnam and its powerful allies, chief among them the United States, with its robust air, sea, and land forces.

After the American withdrawal from Vietnam and the subsequent collapse of the South Vietnamese government, the PRC leadership's perception of the Soviet Union as the primary threat to China's national security created a new problem. Beijing's leaders now found themselves in an awkward position: Vietnam now became not only a place for the CCP to stake its claim to global leadership of world revolution but also a prize for China to secure to prevent Soviet encirclement from the south. As Chinese leaders intensified their views of a Soviet threat, the PRC's increasingly hard-line anti-Soviet position created new tensions between Beijing and Hanoi, adding to the long-standing historical suspicions, territorial and border disputes, and ethnic Chinese problems.

As a result, one of the great ironies of the Cold War and of communism occurred: after many years during which Chinese resources and troops supported Hanoi's war effort to unify South and North Vietnam, the Chinese found they had helped to create a new adversary. For both Beijing and Hanoi, the tragedy of China's involvement in Vietnam provided the two erstwhile "brotherly comrade" socialist countries with too many reasons to engage in a decade of saber rattling and contentious dialogue that ended in bloodshed. Deng played the decisive role in Beijing's decision to go to war with Vietnam, a logical outcome of his sincere perception of a Soviet threat to China's security. This perception manifested itself in his relentless (and ultimately successful) pursuit of an anti-Soviet united front as much to gain the West's support for China's modernization as to offset the Kremlin's machinations.

2 Deng Xiaoping and China's War Decision

In late fall of 1978, the spotlight in Beijing was Deng Xiaoping's reascendance and the Chinese leadership's adoption of economic reform as the highest national priority. During that same period, at the headquarters of the General Staff, PLA officers were considering the use of force to resolve border disputes with Vietnam as the relationship between Beijing and Hanoi continued to deteriorate. Their subsequent proposal evolved into a dreadful decision to launch a large-scale invasion of Vietnam in early 1979. Even worse, the two countries would remain locked in a decadelong military confrontation with scores of lives and properties lost on both sides. Since Deng assumed new responsibilities in leading the party and the country at the time, he played the dominant role in China's national strategy, especially in China's decision to attack Vietnam.

Prior to becoming the preeminent leader, Deng served as chief of the General Staff. All important military issues went to him before being passed to others for consideration, so he was the first Chinese leader to weigh in on the General Staff's proposal regarding Vietnam. Unlike his military subordinates, who could afford to consider the issue simply in terms of military affairs, Deng had to ponder a series of more fundamental and weighty strategic issues before reaching any decision. These questions involved the rationale for China's use of force against Vietnam, a former communist ally, and the possible international and domestic repercussions of such a decision. Factors that influenced the strategic thinking of Chinese leaders included Vietnamese policy opposing China, the SRV's invasion of Cambodia, and the Soviet-Vietnamese alliance. Deng, however, had to contrive a thoughtful rationale that would convince the entire country that the use of force against Vietnam would improve China's strategic position and advance domestic economic reform. The most daunting challenge Deng faced was his own country: a nation torn by factionalism, its people weary of the seemingly endless internal fighting of the preceding decade. The newly adopted economic reform and opening-up policy brought great hope for a return to normalcy and increasing prosperity. While tackling such a domestic environment, Deng pondered his decision to go to war with Vietnam.

China's Response to Border Incidents

After North Vietnam's military victory over South Vietnam in the mid-1970s, CCP leaders became increasingly concerned about Hanoi's foreign policy. They were already worried about Soviet influence in Indochina, as Hanoi moved ever closer to Moscow for material aid and ideological support.[1] Chinese leaders were also irritated by Hanoi's efforts to forge special relations with Laos and Cambodia, the latter of which also came under mounting military pressure from Vietnam.[2]

Most important, Beijing and Hanoi clashed over territorial issues. China had invaded Vietnam several times to achieve regional domination but had rarely done so to acquire territory. Vietnam, for its part, had never challenged Chinese territorial claims. Now this traditional pattern of behavior changed. In 1975, the rising number of border incidents and disputes with Vietnam became a major issue for the PLA General Staff, which ordered two border provinces and military regional and provincial commands to stabilize the border situation.[3] Yet despite Beijing's claims that it sought a peaceful resolution to such disputes, violence on the border surged in 1978.

It was an ominous development, for territorial disputes historically have been the most common issue over which nations go to war.[4] China's initial move toward war came in mid-1978, amid quarrels over the fate of ethnic Chinese living in the SRV. According to Chinese sources, on 12 August, Vietnamese armed personnel launched a surprise attack on a Chinese border patrol squad near Guangxi Province's ironically named Youyi (Friendship) Pass. Two weeks later, in the same area, more than 200 Vietnamese troops boldly occupied a mountain ridge clearly on the Chinese side of the border and then brazenly fortified their hilltop positions with even more troops.[5] Both the numbers and scale of border incidents subsequently increased dramatically, with PRC officials claiming that the number of border clashes rose from 752 in 1977 to 1,100 in 1978.[6] Until August 1978, most incidents were small and involved few casualties. But the August incidents were fierce and deadly, involving large numbers of Vietnamese troops. By all indications, the violent new character and escalation of the border clashes spurred leaders in Beijing to consider using military force against Vietnam.

In the weeks after the August clashes, the General Staff Department met in Beijing to discuss "how to deal with our territory occupied by the Vietnamese forces." Chaired by the deputy chief of the General Staff, Zhang Caiqian, the meeting included staff officers from the Guangzhou and Kunming Military Regions as well as those from General Staff's departments of operations and intelligence. At the outset, Zhang noted that the General Staff had to advise CCP leaders on how to counter Hanoi's mistreatment of ethnic Chinese and the increasing provocations by Vietnamese military and security troops along China's border.[7] He reviewed the events of 1978, noting that on 8 July, the General Political Bureau of the Vietnamese People's Army had ordered troops to pursue an "offensive strategy" against China and to launch an "attack and counterattack within and beyond the border."[8] Two weeks later, the Vietnamese Communist Party's Fourth Plenary Session had again identified the United States as a "long-term enemy" but had ominously branded China the "most direct, dangerous enemy" and a "new prospective foe." At the same time, the Vietnamese government had created a new military district in northwestern Vietnam, fronting China's Yunnan Province.[9] The PLA General Staff perceived a close correlation between Hanoi's newly expressed animosity and the increasing border tension. While existing scholarship perceives the border issue as "more a venue for confrontation than a matter of serious dispute,"[10] from a Chinese perspective, the border issue was the logical starting point for the PLA to begin contemplating an attack on Vietnam.[11]

From the time the PRC was founded, Chinese leaders had shown a proclivity to use carefully chosen military force in territorial disputes with other countries. The PLA had been employed to uphold claims of territorial sovereignty against India in 1962 and against the Soviet Union in 1969. The PLA General Staff continued this tradition in proposing action against Vietnam. The General Staff's proposal was carefully designed to avoid escalation lest it threaten the PRC's economic progress. The PLA targeted just one isolated Vietnamese regiment at Trung Khanh, a border county adjacent to Guangxi Province, to teach Vietnam a military lesson for its misbehavior. Zhou Deli, the chief of staff of the Guangzhou Military Region, recalled that the General Staff believed that Trung Khanh's isolated geographic location would allow the PLA to separate the Vietnamese outpost from any reinforcements and easily wipe it out.

However, after a day of reviewing intelligence about the prospects of a Vietnamese invasion of Cambodia and discussing the overall situation, the majority of the participants concluded that the current problem with the SRV was not simply a border issue and that any military action by the PLA must have a significant impact on both Vietnam and the overall geostrategic situation in Southeast Asia. Accordingly, they recommended a strike against a regular Vietnamese army unit in a larger geographic area rather than against one small, isolated unit. Though the meeting ended without any specific decision, it set a tone for China's eventual war against Hanoi by linking any PLA attack plan to the SRV's actions in Southeast Asia.[12]

None of the Chinese sources available to date explain how the PLA General Staff modified its thinking and war plan over the subsequent months. On 6 November, the operation department of the General Staff informed the Guangzhou Military Region that the central leadership found it necessary to inflict severe punishments on Vietnam and asking officials to consider what forces would be used and where and when they should act.[13] Over time, officials in Beijing also worried that local PLA commanders might become too aggressive in responding to the mounting border incidents, thus jeopardizing centralized war planning. Accordingly, on 21 November, the CMC ordered the regional commands to comply with the main strategy against Soviet hegemony during their handling of border incidents, reminding them of the maxim "On just grounds, to our advantage, and with restraint" (youli, youli, youjie)—that is, striking only after the enemy had struck.[14]

In his memoirs, General Zhang Zhen, the director of the General Logistics Department, indicates that attendees at a November CMC meeting reached a consensus that force should be used against Vietnam as a response to what had happened along China's border.[15] On 23 November 1978, the General Staff convened another meeting to discuss a new scheme of war. Taking into consideration the earlier discussion, the General Staff broadened the scope and duration of operations, aiming to destroy one or two regular Vietnam divisions in a three- to five-day operation near the border.[16] Some participants believed that these operations would not go far enough because they were still limited to a remote area and posed no immediate threat to Hanoi. However, the doubters remained quiet, deferring to the top commanders' judgment. The General Staff ordered the Guangzhou and Kunming Military Regions to carry out the campaign and authorized the transfer of the PLA's strategic reserves, the two armies of the Wuhan and Chengdu Military Regions, to reinforce the Guangxi and Yunnan fronts.[17] The war plan later changed significantly in response to Vietnam's invasion of Cambodia. But the fact that the CMC and the PLA General Staff were planning a major military campaign even before the Vietnamese forces crossed the Mekong suggests that at least initially, the war was intended to force Vietnam to accommodate China's demands regarding border disputes and the expulsion of ethnic Chinese.

Deng's Return to the Center of Power

How did Chinese leaders view the war plan? A speech by the CMC general secretary, Geng Biao, on 16 January 1979 shed light on Beijing's deliberations about how to counter the Vietnamese invasion of Cambodia. In November 1978, Wang Dongxing, the CCP vice chair, and Su Zhenghua, the first political commissar of the navy and a CCP Politburo member, proposed that Chinese troops or a naval detachment be sent to Cambodia. Xu Shiyou, the commander of the Guangzhou Military Region, requested permission to attack Vietnam from Guangxi Province.[18] Geng Biao reported that after careful consideration CCP leaders rejected all the recommendations.[19] King C. Chen contends that Geng Biao, who clearly would have been aware that the PLA had already marshaled troops along the Vietnam's border, was deliberately concealing Beijing's military plans.[20] Geng Biao's report also failed to reveal Deng Xiaoping's role in the decision making as he consolidated his position as a principal leader of the party as Wang's and Su's political influence was waning.[21] The PRC's initial decision on Vietnam coincided with a new round of power struggles inside the CCP.

Deng Xiaoping, a long-standing Chinese party leader and statesman, re-emerged in the country's political arena in July 1977 as CCP vice chair, vice chair of the CMC, and deputy premier and chief of the PLA General Staff. Deng's rehabilitation did not initially mean that he had overwhelming authority within the CCP. Rather, Hua Guofeng, as chair of both the CCP and the CMC, assisted by Wang Dongxing, the CCP vice chair, remained in full control of party and state affairs, continuing to carry out many of the late Mao Zedong's ideas and policies.[22] Ye Jianying remained in charge of the CMC. Deng volunteered to take charge of science and education, spheres that were seen as less important than party and military affairs but that, as he recognized, had profound implications for China's modernization.[23]

From August 1977 to December 1978, the power struggle between Hua and Deng intensified.[24] As the chief of the PLA General Staff, Deng was well aware of the war planning, but he seemed uncertain about whether an attack on Vietnam would be supported by the full CCP Politburo. Furthermore, Deng needed to consider the goal the PLA would achieve through military action beyond simply punishing Vietnam. During a visit to Singapore in early November 1978, in answer to Prime Minister Lee Kuan Yew's blunt query about whether China would use force against Vietnamese troops in Cambodia, Deng demurred. On one occasion, he told Lee that China would punish Vietnam, but on another occasion, Deng merely responded guardedly, "It depends."[25]

Deng Xiaoping, chief of the General Staff and vice chair of the CMC, 1979. cpc.people's.com.cn.

The political scale tilted in favor of Deng soon after his return to Beijing. From 10 November to 15 December, leaders from the provinces, military regions, and central party, government, and military organs met in Beijing to attend the Central Work Conference. The original agenda focused solely on domestic affairs—agricultural development and economic policies for 1979 and 1980[26]—and did not include the Indochina situation, contrary to what King C. Chen has claimed.[27] The meeting took an unexpected turn on 12 November, when Chen Yun, an economic planner for Mao, delivered a speech insisting that those in attendance must address the legacies of the Cultural Revolution before anything else. The agenda thereafter shifted to the rehabilitation of senior party cadres who had been prosecuted during the Cultural Revolution and to criticism of the Hua-Wang alliance for pursuing an ultraleft ideological policy. The meeting ended with the convention of the Third Plenum of the Eleventh Party Congress, at which Chen Yun became a CCP vice chair, consolidating Deng Xiaoping's political position. With the change of political atmosphere in Beijing, Deng gradually became China's preeminent decision maker.[28]

One of Deng's first key decisions, announced at the Third Plenum, was to shift China's national priorities to economic modernization and to open its borders to the outside world.[29] In a remarkable turnabout, under this program, the United States was now deemed the main source of advanced ideas and technology and the most favorable model for modernization. A former

PRC deputy foreign minister, Zhang Wenjin, recalled that Deng believed that if China opened merely to other countries but not to the United States, the new policy would be futile.[30] By December 1978, Beijing had invited several major U.S. corporations to help develop natural resources, petroleum, and other heavy industries. Foreign policy issues were not included on the agenda of the Central Party Work conference or the Third Plenum, but a combination of domestic policies and the PRC's deteriorating relationship with Vietnam (symbolized by the SRV's new alliance with Soviet Union) spurred CCP leaders to arrange a special meeting on the establishment of a diplomatic relationship with the United States.[31] Thus what might be termed the American factor played a significant role in Chinese strategic thinking on the eve of its invasion of Vietnam.

Deng's Perceptions of Vietnam

Michael Howard notes that "statesmen can be as emotional or as prejudiced in their judgments" as any social groups, but "it is very seldom that their attitudes, their perceptions and their decisions are not related to the fundamental issues" of national security.[32] Conversely, Raymond Aron suggests that in a situation in which "hostile intentions [exist] on both sides, passion and hatred [are likely to] arise."[33] Unlike earlier Chinese leaders, who maintained close personal relationships with Vietnamese officials, Deng had no "deep individual attachment to the Vietnamese."[34]

Deng's experience with issues related to China's involvement in the Vietnam War and his annoyance with Vietnam's "ungracious" attitude can be traced back to the mid-1960s. According to the available conversation records between Chinese and Vietnamese leaders, Deng appeared to play hardball with his Vietnamese counterparts at least twice, lodging complaints against Vietnam for its anti-China behavior and ingratitude for China's support.[35] The Vietnamese leaders also appeared unable to forgive Deng's attitude toward the Vietnamese national liberation cause, including his attempts to persuade the North Vietnamese to downplay the revolution in the South and to refuse Soviet aid as a condition of continued Chinese aid during the Vietnam War.[36]

One later study, however, contends that Deng might have been able to save China and Vietnam from a "complete break" had Deng not been purged. After his return to work in July 1977, the relationship between China and Vietnam was beyond repair. Soviet-Vietnamese cooperation had increased and China's relationship with both the Soviet Union and Vietnam had deteriorated badly.[37] Despite such a speculative inference, Deng's views about the Soviet threat and

Vietnam's "ungracious" attitude appeared unchanged at the time. All told, China provided Hanoi with $20 billion worth of assistance over two decades, more than any other country supplied.[38]

Understandably, then, when Vietnam moved to force the repatriation of ethnic Chinese living in North Vietnam[39] and then encroached on Chinese territory along the border, many Chinese were angered by what they regarded as Hanoi's ingratitude given China's aid and sacrifice. The PRC witnessed a widespread public outpouring of anger against Vietnam, both genuine and cultivated, spurred on by official propaganda.[40] Those who had assisted the Vietnamese communists in their wars against France and the United States felt particularly betrayed and were eager to "teach Vietnam a lesson." Vice Premier Li Xiannian characterized forthcoming Chinese military actions as "a slap in the face of [Vietnam] to warn and punish them."[41] Deng Xiaoping agreed. As animosity between China and Vietnam intensified, he became increasingly emotional, even once calling Vietnam the *wangbadan* (literally "tortoise eggs" but also "son of a bitch") in front of a foreign leader.[42] There is no evidence showing exactly how Deng's "annoyance" toward Vietnam affected the Chinese leader's decision making. However, Ezra F. Vogel believes that the Chinese leader was "passionately" offended by "Vietnamese ambitions."[43] The emotion factor may also have intensified Deng's concerns about the risk of Soviet expansion in the region.

Confronting increasingly deteriorated relations between China and Vietnam, most Chinese interpreted Hanoi's newly adopted anti-China policy and actions; intensified political, economic, and military cooperation with the Soviet Union; and expansion in the region (including escalating border clashes and the ongoing exodus of Chinese residents) as clear evidence of a disturbing and growing Vietnamese "insolence." These concerns generated public dismay, increased popular anxieties, and created a favorable climate in which Deng and other Chinese leaders could teach Vietnam a lesson by using military force. Although these public sentiments did not play a dominant role in his decision to use force, Deng did resort to emotional rhetoric when speaking of the need to teach Vietnam a lesson, and his words constituted a serious warning to the Vietnamese to beware of the consequences if they continued to ignore China's concerns.

Nevertheless, Chinese leaders' concerns were dominated by the perception of an escalating Soviet threat. Deng and others perceived Vietnam's anti-China policies and acts, the alliance that had emerged between the USSR and Vietnam, and then Hanoi's invasion of Cambodia as a proxy for Soviet expansion. Since Soviet-backed Cuban forces had intervened in the Angolan civil war in

October 1975, China had been increasingly alarmed at the USSR's success in penetrating and influencing conflicts and insurgencies in the "Third World."[44] In June 1978, the Chinese press began to refer to Vietnam as the "Cuba of Asia," implying that Vietnam's expansion would simply mean the spread of Soviet-sponsored military adventurism into Asia.[45] But this time, that adventurism would occur on China's doorstep and against China's best interests, a circumstance intolerable to the Beijing leadership. Deng was so offended by what he saw as Hanoi's challenge to Beijing's interests that it prompted him "to wage a war to teach Vietnam a lesson."[46] Thus, the perception of the Soviet threat, rather than an enduring and innate passionate hatred toward Vietnam, motivated the Chinese leader to use force against his country's former ally.

The Soviet Factor

If China had to consider an "American factor," it likewise had to consider a "Soviet factor." After his return to power, Deng's foreign policy views initially remained under the influence of Mao Zedong's strategic thinking, which regarded Soviet global expansion and growing military power as the main threats to peace. Despite Moscow's attempt to reconcile with China in 1977 and 1978, Chinese leaders distrusted the Soviet Union because of the long-standing animosity between the two countries, reinforced by recent Soviet actions.[47] The USSR continued a major military buildup near China and routinely conducted military exercises with live ammunition in simulated armed conflict on the borders.[48] By the summer of 1978, the growing cooperation between Hanoi and Moscow (especially an expansion of Soviet use of bases in Vietnam) renewed Chinese fears of an eventual Soviet encirclement of China from the south.

Starting in the early 1970s, Mao had pursued the strategy of a global "horizontal line"—that is, a strategic line of defense against the Soviet Union stretching from Japan to Europe to the United States. The basis of Mao's "line" strategy was close cooperation between China and the United States. Washington, however, had not responded to Mao's overtures as positively as Beijing expected, leaving Chinese leaders to conclude that the United States remained primarily interested in extending the Nixon-era policy of détente toward its Soviet rival.[49]

Chinese frustration continued during the early years of Jimmy Carter's presidency. Carter possessed no previous experience in international affairs (or, for that matter, in national government) and came to office vowing to give an even higher priority to American-Soviet détente. This approach did not please Chinese leaders, particularly Deng. He disliked the U.S. tendency to try to ease international tension by negotiations. On 27 September 1977, he met with George H. W. Bush, the former director of the U.S. Liaison Office in Beijing, and frankly criticized the U.S. nuclear arms control agreements with the Soviet Union, which despite much publicity had not prevented the USSR from reaching parity.[50] In May 1978, the Chinese leader repeated the same criticism to Zbigniew Brzezinski, Carter's national security adviser and a student of the Soviet Union, during Brzezinski's visit to Beijing. Deng cautioned him about the Soviets' intentions, stressing their innate hostility toward the United States and warning that agreements or cooperation with the Soviet Union would not prevent Soviet expansionism. Brzezinski seriously misinterpreted Deng's position, suggesting that his anti-Soviet posturing was merely "rhetorical." Likely astonished at this misreading, Deng strongly disagreed, explaining that China had always done things within the compass of its power.[51] It is difficult to be certain whether this exchange influenced Deng, who later stressed that he did not want other countries to perceive China as soft in its dealings with the Soviet-Vietnamese alliance.[52] The Chinese military action against Vietnam was thus expected to demonstrate that Beijing would match its words with action in joining the United States to oppose Soviet aggression.[53]

In November 1978, two major developments increased Beijing's anxieties. First, Chinese leaders now worried about any normalization or improvement of relations between the United States and Vietnam. On 3 November, Li Xiannian voiced displeasure in a conversation with U.S. energy secretary James Schlesinger, stating that closer ties between America and the SRV would not draw Vietnam away from the Soviet Union.[54] To forestall a possible American-Vietnamese rapprochement, the Chinese appeared more anxious than before to accelerate negotiations with the United States on the establishment of diplomatic relations, reviving talks that had stalled in early July.

Second, the strengthening of Soviet military ties with Vietnam after the signing of the Soviet-Vietnamese Treaty of Peace and Friendship on 3 November sparked alarm in Beijing. At the time, the Soviet Union already had heavy military buildup (including the deployment of SS-20 medium-range ballistic missiles, Tu-22M Backfire bombers, and tactical nuclear weapons) in the region close to the Chinese border, posing a serious threat to China from the north.[55] The newly signed security treaty between Moscow and Hanoi further convinced the Chinese that the Soviet Union had not only backed Vietnam's invasion of Cambodia and the stoking of tensions on China's southern borders but also accentuated the military threat from the south.[56] China thus needed to seek a strategic balance through both diplomatic and military actions to counter the newly established Moscow-Hanoi alliance.

China's first move was to rally support from neighboring countries for a united front against hegemony. During the latter part of October 1978, Deng Xiaoping had a triumphal visit to Japan that considerably strengthened the relationship between the two countries. Although Japan maintained a strong neutralist position, seeking the peaceful resolution of international issues, China managed to include an antihegemony clause in the Sino-Japanese Treaty of Peace and Friendship. At a press conference in Tokyo, Deng promised that China would never become hegemonic and emphasized that China would oppose all countries that sought dominance, and he was definitely referring to the Soviet Union and Vietnam.[57] A week later, Deng traveled to Thailand, Malaysia, and Singapore, inviting them to cooperate with China to resist Soviet and Vietnamese expansion in Southeast Asia. In Bangkok, the Chinese leader made it clear that China always opposed Soviet global ambition and Vietnamese regional ambition; China's response to Vietnam's hegemonic policy in the region depended on the extent to which Vietnam invaded Cambodia. He expected that ASEAN countries would play a major role in opposing the Soviet-Vietnamese hegemonic expansion. Deng had no doubt that his visit to these countries served this purpose.[58] To strengthen China's relations with ASEAN, he later proclaimed that if Vietnam invaded Thailand and other ASEAN countries, China would firmly stand by them against Hanoi's aggression.[59]

Despite these diplomatic maneuvers to rally support for China's antihegemony clause from neighboring countries, the Chinese leadership was still not certain how the Soviet Union would respond if China did attack Vietnam. On 7 December 1978, the CMC met for several hours and decided to launch a limited war on China's southern border to "hit back" at Vietnam.[60] Some attendees expressed concern that the Soviet Union might launch a retaliatory attack from the north, forcing China to fight a two-front war. The PLA General Staff's intelligence analysis indicated that the Soviet Union would have three military options in response to the invasion: (1) a large-scale armed conflict including a direct attack on Beijing; (2) the instigation of armed ethnic minority émigrés to attack China's outposts in Xinjiang and Inner Mongolia; and (3) the use of skirmishes to foment border tensions between the two countries.

Although the Soviet Union had deployed fifty-four divisions along the border with China and Mongolia, the PLA General Staff calculated that two-thirds of these divisions were undermanned and inadequately equipped and that the Soviet Union did not have enough troops to mount a large-scale military intervention in China. Any significant Soviet intervention would force Moscow to transfer a large number of troops (at least one million) from Europe, lessening its strength on the NATO–Warsaw Pact fronts. In any case, the PLA reasoned, the USSR would not have enough time to move these troops to attack China because China's invasion of Vietnam would not take long. Further, the Soviet Union also had to consider the fact that an attack on China from the north would place its own national security in Europe at great risk because of a possible U.S. response. For his part, Deng Xiaoping concluded that the Soviet Union would not attack China because engaging in a land war in Asia (as America had done in Vietnam for more than a decade) would not further Soviet interests.[61] China's attack of Vietnam, therefore, offered the prospect of upsetting Moscow's hopes for strategic hegemony.[62] On 8 December, the CMC ordered the Guangzhou and Kunming Military Regions to be ready for military action against Vietnam by 10 January 1979.[63] The PLA had started down the path to war on its own schedule.

Normalization of Chinese-U.S. Relations

But before the cannons roared, China had a matter to resolve with its new-found American friend. As the PLA forces prepared to invade, Deng Xiaoping moved to "quicken the pace" of negotiations to normalize relations with the United States, remarking that doing so "will be to our advantage."[64] Zhu Qizhen, the Chinese ambassador to the United States, later recalled that the main sticking point in normalization discussions was "the sale of [U.S.] weapons to Taiwan" and that "if we had insisted that the United States had to stop selling weapons to Taiwan, we might have lost the chance to establish diplomatic relations with the United States."[65] He did not explain why the establishment of diplomatic relations with the United States was so crucial to China in December 1978. Chinese party historians have claimed that while CCP leaders were planning a limited war against Vietnam and decided to concentrate the party's work on economic construction and modernization, they felt the need to grasp the opportunity to normalize China's relations with the United States.[66] But these historians do not provide any details to support their contentions. Available Chinese sources and American archival records clearly show that Chinese leaders, particularly Deng, considered all these events as part of an interrelated whole.

November 1978 was thus a critical time not only in the PRC's preparation for war with the SRV but also in the normalization of Chinese-U.S. relations. Both sides certainly appeared intent on securing an agreement by the end of the year, and Deng took the lead in championing the establishment of diplomatic relations between the two countries. At a meeting of the CCP Politburo on 2 November, he directed the Foreign Ministry to probe U.S. intentions on normalization, stressing that the PRC "should accelerate the normalization of relations with the United States in terms of economy."[67] In the meantime, the Chinese leader underscored to American visitors that normalization of relations with the PRC "would do more for American security than any number of arms control treaties signed with Moscow."[68] At a special meeting on 27 November, Deng emphasized "the importance of not missing the opportunity" for normalized relations and gave instructions regarding the next round of negotiations.[69] He apparently had made up his mind by this point, even though some thorny questions still demanded resolution. In early December, Deng told the party leaders in some provinces and the commanders of several military regions that China and the United States would establish a diplomatic relationship on 1 January 1979. He did not want to see the Americans "stick their tails up" (*qiaoweiba*) and therefore would get directly involved in the negotiations until the Central Work Conference was over.[70]

The chief sticking point remained U.S. arms sales to Taiwan. The Chinese understood well from President Carter's forceful September statement to Chai Zemin, the director of the Chinese Liaison Office in Washington, that the United States would continue to provide Taiwan with defensive weapons.[71] On 4 December, the Chinese negotiator registered the PRC's "emphatic objection" to this position. Carter administration officials misinterpreted Chinese objections and misread the PRC's strategic intent, believing that the dispute over arms sales would not prevent China from normalizing its relations with the United States. Their misguided belief soon created confusion in Washington as well as in Beijing.[72] In November, U.S. policymakers struggled to work out a final agreement. High-ranking Chinese officials, for their part, were intent on eliminating the ultraleftist influence at the Central Work Conference, and Deng himself was mulling over the policy guidelines for domestic reform and an opening to the world.[73]

Against the background of this diplomatic dance, the PRC's leaders went ahead with plans to attack Vietnam. In early December, the Chinese leader signed an order to mobilize PLA forces to prepare the attack.[74] Deng then took negotiations into his own hands, holding four talks with Leonard Woodcock, the Carter administration's director of the U.S. Liaison Office in Beijing, from 13 to 15 December. According to Woodcock's reports, Deng gave no indication that he would acquiesce in U.S. arms sales to Taiwan. When, in turn, Woodcock stated that the United States would "refrain from selling weapons to Taiwan" after the Taiwan Defense Treaty became invalid in 1979, Deng mistakenly assumed that Woodcock meant that the United States would stop selling arms to Taiwan.[75]

Thus, on the eve of the unveiling of the normalization agreement, Deng was greatly surprised to learn that the United States fully intended to continue selling arms to Taiwan after establishing relations with China. The Chinese leader strongly objected but nevertheless agreed to accept the U.S. negotiator's recommendation that the two sides could "continue to discuss this question later on without affecting the issuance of the communiqué."[76] Chinese scholars argue that Deng's decision not to "quibble" over the arms sales issue was in keeping with his strategic and domestic objectives.[77] The PLA's preparations for an invasion of Vietnam certainly required a favorable relationship with America, particularly as they were designed in part to promote Mao's "horizontal-line" strategy against Soviet expansionism. Li Shenzhi, Deng's foreign policy adviser, later explained that the Chinese leader regarded an attack on a Soviet ally as "a vital move" to prove that China's national interests were consistent with those of the United States.[78] From Beijing's perspective, then, the establishment of diplomatic relations with Washington on 1 January 1979 had altered the global balance of power in China's favor. Beijing was now free to move against its southern neighbor.[79]

Deng Xiaoping Makes a Decision

Various scholars have claimed that some Chinese leaders opposed the decision to attack Vietnam, but they disagree among themselves about which leaders were involved and what form their opposition took.[80] Chinese archives on the matter are currently inaccessible, and existing Chinese publications offer few clues. In 1978, in addition to Hua, Deng, Chen, and Wang, other powerful PRC leaders included Marshall Ye Jianying and Li Xiannian, both of whom were CCP vice chairs. Marshals Xu Xiangqian and Nie Rongzhen served as vice chairs of the CMC. Their biographies and other available records make no mention of the roles that Ye, Li, and Nie played in China's decision to attack Vietnam, even though all of them had long careers with the PLA.[81] In interviews with foreign journalists, Li was a vocal supporter of the war.[82] But some other veteran revolutionaries were uncomfortable with the drastic change in China's foreign policy toward the long-reviled United States. The authors of Marshal Xu's biography indicate that the minister of defense opposed Mao's horizontal-line strategy of alignment with the United States.[83] Marshal Ye reportedly opposed Deng's decision to use military force against the SRV.[84]

As a result, Ye discreetly traveled to Shanghai and thus did not attend the expanded CCP Politburo meeting on New Year's Eve, when Deng's war proposal was scheduled to be discussed.[85]

All of these policymakers were reduced to the second rank at best compared to the increasingly powerful and dominant Deng. Understanding the PRC's progression toward war during 1978 requires understanding the position and place of Deng. To a degree unknown to other participants (however important they might be), the decision to go to war was largely his alone. He formulated the arguments, he made the case, and he had the faith and confidence of the PLA. His will carried the day.

The CCP's Third Plenum had positioned Deng as number 3 among Chinese leaders, behind only Hua, the nominal leader of the party, and the elderly Ye, who had already transferred his military responsibilities to Deng. After Mao, Zhou Enlai, and Zhu De died, the PLA's leadership and officer cadre saw Deng, like Marshals Peng Dehuai and Lin Biao earlier on, as the only individual inside the CCP and PLA leadership with the status and reputation to exercise absolute control over the military.[86] Marshal Ye once acknowledged that Deng was not only a *lao shuai* (old marshal) but also the "foreman of old marshals."[87]

In short, Deng's seniority and prestige in the CCP and the military meant that his decisions as chief architect of the invasion of Vietnam were unlikely to be challenged. Moreover, Ye shared Deng's strategic views and echoed China's support for Cambodia with the same rhetoric used by the Chinese government.[88] He might disagree with the decision to use force to resolve the differences between China and Vietnam, but Ye abided by the party's rules, which required the minority to be subordinate to the majority. During the subsequent invasion, he reportedly spent almost every day at the PLA General Staff's command center, listening to reports and giving instructions to ensure that operations went smoothly.[89] Xu's opposition to the one-line strategy received no support from his colleagues, and he ultimately backed the war decision and devoted his efforts to furthering war planning. Overall, Deng's control of the PLA General Staff provided him with a convenient vehicle for exerting his own desires and will on military planning, which he pushed through the CMC in November, one month before the central CCP leadership formally decided to strike in December.[90]

Deng offered his colleagues three reasons why China should use force against Vietnam:

First, the current international antihegemony struggle against the Soviet Union was weakening because the United States, Japan, and Europe were afraid to confront the USSR even as the Soviet Union geared up for war and expanded rapidly. Thus, in light of Vietnam's invasion of Cambodia and its continuing provocations along China's border, the PRC itself must take a leading role in the struggle. The PRC's "self-defense counterattack," Deng argued, was aimed not at mere border disputes but at the wider situation in Southeast Asia and even the entire world.

Second, China needed a safe, reliable environment if it were to undertake its Four Modernizations. The PRC could not allow itself to be "wedged in" by the Soviet Union from the north and Vietnam from the south. China, he believed, should expose the hollowness of Vietnam's boast of being "the world's third-strongest military power" and of "being ever victorious." A Chinese failure to act, Deng claimed, would simply fuel Vietnamese aggression and might encourage the Soviet Union to move from the north. China's preemptive counterattack would thus be seen as a warning to the Soviet Union to curb its own adventurism.

Third, the PLA had not fought a war in thirty years. The world doubted China's capability to defeat Vietnam, and even Chinese leaders could not be "sure that our military is still good enough." While this might seem an odd reason for military intervention against Vietnam, Deng believed that it would demonstrate that China was a power to be taken seriously. Deng agreed with the CMC's recent decision to increase troop training but believed that real combat would be even more beneficial. He also worried about the PLA's reputation, which had suffered a great deal in recent years as a result of the Cultural Revolution. In sum, Deng was convinced that a successful war against Vietnam would help restore the military's reputation and provide more officers with war experience. Moreover, the experience earned on the battlefield would force the PLA to become more streamlined and efficient.[91]

If these reasons seemed inadequate to persuade those who feared the intervention would unwisely divert China's scarce resources (which were sorely needed for modernization), Deng tied the potential action against Vietnam to securing foreign financial and technological support for its modernization drive. He argued the United States, Western Europe, and Japan would be willing to provide money and equipment for China's modernization since they all wanted a powerful China to "contain Soviet revisionism." The use of force against Vietnam would demonstrate that China carried substantial weight in the international antihegemony movement. He further stressed this policy was not new and had already been endorsed by Mao, thus wisely linking his own actions to those of China's still-venerated leader.[92] In the end, the combination of Deng's authority and his clearly expressed convictions prevailed.

On 25 December 1978, more than 150,000 heavily armed Vietnamese troops crossed into Democratic Kampuchea. The Cambodian army's resistance was disorganized and ineffective, and in less than a week, it was on the verge of collapse. Two days before New Year's Eve, the Cambodian government informed the Chinese embassy that its diplomats and advisers should evacuate Phnom Penh immediately.[93] At the same time, Khmer Rouge leaders decided to carry out a protracted resistance against Vietnam's invasion. They requested that Beijing act to divert Vietnamese military pressure on Cambodia from the north.[94] Chinese leaders felt a mounting sense of urgency to respond assertively.

On the evening of 31 December, at an expanded CCP Politburo meeting that included not only its members but also high-ranking party and government officials, Deng formally proposed a punitive war against Vietnam.[95] Deng had already made up his mind to launch military action against Vietnam and had cleared this decision with other senior leaders before the expanded Politburo meeting. At this moment, he was not asking for approval. Rather, he was simply informing a larger inner circle of the party of his decision and involving them in discussing details about the war's execution. Apparently influenced by Vietnam's invasion of Cambodia, all participants, including Hua Guofeng, not only unanimously accepted Deng's proposal for attacks on Lang Son, Cao Bang, and Lao Cai but also enthusiastically advocated several changes to the original war plan by including a deployment of two additional armies to attack the iconic Dien Bien Phu from Mengla, Yunnan, via Laos, to more directly threaten Hanoi.[96] The Politburo also decided to extend the operations by fifteen to twenty days so that between three and five Vietnamese divisions would be obliterated.[97] Thus, the scope, duration, and intent of the operation steadily expanded. From one targeted SRV division, the PRC had now determined to target up to five; from a short five-day incursion, the PRC was now determined to spend approximately three weeks at war.[98] At the meeting, Deng appointed Xu Shiyou to command operations from Guangxi in the east and Yang Dezhi (the commander of the Wuhan Military Region) to command operations from Yunnan in the west, sidestepping Wang Bicheng, the commander of the Kunming Military Region.[99]

The reason for the change of command in Yunnan has not been disclosed. One early study suggests that Wang was removed from the top command position of the Kunming Military Region because of his heavy involvement in a factional struggle with other leaders in Yunnan that made him unpopular at a time when "utmost unity was demanded" from both military and civilian leadership. In addition, Wang may have been bypassed as a payback for having repeatedly and publicly criticized Deng following his 1976 purge.[100] Other rumors alleged a bad personal relationship between Xu and Wang that caused

Xu to recommend that the Politburo drop his rival.[101] For whatever mix of reasons, Deng summoned Yang (then attending a CMC meeting in Beijing) to the Great Hall of the People in the midst of the Politburo war meeting on New Year's Eve, appointing him commander in place of Wang.[102]

After returning to power, Deng had become increasingly worried about the political quality of the PLA and particularly the loyalties and unity of senior officers.[103] The political purges since the late 1950s and the Cultural Revolution from 1966 to 1976 had fractured many long-standing relationships among China's aging general officers. Indeed, an expanded CMC meeting (attended by senior officers from three headquarters, all of the PLA services, and the military regions) on 20 December 1978–3 January 1979 dissolved into bitter acrimony, with Marshal Xu failing to maintain any collegiality or order. An undoubtedly frustrated Deng (now confident in his views about the post-Mao discord affecting the PLA) brought it to an end without reaching any consensus.[104]

Ironically, the specter of conflict with Vietnam imposed an order and unity on the PLA that it sorely lacked in the post–Lin Biao era. Zhang Sheng, an officer on the General Staff (and son of General Zhang Aiping, a senior PLA leader) later argued that without the war with Vietnam a few weeks later, this turmoil among senior military officers might have continued.[105] The PLA in 1979 was clearly not the capable military force that had fought in the Korean War and that had prevailed in border clashes with India and the Soviet Union. PLA generals had lived a comfortable well-fed life and were divided because of their long-standing service branch and field army loyalties as well as political grievances arising from the Cultural Revolution. Indeed, many Chinese later tended to believe that Deng used the war against Vietnam to reinstate political control over the military.

But recently available Chinese documentation also suggests that Deng worried that the ongoing internal struggle would rob China of stability and unity. According to Deng, foreign countries would not increase their trade with China unless they saw it as a stable country.[106] Thus, Deng needed the military not only to back him during his power struggle within the CCP but also to achieve his economic reform policies. As of late 1978, he was uncertain about whether he could count on the military's unconditional support.

The PLA's factionalism had deep roots, having been nourished during the revolutionary period and then enjoyed accelerated growth during the political struggles attending the Cultural Revolution. According to Deng's remarks delivered at a CMC forum on 3 January 1979, trust between superiors and subordinates had always been a key component in ensuring the PLA's steadfastness and combat effectiveness. However, by the end of the Cultural Revolution, this relationship had been severely damaged.[107] He later acknowledged that the war against Vietnam could help restore the PLA to its past vigor.[108]

A series of changes in the PLA leadership in the early 1980s might at first glance suggest that the 1979 war with Vietnam inspired this reorganization, but streamlining the PLA and its command system had been under consideration well before the war. Certainly, The PLA's long-standing problems defied easy or swift resolution. Deng opted for a methodical rather than dramatic approach to reform, reflecting more broadly the priority he placed on national stability and unity. The PLA's subsequent dismal performance in the war merely confirmed Deng's belief in the need for sweeping changes.[109] Wang's replacement by Yang on the eve of the war, however, prompted Deng to send two of his deputy chiefs to Kunming to supervise the transition and war preparations.[110] In Beijing, the Chinese leader designated two aides, Yang Yong and Wang Shangrong, to coordinate operations between the two military regions, which would carry out their missions independently.[111]

Even though Deng was increasingly seen as the supreme leader akin to Mao, he remained obliged to consult trusted senior colleagues before making a decision. They were mindful of several key risks—that the Soviet Union would launch a retaliatory attack on China; that the United States would seek to profit from the situation; that world opinion would condemn the PRC; and that the war with Vietnam would impede China's drive for economic modernization.[112] To test his assumptions and acquire independent, dispassionate counsel, Deng invited one of his closest colleagues, Chen Yun, to weigh the advantages and disadvantages of a war against Vietnam. After contemplating the matter, Chen not only offered his full endorsement but also took a reassuring tone.[113] He evidently helped to convince Deng that a defensive, limited, and brief military action against Vietnam would not provoke Moscow's intervention and would have little impact on domestic economic reform.

Chen Yun's advice came at a propitious time. Plans for the incursion had already moved from attacking one division over a few days to attacking up to five divisions over three weeks. Now, to prevent the situation from spinning out of control, the CCP Politburo decided that no matter what results were reached on the battlefield, after the seizure of two Vietnamese border provincial capitals, Lang Son and Cao Bang, the PLA forces would halt their advance, disengage from the fighting, and withdraw.[114] The promise of a short war was designed to allay concerns and undercut domestic opposition. It was also perhaps a way to avoid unseen troubles by bringing the war to a close before the shock of the incursion had triggered the full fury of an SVR military response. Moreover, a short war would reassure the Soviet Union that China did not desire to invade Hanoi and overthrow Moscow's ally, as Vietnam had done in Cambodia, thus reducing the likelihood that the Soviet Union would escalate and retaliate against China. Conventional wisdom holds that "since war plans tend to cover only the first act, the national leadership, in opting for war, will in fact be choosing a plan without an ending."[115] To preclude being entrapped in a prolonged conflict, the Chinese leadership implemented restraints to both the means and ends of warfare. Nevertheless, in the interim, Chinese leaders could not lower their guard, and they ordered troops in the northern and northwestern military regions to step up combat readiness for possible Soviet strikes. Officials also stressed that if Soviet forces invaded, Chinese troops must "hold out firmly while not giving the impression of weakness."[116]

The New Year's Eve meeting deferred the timing of military action. Some Western analysts argue that the PRC was still inhibited by concerns about international reaction and that Deng's scheduled trips to the United States and Japan were intended to test the waters.[117] In fact, Chinese leaders were mainly worried about whether their forces had enough time to adequately prepare for the invasion. The initial mobilization and deployment orders to Guangzhou and Kunming required all units to "reach their designated positions by 10 January 1979 and complete combat preparations at once."[118] However, Chinese soldiers had not engaged in any war since 1969, and many of them could not comprehend going to war against a traditional ally and a small neighboring state.[119]

Shortly after the New Year's Eve meeting, Deng sent Yang Yong, the deputy chief of the General Staff; Wei Guoqing, the director of the General Political Department; and Zhang Zhen to inspect troops' combat readiness at Yunnan and Guangxi. The evident lack of preparation appalled them, and Zhang immediately recommended the postponement of the war for a month. The CMC agreed to defer military action until the middle of February.[120] On 22 January, Deng met at home with the chief leaders of the CMC, Xu Xiangqian, Nie Rongzhen, and Geng Biao. Yang reported on his recent trip to the front and offered suggestions on the war.[121]

At this gathering, the Chinese leadership likely not only reaffirmed the war decision but also suspended the plan to attack Vietnam from Yunnan via Laos. Vietnamese forces had already occupied most of Cambodia, and CCP leaders did not believe that a PLA attack from the north would significantly influence Hanoi's operations in the south. Two days later, the General Staff summoned the chief of staff of the Guangzhou Military Region to Beijing to finalize the war plan, conveying Deng's instructions that troops must be ready by 15 February to embark on their mission of eliminating enemy forces at Lang Son and

Cao Bang. To assist the operation, the two additional armies freed from the abandoned northwest invasion plan were transferred to reinforce the attacks from Guangxi. The participants in the meeting characterized the forthcoming operation as a "self-defense counterattack against Vietnam."[122]

Seeking Washington's Support

On 28 January 1979, as Chinese troops prepared for war against Vietnam, Deng Xiaoping boarded a Boeing 707 to Washington for his historic visit to the United States. He sat taciturn in his own cabin, evidently immersed in thought and aware of the gravity of the trip.[123] His visit would complete a journey initiated by Mao nearly a decade earlier to forge a strategic relationship with United States.[124] Deng appeared unsure about how the Americans would react to the planned war against Vietnam. Chinese leaders apparently assumed that China and the United States had similar strategic aims and would form a united front against Soviet hegemony. One of the major (if unstated) purposes of Deng's trip was to ally the United States with China to counter the Soviet-Vietnamese alliance in East Asia.[125] Deng's trump card was the Chinese military plan against Vietnam, for which he wanted American support. According to Geng Biao, Deng proposed that the United States dispatch ships to the South China Sea to contain Soviet naval activities while helping China with intelligence on Vietnamese vessels. Chinese leaders seemed convinced that giving the U.S. Navy access to the naval base at Yulin on Hainan Island "will be conducive to the stability of Southeast Asia."[126]

Deng's schedule in Washington included three official meetings with President Carter. During the first two, the two men exchanged views about world issues, and at the third they planned to discuss the development of bilateral relations.[127] On the evening of 28 January, a few hours after arriving in Washington, at the dinner table in Brzezinski's house, Deng surprised his American hosts by requesting a special meeting with Carter to discuss the Vietnam issue.[128] The meeting, held in the Oval Office late on the afternoon of 29 January, immediately after the second official session, was attended by Deng, Foreign Minister Huang Hua, and Deputy Foreign Minister Zhang Wenjin on the China side and by Carter, Vice President Walter Mondale, Secretary of State Cyrus Vance, and Brzezinski on the U.S. side.[129] According to Brzezinski, the Chinese leader spoke in a "calm, determined, and firm way" about China's decision to attack Vietnam, informing the Americans that to counter Soviet expansion, the Chinese leadership "consider it necessary to put restraint on the wild ambitions of the Vietnamese and to give them an appropriate limited

Deng Xiaoping at a dinner hosted by Zbigniew Brzezinski, 28 January 1979. Courtesy Jimmy Carter Presidential Library, Atlanta.

lesson." Without divulging specific details about China's plan, Deng outlined possible Soviet responses and the ways to counter them. He said that if "the worst possibility" were to happen, China "would hold out" and would simply ask for U.S "moral support" in the international arena. Carter did not offer an immediate response and instead merely reminded his Chinese guest to exercise restraint in dealing with such a difficult situation.[130]

The next day, Deng received a handwritten note from Carter, who sought to discourage a Chinese attack on Vietnam. The president argued that a limited punitive war would have no effect on Vietnam's occupation of Cambodia and might drag China into a quagmire. Carter also predicted that an invasion of Vietnam would stymie China's effort to foster a peace-loving image and might cause Americans to worry that future Chinese military action would impair U.S. interests in the region.[131] On 30 January, at another private meeting with Carter, Deng was determined and tough, insisting that China must punish Vietnam and that the PLA would limit its action to a short operation. He acknowledged that international reaction might be divided but remained confident that opinion would favor China in the long run.[132] The potential international backlash would not deter the Chinese leader because he would yield to nothing after having made up his mind.[133] Despite Carter's unsupportive comments, Deng did not believe that the United States would endorse a condemnation of China for its military action.[134]

Deng Xiaoping and Jimmy
Carter at the ceremony
honoring Deng's arrival in
the United States, 29 January
1979. Courtesy Jimmy Carter
Presidential Library, Atlanta.

If Deng was disappointed by Carter's cool response to the proposed military action against Vietnam, he was undoubtedly pleased by something else—the American administration's eagerness to exploit its new relationship with China to work against Soviet interests. Before leaving Washington to tour other parts of the United States, Deng was surprised to learn that the United States was interested in a joint U.S.-Chinese listening post in the Xinjiang area targeted against the Soviet Union. The Islamic Revolution that was gathering pace in Iran had cast doubts on the future viability of U.S. bases located in that country, and according to Brzezinski, the proposed installation in China was intended to help the United States verify Soviet compliance with the Strategic Arms Limitation Treaty (SALT) via monitoring of missile tests.[135] Unlike Mao, who in the 1950s had rejected the Soviet Union's proposal for a joint long-wave radio transmission and receiving station in China, Deng showed great interest in the idea and agreed to consider it.[136]

During this final private discussion among Carter, Brzezinski, and Deng, the two sides apparently reached a tacit understanding that the United States would help China with intelligence monitoring of Soviet forces in the Far East.[137] Deng told the CCP Central Committee in March 1979 that American officials publicly "spoke with official tone" (*daguanqiang*) against China's military actions but "in private had spoken [to him] differently" and "provided us with some intelligence" showing that (as PLA experts already suspected) none of the fifty-four Soviet divisions on the country's border with China were at full strength. More important, the Chinese leader believed that he made it clear before the Americans that "what China said is reliable; China has given careful consideration to its actions; [and] China will not act impulsively."[138]

Jimmy Carter meets Deng Xiaoping in the Oval Office, 29 January 1979. Courtesy Jimmy Carter Presidential Library, Atlanta.

Thus, in contrast to his tense demeanor during his flight to America, Deng was visibly relaxed on the trip home.[139] Indeed, he had every right to be pleased. He had told his colleagues in Beijing that his trip to the United States would yield positive results for a joint alliance against Soviet expansion and Vietnamese aggression.[140] He now sensed that a new strategic relationship between the PRC and the United States was developing on the basis of the two countries' shared interest in countering Soviet expansionism. On the issue of Vietnam, the Americans had not rejected or directly criticized the Chinese plans and had instead called for future intelligence cooperation.[141] Deng became even more confident, as he later told other Chinese leaders, that Beijing's scheduled military action against Vietnam would prove China's value for both curbing the Soviet Union and receiving assistance for its modernization from the United States and other Western countries.[142]

Conclusion: Assessing China's Decision to Go to War

Deng's trip to America effectively green-lighted his already-firm decision to go to war. On 11 February 1979, two days after Deng Xiaoping returned to Beijing, the CCP Politburo met in an expanded session. Deng explained the nature and goals of the attack on Vietnam and its basic rationale. The local military commands in Guangxi and Yunnan subsequently received orders to launch attacks on Vietnam.[143] On 14 February, the CCP Central Committee dispatched a document to the party organizations of the provinces, military regions, PLA general departments, and government ministries explaining its decision to launch a self-defense counterattack. The document informed the party organizations about the imminent war and instructed them to share the news with party members at county and military regimental levels. To counter any opposition and concerns, it stressed that the war would be limited in space, time, and scale. Citing the Chinese-Indian border conflict of 1962 and the Chinese-Soviet border clashes of 1969, the CCP document insisted that China would not take a single square inch of Vietnamese territory and would not allow the SRV to occupy a single square inch of Chinese land. The document concluded by noting that the military action would bolster peace and stability along the border and would facilitate China's Four Modernizations.[144]

Third-party observers had anticipated that the strike would be timed based on weather factors. The PRC would not want to conduct military operations in the rainy season, usually beginning in April, or attack too early, when Soviet armed forces could still cross the frozen rivers along the Sino-Soviet border. The day came on 17 February.[145] Deng and other Chinese leaders had weighed the alternatives as well as the likely consequences after their troops crossed Vietnam's border, including a possible confrontation with the Soviet Union. They were confident that the limited scope and duration of the "self-defense counterattack" would forestall negative reactions at home and abroad. No one, however, seemed to anticipate that the 1979 war would trigger more than a decade of continuous military confrontations on the PRC-SRV border.

According to Chinese scholars, the PRC's decision to wage war against Vietnam was influenced by Chinese leaders' reaction to the Soviet Union's genuine threat, which caused them to pursue strategic cooperation with the United States against the Soviet Union. Because this policy emphasized confrontation, Beijing's approach to international crisis in the region became both adamant and militant. Chinese policymakers believed that a punitive attack on Vietnam would deal a blow to the USSR's global expansion strategy.[146] Nevertheless, these studies by the Chinese scholars criticize their leaders for exaggerating the Soviet threat but do not adequately explain why those leaders did so.[147] They also do not elucidate why Deng was so eager to inform the Carter administration of Beijing's decision to attack Vietnam, something that normally would only have happened between two closely allied countries (for example, Churchill and Roosevelt in the Second World War or Stalin and Mao in Korea).[148] However, Deng's 1979 assessments of the Soviet threat were extraordinary. First, he believed that Moscow would wage war in 1985 as a consequence of its sustained military expansion and the deteriorating economic conditions and intensified ethnic problems between Russians and ethnic minorities at home.[149] Second, the Chinese leader worried about the decline of U.S. strength and influence and concluded that the Soviet Union could act even more recklessly after its invasion of Afghanistan.[150] Although the Soviet factor was influential in Chinese decision making, other second-order factors, including domestic politics and the country's evolving relationship with America, also played a role.

First, Vietnam's "misbehavior" toward China, particularly its alliance with the Soviet Union, had affronted the Chinese, who wanted to punish their treacherous erstwhile ally. This sentiment played a significant part in generating a broad consensus among Chinese political and military leaders to support Deng, the key figure pushing for military action against Vietnam. Second, on questions of territorial sovereignty, which often stir Chinese emotions, the military view seemed to be the determining factor in the initiation of actual hostilities. The September PLA General Staff meeting that produced recommendations for remedying deteriorating relations with Vietnam provided the starting point for a major military operation. Deng used these recommendations for both strategic and domestic objectives. Further, the 1979 war demonstrated that the PLA always played a critical role in the PRC's national security.

The historical-cultural element along with national sentiment induced Chinese leaders to launch a war that would "teach Vietnam a lesson." Last but far from least, Deng was guided by manifold considerations ranging from China's strategic posture when confronted with an increasing Soviet threat to Beijing's adoption of economic development as the national priority. In the late 1970s, Deng abandoned many of Mao's radical domestic policies but adhered staunchly to the late Chinese leader's "horizontal line" strategy of forming a common front with the United States against the Soviet Union. The new Soviet-Vietnamese military relationship, the Vietnamese invasion of Cambodia, and Vietnam's growing hostility toward China stoked Beijing's concerns about an increasing Soviet threat. Since the late 1970s, Beijing had increasingly perceived Vietnam and even all of Southeast Asia as a new battleground for the fight against Soviet hegemony. Niu Jun concludes that the PRC's policy toward Indochina consequently evolved from serving Mao's "ever-growing ambition for promoting world revolution" in the 1960s to "seeking geopolitical security as major objective" under Deng in the late 1970s.[151] Beijing's decision to go to war with Vietnam in 1979 was largely based on Deng's assessment of China's strategic situation, with a focus on what Soviet expansion meant to global security and what responsibility China should share for maintaining the balance of world power.[152]

China's market-oriented economic reforms also reinforced the importance of pragmatic power politics to Chinese strategic thinking. Deng staked the success of economic reform on Western technology and foreign investment, particularly from America. Deng's acceptance of U.S. terms during the establishment of diplomatic relations between the two countries in mid-December 1978 was crucial in achieving these two strategic objectives both externally and internally. Despite Deng's pragmatic calculation of national interests with few ideological restraints, he harbored the naive hope that the issue of arms sales to Taiwan would resolve itself as China developed more favorable relations with the United States.[153] China's decision to launch a punitive war against Vietnam was intended to display Beijing's usefulness in countering Soviet expansionism. In Deng's own words, China was "a reliable friend," and it therefore deserved Western economic and technological assistance.[154]

After repeatedly associating Vietnam's regional hegemonic desire with Soviet global expansionism and with China's important role in the ongoing opposition to Soviet world hegemony, Chinese leaders found it imperative to show that ignoring Chinese statements had serious consequences. For Beijing, Vietnam's dismissal of repeated Chinese warnings not to invade Cambodia had challenged Chinese credibility, both in the West and in the ASEAN countries. Therefore, China had to "teach" Hanoi to take Chinese warnings seriously or pay a heavy price. In view of all these factors, China's decision to use force assumed far greater importance than many observers initially realized. Furthermore, the decision to go to war is hard to assess without a careful evaluation of geopolitical circumstances and China's drive for economic reform, conditions that in 1979 fundamentally differed from those in 1950. In addition, the ongoing power struggle inside the party leadership and factionalism within the PLA served as catalysts for Deng's increasing willingness to employ military action against Vietnam. In his view, doing so would rally domestic and foreign support to China's side and create a safe and stable environment for modernization. These second-order factors obviously complicated China's decision to use force against Vietnam. Finally, whatever the rationale for the war, Deng's dictatorial leadership style allowed him to dominate Beijing's decision making, allowing no serious debates on the decision to go to war. It is understandable, therefore, that historians and policy analysts focus on Deng when considering the wisdom of China's decision to attack Vietnam.

3 Planning and Preparation for the Invasion

On 9 December 1978, both the Guangzhou and Kunming Military Regions received orders to deploy troops on the Vietnamese border by 10 January and prepare to fight a war "in limited time and space" with "overwhelming force." Many Chinese soldiers doubted whether China should attack Vietnam and whether they would be victorious. The PLA forces had not fought a major war in almost thirty years. Thus, no officers at or below the battalion level had any combat experience. Moreover, the Cultural Revolution had left the PLA's morale and reputation at all-time lows. Chinese leaders, including Deng Xiaoping himself, were unsure about the PLA's combat capability. In the midst of these doubts and uncertainties, the Guangzhou and Kunming Military Regions embarked on detailed planning and preparations for the invasion of Vietnam.

This chapter explores the PLA's implementation of the invasion operations at the campaign and tactical levels in the context of Cold War history. The PRC never planned to engage in a fight with the SRV, and the PLA had never before prepared for such a military action. Chinese forces were undermanned, underequipped, and poorly trained. The most serious difficulty was the lack of enthusiasm among the rank and file. Many soldiers did not understand why they would attack a country that seemed like—and had often been compared to—China's "little brother."

The PLA had developed its own approach to war and its own unique institutional culture. Much of the continuity found in the PLA's military doctrine, strategy, and operational concepts was based on adherence to Maoist principles, even when fighting a weaker enemy like Vietnam. Mao's military thought, the PLA's "political work system," and the mobilization of society to support military actions all played vital roles in guiding the planning and preparations for invasion. The characteristics of the PLA's operational art in military campaigns during the invasion foreshadowed both continuities and changes for years to come. Preparations for war against Vietnam were a national undertaking in support of the Chinese leadership's strategic objectives.

The PLA's Doctrinal and Institutional Traditions

In 1979, the PLA's senior military officers were still Mao's generals, with combat experience from the war against Japan, the civil wars against the Nationalists, and the Korean War. They were intimately familiar with Mao's approach to conflict. In planning and preparing to invade Vietnam, they hewed to the principles developed by the late Chinese leader in the 1930s and 1940s. The CMC's order included some of these principles, requiring both the Guangzhou and Kunming Military Regions to "concentrate a superior force," to employ "encirclement and outflanking" tactics, and to engage in a decisive "battle of annihilation."[1] Understanding how the PLA applied Maoist doctrinal and institutional traditions in the planning and preparation phase of the 1979 invasion of Vietnam requires us to examine the traditions themselves.

Mao's military thinking focused on how a force inferior in arms, equipment, and training could defeat a superior adversary. The essence of his approach was creating a political environment for mobilizing the whole country and rallying popular support for a protracted war. One key doctrinal principle Mao invoked in his approach to warfare was "active defense" (*jiji fangyu*) through "decisive engagements," using the three operational principles of *initiative*, *flexibility*, and *planning*. First, he believed that gaining and retaining the initiative were essential for a weaker force in asymmetric warfare. Second, he asserted that flexibility was essential for achieving the operational initiative. Third, he contended that making clear plans and later necessary changes during the fight helped overcome the confusions, obscurities, and uncertainties peculiar to war.[2]

Mao believed that applying these principles necessitated having commanders who "use all possible methods of conducting reconnaissance" and "ponder information" by "discarding the dross and selecting the essential, eliminating the false and retaining the true" and then "proceeding from one to the other and from the outside to the inside." By carefully considering the interrelationships between conditions of his own army and those of the enemy's army, a wise commander could "reach to his judgment, make up his mind, and work out his plan."[3]

In the late 1940s, as the communist forces were growing in size and strength after more than ten years of fighting against internal and external enemies, Mao redefined Chinese military strategy and operational doctrine, extracting four additional principles: (1) annihilate the enemy's effective strength (*yousheng liliang*) rather than seizing or holding a city or a place; (2) concentrate the superior force (*jizhong youshi bingli*) with concurrent frontal and flank attacks and avoid becoming bogged down in a battle of attrition; (3) make preparations that will ensure victory in any given situation; (4) fight courageously in continuous battles without fear of sacrifice or fatigue.[4] The PLA employed these military principles in its 1949 victory against the Nationalist regime, and they became enduring features of the PLA's tactical and operational style.

Since the founding of the Red Army in the later 1920s, Mao had attached great importance to the CCP's absolute control over the military. He advocated embedding the party organization inside the army at all levels to guarantee that troops would comply with the CCP's directions. He particularly stressed the importance of the party's role at the company level. Because his army was very weak and experienced extreme hardship, Mao was convinced that only a politicized army could keep up morale and maintain solidarity among the rank and file. The CCP had to play an active and decisive role in making rules, regulations, and decisions for the military. Troops must act on orders from the party instead of orders from an individual commander.[5] This advocacy gave rise to the creation of a distinctive institutional characteristic of the communist-led armed forces—the political work system—to ensure one of Mao's other key principles for the military: the gun must be under the control of the party, not the military.[6]

The most critical components of the political work system were the *party committee system* and the *political commissar system*. The party committees were designated to provide leadership, guidance, and unity for troops, conveying directives and orders to lower-level party organizations and making sure that troops carried out orders. Under the leadership of the party committees, a *collective* decision-making authority was established in which military commanders and political commissars jointly shared responsibility for the work of their units. Except in tactical and emergency situations, the party committees discussed and made all important decisions.[7]

Under the collective leadership of the party committee, a dual commandership system gave the military commander and the political commissar equal ranks. The former was responsible for all military affairs, while the latter, who usually served as the secretary of the party committee, was in charge of promotion, security, propaganda, public service, and ideological indoctrination. The basic principles of political work—unity between officers and soldiers, unity between the army and the people, and (consequently) the disintegration of enemy forces—constituted the political basis for unifying the troops and defeating the enemy. The CCP leadership and the PLA were convinced by their shared experience from the 1920s that the political work system played a significant role in ensuring that the troops were loyal to the CCP and in providing the troops with motivation sufficient to enhance their combat effectiveness.[8]

The CCP-led forces consisted of three basic components: main forces, regional forces, and militia. The main forces operated unconstrained by geographical concerns, whereas the regional and militia forces were restricted to their own localities. Consequently, over the years, regional and militia forces developed strong social networks in their areas that translated into detailed knowledge of local conditions and thus of how to conduct operations there.

In late 1948, following the significant expansion of communist forces in the final years of the civil war, the CMC reorganized its troops into four field armies.[9] By the time that the People's Republic was founded, the first field army, under Marshal Peng Dehuai and Marshal He Long, had established a strong presence in northern and northwestern China. The second field army, under Marshal Liu Bocheng and Deng Xiaoping, dominated central and southwestern China. The third field army, under Marshal Chen Yi and General Su Yu, occupied eastern China. Finally, the fourth field army, under Marshal Lin Biao, swept from northeastern to southern China.[10] The field army became an institution with which the rank and file personally identified. This individual affiliation as well as the longtime service of soldiers in a particular unit also laid the foundation for valuable mentor-protégé relationships between senior officers and trusted subordinates and for fostering less desirable factionalism in leadership politics. These traditions and institutional characteristics, deeply embedded in the PLA by 1979, strongly influenced China's decision to go to war against Vietnam.

Planning the Invasion

Gerald Segal has claimed that China's prime motives for attacking Vietnam were checking Vietnamese ambition and aggression in Southeast Asia, halting a Vietnamese threat to Chinese national security, and exposing Soviet weakness. However, poor political calculation meant that by attempting to create a strategy to punish Vietnam, the PRC's leaders had actually put themselves in an unwinnable position—that is, one in which China never stood a chance of success.[11] China's clearly stated desire to "teach Vietnam a lesson" created a misleading impression that its main war objective was simply an "act of revenge."[12] This impression was unfortunate, because the attack was hardly impulsive or merely vengeful. At the outset, Beijing had strictly limited the objectives and the duration, scope, and conduct of the war to avoid going beyond a bilateral border conflict. However, following Vietnam's invasion of Cambodia, the CMC broadened its objectives to include invading northwestern Vietnam.[13]

Practical or not, this scheme revealed both that considerable thought had gone into crafting the plan and that China's leaders were willing to gamble, seemingly no matter what the cost. In addition, the plan reflected the moderating influence of the CCP leadership on the PLA's seething anger. PLA officers wanted to use force to strike hard at Vietnam, which they perceived as nothing less than a traitorous former ally that must be punished. Instead of offering the military an unconstrained framework in which to inflict the desired punishment, CCP leaders limited their operations in both time and space by directing the military leadership at Guangzhou and Kunming to derive an operational strategy that could meet the CCP leadership's strategic objectives. Local military planners were concerned about the extent to which their objective of teaching Vietnam a lesson could actually be achieved or even measured.

The CMC initially asked the Guangzhou Military Region for two armies (the 41st and 42nd) and one division (the 129th of the 43rd Army) to attack Vietnamese forces in the Cao Bang area, while two other armies (the 43rd and 55th) would engage in diversionary attacks against Dong Dang and Loc Binh prior to the final assault on Lang Son.[14] The Kunming Military Region was ordered to employ two armies (the 13th and 14th) to destroy one Vietnamese division at Lao Cai as well as other local units near the Yunnan border.[15] The CMC apparently granted operational autonomy to regional commanders but kept the duration and space of the fight under the command of the central leadership in Beijing. Deng Xiaoping was determined to avoid having the invasion turn into a quagmire for China.

According to General Zhou Deli, General Xu Shiyou, the commander of the Guangzhou Military Region and a veteran PLA warrior, received the planning task on 9 December 1978 and then began to consider his military strategy against Vietnam. He immediately thought of an overwhelming surprise attack on the Vietnamese army, seizing the initiative and preventing the Vietnamese from recovering their strength. Drawing on his own combat experience, Xu's suggested plan was known as *niudao shaji* (using a butcher's knife to kill a chick), a description suggestive of its massive violence. As a student of Mao's approach to war, Xu believed that this approach fittingly applied Mao's doctrine to fight wars of annihilation. There were three components: (1) concentrating strikes on the vital parts of the enemy's defense but not on the enemy's strong point, (2) employing overwhelming force and firepower to crush the enemy defense at the point of engagement, and (3) quickly and deeply striking at the enemy's heart. In this way, Xu expected the PLA to cut the enemy defenses to pieces and then destroy the targeted forces one by one.[16]

On 11 December 1979, Xu convened his first war meeting. Participants included the vice commanders, the deputy political commissars, the chief of staff, the political director, the logistical director, and the commanders and political commissars of the 41st, 42nd, and 55th Armies from the Guangzhou Military Region.[17] At the meeting, the 41st and 42nd Armies were designated to conduct a two-pronged offensive against Cao Bang, while the 55th would launch attacks on Lang Son. Because the Guangzhou Military Region did not have enough troops, the CMC transferred the 43rd Army from the Wuhan Military Region as Xu's reserve.

After General Zhou announced his assignments, the participants raised many questions because their troops had not engaged in such large operations for many years. The main problem was how to transport their troops—especially the two armies and two artillery divisions from the Guangdong area—from their home barracks to the border region in Guangxi by the end of December.[18] Few people had the knowledge and experience to arrange in such a large-scale movement of troops, particularly in light of the limited means of transportation. Another pressing issue was that all units involved in the invasion were undermanned and underequipped. Those in attendance at the meeting agreed that no more than 5 percent of personnel would be left in the rear and required all troops to prepare to fight with the equipment they had on hand.[19]

At the end of the meeting, Xu urged senior officers to serve as exemplars by changing their work habits from the routine of a peacetime regimen to the total focus of wartime—to act swiftly and on time and to work hard. He made clear that he would punish those who failed to perform their jobs. Then Xu requested that his deputies go to the troops and help them prepare for the invasion.[20]

Xu had been the commander of the Nanjing Military Region (the third field army) for eighteen years before taking up command in the Guangzhou Military Region in 1973, when Mao became increasingly apprehensive about the loyalty of his military regional commanders.[21] Because Xu inherited most of his deputies and troops from the fourth field army, many of them were not comfortable with his leadership style. After the meeting, chief of staff Zhou Deli felt it necessary to bring his department heads together to discuss details about how to deploy troops to the border region. For security reasons, Xu asked his chief of staff to discuss assignments and mission objectives with each department separately.[22]

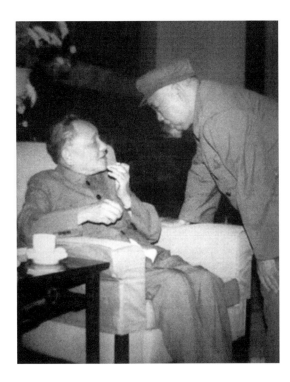

Deng Xiaoping
and Xu Shiyou, 1984.
cpc.people's.com.cn.

Deng did not seem confident in the Guangzhou Military Region's leadership, as the purge of the Gang of Four's supporters was then under way. Most of the senior officers had been the subordinates of Marshal Lin Biao, who was killed in a September 1971 plane crash in in the Mongolian desert, allegedly after a failed coup against Mao. Lin was subsequently condemned as a traitor and labeled the chief designer of a series of political purges against many CCP and PLA leaders—including Deng—during the Cultural Revolution.[23] In early December, one of Deng's longtime subordinates from the second field army, Liu Changyi, was appointed Xu's deputy to command the war, even though he already had five deputies. However, this appointment did not make Xu feel uneasy, since his personal connections with Liu extended back to their days in the Red Army.[24] Nevertheless, the lack of personal connections between the rank and file and their commander would lead to complaints about Xu's leadership style when operations did not go as expected.[25]

On 21 December, the Guangzhou Military Region set up a forward command post in an air force cave depot near Nanning, capital city of Guangxi Autonomous Region, since the attack would be launched from three directions from the Guangxi side. The post comprised seven functional groups: the headquarters (Group 1), the political department (Group 2), the logistics department (Group 3), the artillery corps (Group 4), the engineering corps (Group 5), the air force (Group 6), and the navy (Group 7). Staff officers were divided into three teams, with each team supporting the operations of one direction of attack. In his memoirs, General Zhou claimed that this command structure was effective for directing one army group, thus avoiding chaos during the campaign.[26]

On 5 January 1979, the members of the Guangzhou forward command held their second war meeting in Nanning. In addition to those who attended the first meeting, attendees now included senior officers from the air force and the navy as well as local CCP leaders. After reviewing the preliminary operational plan, the participants recommended several revisions. The final plan divided the campaign into two stages: first, two armies would be employed to mount attacks on Cao Bang, and then one army would take on Lang Son. The plan also called for two divisions to thrust into the enemy's rear, to encircle Cao Bang from the west and south. The PLA General Staff endorsed the plan, recommended additional training, and instructed that units assigned to deep-penetration tasks carry as much ammunition as possible, even by reducing their other provisions to no more than three days' worth. On 5 February, attendees at the third meeting proposed that a simultaneous attack should be launched on Dong Dang, the gateway to Lang Son, once the battle against Cao Bang began. Xu approved this final revision. Because the PLA possessed only limited knowledge about the SRV's military and local social and natural conditions, Zhou Deli later acknowledged that the plan was flawed from the outset. Otherwise, the subsequent military campaign would have secured more victories.[27]

No personal recollections similar to Zhou Deli's are available to provide information about how the Kunming Military Region prepared for its actions. We now know that a change of leadership occurred on the Yunnan front, and the plan for attacking Dien Bien Phu was scrapped. On 7 January 1979, Yang Dezhi replaced Wang Bicheng, who was also from the third field army but had a bad relationship with the commander in Guangxi.[28] However, four days after the Chinese forces invaded Vietnam from Yunnan, Yang was rushed to the hospital in Beijing with serious stomach bleeding.[29] The campaign was thus originally planned by Wang Bicheng but executed by Yang's two deputies, supported by a team of staff officers from the PLA General Staff.[30] Nevertheless, it is misleading to assert that Yang would have been a better choice for military leader than Xu.[31]

From 8 to 10 January, the Kunming Military Region held planning meetings for the invasion. The 13th and 14th Armies would attack one regular Vietnamese division in the Lao Cai and Cam Duong area and then seek to engage another Vietnamese division in the Sa Pa area. The 11th Army would undertake an independent operation in the Phong Tho area. A forward command post was to be set up at Kaiyuan, a county town between Kunming and a border town, Hekou. The operations would involve a total of three armies, along with artillery units, tank units, engineering units, and independent units (150,000 troops).[32] A western command was created to direct the 50th and 54th Armies as they conducted an outflanking operation in northwestern Vietnam. After the Vietnamese military forces had seized most of Cambodia by mid-January, however, the CCP leadership aborted this campaign and redeployed these two armies (except for one division from the 50th) to the Guangxi front as reserves.[33] No sources ever mention any coordination between the two military regions: they carried out their attacks independently.

Deployments and Preparations

In mid-December 1978, the armies of the Guangzhou and Kunming Military Regions began deploying to their positions along the border with Vietnam. Troops moved in by road, while their heavy equipment and supplies came by rail. Engineering units built three pontoon bridges on two main rivers in Guangdong. A total of more than 168,100 troops along with 7,087 tons of materials were transported from Guangdong to the front.[34] Four armies from other military regions traveled to their destinations in Guangxi and Yunnan by rail. The 13th Army—a total of 35,000 troops, along with 873 pieces of artillery, 1,950 vehicles, and other equipment—traveled 1,700 kilometers from Chongqing, Sichuan Province, by ninety trains.[35]

Although the PLA moved by night, such heavy rail and road traffic disrupted normal train schedules and piqued the curiosity of many passersby and travelers. All vehicles used Guangxi license plates to conceal their identification, and troops maintained radio silence during their deployment. The rear bases operated their transmitters on their routine schedule to deceive Vietnamese and other foreign intelligence collectors. By the end of the month, all armies of the Guangzhou Military Region, including the 43rd Army from Louyang, Henan Province, in the Wuhan Military Region, had taken up their positions near the border. Zhou Deli later recalled that the troop movements were completed on schedule. Only one accident had occurred, leaving an artillery piece damaged and two soldiers injured.[36]

According to Zhou, the air force and navy deployed their troops at the same time.[37] Thirteen air force aviation regiments plus another six flying groups, along with their support units, antiaircraft artillery (AAA) and surface-to-air missile (SAM) units, were brought to the airfields in Guangxi, near the border.[38] The air force command and control systems were inadequate in these two provinces. Though unified command is essential for effective military performance in military strategy, two air force forward command posts were created under the existing military region system: regional air force commander Wang Hai was placed in charge in Guangxi, and Hou Shujun, the Kunming Military Region Air Force command post director, took command in Yunnan.[39]

To avoid escalating the conflict, the CCP leadership confined the use of air power to Chinese territory, ordering the air force units to prepare to provide support for PLA ground operations "if necessary." However, the leadership gave no clear definition of what a "necessary" situation might be or when it might occur; instead, leaders mandated that any operations outside China's airspace must be authorized by the CMC. Based on this principle, the PLA Air Force (PLAAF) came out with a strategy that required its units to be prepared to provide both air defense and ground support at any time and to fly as many sorties as possible over the border airspace to deter the Vietnamese air force from taking action against China. Air force operational teams were sent to both military regions' forward command posts, and target guiding groups were attached to ground force army and division headquarters.[40]

The PLA Navy (PLAN) deployed a task group, designated the 217 formation, consisting of two missile frigates, one missile boat group, one torpedo boat group, and one subchaser group, to the Paracel Islands and ports in Guangxi to prepare to attack the Vietnamese navy in Tonkin Gulf. The naval aviation units on Hainan Island were assigned to keep watch on Soviet naval activities in the South China Sea. In case it had to fight against the Soviet cruisers, the PLAN adopted a defensive strategy of using the islands and shores to mask its missile boats, enabling them to launch surprise attacks from hidden positions.

Because no sea engagements actually occurred during the invasion, it is difficult to determine whether this strategy would have worked against the Soviet flotilla. However, the after-action report by the Political Department of the South Sea Fleet admitted that the seamanship was not professional at the time and that only 20 percent of the shells fired by the gun crews hit their targets in training. Another incident demonstrated that the ships worked badly in flotillas. In one exercise, a signalman reportedly sent the wrong signal, throwing the whole formation into confusion.[41]

The regional military leadership was increasingly concerned about operational security, particularly leakage of information about troops' movement toward the Guangxi border areas. General Xu was irritated to learn that his presence in the capital city of Guangxi, which was supposed to be secret, was broadcast by foreign journalists. He was further alarmed to learn that the rail line between China and Vietnam remained operational on a normal schedule, and cross-border trade continued between the two sides. In both situations, Vietnamese intelligence agents could obtain information about Chinese military movements in the border area. Xu asked the Guangxi government immediately to halt all border trade activities and close the border. He also requested that Beijing close rail operations between the two countries and expel Vietnamese railroad staffs from the border town of Pingxiang. Beijing approved this request. On 26 December, the Guangxi-Vietnamese border was closed as the troops started arriving in their assembly areas nearby.[42] While this series of initiatives undoubtedly solved his immediate problem, these actions themselves may well have alerted Vietnamese authorities to the imminence of military action from Guangxi.

PLA forces had not engaged in such large-scale military action for more than two decades. The Guangzhou Military Region forward command promulgated a detailed directive requesting the troops to pay close attention to five issues when they were preparing for the invasion. First, all troops needed to construct defensive works and camouflage vehicles and equipment against the possibility of a surprise Vietnamese attack from the air and ground. Second, commanders at all levels needed to familiarize themselves with the enemy and with geographic conditions in northern Vietnam along the China border and start gathering target information for their artillery. Third, all forces needed to increase their units to full strength and maintain weapons and equipment in good condition. Fourth, all units needed to practice good communications security, especially assignment orders given in person instead of by wire and wireless communications. Finally, all units needed to train new recruits in grenade throwing and rifle marksmanship and draw up plans to accomplish their combat missions.[43]

This directive reflected several critical problems the PLA confronted on the eve of the invasion. Most seriously, its forces were far from ready for operation; indeed, they were not yet fully manned and equipped. For years, the PLA's ground forces had maintained a peacetime organizational structure: within each army, only one division—the Category A division (*jiazhongshi* or *quanzhuangshi*)—was kept at full strength, while the other two divisions—Category B division (*yizhongshi* or *jianbianshi*)—were below strength. Local authorities conducted two wartime drafts. Given the shortage of veteran soldiers, the second draft specially conscripted well-trained militiamen and ex-servicemen.[44] In Guangdong Province alone, nearly 400,000 young men responded to the call. A total of 15,000 new recruits were drafted, and 1,512 demobilized soldiers were reactivated.[45] The PLA also quickly promoted officers to fill leadership vacancies at all levels. Specialized personnel from other military regions were transferred to staff technical jobs in artillery, engineering, communications, armor, and anti-chemical-warfare units.[46]

The 42nd Army promoted eleven officers to be commanding officers at division level and eighty-two officers at regiment level, while the 55th Army advanced fifteen individuals to be division leaders and seventy-six people to be regiment leaders.[47] To fill leadership positions at the platoon level, the 42nd Army commissioned 1,045 enlisted men to be officers on the eve of the invasion.[48] The 13th Army received 15,381 recruits, of which 11,874 were new conscripts.[49] These statistics demonstrate the training problems faced by the PLA as it prepared for war.

Training Troops before Fight

In his book, General Zhou Deli's use of an expression, "Sharpen one's sword only before going into battle—start to prepare for war only at the last moment" (*linzhen modao*), suggested that the PLA was in an embarrassing condition at the time.[50] Indeed, in 1978, only 42 percent of military units undertook military training.[51] The air force had some 800 pilots who conducted firing and bombing practice, but only 36 percent hit their targets.[52]

But the actual situation of the PLA was even more shocking. General Zhang Zhen, director of the General Logistics Department, inspecting war preparations on the Guangxi front in mid-January 1979, found that the PLA forces had numerous problems that indicated a serious lack of combat preparation. According to his memoirs, the Company 2 of the 367th Regiment of the 41st Army had 117 men, of whom 57 were new recruits. In a little over two weeks of training, 44 soldiers had three firing practice sessions, 41 had two, and the rest had only one. Thirty-three soldiers received training in offensive tactics as a squad, but no defensive tactical training was offered because no military officers knew how to do it. General Zhang recommended that each division set up a field that could be used to train units to operate at the squad level as well at the company and battalion levels. Trainees would focus on infantry attacks along with artillery and tank units. The infantry units should especially be taught how to call fire support. The general promised that the

GLD would allocate 10,000 yuan so that each division could construct such a training field.[53]

Based on these recommendations, the troops began training themselves in accordance with their assigned missions. The 121st Division, which was designated to undertake a deep-penetration mission in Vietnam, focused on how to move through jungles and mountain trails against the enemy's ambushes and then how to attack the enemy positions on hilltops. At least three soldiers from each company were trained to read maps. The division organized three exercises under environmental conditions similar to those in northern Vietnam to teach the troops to maneuver with little rest and food.[54] The 163rd Division, which was assigned to conduct front attacks on the enemy's strongholds, concentrated on training individual soldiers and squads in combat tactics as well as conducting live-ammunition exercises at the platoon, company, and battalion levels. The division carried out joint exercises with an infantry battalion plus artillery and tank units.[55]

Such desperate last-minute training efforts, though somewhat helpful, were woefully insufficient because there were too many new recruits and too many of them were peasant farmers. Despite the goal of teaching military skills, most of the soldiers completed only one to two live practices on the shooting range and only one live grenade-throwing practice. Few units conducted serious tactical training exercises at the regiment or division level. Many officers reported that they were still uncertain about their troops' fighting ability when battle began.[56] In short, the PLA invasion troops were poorly trained and inadequately prepared for a modern war against the SRV's forces. The PLA's subsequent poor battlefield performance was ascribed to lack of training rather than the enemy's strength and twenty-five years of combat experience.[57]

Repairs and maintenance of weapons and equipment were other nagging problems for the PLA forces. Since 1975, Deng Xiaoping had called for improving the quality of the PLA's equipment and supplies, but no significant changes seem to have been made.[58] Military professionals believe that sustainable logistical support guarantees military success. General Zhang Zhen recalled that his worst problem was the insufficient amount and poor quality of ammunition.[59] Initial inspections showed that some artillery shells misfired, and a third of all grenades failed to explode. Cadets from the armament school were sent to assist the army depots in thoroughly checking their stock. The GLD also urgently ordered defense industries to increase production—in particular, of large-caliber artillery shells, rockets, and armor-piercing rounds.[60]

The supply of oil was another of the GLD's concerns. Not only were both

Guangxi and Yunnan Provinces far from China's petroleum industries in the northeast and northwest, but demand for oil would rise sharply if the Soviet Union retaliated against the attack on Vietnam. In addition, southern China had a shortage of oil storage facilities. Because outdoor oil facilities could be easily attacked, the GLD suggested using Guangxi's numerous karst caves to store fuel. More than 428 kilometers of temporary pipelines were laid to supply fuel to four airfields in Yunnan.[61] Each army received assistance from a motor transport regiment to ensure that the troops received supplies, but as of mid-January, tons of supplies remained piled up at division headquarters, leading the GLD to rush in three additional motor transport regiments from the Nanjing and Fuzhou Military Regions.[62] In its first attempt at conducting military operations with a significant amount of technical equipment, the PLA had to seek civilian technicians to assist in maintaining autos, tanks, and other machinery. Nevertheless, the logistical problems continued to crop up, thwarting the PLA's operations once the invasion began.

Political Mobilization

Despite the urgent need for training, the PLA continued the tradition that Mao had advocated forty years earlier—that is, the idea that the war could not be won without political mobilization.[63] On 12 February 1979, the CMC issued an order emphasizing the importance of political mobilization in the PLA's military operations in Vietnam.[64] Western analysts have criticized the PLA's decision to devote "so much time, energy, and attention" to this effort when Chinese soldiers badly needed training in military techniques.[65] This criticism overlooked the long-standing significance of political mobilization, which had become institutionalized and thus culturally accepted in the reflexive framework of the PLA's war preparations. One notable characteristic throughout the PLA's history was that many of its soldiers were poor, illiterate peasants. The political indoctrination system had been instituted to mobilize them to fight against a strong enemy, proving its value repeatedly over the years.

By 1979, the PLA had changed only slightly; the members of the rank and file still came overwhelmingly from rural areas and were uneducated, inadequately equipped, and poorly trained. At the same time, the PLA's invasion of Vietnam did not correspond with a Chinese cultural tradition that supported the use of force only if it could be morally justified. Shortly after receiving Beijing's order, the local military leadership noticed that the Chinese forces were ideologically ill prepared. The immediate question was whether China should attack a small neighboring country such as Vietnam. According to Mo Wenhua, political commissar of the PLA's armored forces, Chinese soldiers lacked an understanding of the significance of the war against Vietnam. They were not only apprehensive about Soviet military intervention and their own possible inability to defeat Vietnam but also worried that the war would be detrimental to China's Four Modernizations and that other countries would use it to condemn China as an aggressor.[66]

Despite China's quantitative dominance over Vietnam, Chinese soldiers were concerned that they did not have a technological advantage over Vietnam's Russian-made weapons and American equipment captured from the Saigon regime in 1975.[67] China's air force pilots were particularly concerned that their J-6s could not match the Vietnamese MiG-21s, many flown by pilots who had already flown—and scored against—the U.S. Air Force and U.S. Navy.[68] In addition, Vietnam possessed a robust SAM threat, with skilled crews who were highly practiced in air defense operations. When the Chinese government ordered the invasion of Vietnam, Chinese troops appeared more knowledgeable about construction and agricultural production than about operating their weapons.[69]

Soldiers' trust in the central leadership's decisions and obedience to orders was deemed fundamental to victory. On 12 December, the General Political Department (GPD) issued guidelines for political mobilization. Unlike the Western military, which depends on professional ethics and training to ensure soldiers' compliance with their duties in war, the PLA opted for political indoctrination of troops, attempting to make them understand why the war must be fought and how it would matter to them. Under the influence of Confucian philosophy, the Chinese were accustomed to viewing themselves as a peace-loving people, not violent or expansionist, and only using force in self-defense. The concept of the just or righteous war was prevalent throughout Chinese society. For Chinese soldiers, this cultural tradition seemed to pose a barrier to conceiving a socialist neighboring country as a dangerous enemy that threatened national security. The GPD therefore urged all troops to study the CCP leadership's directives and speeches as well as the CMC's war and political orders, making them believe that the decision to attack Vietnam was correct.[70]

According to the GPD's propaganda outlines, the war against Vietnam was just and necessary because the SRV's expansionist ambitions had led it to degenerate into the "Cuba of the East," the "hooligans of Asia," and the "running dogs of the Soviet Union." The two countries' shared political ideology did not prevent the PLA from launching self-defense actions against a neighboring small state that had violated China's national interests. Equally important, the directive pointed out that the SRV had already viewed the PRC as its primary enemy and called for "doing everything to defeat China."[71]

From 10 December 1978 to 15 January 1979, the political apparatuses at all levels ran full steam ahead to politicize the soldiers' minds, using lectures, denunciation meetings, and visual exhibits to serve the purpose.[72] These strategies included appeals to "just war" theory, punishing "ingratitude," defending the Four Modernizations, and confronting an emerging Vietnamese-Soviet quest for regional hegemony. The 43rd Army's political department attempted to convince troops that they were fighting a just war because Vietnam had invaded China and had fired the first shot; as a result, counterattacks were justified.

Another tactic involved reminding soldiers that China had made tremendous sacrifices to support Vietnam for many years, while Vietnam had returned kindness with ingratitude. Vietnam, the argument continued, thought that China was easy to bully and therefore, would further challenge China's territorial sovereignty. Therefore, Vietnam was a main threat to China's Four Modernizations and deserved to be punished.

Political officers also linked Vietnam's policy against China and hegemonic desires in Indochina to the Soviet social-imperialist global strategy. According to this line of argument, China's counterattack against Vietnam would frustrate Soviet hopes to encircle China. Vietnam's invasion of Cambodia and policy against China had been unpopular in the world, so China's punishment of Vietnam would receive global support.[73]

The mobilization program emphasized arousing the troops' animosity toward the enemy. The PLA's peasant soldiers had always been encouraged to pour out their grievances against despotic landlords at denunciation meetings designed to stir up class consciousness so that they could be mobilized to believe that they were fighting for their own interests. In 1979, the political departments convened denunciation meetings, inviting the soldiers from the border guard units, the villagers from the border area, and the ethnic Chinese who had returned from Vietnam to use the facts of their personal experience to denounce the "hate-China, anti-China" crime committed by the Vietnamese revisionists.[74] In this way, the political propaganda not only sowed the seeds of hatred in soldiers' minds but also strengthened their convictions about carrying out their obligations as PLA soldiers to protect the people and their interests.[75] To encourage troops to (if necessary) willingly sacrifice their lives in combat, the 13th Army political department organized rallies at which officers and soldiers took an oath together by holding their guns in the air and shouting slogans. In powerful, emotional scenes that ignited patriotic fervor, all the soldiers pledged to take on dangerous and difficult tasks.[76]

Given the fact that the PLA troops were not professional soldiers, political work served as a psychological means to prepare them to confront unpredictability and uncertainty and to fear neither hardship nor death on the battlefield. Ceremonies highlighting the heroes of the units' history encouraged troops to continue that glorious tradition. The 43rd Army demanded that all companies take an oath to carry on the tradition: "Learn from heroes, become a hero, and add new glories to the heroic war banners."[77] Cadres and CCP members were urged to set themselves up as role models. Recognizing that its troops had not fought for a long time, the Guangzhou Military Region forward command conducted a survey identifying the officers who had participated in the wars against Japan and the Chinese Nationalists, the Korean War, and the Vietnam War as well as in the border conflicts with India.[78] These veterans were asked to give lectures about their personal experience in combat. Having commanding officers show up on the front lines had been a PLA tradition, assuring troops that their superiors were sharing the risks and hardships. While sending his deputies to each army under his command, General Xu requested that the commanding officers at the army, division, and regiment levels send their deputies to lower-level units to assist with the command.[79]

Political work also reportedly played a role in dispelling the skepticism of sailors and pilots about their chances against better-equipped opponents. The navy crews initially thought that they could easily defeat the Vietnamese navy. However, once they learned that they might have to confront Soviet missile cruisers, many of them became less confident in their own capabilities. Soviet ships were far bigger and had vastly more firepower and better communication technology. Chinese sailors grumbled that their small guns would only scratch the rust off the Soviet ships. In response, navy political officers used ideological indoctrination to stimulate sailors' patriotism. They also talked about the Soviet navy's weakness, noting that the ships had traveled far from their homeland and were dependent on a greatly stretched supply line. The Chinese crews became somewhat satisfied only after their commanders decided to use a surprise antishipping missile blitz against the Soviet cruisers.[80]

The air force also convened meetings to deal with skepticism among its pilots by emphasizing Mao's teaching that "weapons are an important but not decisive factor in war, and man is the decisive factor." According to a report by the party committee of the 44th Air Division, the Korean War veterans were invited to tell their stories of flying against American F-86 Sabres to prove Mao's teaching right. Political officers also used the stories of the Pakistani air force, which had defeated India's Soviet-made MiG-21s with Chinese-made J-6s, to build up pilots' confidence against the Vietnamese air force. They particularly noted that the Chinese aircraft could outmaneuver the enemy's MiG-21s at medium altitudes if the pilots used correct tactics.[81] Nonetheless, the air force leadership could not overlook the superior capability of the Vietnamese MiG-21s and did deploy all 73 of its J-7s (Chinese made MiG-21s) to Guangxi and Yunnan. Some J-6s were upgraded with air-to-air missiles, giving the Chinese air force firing capability than its Vietnamese counterpart.[82]

While political work played the pivotal role in mobilizing soldiers' minds, the political system also helped the PLA deal with the problems its troops might face in fighting. One immediate concern was the leadership vacancies, especially at the platoon and company levels. In mid-December 1978, the GPD instructed participating units to fill all leadership vacancies and develop a plan to avoid leadership interruptions during military operations.[83] The CMC transferred authority to promote divisional officers to the CCP committees of military regions and armed services levels.[84] The political departments in military regions requested units at all levels to generate lists of candidates who could take leadership positions in the midst of the fighting. Each battalion and company received an extra deputy billet to ensure uninterrupted command operations. The PLA tradition trusted the CCP organizations to play a vital role in maintaining combat effectiveness. The party branch in the company urged party and youth league members to play a vanguard role in combat and to assume leadership roles when vacancies occurred.[85]

Political work also included preparing Chinese soldiers to distinguish Vietnamese civilians from military personnel and to use political and psychological strategies (winning the hearts and minds of civilians) to dismantle the enemy's forces. The GPD issued a number of combat disciplinary regulations regarding operations in Vietnam, emphasizing that Chinese troops must attempt to win support from the Vietnamese masses. During the preparation phase, Chinese troops studied local customs and lifestyle as well as the significance of working with the Vietnamese masses in the war zone. Just as PLA troops traditionally did while fighting inside China, those in Vietnam were expected to show concern for civilians and be kind to them. The GPD required every unit to organize a work team to use propaganda to improve local Vietnamese civilians' attitude toward China and the PLA and to damage the enemy's fighting will and morale. In addition, the GPD instructed troop leaders to teach soldiers the Vietnamese language so that they could shout propaganda slogans at enemy troops. They also trained soldiers to wage psychological warfare by distributing leaflets and broadcasting. Avoiding abuse of Vietnamese captives was another important battlefield rule. The GPD reiterated the PLA's POW policy, specifying that after being captured, Vietnamese militia fighters should be released immediately after receiving indoctrination. However, this rule would soon prove difficult to implement in a hostile country. The circumstances of the Chinese invasion of Vietnam differed vastly from the PLA's experience in the Chinese Civil War and, for that matter, from its experience in Korea from 1950 to 1953.[86]

Mobilizing Support from the Society

The CCP traditionally mobilized Chinese society in support of war, although few studies have examined this practice.[87] Western scholars recognize that Chinese citizens held "varying opinions" about the 1979 conflict and that little "public enthusiasm" for the war existed in the provincial capital cities of Guangxi and Yunnan.[88] It was almost impossible for the PLA forces to operate outside the country without mobilizing public support for the war at home. Newly available Chinese records demonstrate the government's enormous effort to mobilize local populations to support the PLA's invasion. Since the PRC's founding, the PLA traditionally had been considered a positive role model for Chinese society, but its reputation had been severely damaged when the military abused its power during the Cultural Revolution. Therefore, the public's attitude toward the PLA had to be improved. Persuading the public to support the invasion required making people feel proud of the PLA's soldiers and patriotic toward China.[89]

Despite the lack of widespread support for the invasion of Vietnam throughout China, CCP leaders in both Guangxi and Yunnan Provinces paid particular attention to the mobilization of support in their local communities. Public opinion in these two provinces was pessimistic about Beijing's war decision. The local communities had undergone much hardship in the Cultural Revolution and had made considerable sacrifices for the Vietnamese war effort. These two provinces had not been on the priority list for investments from the central government.[90] Thus, these areas remained socially and economically backward. Nevertheless, citizens there hoped that economic reform— now the highest national priority—would bring peace, development, and better standards of living. The people and local governments in these two provinces seemed unenthusiastic about the Chinese attack on Vietnam and feared that the military action would conflict with the economic development agenda.

Given this mind-set, the two provincial governments resorted to their propaganda machines to persuade people to support Beijing's decision to go to war with Vietnam. The CCP propaganda departments of both provinces sent city, district, county, and subdistrict party organizations long lists of Vietnam's alleged crimes against China, requiring that the information be used to educate the local populace and arouse their patriotism in support of the war. Guangxi Autonomous Region held more than 530 mass meetings with a total attendance of 263,400.[91] The CCP committee of Yunnan Province issued a mobilization order that stirred up the whole province to "do all for the front and do all for victory."[92] Preparing for war and providing support for the front were the top priorities of party work and government work in both Yunnan and Guangxi. Both provinces created Aid-the-Front Committees to supervise and coordinate war preparations.[93] Similar offices were also set up in lower-level government organizations.[94] Twenty-one of Guangxi's cities and counties and fourteen in Yunnan were mobilized to support the front lines.[95]

This approach not only demonstrated the PLA's commitment to continue Mao's "people's war" doctrine but also reflected the PLA's unequivocal weaknesses. PLA leaders realized that they lacked a modern logistics system to sustain the war effort, and their standard solution was the mobilization of popular backing. In November 1978, Zhang Zhen wrote that local support for food, lodging, and other supplies was critical in both total war and small-scale operations. He specifically noted that civilian support had accounted for almost 80 percent of the support for military operations during the 1969 border conflicts with Soviet forces, and civilian vessels had helped with the shipment of 65 percent of oil supplies during the 1974 sea battles against the South Vietnamese navy. Even in today's modern warfare, Zhang concluded, the armed forces would continue to depend on local governments to provide personnel and food, and military logistics would be determined by the strength of the national economy.[96]

Since mid-December 1978, prefectural cities and counties in Guangxi and Yunnan Provinces had rushed to set up military reception centers (*junren jiedai zhan*) along rail lines and highways leading to the border so that troops could rest and receive meals and hot water. Each county government was responsible for housing troops at designated assembly areas near the border. Because border counties were small and economically backward, the tasks of frontline support often stretched beyond their capacities. Within a few weeks, more than 100,000 military and militia soldiers swarmed into Hekou County, opposite the Vietnamese city of Lao Cai, which had a population of 50,000 in 1978.[97] Local authorities had to vacate offices, warehouses, and their own living quarters to accommodate the troops. Villagers and township dwellers were encouraged to "volunteer" their houses for military usage. Some local authorities mobilized office workers, students, and teachers to construct sheds with bamboo poles and cogon grass as military lodging facilities.[98]

At the time, the PLA still had a hodgepodge supply system that required every unit to be self-sufficient in "retail logistics." The sudden surge in demand for food and other supplies presented a considerable challenge to local economic and commercial service authorities, which had to manage supplies for local residents as well as troops. Local vendors were required to provide more livestock to the troops, while purchasing agents were sent to other provinces to guarantee every soldier a half pound of pork per day.[99] Following an emergency request from the military, food producers in both Guangxi and Yunnan rushed to furnish troops with 1.25 million kilos of crackers prior to the invasion.[100]

Since 1976, Yunnan had suffered from decreasing grain production. Food supply was a particularly acute problem. The troop assembly areas were situated in the poorest remote regions where local residents could not even produce enough food for themselves. The provincial government urgently appealed to Beijing for permission to use food reserves to meet the abrupt increase in demand and cut 40 percent of food supplies to urban dwellers to guarantee adequate supplies for the front. To overcome the problem of cooking rice during military operations, the local government imported a food production line for instant rice.[101] Records from Guangxi and Yunnan Provinces show that the mobilization was carried out throughout the whole province and involved almost every government bureaucracy and every sector of society. A total of about half a million civilians served in either combat operations or aid-the-front work.[102] The most notable undertaking was the organization of hundreds and thousands of militias to provide direct support for the PLA's operations beyond the border.

Mobilization of the militia forces to engage in combat and provide support for the front was a tradition of the communist-led armed forces stemming from Mao's "people's war" doctrine. The Chinese military's dependence on the aid-the-front militia units also revealed an awkward situation for the PLA, which was incapable of sustaining any expeditionary operations on its own. General Zhou Deli recalled that the PLA invasion forces did not feel safe conducting operations in Vietnam without a secure rear, and the militias and the local populace played a critical role in rear-echelon security.[103] Both provinces had been the first line of national defense during the Cold War. Transportation infrastructure was inadequate for the large-scale troop movements needed for the invasion. In October 1978, Yunnan Province mobilized more than 100,000 militiamen from the capital city and seven prefectures to build two highways leading to the border. They completed the project in three months and thereby ensured the deployment of troops to the border areas on schedule.[104]

In early January 1979, the militia forces received full mobilization. The well-organized and better-trained militia units from other parts of the two provinces were deployed to the border areas to provide direct support for military operations. Qujing Prefecture, located in northeastern Yunnan, deployed between 500 and 600 young militiamen from each county to serve in the war.[105] Men aged between eighteen and fifty-five in all border counties were conscripted into the militia.[106] According to the Yunnan provincial government's final report dated 6 September 1979, more than 87,000 militiamen (630 companies) plus 5,000 civilian horses and mules were called to serve, primarily as stretcher bearers, security guards, and porters. More than 21,000 militiamen operated side by side with the regular units in combat action.[107] The employment of nonuniformed militia soldiers in a hostile country along with the PLA units later created confusion during encounters with Vietnamese defenders, who were also dressed in civilian clothes on the battlefield. On a few occasions, PLA soldiers found themselves with no choice but to kill anyone not in a uniform, even some of those men might be Chinese comrades.[108]

General Zhou also asserts that more than 215,000 residents of Guangxi Province served in the war, with 60,000 were involved in military actions as stretcher bearers, security guards, and porters and more than 26,000 engaged in combat activities.[109] The PLA forces transferred several thousand automatic assault rifles and various types of heavy weaponry to the local militia units. By the time the invasion commenced, the militia forces in border counties were well equipped with machine guns, antiaircraft guns, mortars, rocket-propelled grenade launchers, and recoilless guns.[110] The local militias bore responsibility primarily for constructing defense works, transporting ammunition and supplies to the front, and looking after the wounded.[111] The militias' air defense units also protected border county towns and key industrial facilities such as hydroelectric stations and reservoirs.[112]

Mao's "people's war" strategy was called into question since such a strategy of total war had not applied to the limited local conflicts in which China had engaged since Korea.[113] King C. Chen in particular points out that China failed to engage in a people's war against Vietnam in 1979 because the necessary environment, which included "a strong sense of nationalism and massive people's participation," never existed.[114] Mobilization of society to support the war was the pivotal Chinese strategic tradition, and the 1979 war proved that the PLA still operated within the people's war ideological framework.

Conclusion

There is no way to overstate the level of intensity involved in PLA planning and preparation for military operations against Vietnam. This process reflected the PLA's strategic and institutional cultures, which were heavily influenced by Mao's military theory. The central military principles worked out by Mao and the operational style the PLA had developed still essentially guided its approach to the 1979 military campaign. The war plan created by the regional commands demonstrated an operational preference for seizing and maintaining the initiative by deploying superior force coupled with surprise attacks. Despite the urgent need for training, the PLA continued its established traditions, using political indoctrination as a primary means of boosting morale and improving combat effectiveness.

Political indoctrination activities probably made no sense to Western military professionals. However, from a Chinese perspective, such political work played a crucial role in persuading ordinary, undereducated Chinese soldiers that China should launch military attacks against Vietnam, long considered a brotherly, even comradely, country. The mobilization of society to provide support for the war reflected the essence of China's "people's war." The PLA seemed unable to perform any large-scale military operations without mobilizing local governments and civilians for support. (Indeed, even now, more than three decades later, this critical characteristic continues to characterize China's approach to warfare and will likely do so in the future.) Despite detailed planning by Chinese military staffs, many events on the battlefield would remain unanticipated, a failure that would rapidly prove how deadly and costly an invasion of Vietnam could be.

4 Bloodshed over Vietnam's Northern Border Region

China's 1979 invasion of Vietnam can be divided into three phases. During the first phase (17–25 February), Chinese forces broke through the Vietnamese first line of resistance and captured the provincial capitals of Cao Bang and Lao Cai and a key border town, Dong Dang, the gateway to Lang Son. The second phase (26 February–5 March), consisted of a full-scale Chinese assault on Lang Son in the east and additional military engagements in the areas of Sa Pa and Phong Tho in northwestern Vietnam. The final phase(early to mid-March) saw a continued mopping-up campaign against sporadic enemy resistance while Chinese forces razed military and economic installations before withdrawing from Vietnam on 16 March.

The Chinese invasion consisted of nine field armies, three regional divisions, three artillery divisions, two antiaircraft artillery divisions, one railroad engineering division, and five engineering regiments—more than half a million combatants. Unlike Mao, Deng Xiaoping did not interfere in daily battlefield operations by giving detailed instructions from the national capital far removed from the fighting front. He did, however, spend a few hours every day in the General Staff war room reviewing battlefield reports.[1] The Chinese leader believed that only if the PLA mounted a successful operation would Western nations believe that China was a reliable friend in their struggle against Soviet expansionism. At the same time, a PLA victory would send a strong signal to Hanoi and Moscow not to undermine China's security.

But the PLA had not engaged in any large-scale operations since the Korean War and thus continued to employ older tactical and operational styles developed in its now very distant war experience. In contrast, the PAVN was a battle-hardened force that had fought almost endlessly for decades against Western powers France and the United States. Yet this disparity was not as great as it might seem: most of Vietnam's elite units were involved in the invasion of Cambodia, while many of the forces that the PLA fought in 1979 were

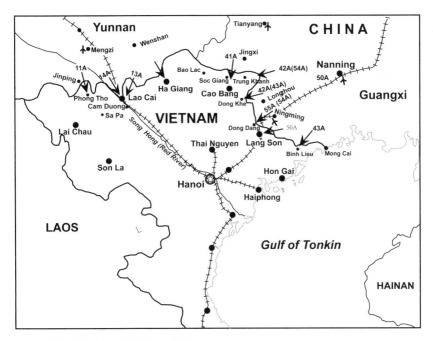

MAP 2 China's Invasion of Vietnam, 1979

filled with new recruits and were distracted from combat by their long-term engagement in the country's economic reconstruction. Even so, the invasion quickly highlighted serious deficiencies in the PLA, preventing it from living up to its leaders' expectations. The most notable problem was the outdated doctrine, command and control system, operational tactics, and force structure, and the military's performance convinced the Chinese leadership that the PLA had to be reformed.

The Lost Opportunity at Cao Bang

During the first phase, the PLA forces fought two crucial engagements, the Battle of Cao Bang and the Battle of Dong Dang. PLA planners had conceived this stage of military operations to destroy the Vietnamese forces in the Cao Bang area while conducting a simultaneous attack on Dong Dang, thereby confusing the enemy about Chinese intentions. Moreover, the seizure of Dong Dang would better position the Chinese forces to stage subsequent attacks against Lang Son.

On 17 February, the 41st and 42nd Armies plus the 129th Division of the 43rd Army engaged in a multipronged offensive toward Cao Bang. They ad-

PLA infantrymen ride on tanks during the invasion of Vietnam, 1979. Courtesy Xiaobing Li.

vanced from the north, east, and south, respectively, seeking to clamp down on and destroy the Vietnamese defenders in the area.[2] Following an extremely intense thirty-minute preparatory artillery barrage, the 41st (the north group) crossed the border along several axes between Pingmeng in the west and Longbang in the east. One of its divisions, the 122nd, attacked Soc Giang. At the same time, its main thrust drove toward Cao Bang through the border town of Thong Nong. After reaching Thong Nong, this force divided into two columns. One column (the 121st Division) went all the way to Ban Trang while trying to block Cao Bang from the Dong Dua area in the west. The second column (the 123rd Division minus one regiment) turned toward Hoa An to press on Cao Bang from the north.[3] To divert the enemy's attention, one regiment of the 123rd attacked Tra Linh, the primary axis of Vietnamese defense in this border sector.[4]

The south group (the 42nd Army's 124th and 126th Divisions plus the 43rd Army's 129th Division) entered Vietnam from the small village of Buju, advancing toward Cao Bang along Highway 4 through Dong Khe and Khuoi Kong. Simultaneously, the 125th Division of the 42nd attacked Phu Hoa (a border district town) from Shuikouguan, pressuring Cao Bang from the east. The 129th Division was assigned to seize That Khe to prevent PAVN forces from attacking the south group from the rear.[5]

The defenders in the Cao Bang area were the PAVN's 346th Infantry Division, which had converted from an economic construction unit to a combat unit in April 1978.[6] It had three infantry regiments and one artillery regiment under its command. The 246th Regiment was positioned at Soc Giang, a northwestern approach to Cao Bang; the 677th Regiment defended Tra Linh and its surrounding area; and the 851st Regiment served as reserves in the Hoa An area. The 188th Artillery Regiment was deployed between Lung Loi and Phu Ngoc to provide fire support for its infantry units.[7]

In addition, three independent regiments were in the region: the 31st at Phuc Hoa, the 567th at Trung Khanh, and the 576th at Tra Linh. Complementing these were local forces (one public security regiment, five independent battalions from border counties, and eleven public security stations), with a combined total of 15,000 troops.[8] These local units had been well trained and well equipped, and they possessed formidable combat capabilities. One Chinese source later concluded that they even "might have been superior to some of the Chinese regular units."[9]

Chinese planners thought they had assembled an overwhelming force in the Cao Bang area, but they failed to account for the tens of thousands of PAVN militia soldiers, who seriously constrained the Chinese advance on their home territory. This miscalculation became a primary reason why the PLA invasion forces failed to achieve their objectives. Despite the PLA's initial breakthrough of the first Vietnamese defensive line, difficult terrain and the enemy's tenacious resistance held the Chinese forces at key locations during the first critical days of the invasion.

The Chinese invasion forces suffered their worst losses during the first four days of the war at Soc Giang. This border town, four kilometers from its Chinese counterpart, Pingmeng, is situated on a highway north of Cao Bang. It is surrounded by limestone mountains riddled with caves, which historically constituted a natural barrier against invaders. The 122nd originally planned to take Soc Giang in two days, but five days were ultimately needed to eliminate Vietnamese resistance. On 20 February, on two separate occasions, Vietnamese defenders pinned down two Chinese companies and their support elements by interconnecting fields of fire. One was in a rice field, and the other was at a narrow pass. The first encounter ended with 122 Chinese troops killed and 66 wounded, including a deputy regiment commander; the second battle lasted for a little over ten minutes, but six Chinese tanks were damaged and 108 soldiers were either killed or injured.[10] Not surprisingly, the 41st Army fell behind schedule for reaching its attack position.[11]

The PLA's punitive invasion attached importance to encircling Cao Bang, but the 121st and 124th Divisions failed to penetrate to their destinations within the allotted twenty-four hours. The mountainous terrain, dense jungle, lack of roads, and frequent PAVN ambushes gave rise to all sorts of unimagined difficulties. The PLA troops not only literally had to fight their way through but also had to climb mountains and hack through forests. The 121st Division needed six days to arrive at its designated position at Khau Don, southwest of Cao Bang. This delay not only allowed one Vietnamese regiment to escape from encirclement but also forced General Xu to hold back an immediate attack on the provisional capital city of Cao Bang.[12]

Xu had even greater problems from another unexpected direction: internal PRC politics. By 20 February, troops from the 42nd Army, under the command of one of Xu's deputies, Wu Zhong, had already closed in on Cao Bang. But an ongoing investigation of Wu's political affiliations in the Cultural Revolution resulted in his removal from command right in the midst of the campaign. In a cable on 20 February, Xu reiterated that the campaign should remain under the command of his other deputy, even though the latter and his troops (the 41st Army) were still battling their way to Cao Bang from the north.[13] Not until three days later did Xu and his staff officers realize that the city was defended only by a small number of Vietnamese troops who were trying to hold off the Chinese advance so that military leaders and governmental officials in Cao Bang could retreat to safe areas. He then ordered assaults on the city, which was taken by the Chinese forces after several hours of fighting.[14]

The Battle of Cao Bang was a frustrating and unsatisfactory operation for the Chinese military leadership. The PLA's original battle plan was to seek quick and decisive engagements with regular PAVN units and then obliterate them. But except at Soc Giang, most of the battles the PLA forces fought were against the militia and citizen-soldiers, and the Vietnamese regional forces, which operated in small units, resisted fiercely. The PLA's 126th Division took over Dong Khe, a district town fifty kilometers south of Cao Bang on Highway 4, in the first hours after the invasion commenced. But its defenders, the Thach An district independent battalion supported by militia soldiers, inflicted heavy casualties on Chinese troops.[15] After the first echelon of the 124th Division passed through Dong Khe, it breached a reservoir, creating a quagmire that hindered the follow-up Chinese motorized column's forward movement. The reinforcement forces had to detour from Shuikouguan via Phu Hoa. The defense of Phu Hoa by a PAVN local unit had blocked the 125th Division in its tracks for more than two days.[16] The arrival of the powerful 54th Army from the Wuhan Military Region on 12 February finally enabled the

Chinese forces to break through the Vietnamese defensive line in the Phu Hoa area and then close in on Cao Bang from the east.[17]

Nevertheless, the belated capture of Cao Bang seriously upset the PLA's original campaign plan. For a whole day, the PLA forces searched the Ke Map Nua area, three kilometers north of Cao Bang, but could not find any regular Vietnamese force units. The military leadership in Guangxi realized that PAVN forces had broken up and ordered the PLA forces in the area to conduct a mop-up operation. According to captured Vietnamese documents, not until March 6 was the PAVN's 346th Division defeated.[18] The unit history of the 346th indirectly supports this, giving no account of its forces still fighting after 27 February.[19] Despite this success, the PLA's heavy losses meant that the operation during this phase was much less successful than its after-action reports optimistically suggested.

The Seizure of Dong Dang

Although the Vietnamese local and militia forces did most of the fighting in the Cao Bang area during the early stage of China's attack, Vietnam relied on its regular units to counter the invasion in the Lang Son area, which Chinese imperial armies had historically used to invade Vietnam. From a military point of view, Lang Son (a capital city 18 kilometers from the border and 135 kilometers from Hanoi) was the most important objective. Capturing this city would allow the PLA to use railroad and highway networks to reach Thai Nguyen and Hanoi from the border. However, Lang Son was screened by three mountains: Khau Khao Son, Khau Ma Son, and Khau Phai Son, each towering some 850 meters above sea level. Sloping down from their highest peaks is a series of rugged crisscrossed ridges and fingers, honeycombed with limestone caves and blocked with massifs, all blanketed in trees and elephant grass. The terrain was far more advantageous to its defenders.

Lang Son was an obvious objective for any Chinese incursion; consequently, as early as the summer of 1978, the PAVN leadership set up the town's defense by deploying the 3rd Division (one of the PAVN's most combat-experienced and well-equipped units), supported by the 166th Artillery and 272nd Antiaircraft Artillery Regiments of the First Military Region, there.[20] The 3rd Division's full complement was three infantry regiments (the 2nd, 12th, and 141st), one artillery regiment (the 68th), one public security regiment (the 12th), and two local force battalions—a total of 12,000 troops.[21] By January 1979, some 20,000 field fortifications, including camouflages, bunkers, prepared fields of fire, and minefields, had been built.[22] The defensive line stretched for 60 kilometers, with the 12th Regiment defending the Dong Dang-Van Lang sector and the 141st Regiment defending Ban Ngua, Thong Dat, and Po Lieu, the northern and northeastern approaches to Lang Son. The 2nd Regiment defended the railroad and highway running from Lang Son to Ba La. The batteries of two artillery regiments were emplaced at Dan Nhuang, Tha Ta, and Ban Nac to provide fire support.[23] The 327th, 338th, and 337th divisions constituted an immediately available ready reserve to reinforce the defense of Lang Son.[24]

The original Chinese plan, which focused primarily on Cao Bang, did not include Dong Dang during the first phase. Not until early February did Xu and his associates realize that a simultaneous attack on this border town would confuse the Vietnamese defenders, rendering Chinese intentions unclear and thus complicating the PAVN's ability to assess and thereby grasp the PLA's intentions. In addition, the attack on Dong Dang would prevent the PAVN from sending reinforcements to assist the defense of Cao Bang.[25] The 163rd Division of the 55th, supported by the 164th and 165th Divisions, was ordered to attack Dong Dang and wipe out PAVN forces in the area within five days.[26] Given the fact that the Vietnamese defensive positions were well sited and constructed and that no PLAAF airpower would support the PLA's ground operations, the largest artillery force possible (totaling 270 large-caliber cannons) was assembled to support the infantry attacks on Dong Dang.[27]

On the morning of 17 February, the Chinese attack on Dong Dang started with an extensive artillery barrage—more than 6,000 shells dumped on thirty-four enemy strongpoints and artillery positions. At the same time, some 400 smaller caliber cannons fired at close-range targets.[28] Nevertheless, scores of undetected enemy defensive positions rendered the PLA's artillery preparation ineffective. The Battle of Dong Dang demonstrated the innate cost and cruelty of close-combat ground warfare, with Chinese casualties increased by frequent and wasteful infantry assaults up steeply sloped hills against the well-equipped and firmly entrenched Vietnamese defenders. It is no exaggeration to call Dong Dang the Chinese equivalent of the well-known American Hamburger Hill a decade earlier.[29]

Existing English-language literature fails accurately to depict of Chinese operations in the 1979 war against Vietnam, particularly the Battle of Lang Son.[30] A major part of the problem is that the Chinese and Vietnamese battle accounts do not match.[31] Such discrepancies, of course, are not surprising: as in numerous other conflicts, battlefield complexity and Clausewitzian "fog of war" frequently mislead belligerents into giving widely differing accounts of the same action. This account of the events at Dong Dang and Lang Son is not intended to discredit the Vietnamese side of story but rather seeks to make available a Chinese perspective on the action.

The 163rd Division attacked Dong Dang from the ironically named Friendship Pass. The PLA launched a two-axis frontal attack and a single-axis penetration to establish a blocking position between Dong Dang and Tam Lung. The 165th Division sent two of its regiments on a wide flanking movement to isolate Dong Dang and prevent it from receiving supplies and reinforcements from Lang Son and Thai Nguyen. Two regiments of the 164th Division attacked the defended hills in the Ban Nhien area.[32] In addition, two divisions of the 43rd advanced toward Chi Ma and Long Dau to secure the 55th Army's flank from the east.[33]

By the end of the first day, the PLA had seized Hill 303 and Hill 409, followed by Hill 386 and Hill 423 along Highway 1A, offering deceptive success.[34] But the Vietnamese defenders fought viciously in holding Hill 339, the French Fort, and Tham Mo, turning the battlefield of Dong Dang into a meat grinder.[35] Scores of lives were lost on both sides. No detailed Vietnamese accounts of the conflict are available, though the unit history of the PAVN 3rd Division notes how fiercely troops defended their positions, with pages waxing lyrical about soldiers' heroism in the face of Chinese attacks. However, it provides no details about Vietnamese losses.[36] The PLA after-action report admitted that the 163rd Division attacks were thwarted at these three positions, including the loss of half of its tanks.[37] It attributed such setbacks to the Vietnamese defensive positions at Hill 339, the French Fort, and the village of Tham Mo, which served as "a mutually supporting entity" with the PAVN defensive forces.[38]

At the same time, the Military Region's intelligence analysts wrongly informed the 55th Army that the Vietnamese forces (consisting of four divisions supported by two artillery brigades) had moved forward and were prepared to counterattack Chinese positions near Friendship Pass.[39] On 18 February, the 55th Army leadership responded by moving the bulk of its attacking forces back into China to prepare for the anticipated Vietnamese counterattacks, leaving only a small number of troops to hold their positions near Dong Dang.[40] This unfortunate and unnecessary withdrawal left PLA units defending their positions at Tam Lung without food and water for two days.[41] Although the Vietnamese forces failed to retake full control of Highway 1A to Dong Dang and Highway 1B to Tham Mo and the French Fort, they claimed some successes in counterattacks against the Chinese-occupied heights in the Chao Canh Hill area (which the Chinese referred to as the north side of Tam Lung).[42]

By the afternoon of 18 February, the forward command at Nanning realized that it could have been deceived by the Vietnamese, and leaders subsequently ordered the 55th Army to resume offensive operations the next day. Having recognized that Tham Mo, the French Fort, and Hill 339 were heavily fortified, the forward command also decided to use a small number of forces supported by direct-fire artillery combat groups and tanks to mount successive assaults from multiple directions against the enemy positions.[43]

These three Vietnamese strongpoints were situated in a triangle around the intersection of Highways 4A and 1B and the railroad tracks that run from Lang Son in Vietnam to Nanning in China. At the center of this defensive position lay the French Fort, perched on a low hill some hundred meters southwest of Dong Dang. To the south of the French Fort lay the rail station and Tham Mo. Hill 339 was "about 750 meters to the west of Tham Mo, across a gap through which ran Highway 1B and the railroad."[44] Any attempt to capture Dong Dang would draw fire suppression from the French Fort, Tham Mo, and Hill 339. The fort, built by the French in the early 1940s, was a concrete reinforced semiunderground bunker with a 1.5-meter-thick wall enclosing an area about three hundred meters long and one hundred meters wide. Troops could fire small arms and machine guns from three hundred embrasures. A trench was built around the bunker with links to its outlets. Vietnamese soldiers boasted that it constituted "an impregnable fortress."[45] Defending the French Fort was one infantry company of the PAVN's 12th Regiment, reinforced subsequently by one border force unit and an uncounted number of local civilians who retreated into the fortress.[46]

On the evening of 19 February, the Chinese forces launched vicious assaults on these three places: one company on the French Fort, one battalion on Tham Mo, and one battalion on Hill 339. The 55th Army also divided its troops into small units to engage in a pacification campaign against Vietnamese soldiers hiding in caves in the area taken by the Chinese. However, the Vietnamese defenders held their positions at the French Fort and in the Tham Mo hills, fending off the initial Chinese attacks. The PLA's losses were heavy: the company of the 489th Regiment attacking the French Fort lost almost half of its strength.[47]

On 21 February, after receiving reinforcements consisting of two platoons from other units, the company launched another assault on the French Fort, supported by artillery and rapid-firing high-velocity antiaircraft machine guns. This assault bore fruit following an intense four-hour fight. By the middle of the day, Chinese forces had secured all the ground around the French Fort. After attempting to persuade the Vietnamese soldiers and civilians inside the fort to surrender, Chinese troops blew up its tunnels using gasoline, explosives, and flamethrowers.[48] Even now, the exact number of troops and civilians hidden inside the fort remains unknown, although the sole Vietnamese survivor testified that approximately 800 people perished.[49]

Last to fall to Chinese assault was Tham Mo, a village stronghold surrounded by a cluster of eighteen connected hills ranging between 280 and
300 meters above sea level. The Chinese takeover of these Vietnamese defense
positions, Tham Mo included, came only after the PLA paid a heavy toll in
dead and wounded. Since the conflict, Vietnamese accounts, however, have
exaggerated the size of the Chinese forces, claiming, for example, that the PLA
employed "almost an entire division to attack positions being held by less than
two battalions of our troops" and stating that when "we crushed one of their
regiments they simply sent a new regiment to take its place."[50]

But according to Chinese accounts, only one battalion assaulted Tham Mo,
sustaining 40 dead and 152 wounded during the three days and four nights of
fighting. After receiving reinforcements of 300 troops on 21 February, the PLA
finally sacked Tham Mo a day later. Based on Chinese records, PAVN losses
were appalling: 456 troops killed and 6 captured. The Chinese also seized ten
37mm antiaircraft guns, ten 12.7mm antiaircraft machine guns, two 85mm
field guns, two 75mm recoilless rifles, three trucks, one bulldozer, and a score
of small arms.[51]

According to the Vietnamese 3rd Division history, its 12th Regiment lost all
reserves during the first five days of battles, and by the final hours of its defense
of Tham Mo, only 10 soldiers remained still alive.[52] Such Custer's Last Stand–
type stories reinforce Chinese claims that the PLA annihilated the entire 12th
Regiment and its affiliated units, killing a total of 3,973 enemy troops in the
Dong Dang and Ban Ranh areas.[53] On the early morning of 23 February, Dong
Dang fell into Chinese hands, but only after the 55th Army suffered 2,220 casualties, including 531 killed. This victory represented the end of the first stage
of the eastern campaign, rendering Lang Son vulnerable to imminent PLA
assault.[54]

Chinese Attacks from Yunnan

Across the Yunnan border, Lao Cai, capital city of Hoang Lien Son Province,
also suffered from Chinese attacks in the 1979 war. However, available English
accounts about this attack remain dependent on journalist reports.[55] The official history of the PAVN 316th Division, one of the Vietnamese units battling
against the Chinese invasion in the area, is silent on its role in the conflict.[56]
Not until Nguyen Tien Hung published *History of the Second Military Region
Armed Forces* in 2006 did a brief sketch discuss the role of PAVN regular units.[57]

Although Lao Cai was a nexus of rail, road, and river traffic to Hanoi in remote northwestern Vietnam, its long distance from the national capital made it

strategically less significant than Lang Son. China's attacks in the area focused not on seizing cities and territory but instead on destroying a significant portion of the Vietnamese military forces and their defense facilities. Operational principles emphasized the application of Mao's strategy of tactical dominance via mass concentration, the idea that "every battle concentrates an absolute superior force to eliminate the enemy's effective strength."

China assembled the 11th, 13th, and 14th Armies, along with a considerable number of support units, to conduct the invasion campaign with the 149th Division of the 50th Army as reserves.[58] They were the best PLA forces capable of operating in jungle and mountain terrain, and their combat performance differed substantially from that of the troops in the Guangzhou Military Region. The invasion took place along the 250-kilometer border from Moung Khang in the east to Phong Tho in the west. Chinese forces did not penetrate more than 40 kilometers across the border. The Vietnamese forces in the area were the 345th Division, which had recently converted from an economic construction division to an infantry combat division and was located at Bao Thang, and the 316th Division, an elite force unit stationed in the Binh Lu area.[59] In addition, about 20,000 members of provincial local force regiments and district local force battalions as well as militia self-defense forces were present.

The PLA's attack from Yunnan was divided into two fronts: the 13th and 14th Armies concentrated their operations in the Lao Cai, Cam Duong, and Moung Khang area as the main direction of attack, while the 11th Army acted independently against Phong Tho as a secondary offensive front. The 13th and 14th Armies launched a two-pronged invasion with the former to attack the Vietnamese positions on the west side of the Red River and the latter to fight the enemy forces on the east side. They jointly intended to encircle the Vietnamese forces in the Lao Cai, Cam Duong, Coc Leu, Sa Pa, and Bao Thang areas and then to annihilate them.[60]

On 16 February, the night before the invasion, the PLA secretly ferried troops across the Red River. In addition, three pontoon bridges were erected between Hekou and Bax Xat. Thus, more than 20,000 troops from the 13th Army had already crossed the river by dawn the next day. Just hours after this masterstroke of surprise, they broke through the PAVN's defensive line, held by the Hoang Lien Son local-force units (the 192nd Regiment, 2nd Independent Battalion, and Lao Cai Independent Battalion) and militias.[61] By nightfall on 18 February, Chinese forces claimed to have killed nearly 1,000 Vietnamese defenders and secured a 50-kilometer section of the border west to Hekou.[62]

Prior to the Chinese attacks, Hanoi appeared to have little knowledge about Chinese deployment and strategic intent.[63] The PAVN sought to hold a defensive line along the border and destroy the Chinese invaders as soon as they attempted to cross. A significant number of the Vietnamese regular and local forces (including the 121st Infantry and 190th Artillery Regiments of the 345th Division and the 148th Regiment of the 316th Division) were deployed to defensive positions along the border to guard against Chinese invasion. Relying on their fortified positions and hilly terrain, they momentarily stopped the two regiments of the PLA's 13th Army at Mong Xen and in the area south of Chu Dang and west of Nhac Son. Upon encountering this resistance, the Chinese forces instantly changed their mission from one of penetration to one of fighting against the Vietnamese strongholds. By the late afternoon of 18 February, they had completely encircled the PAVN forces in the Coc Leu and Bao Thang areas.[64] On the battlefield of Lao Cai, the 40th Division of the 14th Army engaged in massive infantry attacks, attempting to break through the PAVN's defensive lines.[65] On 21 February, the provincial capital fell to Chinese forces. By then, the PLA claimed to have destroyed the PAVN's 192nd Regiment and Lao Cai Independent Battalion and to have inflicted heavy losses on the 345th Division's infantry regiment (the 121st) and its affiliated artillery regiment (the 190th), killing and wounding approximately 2,000 Vietnamese troops.[66]

On the same day that Lao Cai fell, Hanoi ordered the Vietnamese forces at Cam Duong to make a last-ditch defense of this mining town (a source of apatite, used for extraction of phosphorous and for fertilizer production) 12 kilometers south of Lao Cai. The 345th Division hastily sent one battalion from the 118th Regiment from the east side of the Red River to reinforce the 121st Regiment's defensive positions in the area of Coc Tha, Dien Na, Dung Ha, and Chan Uy. The 316th Division moved eastward from Binh Lu to Sa Pa along Highway 10A to reinforce the defense of Cam Duong while awaiting an opportunity to retake Lao Cai and Coc Leu. Still uncertain about Beijing's strategic intentions, Hanoi obviously was extremely concerned about the breakdown of the defensive line along the Red River.[67]

Based on these developments, the PLA's Kunming Military Region moved the 149th Division and one regiment from the 11th Army to reinforce the 13th Army, warning them to prepare for a "big and fierce battle" at Cam Duong. To prevent the PAVN's 345th Division from receiving reinforcements, the 39th Division of the 13th Army rushed a force of four companies to set up blocking positions at Thay Nai, where Highway 10 winds its way through an opening in the mountains. The narrow pass was an ideal area in that even a very small force could prevent the Vietnamese from sending reinforcements to Cam Doung. From 22 to 25 February, PLA forces fought furiously at Thay Nai against the 148th Regiment of the 316th, which attempted to break through

PLA troops repulse Vietnamese forces at Thay Nai, 1979. Courtesy Wang Huazhang.

to Cam Doung. Hundreds of Vietnamese soldiers were sent forward in twenty human-wave attacks, all of which failed. Two PLA companies later received the highest commendations from the CMC for their courage and steadfastness in standing firm and repelling these repeated assaults.[68]

The 37th and 38th Divisions of the 13th Army attacked the 345th Division's defensive positions in a narrow area north of Cam Duong. A total of 564 artillery pieces were assembled to provide fire support for ground assaults.[69] On the evening of 23 February, the Chinese intercepted a radio call from Col Ma Vinh Lan, commander of the 345th, desperately appealing to the 2nd Military Region for assistance because "his troops' positions are badly beaten; it is difficult to reconfigure [defense]; and the situation is further deteriorating."[70] With no hope of receiving reinforcements, he deserted his command post, crossing the Ngoi Bo River with a few of his staff before dawn.

Following another day of fighting, the Chinese forces seized Cam Duong, triumphantly declaring that they had crushed Hanoi's diehard attempt to defend this important mining town. The victory brought the Chinese closer to achieving their campaign objectives, which emphasized the elimination of a significant number of enemy forces. According to Chinese records, one-third of the 345th Division was rendered combat-ineffective, with casualties including two battalions of the 121st Regiment, one battalion of the 118th Regiment, and even the division's independent rocket artillery battalion. This example was not isolated: the PAVN's 978th Public Security Battalion was totally depleted, and the 190th Artillery Regiment lost 40 percent of its strength.[71]

Thus encouraged, the Chinese campaign leadership in Yunnan now targeted the PAVN's 316th Division. Having failed to break through the Chinese defensive positions at Thay Nai, the Vietnamese reconfigured their defensive line along Highway 10 and other trails, following the steep climb into Sa Pa from the north. The terrain consists of rolling and densely forested hills connecting to the Hoang Lien mountain range, where Vietnam's highest mountain, Phan Xi Pang (3,143 meters), rises.

On 24 February, the Kunming Military Region ordered the 149th Division, which had been held in reserve, to join the fight against the 316th in the Sa Pa area. This PLA division had not received its deployment order until 14 February, just ten days earlier, and had to be rushed to Yunnan from its barracks in far-off Sichuan between 18 and 21 February. Moreover, it is still unclear why the PLA General Staff hastily committed this non-combat-tested unit into battle against one of the best of the PAVN's units, particularly since the 13th Army was still in good condition after its battle for Cam Duong.[72]

The PLA returned to the tactics that it had employed since the beginning of the conflict. One reinforced regiment (the 447th) was ordered to penetrate to the Hoang Lien Son Pass near Sin Chai to cut off the 316th's retreat route to Binh Lu. Simultaneously, the main force of the 149th advanced to Sa Pa in two avenues of approach along Highway 10. On 25 February, it crossed the border from Mong Xen, but hostile artillery fire, difficult terrain, and heavy rain seriously slowed its advance. In addition, time pressures began to mount: on 28 February, the Kunming Military Region urged attack forces to seize Sa Pa in two to three days at most since the invasion was approaching the deadline for withdrawal.[73]

Ironically, Sa Pa, a small district town, possessed no strategic importance. However, since the two sides committed an almost equal number of forces in a duel between their regular units, the Battle of Sa Pa became the bloodiest and most furious of the western front.

In the bitter fighting that followed, the PAVN's 316th Division demonstrated both excellent offensive and defensive mastery, fighting from fortified positions to thwart the Chinese advance, though typically without showing much evidence of coordinated or mutually supported action. The Chinese attacks were relentless and massive, and the Vietnamese ultimately admitted that they lacked the forces "to block the enemy's advance" and had to "retreat to preserve our own forces."[74] On 3 March, the PLA captured the town, bringing the battle to a close. The 149th had engaged in continuous fighting for seven days, enduring losses of 420 of its soldiers.[75] In turn, it had inflicted heavy casualties on the 316th Division and the Sa Pa Independent Battalion, with 1,398 Vietnamese troops killed, 620 wounded, and 35 captured.[76]

Even so, the Chinese campaign in the west did not end with a notable victory such as the seizure of Lang Son (which, unlike Sa Pa, was a strategically located border city) in the east. From a Western military perspective, Chinese soldiers had made sacrifices merely to attain insignificant "tactical objectives."[77]

But given the limited access to Chinese or Vietnamese records, this prevailing Western narrative appears excessively Eurocentric and therefore misleading. Hanoi's commitment of regular force units (two full divisions) to the fight in the Lao Cai–Cam Duong–Sa Pa corridor played into the hands of Chinese war planners, who had prioritized the destruction of PAVN forces as a key campaign objective. Furthermore, from the Beijing leadership's perspective—especially Deng Xiaoping's—the battlefields across the Yunnan border were a brutal training ground in which the Chinese forces could gain combat experience. True, they had paid a heavy price, losing 7,886 troops, including 2,812 killed. But the Vietnamese forces suffered heavy losses as well. According to Chinese claims, the invasion ended up with the defeat of one Vietnamese division, five Vietnamese regiments, and eight Vietnamese battalions, amounting to more than 13,500 Vietnamese troops, a figure dwarfing the PLA's own fatalities by nearly a factor of five.[78]

The Battle of Lang Son

The ultimate target of the 1979 war against Vietnam was Lang Son, whose capture would endanger Hanoi itself. Immediately after the seizure of Dong Dang, Beijing had urged the PLA forces in Guangxi to initiate the attack on Lang Son. The Guangzhou Military Region Forward Command responded that it would take three days to regroup its forces for the assault. At a 25 February meeting, the forward command determined that pursuant to the CMC's order, it would commit seven divisions totaling 80,000 troops.[79] Taking the main axis of advance would be the 55th Army, supported by the 161st Division of the 54th Army and striking from the north. Two divisions of the 43rd Army (assisted by two regiments from the 50th Army) formed a secondary attack axis that would conduct a flanking assault on Loc Binh and then press on toward Lang

PLA artillery positions on the Guangxi front, 1979. Courtesy Xiaobing Li.

Son from the southeast.[80] Drawing lessons from the battle for Dong Dang, the Guangzhou Military Region Forward Command decided to first clear out Vietnamese defensive positions around Lang Son while moving the main attacking forces along Highway 4A toward the city. General Xu ordered his force to commence the attacks early on 27 February.[81]

The Battle of Lang Son began with a four-pronged attack on Khau Ma Son, Hill 417, Pa Vai Son, and Khau Khao Son. This attack bought time for other units to outflank Lang Son from the southeast and southwest, respectively. For the first two days, the Chinese forces mounted multicompany assaults, each of which incurred heavy casualties. One company of the 163rd was almost entirely depleted in the battle for Hill 417, located 1 kilometer south of Tham Lung, on Highway 4 to Lang Son.

But if the PAVN was inflicting heavy casualties on the PLA, it was taking them as well, for the PLA was no less determined or remorseless in combat. Consequently, the PAVN 3rd Division's strength was steadily reduced. On the afternoon of 27 February, Chinese forces seized Khau Man Son, which had a Vietnamese artillery command post on its 800-meter peak that had effectively directed artillery fire against the PLA forces during the Battle of Dong Dang.[82] The loss of this artillery command post constituted a serious blow to the PAVN. The 493rd Regiment of the PLA's 165th Division pushed forward for 13 kilometers after overrunning Khui Phat (about 1 kilometer south of Khau Ma Son). Around Khau Lau Son, Khau Bo Son, Khau Tang Son, and Pa Vai

Son (which sheltered Lang Son from the northeast), two regiments of the PLA's 164th Division fought a series of intense and desperate engagements against the 141st Regiment of the PAVN's 3rd Division. By the afternoon of 28 February, the PLA controlled all these positions and claimed to have killed 252 Vietnamese soldiers at Pa Vai Son alone. As a result, Lang Son was now vulnerable to PLA attacks from the east.[83] Although the Vietnamese continued to hold out in isolated pockets on the outskirts of Lang Son, the PLA forces were ready to engage in a massive assault on the city proper from three directions.

For the first time, the Guangzhou military leadership felt satisfied with the PLA's battlefield progress. General Xu had been disappointed by his troops' performance since the beginning of the invasion, but the successive triumphs culminating in the fighting for Khau Lau Son, Khau Bo Son, Khau Tang Son, and Pa Vai Son convinced him the time had now come to redeem his credentials as a warrior.[84] Accordingly, he ordered a dense concentration of his artillery forces, totaling 306 large-caliber cannons, to bombard Lang Son City, cued by an artillery command post on the top of Khau Ma Son, from which PLA observers could direct fire onto the PAVN's defensive positions in the city and even beyond.[85] According to Xu, he wanted to use his artillery "to raze every house in Lang Son."[86]

On 1 March, the Chinese artillery forces laid down an intense thirty-minute barrage against the provincial capital. That day, however, the Chinese forces met strong Vietnamese resistance and the 163rd's advance toward the Ky Cung River Bridge was checked 1 kilometer from the destination, in front of Hill 279 and two rock hills near Dong Uyen. One battalion of the 489th Regiment was pinned down in an open area by concentrated fire from antiaircraft cannon, antiaircraft machine guns, and heavy machine guns. Only later did the Chinese discover that Hill 279 and the rock hills constituted a veritable hornets' nest: Hill 279 was the site of the command post for the 42nd Regiment of the PAVN's 327th Division, and the rock hills were defensive complexes consisting of tunnels, firing points, and a score of caves. Together they shielded the northern and northwestern approaches to Lang Son City.[87]

Even so, the PLA made steady progress against the defenders of Lang Son. At Lam Truang (about two kilometers northwest of Lang Son), the PLA's 165th Division broke through the defensive line held by the PAVN's 42nd Regiment and an element of the 166th Artillery Regiment, claiming to have killed more than 300 Vietnamese troops and captured eleven trucks. By noon on 1 March, the PLA's 164th Division had seized the headquarters of the Vietnamese 141st Regiment at Po Leo (about 1.5 kilometers northeast of the northern district of Lang Son), capturing a significant cache of weapons, including Soviet-made antitank missiles and American-made rockets. By the end of that day, the Vietnamese defensive lines in Lang Son City were on the verge of collapse.[88]

The official PAVN history states that on 2 March, Vietnam's military leaders decided to abandon the city and pull the battered 3rd Division back to serve as the last-ditch reserve force.[89] The order came too late for Lang Son's defenders, however. That same morning, the PLA resumed attacks on the hill positions, and after a daylong fight, Chinese forces had secured both the heights and all government buildings in the northern part of the city, including the provincial government office. They blasted the PAVN's rock caves at Nhi Thanh Dong and Tam Thanh Dong with explosive charges and flamethrowers and brought rapid-fire 85mm artillery guns to fire at what was, for these cannon, extremely close ranges of between 500 and 800 meters.[90] The PLA claimed the PAVN lost 350 soldiers and had three tanks and six armored vehicles destroyed or captured.[91]

Beijing originally planned to halt operations after the PLA reached the Ky Cung River, which separates the city of Lang Son into northern and southern districts. But because Hanoi's propaganda machine refused to accept the PAVN's defeat at Lang Son, the CMC ordered the PLA to cross the river in search of more victories.[92] On 4 March, an attack force of six battalions from the 163rd Division crossed the river between Khui Khuc and Khon Pat. They not only quickly seized Lang Son's southern district but also reached Pac Meng, five kilometers south of Lang Son. The 163rd's advance across the Ky Cung and consequent drive down Highway 1A to Pac Meng constituted the PLA's deepest penetration toward Hanoi.

Two battalions from the 50th Army (which had been kept in reserve) were also now thrown into the battle. They crossed the Khon Pa Bridge; took Hills 332, 317, and 382; and engaged in a fight against a Vietnamese armored unit (presumably the 202nd Tank Brigade of the Vietnamese First Army Corps), allegedly destroying two tanks, one armored vehicle, and one towing tractor.[93] To the east, a regiment of the 127th Division crossed the river at Phieng Phuc, defeated a unit of more than 480 troops from the 155th Regiment of the PAVN's 327th Division, and then went on to seize Me Mai Son, approximately 5 kilometers southeast of Lang Son, where a country road leads onward to Hanoi.[94] The Chinese military leadership subsequently asserted that the occupation of this mountain created a threatening military posture toward the Vietnamese capital.[95]

In *Chinese Military Strategy in the Third Indochina War*, Edward O'Dowd argues the Chinese conducted an ineffective military operation against Lang Son. His criticism covers the PLA's artillery doctrine, personnel system, and logistics system.[96] The Chinese offered a different assessment. The 55th Army's after-action report admitted that 1,271 Chinese troops had been killed and 3,779 wounded at Dong Dang and Lang Son. In addition, thirty tanks and thirty artillery pieces had been lost. However, the Chinese credited themselves with having inflicted 10,401 casualties on the Vietnamese defenders, most of them from the PAVN's 3rd Division and the local units under its command along with a small force of the PAVN's 327th Division. This number did not include those killed by gasoline, explosives, and flamethrowers in the tunnel complex of the French Fort and the caves at Lang Son. The 55th Army also recorded the destruction of forty-four PAVN tanks and six armored vehicles and the capture of a significant number of weapons, including 3 tanks, 3 armored vehicles, 29 trucks, 32 motorcycles, 99 artillery pieces, 2,200 small arms, 17,000 artillery rounds, and tons of other military supplies. Prior to withdrawing from Lang Son, the 55th destroyed 2,920 military and public facilities, literally turning the city into a ruin.[97] General Xu's forces returned to China convinced that the combination of artillery fire and fierce ground combat at Lang Son had taught Vietnam a harsh and unforgettable "lesson."[98]

Hanoi's Response as Seen from the Vietnamese Perspective

With limited access to Vietnamese records, it is difficult to give an objective account of the Vietnamese response to the Chinese attacks. The published PAVN history presents at best a sketchy depiction of the 1979 conflict.[99] Since the unification of Vietnam in 1975, Hanoi had adopted a policy that regarded America as the "long-term fundamental enemy" but China as the "most direct, dangerous enemy," and the "new prospective foe" against which Vietnam needed to prepare to fight.[100] In July 1978, the Vietnamese central party leadership promulgated a resolution calling on the Vietnamese people to carry out economic construction while preparing for war at any time.[101] To defeat China, the resolution urged, "Every person must be a soldier, every district must be a battle position, every district must be a fortress, and every province must be a strategic area." Hanoi's military strategy stressed the tenacious defense of the border by winning victories on the first line.[102] Regular troops were deployed to the border region, and people living there were mobilized, equipped, and trained to fight against the Chinese invasion.[103] Field fortifications including trenches, bunkers, tunnels, and minefields were constructed at such strategically important areas as Dong Dang, Cao Bang, Lang Son, and Lao Cai.

According to the Vietnamese perspective, the PLA and Chinese border forces increasingly triggered border provocations starting in early 1979. (For their part, the Chinese blamed the rise in incidents on the Vietnamese, but the Vietnamese were probably correct since the PLA sent many scout teams to acquire information).[104] Immediately after the new year, the Vietnamese Central Military Commission directed the PAVN forces in the northern border region to keep at the highest state of readiness for combat, requiring one-third to two-thirds of the forces to stay in their battle positions around the clock and to fire on the enemy as soon as it appeared.[105] In the meantime, Hanoi engaged in a vigorous public relations campaign. On 14 February, the Foreign Ministry issued a memorandum accusing China of creating a tense situation along the border while massing large numbers of troops and war materials there.[106] However, Hanoi continued to believe that "a fraternal socialist country" would never attack another socialist nation; it was also confident that the equipment it had captured from the Americans and received from Russia [was] "superior to that of the PLA" and that "the Cultural Revolution [had] lowered PLA combat readiness."[107]

Despite Beijing's several months of saber rattling, China's invasion still caught Hanoi off guard. When the massive numbers of Chinese troops crossed the border, both Premier Pham Van Dong and the chief of the PAVN General Staff, Van Tien Dung, were visiting Phnom Penh. On the northern front, the military leadership did not seem to anticipate the Chinese attacks that day. The commanding officers at all levels of the 3rd Division were taking a training class at division headquarters. After the PLA attack was reported, they were ordered to immediately return to their command posts. However, Nguyen Xuan Khan, commander of the 12th Regiment, and his staff officers could not reach their command post because Chinese artillery had severed communications between troops and higher headquarters. The history of the 3rd Division concedes that the PLA immediately "rendered us deaf and blind."[108]

As the PLA planners had intended, the massive assaults prevented the Vietnamese high command from identifying both the main axis of the invasion and the real objectives of the attack. One Vietnamese diplomat later recalled that the government had anticipated the Chinese invasion but was stunned by the timing, the large scale, and the massive force employed.[109] The PLA's deep-penetration flanking and envelopment attacks caused particular concern, as both went well beyond what the PAVN had anticipated.[110] The Vietnamese were soon convinced that the main direction of the Chinese attacks was Dong Dang and Lang Son, with the assault on Cao Bang by two PLA armies constituting only a secondary front.[111] Hanoi's immediate response was "to improvise, to throw up whatever resistance might delay the Chinese advance" in this direction.[112]

Hanoi also urgently appealed to Moscow to fulfill its obligations under a recently signed treaty of friendship and cooperation between the two countries. The Soviet leadership responded by sending a group of military advisers to assist the PAVN General Staff in conducting operations. Colonel General Gennadi I. Obaturov was charged with leading the group, which consisted of twenty officers, including two lieutenant generals and at least eleven major generals. On the morning of 19 February, they flew to Hanoi and met with the chief of the PAVN General Staff to hear about the increasingly grave situation at the front. The following day, Obaturov traveled to Lang Son to see for himself, and his motorcade came under intense shelling by Chinese artillery. No one was hurt. Waves of refugees were fleeing from Lang Son to Hanoi, and the situation on the front was dire and uncertain. Vietnamese resistance was uncoordinated, and guerrilla-type ambushes and action predominated. Even worse, a significant number of PAVN forces were already surrounded by the invading Chinese. To the Russian general, the entire Vietnamese defensive line at Lang Son was almost collapsing; nothing could stop the Chinese forces from advancing toward Hanoi once it fell. He recommended building a new defensive line between Lang Son and Hanoi. This move required withdrawing some troops from Cambodia, but only Le Duan, the party secretary-general, could make such a vital decision. Soviet sources indicated that General Obaturov went to great lengths to try to see the Vietnamese leader and then to persuade him to take action.[113]

On 27 February, the PAVN 2nd Corps (30,000 soldiers) in Cambodia received orders to go defend the northern border of Vietnam.[114] In keeping with Obaturov's recommendation, the Vietnamese leadership also rushed a rocket artillery division with the newly received BM-21 Grad Russian rocket launchers to the border area to help relieve the division under the Chinese siege.[115] One regiment of the PAVN 327th Division, which had been held as a reserve in the area south of Lang Son, moved up to join the 3rd Division to defend the city. The PAVN's 308th, 312th, and 390th Divisions were deployed along the roads between Hanoi and Lang Son.[116] With the reinforcement of the 304th, 306th, and 325th Divisions from Cambodia in early March, the General Staff in Hanoi allegedly planned to conduct a massive counterattack against the Chinese occupation forces at Lang Son. Soviet advisers were dispatched to the Vietnamese front units. One Soviet signal company was airlifted to Hanoi to provide communication for Soviet advisers working with the PAVN General Staff. On 5 March, Beijing, however, declared its withdrawal from Vietnam.[117] The same day, Hanoi called for a nationwide general mobilization for the war against the Chinese invasion. It provided that male citizens between ages eighteen and forty-five and females between eighteen and thirty-five must join the militia forces to prepare to fight, and all walks of life must operate under the military system. The whole country returned to wartime status only a few years after the war against America ended. But the mobilization came too late.[118]

Without ascertaining Beijing's war objectives, Hanoi appeared slow in responding to the fast-changing and fluid situation on the battlefield. Apparently following the recommendations of the Soviet advisers, Hanoi began reorganizing its defense against the Chinese threat. On 2 March, the PAVN established a 5th Corps to pull all units together in the Lang Son area under one command. Three days later, it created a Capital Military Region for the defense of Hanoi. During the Chinese invasion, Quang Ninh, at the eastern side of Vietnam's border with China, had never been a key battleground. On 8 March, the Quang Ninh front, separated from Military Region 1, was created under the direct leadership of central military authorities. In the northwestern border area, the Vietnamese General Staff established the 6th Corps, headquartered at Tri An and consisting of seven divisions (the 313th, 314th, 316th, 326th, 345th, 355th, and 356th).[119] Although this military reconfiguration in the northern border did not seem to hamper Vietnamese operations in Cambodia, Hanoi's effort to fight two wars simultaneously drained the country's resources. That the Vietnamese leadership failed to grasp the gravity of the situation was increasingly evident as it continued a militaristically futile policy.

All these military reconfiguration efforts came too late to influence the battles for Cao Bang, Lao Cai, and Lang Son. The fall of Lang Son City signaled the PLA's achievement of its military objectives. The Vietnamese subsequently argued that only their withdrawal had enabled the Chinese to enter the city. Yet no information suggests that the badly battered PAVN 3rd Division could have held on in Lang Son any longer than it did without receiving significant numbers of fresh reinforcements. The occupation of the city's northern district helped the Chinese forces obtain a favorable position for on further strikes. Particularly from the heights on the north bank of the Ky Cung River, the Chinese artillery observation posts provided their gunners with increasingly reliable targeting information. On 3 March, the 122mm howitzer batteries of 164th Division undertook an eighteen-minute barrage against one Vietnamese infantry battalion, one howitzer battalion, and one tank company as they were assembling on the east side of Hill 391, south of the river. The Chinese gunners claimed that they destroyed six artillery pieces, five tanks, four towing tractors, and three trucks and killed or wounded approximately 300 PAVN troops.[120]

With the fall of Lang Son, Hanoi's leadership became alarmed about possible further Chinese incursions. Even though Vietnam maintained that its savage resistance had brought about Beijing's withdrawal announcement, the future attacks now seemed possible. All political and military measures taken by Hanoi were warranted at the time. But in the long run, Vietnam's anti-China policy, built on the basis of Soviet support, was questionable, and actually worked against the national interest.

The Last Stage: Withdrawal from Vietnam

In the last stage of the 1979 war, the Chinese continued a mopping-up campaign against Vietnamese resistance that lasted nearly two more weeks. During this stage, the brutalities and predatory nature of war—even between two "fraternal" countries—were further revealed.

On 5 March, Beijing announced that its counterattack in self-defense had "achieved the expected objectives," and that it was beginning "to withdraw all troops back to Chinese territory."[121] At the time, Chinese troops were still engaged in furious battles against Vietnamese defenders south of the Ky Cung River and in extensive and ruthless mop-up operations in a vast area running from Lang Son to Cao Bang and then to Sa Pa and Phong Tho. General Xu allegedly resented the withdrawal order's timing. Although the CMC's order allowed some leeway for PLA troops still undertaking operations against isolated pockets of lingering Vietnamese resistance, the deadline for PLA troops in the Lang Son and Cao Bang areas mandated their withdrawal on 11 and 13 March, respectively. Xu made a few changes that allowed his troops to exploit the victory for two more days in the area south to the Ky Cung River and postponed the deadline for a few additional days to complete an orderly withdrawal from the Cao Bang area.[122] He also ordered PLA troops to destroy everything they could along their way home.[123] This organized destruction and looting became another new phenomenon for the PLA.

No Chinese official sources give accounts of the PLA's wanton acts of destruction in Vietnam. According to fragmentary personal recollections, the PLA units engaged in an economic sabotage operation on their way back to China, the long-term effects of which allegedly crippled Vietnam for the next fifteen years. Combat engineering units blew up bridges, factories, shops, granaries, and government buildings. Military trucks hauled various sorts of seized merchandise—bicycles, tractors, sewing machines, tons of rice—back to China.[124] Apatite production at Cam Duong, which reportedly accounted for one-third of all Vietnamese export earnings, was savaged. The PLA not only destroyed the mining facilities but also confiscated 2 East German caterpillar excavators along with 250 dump trucks that Vietnam had recently imported from Romania.[125] King C. Chen concludes, "The immediate reaction of the Vietnamese people who suffered from the devastation was undoubtedly an intensive hatred for the Chinese."[126]

Following the fall of Cao Bang, the Vietnamese forces had drawn on their Viet Minh heritage, dispersing into company- and platoon-sized units; hiding in the mountains, forests, and caves; and venturing out to counterattack when circumstances became favorable. The PLA immediately had to amend its operational tactics, and in a response American veterans of the Vietnam War would have recalled with some grim irony, now divided their forces into battalion- and company-sized formations to engage in U.S.-style search-and-destroy operations in the Cao Bang, Tra Linh, Trung Khanh, and Guang Hoa areas. They imposed roadblocks, combed hills, searched caves, torched the ground, and blew up any tunnels they discovered. Unprepared for such operations, the PLA initially tried to assault caves with conventional infantry attacks but took heavy casualties. It then resorted to simply deploying artillery at close range, together with a large number of combat engineering teams skilled with explosives and flamethrowers, blasting and burning any caves they encountered. Hundreds of Vietnamese soldiers and civilians concealed in the caves were killed.[127] At the end of these operations, the Chinese had captured the headquarters of the PAVN's 346th Division in a cave at Na Hoai and had destroyed the 567th Regiment, a PAVN regional unit, in the Phu Ho area.[128]

During the withdrawal operation, the PLA undertook a carefully staged pullback, with frontline units withdrawing through rear covering units, then the rear units (now the frontline units) withdrawing in turn. The Guangzhou Military Region sent the 58th Division of the 20th Army and the 150th Division of the 50th Army, which were held in reserve, to join mop-up operations in the Lang Son–Cao Bang area.[129] General Xu also ordered his troops to set up ambushes against any PAVN forces tailing the Chinese.[130] The editorial in the 7 March issue of the Vietnamese party journal *Nhan Dan* declared that Vietnam would allow the invading Chinese forces to withdraw but that there would be no "red carpet exit" treatment for the Chinese.[131] Indeed, the PAVN's 338th Division closely followed the withdrawing PLA forces, harassing them constantly on their way out of the country. (In the early stage of the war, one battalion went into China itself to attack a PLA position.)[132] But the harassing actions themselves resulted in substantial Vietnamese casualties. On 9 and 10 March, the PLA's 43rd Army ambushed two battalions from the 338th Division, killing approximately 600 troops.[133] Tactical intelligence deficiencies added to the PAVN's woes: a Vietnamese company tailing withdrawing Chinese troops one dark night pretended to be a PLA unit by singing Chinese songs that had been popular during the Cultural Revolution. But Chinese troops no longer sung these songs, so the PAVN soldiers inadvertently gave away their identity, alerting the PLA, which promptly attacked.[134]

However, the Chinese withdrawal was marred by a disastrous miscalculation that has not been adequately discussed in subsequent historical accounts of the last stages of the war.[135] With an overwhelming PLA victory in hand, the leadership of the 150th Division made an earnest plea to join the fight before the incursion came to an end so that soldiers could gain battle experience. But the 150th was poorly prepared, and on 11 March, its 448th Regiment was encircled and cut to pieces in a Vietnamese ambush at Ban Ngan, about 2 kilometers northwest of Cao Bang. After two days of attacks and counterattacks, the regiment disintegrated. Its commander lost contact with his troops and division headquarters, abandoned his command post, and left his troops to break out on their own. As a result, the 448th lost 859 troops—96 killed, 544 missing in action, and 219 captured, including a whole company ordered to surrender by its commander.[136] The Vietnamese later used these captured PLA soldiers for propaganda and psychological warfare against China. This defeat shocked Xu, who immediately ordered all units in the Cao Bang area to suspend their retreat and rescue the dispersed troops of the 448th. Consequently, PLA forces in the Cao Bang area did not return to China until 16 March.[137]

Conclusion

From 17 February to 16 March, a total of twenty-seven Chinese army divisions undertook a monthlong invasion of Vietnam, seizing three provincial capital cities—Lang Son, Cao Bang, and Lao Cai—and seventeen other district towns. Beijing subsequently claimed that its forces had achieved their operational objective. China's invasion of Vietnam constituted the PLA's largest military operation since the Korean War. In retrospect, it was two-dimensional (air and naval forces did not participate) and was fought in a narrow border area against a weaker enemy. The PLA's performance was uneven, revealing many deficiencies, including poor planning and intelligence, inefficient command and control, outdated operational tactics, and a backward logistical support system. Most of these shortcomings may have been closely associated with the PLA's erroneous military thinking and traditions. A further assessment of the PLA's experience in 1979 is needed to address the questions of why the PLA did so poorly and how this poor performance actually served the Chinese leadership's strategic intent. Moreover, this narrative suggests that there is a unique set of Chinese characteristics in warfare.

5 Reassessing the 1979 War

The classic Sun Tzu adage of war, "Know the enemy and know yourself," writ large, is a fundamental tenet of Chinese military strategy. The PLA always maintained an active self-evaluation program to be fully aware of its strengths and weaknesses. Deng Xiaoping reckoned that the invasion of Vietnam was a remarkable experience for the PLA since so many troops endured the combat test. Shortly after military operations ended, he ordered all troops involved in the conflict to write summaries of their combat experience as their primary job.[1] The *PLA Daily* subsequently published an article, "Transforming the Self-Defense Counterattack Experiences into the Treasury of the Whole Army," suggesting that the combat experience gained in the war against Vietnam would hold tremendous significance for the PLA.[2] Special teams were assigned to help units document almost all aspects of the military operation in Vietnam, including planning, intelligence, command and control, operations and tactics, logistics, political work, and the aid-the-front work. Since the PLA was a highly politicized military force, analysts paid particular attention to the political work, the principal mechanism for mobilizing Chinese forces.

China claimed military victory on the basis of the geopolitical outcomes that resulted from the PLA's performance on the battlefield, reflecting the peculiarities of how the PLA undertook its postwar "lessons learned" analysis of the conflict. China's approach to evaluating military operations differs from Western approaches largely as a result of China's preference for "subjective measures versus quantitative indicators of performance."[3] But the differences are at once less and more subtle than such a simplistic interpretation suggests. The PLA does employ quantitative measures, using them to evaluate the direct results of military operations and to understand to what extent the enemy's effective strength has been annihilated or paralyzed. However, this use of quantitative indicators is secondary to the subjective factors that are embedded in Chinese strategic culture—most notably, the emphasis on "wits, wisdom, and strategy" that largely determine a war's outcome.[4]

Though the PLA conducted a thorough evaluation with both quantitative and subjective measurements, it failed to disassociate the lessons learned from the conflict from the army's outdated military philosophy and tradition. Consequently, this failed process restricted the PLA's subsequent modernization and transformation.

Early Assessments

Various scholars and intelligence analysts undertook a series of early assessments of the PLA's performance in the 1979 war. These early assessments offer a foundation for better understanding the PLA's assessment process and methodology. Harlan Jencks, a postdoctoral researcher at Berkeley, published the first scholarly analysis of the war in August 1979.[5] Jencks acknowledged that "many critical facts remain unknown" and analyzed China's military performance based solely on media reports. As late as 2002, lack of access to Chinese sources meant that Jencks's study was described as the "very best work" on the 1979 war.[6]

Jencks examined China's war objectives and military operations, including timing, command arrangements, forces committed, strategy, and tactics. He found that China had achieved some positive results: Vietnamese military and civilian installations in the border area had been completely destroyed; the PLA had inflicted significant casualties on some Vietnamese regular units; troops had gained valuable combat experience; and the invasion demonstrated to foreign powers that China meant what it said. Nevertheless, he concluded that China had lost more than it had gained. Strategically, the Chinese invasion strengthened the Soviet-Vietnamese alliance, intensifying regional tensions and consequently disturbing East Asian and Southeast Asian countries as well as the United States. Overall, the war proved that the PLA remained an ineffective force, fighting with outdated strategy and tactics in "two-dimensional" ground warfare and suffering heavy losses as a consequence.[7]

Other initial assessments emphasized that Vietnam's combat-seasoned force, equipped with modern Soviet weapons, outperformed the inexperienced PLA.[8] However, the lack of transparency in both China's and Vietnam's military establishments made these assessments more speculative than factually insightful. Those writing English-language accounts seemed unwilling to include information from Chinese newspapers, even though they printed a significant number of reports about the PLA's performance. Though these accounts were often filled with political propaganda, ignoring them meant that scholars missed an opportunity to obtain an analysis untainted by an inadvertent pro-Vietnamese bias.

Complementing these academic and popular assessments, American government agencies undertook more official studies of China's war with Vietnam. In March 1980, the Central Intelligence Agency (CIA) produced a highly classified assessment of the PLA's combat performance and obvious lessons China learned from the war with Vietnam.[9] Since the invasion failed to oust Vietnamese troops from Cambodia, the CIA report concluded that China achieved few of its political objectives. It noted that the PLA's conservative tactics limited the operation's scale, depth, and duration. The report asserted that the PLA's slow advance was more a product of Chinese "cautiousness and concern for reducing casualties" than a consequence of "the difficult terrain and tenacious Vietnamese defense." Given the fact that it was a short conventional military action with no air and naval power involved, CIA analysts concluded that China's war with Vietnam did not present enough information for them to assess the PLA's overall war capabilities.[10]

The CIA's assessment obviously included information furnished by Beijing. Two weeks after Chinese troops withdrew from Vietnam, Chinese ambassador Chai Zemin visited the White House, where he briefed national security adviser Zbigniew Brzezinski about the war. Chai discussed Vietnamese strength at the border, the PLA's deployment, operations and casualties, and combat highlights.[11] Chai tried to convince the Americans that China had achieved victory over Vietnam, emphasizing that the PLA had annihilated two Vietnamese divisions and four regiments, seriously weakened four other regiments, and inflicted five Vietnamese casualties for every one suffered by the PLA. According to the Chinese ambassador, Vietnamese troops performed poorly when fighting large battles but did well when using guerrilla tactics and sabotage attacks, something consistent with America's experience in the 1960s and that of the French a generation earlier. The biggest lesson the PLA learned was that the hilly and jungle-like terrain impeded large-unit maneuvering, making it necessary to devise on-the-spot mid-battle adjustments that favored small-unit tactics against the Vietnamese guerrilla-type resistance. In conclusion, the Chinese were convinced that Vietnam would be more restrained after having suffered such severe punishment.[12] In retrospect, Chai's report was itself an incomplete assessment, containing inaccurate casualty information, but it was what Beijing was willing to share with Washington at that moment. Beijing appeared unwilling to furnish insights as to why the PLA did not perform as well as expected because the Chinese did not think it necessary to share anything beyond the outcome of the war with the Americans.

But even at this early point in postwar analysis, a growing discrepancy was evident between a Western view that tended to underscore the PLA's shortcomings and a Chinese position that stressed the PLA's victory over the PAVN. All these assessments suffered from the absence of many critical facts, including information about such basic matters as Chinese strategy and campaign objectives, Chinese operational tactics, and the number of casualties on both sides.

Battlefield Claims and Casualties

The PLA had not engaged in such a large-scale military operation since the Korean War. Based on Mao Zedong's strategy that "in every battle, concentrate an absolute superior force against the enemy," Beijing had deployed nine regular armies along with special and local units, amounting to over half a million troops. Air force fighter units flew 8,500 border air defense sorties, while transport and helicopter units flew 228 airlift sorties[13] and the navy dispatched a task force to prepare for possible Soviet naval intervention.[14] In addition, Guangxi and Yunnan Provinces mobilized tens of thousands of militiamen and laborers to support the PLA's military operation in Vietnam. During the conflict, Chinese forces captured three Vietnamese provincial capitals along with a dozen other border cities and district towns, claiming to have killed and wounded 57,000 Vietnamese troops, severely damaged four PAVN regular divisions and ten other regiments, and captured 2,200 prisoners of war.[15] Chinese victory claims also included the destruction of 340 pieces of artillery, 45 tanks, and some 480 trucks and the capture of 840 pieces of artillery and more than 11,000 small arms, along with many other types of military equipment.[16] On this basis, Beijing asserted that military operations against Vietnam ended with China's triumph.

However, based on the reported heavy casualties China suffered in the war and lack of information about Vietnamese casualties, most contemporary Western studies maintained that Vietnam "had indeed outperformed" the Chinese forces on the battlefield.[17] Such reasoning accepted Hanoi's disingenuous claims that Vietnam had committed only militia and local forces, who executed constant attacks against Chinese invaders. Apologists for the Hanoi regime argued that Vietnam had lost Lang Son and other cities only after Vietnamese defenders had killed a large number of PLA troops.[18] (At the time, Hanoi Radio announced that a total of 42,000 Chinese troops were killed and wounded in the war, a third more than the PLA's actual combat casualties.)[19] Vietnam's 1979 war records remain unavailable. However, the publication of PAVN unit histories reveals that a significant number of Vietnamese regular forces fought against the Chinese invasion, including some that engaged in "last-stand" actions before being overwhelmed by resolute PLA attackers.[20]

A reassessment of the 1979 war based on China's sources is equally one-sided but is still both intriguing and informative. Battlefield casualties are a common measure of combat effectiveness. Beijing publicly acknowledged that 20,000 Chinese soldiers were either killed or wounded.[21] In reality, the PLA lost more than 31,000 soldiers (including almost 8,000 fatalities), divided between the two military regions: 5,103 dead and 15,412 injured in Guangxi and 2,812 killed and 7,886 wounded in Yunnan.[22] Western observers, however, did not accept Chinese numbers and therefore speculated (with a misleading "precision" based on specious media reports) that the PLA could have had as many as 26,000 killed and 37,000 wounded in action.[23] Over time, these figures have become accepted by scholars and subsequently have been widely cited to support the thesis that the PLA did not conduct itself successfully in the fighting.[24] It is true that China's casualties in such a short war were significantly high. However, the Chinese believed that their losses were still outstripped by Vietnamese losses.

The most controversial statistic was the number of soldiers killed. The basis of PLA victory claims were body counts after the Vietnamese positions had been sacked, a practice ironically echoing that of the U.S. Army in South Vietnam a decade earlier. For example, the 163rd Division counted 5,293 Vietnamese soldiers killed and 612 Chinese dead. This claim did not include the unknown numbers of Vietnamese troops killed inside the underground bunkers at the French Fort and inside Nhi Thanh and Tam Thanh Caves.[25]

However, that the figures claimed by the PLA forces may be inflated.[26] The battlefield was a dangerous and chaotic place, and perfectly accurate casualty reporting was always difficult.[27] On 16 March 1979, at a CCP Central Committee meeting, Deng noted that the number of Vietnamese wounded counted by the PLA might not be accurate, since battlefield experiences often supported a high wounded-to-killed ratio.[28] This discrepancy cannot be resolved until the Vietnamese records become available. The Chinese leader, however, did not think that casualties were the best criterion for weighing military success. For him, China's victory was determined by the overall strategic situation, which he thought concluded in China's favor. According to Deng, the war improved China's strategic position and China's world prestige and inspired the Chinese people to be more devoted to the Four Modernizations." He stressed that the PLA's battlefield losses were "small" compared to the heroism and bravery manifested by Chinese troops in the war. Deng also felt a sense of relief, speaking of his satisfaction about the PLA's performance during the invasion with a comment that Chinese troops had not behaved like "ducks" (*fang yazi*) even when they confronted extraordinary challenges and ordeals.[29] The Chinese leader was convinced that any PLA deficiencies were less important than the strategic gains China had achieved.

Assessment from a Strategic Perspective

From a Chinese perspective, the 1979 war with Vietnam was a deliberately orchestrated military response to Vietnamese policy toward China and its expansion in Southeast Asia as well as to Soviet global aspirations.[30] As Deng Xiaoping stressed on 19 February 1979, Vietnam's invasion of Cambodia placed at least some of the ASEAN countries under threat, and the Soviet Union could use Vietnam to create an "Asian Collective Security System" to contain China. "Although China's action to teach Vietnam a lesson just began," the Chinese leader continued, "it was a limited operation to be confined within the border region with a simple objective"—to "warn Vietnam not to be recklessly aggressive in the region."[31] The Chinese leader related China's war with Vietnam to Hanoi's Indochina policy but did not state that Beijing's strategic objective was to compel Vietnam to withdraw from Cambodia. Accordingly, the PLA's performance must be assessed from a perspective that examines to what extent the 1979 war served China's strategic interests.

The Chinese leadership believed that Beijing had met its goals. On 16 March, speaking in front of party, government, and military leaders at the Great Hall of the People, Deng declared China's "victory" over Vietnam. He believed that the war had boosted China's prestige and influence in the world, proving that China stood behind what it said and that the war was important for the fight against hegemony. He also believed that the war had inspired the Chinese people to shift the focal point of their work to economic development programs.[32] Thus, for Deng Xiaoping, the war's outcome had created a favorable situation for China both at home and abroad, enabling China to concentrate its energy and resources on achieving the Four Modernizations. Few Western observers would evaluate the war's outcomes the same way that Deng did because the Chinese leader assessed the war from a larger international and domestic perspective. For him, the war produced the kind of strategic outcomes he had desired and anticipated.

The military campaign revealed the PLA's deficiencies in modern doctrine and tactics, but from beginning to end, China controlled the conflict's initiative and tempo. Beijing, not Hanoi, determined the pace, structure, battlefield and geostrategic engagement, and duration of the war. Beijing surprised Hanoi not only by waging massive attacks but also by its quick withdrawal without becoming bogged down, something that the Hanoi regime, overconfident from its experience against the Americans in a very different kind of conflict a decade earlier, never anticipated.[33] China's gauge of the Soviet response to the invasion also exposed Moscow's inability or unwillingness to back Vietnam. This outcome proved Deng Xiaoping's prophecy that the Soviet Union would not risk its strategic interests in Europe, the Middle East, North Africa, and South Asia to confront China over Vietnam.[34] Hanoi's reliance on the Soviet Union for security was clearly a disappointing and even disillusioning experience.

Even more critical, the 1979 war marked the beginning of Beijing's policy of "bleeding" Vietnam in an effort to contain Hanoi's further expansion in Southeast Asia. While a Vietnamese withdrawal from Cambodia following China's attack was desirable, the PRC's leadership never anticipated an immediate withdrawal. After the war, Vietnamese claims notwithstanding, China still commanded all significant strategic options. It was free to maintain military pressure on Vietnam, including constant verbal threats of a second attack. Nor was the pressure limited to just verbal assaults. For almost the entire 1980s, the PLA engaged in occasional intense artillery shelling and major border battles. Indeed, as one study from the early 1990s concluded, "The war was most successful when seen as a tactic in China's strategy of a protracted war of attrition" against Vietnam.[35]

Similarly, the war did not produce significant international consequences for China. In Cambodia, the invasion not only enabled the Khmer Rouge to escape total annihilation but also encouraged the different political forces to formulate a joint alliance against the Vietnamese occupation as a legitimate course. However, the use of military force against Vietnam raised suspicions in Indonesia and Malaysia, always wary of China's influence in the region. The Vietnamese occupation of Cambodia, which threatened Thailand, enabled the continuing growth of the strong opposition coalition of ASEAN countries against Vietnam.[36] Regarding the Sino-U.S. relationship, China's punitive invasion appeared particularly successful. Washington publicly condemned both Vietnam's invasion of Cambodia and China's invasion of Vietnam but shared China's interest in containing Soviet influence in Southeast Asia. Beijing's willingness to use force, regardless of the casualties suffered, made China "a valuable deterrent" to Soviet-Vietnamese expansionism. Washington thus continued to seek a close relationship with China to counterbalance the Soviet Union.

Perhaps motivated by China's use of force against Vietnam, in July 1979, the U.S. government signed a trade agreement that granted China most-favored-nation status, a significant economic coup for the Deng regime.[37] In the following month, Vice President Walter Mondale visited Beijing and stressed to the

Chinese leadership that the United States had decided to develop close trade and economic ties with China and to treat China differently than the Soviet Union. This new economic relationship, according to Mondale, included the relaxation of restrictions on U.S. exports to China, a two-billion-dollar government loan to China, and export licenses for two sets of advanced equipment (a $1 billion ore-processing complex and a 50 billion electron-volt high-energy accelerator).[38] Deng had wanted an improved relationship with the United States: the war against Vietnam demonstrated China's strategic value and importance to the ongoing struggle against Soviet hegemony (in Deng's own phrase, "to the world anti-hegemony united front"), and, in return, the West "would provide money and equipment for a powerful China to deter Soviet revisionism."[39]

The Chinese leadership also perceived that the 1979 war served China's domestic interests. Beginning in late 1978, the radical ideology and policies of Mao Zedong's disastrous Cultural Revolution were increasingly repudiated. Democratic dissidents called for ideological and political changes in China, posting big-character posters and handbills calling for more democracy and freedom on the "Democracy Wall" in the national capital. This alarmed Deng, who wanted a fresh start for China but also believed that China's new drive for the Four Modernizations required all "citizens being of one heart and one mind."[40] The Democracy Wall, Deng believed, stirred up sentiments corrosive to stability and unity. Moreover, he resented those people who posted letters on the wall requesting that President Jimmy Carter interfere in China's human rights situation and the activists who burst into the Vietnamese embassy in Beijing voicing their opposition to the war against Vietnam. Following the Chinese forces' withdrawal from Vietnam, he directed the Beijing municipal authority to ban all activities that undermined political and social stability and unity.[41]

The Vietnamese leadership never seemed to comprehend the PRC's strategy and war objectives, persistently maintaining that the 1979 invasion simply constituted a prelude to Beijing's long-term scheme of infringing on Vietnamese sovereignty and independence.[42] After China announced its withdrawal on 5 March, Hanoi called for a nationwide general mobilization for the war and began constructing defensive positions in and around Hanoi. By the end of May, the PLA had reverted to its normal alert status.[43] Vietnam, however, remained on guard, stationing a large number of PAVN troops (allegedly 300,000)[44] along border with China at a time when the economy was "in a worse state than at any time since 1975."[45] As a result, Hanoi's attempts to fight simultaneously in Cambodia and on its northern border took a growing

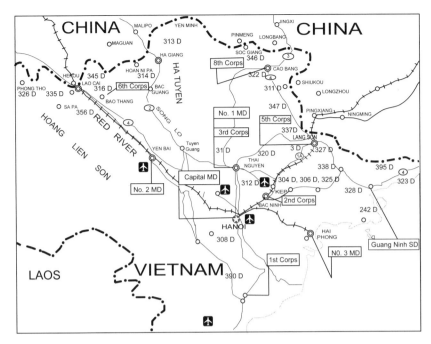

MAP 3 Vietnamese Military Dispositions since 1979

national economic and social toll, subsuming Hanoi's effort to modernize its economy and, more important, undermining its geopolitical ambitions. According to Fred Charles Iklé, "Governments tend to lose sight of the ending of wars and the nation's interests that lie beyond it," and many are "blind in failing to perceive that it is the outcome of the war, not the outcome of the campaigns within it" that determines how well their policies serve the nation's interests.[46] The Vietnamese leadership clearly failed to grasp the gravity of the situation and continued depending on the Soviet Union until its collapse in 1991. If the Vietnamese should draw any lessons from the 1979 war with China, one is, as one Vietnamese general later remarked, "We must learn how to live with our big neighbor."[47]

China's Failure to Use Air Power

Despite China's strategic success, the campaign revealed numerous deficiencies in the PLA's doctrine and tactics. Many were associated with its outdated military philosophy and tradition. The PLA continued to exhibit its preference for mobile operations with deep attack penetrations and flanking maneuvers, seeking battles of annihilation with overwhelming forces and artillery firepower and fighting tenaciously.[48] Such preferred operational character-istics ensured that the 1979 military campaign would remain a classic two-dimensional force-on-force mass-driven struggle with heavy losses on both sides.

One surprising aspect of the war was that neither the Chinese nor the Viet-namese air force actively participated in combat operations. Neither side flew any counterair, interdiction, or battlefield air support missions despite pos-sessing robust air arms. Western analysts believe that the Chinese were aware that their air force would have been at a disadvantage in any engagement with Vietnamese air units.[49] (Indeed, at least in theory, Vietnam's air force and an-tiaircraft forces were highly experienced from almost a decade of war against the world's finest air power.) However, this Western conclusion appears to have been drawn prematurely, resulting in an unbalanced assessment of the prob-lems that both the Chinese and Vietnamese air forces were facing.

In 1979, the Chinese and Vietnamese air forces were almost identical, flying the same aircraft and operating under the influence of Soviet air doc-trine, which stressed no independent air actions but rather a strongly cen-trally controlled effort heavily dependent on radar-cued and radio-directed ground-controlled operations from takeoff through landing.[50] The PLAAF had a numerical advantage but no technological edge because Vietnamese MiG-21s were better than Chinese J-6s (a MiG-19 derivative) and J-7s (an early MiG-21 derivative).[51] The Vietnamese MiG-21 pilots were allegedly combat-experienced with impressive claims against American pilots during the Viet-nam War.[52] However, this combat record had been exaggerated.[53] Moreover, the combat environment was different in the 1979 war. The MiG-21s were short-ranged and point-defense interceptor aircraft unsuited for long-range missions; in any case, they had very limited air-to-ground weapons capabili-ties. Hanoi's strategy was thus to husband its air resources to defend vital tar-gets (largely in the Hanoi area) rather than send them to engage the Chinese air force at the border.[54] According to the PLAAF records, the Vietnamese air force took no action until the fourth day of the Chinese invasion. Each time the MiG-21s scrambled from their base near Hanoi, ground controllers repeat-edly urged pilots not to fly too close to the border to avoid direct confrontation with the Chinese.[55]

On the other side of the border, the PLAAF deployed around 700 air-craft—including all its J-7 units, six bomber and attack aircraft regiments—to Guangxi and Yunnan. The forefront airfields on the border alone fielded more than 200 fighters.[56] During the first day of the military campaign, the Chinese air force flew 567 defensive counterair sorties along the border as part of an effort to deter its Vietnamese counterparts; the PLAAF then flew an average of 300 sorties each day for the duration of the war.[57] Although the PLAAF conducted no aggressive cross-border air operations, it flew 52 reconnaissance overflights, some of them deep into Vietnamese airspace, reportedly collecting valuable intelligence information for PLA ground operations.[58]

The Chinese believed that their numerical superiority demonstrated the might of the PLAAF and accordingly deterred the Vietnamese air force from challenging the Chinese air force. One Chinese J-7 regiment commander later recalled that the Vietnamese air force could launch their MiG-21s only singly or in pairs, while his unit always flew formations of four, eight, twelve, or sixteen.[59] Operating out of their bases near the border also gave Chinese pilots a fuel advantage: Vietnamese MiG-21s could only make one pass before returning to base at Hanoi.[60] During the invasion of Cambodia, Vietnam's U.S.-made Northrop F-5s and Cessna A-37s captured in 1975 had seen action against the Khmer Rouge forces.[61] The PLA ascribed the Vietnamese air force's inaction in the 1979 war to superior numbers of aircraft deployed by the PLAAF to the border. In any case, by 1979, many of the aging F-5s likely were no longer airworthy, and some had already been sent to other communist-bloc nations for study and technical analysis, and the A-37s (a light-attack derivative of the T-37 trainer) were incapable of surviving the intense antiaircraft and missile fire the PLA could have brought to bear.[62]

Still, Chinese leaders failed to permit their air force to provide support for ground operations when that support was badly needed. China justified its failure to conduct aggressive air operations on that grounds that doing so might have escalated the conflict to an unmanageable level. The PLAAF, however, maintained that flying a large number of patrol sorties over the border airspace helped to dispel ground troops' fears about enemy air threats, thus inspiring them to fight. As a matter of fact, on several occasions, both the Guangzhou and Kunming Military Region forward commands urged direct air support when the ground assaults encountered intense opposition from the Vietnamese.[63] The CMC leadership refused to grant such permission. Nevertheless, the question remained whether the Chinese air force could have provided effective support for ground operations. On the early evening of 8 March, for example, one squadron leader flying a J-6A failed to intercept a Vietnamese IL-14 transport over Cao Bang because of poor air-ground communication.[64]

Despite the PLAAF's questionable capability, the Chinese also maintained a fallacy generated by Mao's "people's war" doctrine, which did not envision the need for offensive air power. The PLA experience also suggested that air power had little impact on the victories claimed by China in the past (that is, the Korean War). It was, therefore, not surprising that Chinese political leaders and generals maintained that the war did not require active air participation. Furthermore, given their faith in their war experience, Chinese leaders were convinced that ground forces could overwhelm any opponents. Thus, the 1979 war featured primitive, bloody ground warfare even though China had one of the largest air forces in the world (and, as it subsequently claimed, maintained theater air superiority). The PLA and its generals came from an institutional tradition that was accustomed to fighting infantry warfare with artillery firepower and numerical superiority; thus the "spirit of the bayonet" continued to prevail. Consequently, the 1979 Sino-Vietnamese War was particularly deadly and atrocious because both sides engaged largely in traditional ground warfare with many close-quarter battles.

Chinese Operational Characteristics

Chinese tactical and operational styles remained fixated on large-scale two-dimensional army warfare, ground maneuvers, and adeptness in ground combat operations. That was, in many respects, hardly surprising: Deng Xiaoping and his generals were ground-war veterans and faithful students of Mao Zedong's combat principles, which emphasized the concentration of superior firepower and numbers to conduct a "battle of annihilation" with a willingness to absorb heavy losses.[65] But again not surprisingly, such a combat preference determined that although the 1979 war was in many respects a low-intensity conflict, it nevertheless featured exceedingly high casualties. Western analysts criticized the PLA's employment of human-wave tactics in classic "meat-grinder" operations as irrational and anachronistic.[66] One study was particularly critical, asserting that this Chinese way of warfighting not only was costly but also often failed to accomplish its tactical objectives.[67] The author of that study describes the Chinese human-wave assault as an attack "without attempting to mask or shield its movement."[68]

The Chinese have objected to the Western characterization of the PLA's operational tactics as human-wave attacks. According to Zhang Wannian, commander of the 127th Division and later vice chair of the CMC, mustering superior force (*jizhong bingli*) and human-wave (*renhai zhanshu*) assaults are two essentially different operational concepts. Human-wave attacks were conducted by the massed groups of infantry soldiers without trying to use fire and maneuver tactics. In the 1979 war, he sent seven battalions to attack one Vietnamese battalion (belonging to the 123rd Regiment of 304B Division) at Chi Ma. His attacking troops were divided into groups and advanced in echelons, with each group supporting the other while engaging in consecutive assaults. Zhang admitted that massed formation occurred as the Chinese used human-wave attacks during the fighting, but he argued that the problem was caused mainly by inept leadership rather than by tactics per se.[69]

Another well-known operational tenet used to obliterate the enemy's effective strength in the 1979 war was the "one point, two flanks" tactic. Marshal Lin Biao summed up this principle as the PLA's preferred operational art for surrounding and exterminating the enemy with simultaneous frontal and flank attacks. This operational preference was responsible for the PLA's success in the Dong Dang and Lao Cai–Cam Duong battles. A unit was assigned to a defensive position as a blocking force to prevent the enemy force from conducting a retrograde operation. Western scholars concluded that Chinese operational success came only after their attacks "with a battalion where a company failed, and a regiment where a battalion failed."[70] The Chinese reported that each time Vietnamese reinforcements attempted to breach a Chinese blocking position, wave after wave of assaults were conducted, often leaving several hundred dead bodies. PLA studies no longer used the "one point, two flanks" tactic to characterize its military operations in Vietnam after the dramatic fall of Lin Biao in the early 1970s and the subsequent purge campaign directed against him.[71]

The 1979 war offered ample evidence of the PLA's continuing obsession with artillery and its adeptness in using artillery to provide covering fire to support infantry troops to either maneuver themselves out of difficult situations or press forward toward their objectives. During the 1979 invasion, more than 7,000 pieces of large-caliber artillery were deployed, and they fired a total of 880,000 shells. The Dong Dang and Lang Son battles alone witnessed 1,400 tons of artillery shells dumped on enemy positions.[72] The PLA's preference for extremely close-range artillery engagement—with gun crews encouraged to site their guns at the closest possible range from their targets—represented a unique PLA form of infantry and artillery cooperation. The PLA's zealous passion for artillery fire, however, concealed another reality—that is, the PLA's failure to recognize air power as a main striking force in modern conventional warfare.[73]

Political Work on the Battlefield

In the PLA tradition, political work has been regarded as vital for combat effectiveness and victory. During the preparatory stage prior to invasion, in-depth ideological mobilization and political education increased the troops' morale and enthusiasm for going to war. After the war commenced, political work was a key mechanism for maintaining high combat morale and ensuring troops' battlefield performance, which, from a Chinese perspective, was determined by the bravery of soldiers and their obedience to orders and compliance with discipline.

At the core of the effort lay party committees and political organs. Since the early years of the Red Army, the CCP had established committees at all levels of the military apparatus. In particular, the party branch committee at the company level ensured that the party served as a role model during combat. Both rewards and punishments shaped and influenced the troops' morale. As a result, political work strongly shaped the PLA's operational tactics.

One recent study by a retired U.S. army officer harshly criticizes the PLA's political focus in the war against Vietnam. The PLA's political motivation, he argues, impressed on its troops "the imperative to advance straight at the enemy" but required no "development of professional skills" for combat.[74] In his evaluation, the PLA, an army that had defeated American troops in Korea during the winter of 1950–51, was by 1979 no longer capable of brushing aside a much weaker opponent. A professional soldier might have difficulty agreeing completely with the PLA's political work system and its importance. Thus, without giving any detailed analysis of how the PLA used political work in combat, the author simplistically equated it to human-wave tactics and concluded that it had led to a PLA defeat.[75]

The PLA certainly was not properly trained and prepared for war, making political work all the more crucial. The political work system arguably motivated Chinese soldiers to fight courageously in the face of intense PAVN and militia resistance. From a Chinese perspective, bravery was the essential element in fighting the war. According to Deng Xiaoping, if properly politically motivated and therefore courageous, poorly equipped PLA troops led by largely inexperienced commanders might suffer severe losses at the beginning of the fight but would gain experience and combat skills. After the war, Deng was gratified to learn that the PLA's current soldiers had fought as courageously and tenaciously as their predecessors, thereby confirming his faith in them and in the political system of warfare.[76] Since that time, political work has remained an indispensable mechanism of China's armed forces. Thus, the value and significance of political work to motivate the PLA's combat forces and thereby ensure victory in the 1979 war cannot be overemphasized.

In 1980, the General Political Department compiled a collection of the PLA's political work experiences in the war against Vietnam, emphasizing twelve different aspects, among them inculcating understanding of the high authorities' resolve, strengthening patriotism and "revolutionary heroism," emphasizing firing-line promotion as a consequence of good combat performance, and stressing the important role party cadres and Communist Youth League members could play on the battlefield. The remainder addressed issues involving different army branches, the front and the rear, and the civilian and military hierarchies, including psychological warfare, the militia forces, and the aid-the-front work.[77] These experiences were compiled and written by political officers who regularly disseminated propaganda, meaning that exaggeration and lack of authenticity were unavoidable. Nevertheless, this 800-plus-page document suggested that the political work system was inseparable from the PLA military system and its combat missions. Without political work, the PLA believed, Chinese forces would have almost no chance of accomplishing any of their tasks. As a result, political officers and party organizations bore responsibility for making sure that soldiers understood their assigned tasks before battle and for helping military officers deal with problems that arose during battle. The troops assigned to deep-penetration maneuvers feared that they were vulnerable to enemy attacks. While explaining that penetration was essential for creating a favorable position from which to annihilate enemy forces, political officers drew up contingency measures for problems that might occur during the operation.

According to a report by the 488th Regiment, to curb the fear of troops in blocking operations, political officers repeatedly reminded them that they did not fight alone because their brother units were fighting to destroy the enemy's defenses. This regiment later reported that political work played a decisive role in ensuring that the troops would accomplish their blocking mission after they repelled thirteen Vietnamese attacks and killed 779 enemy troops.[78]

Political work also encouraged the rank and file to act in ways that would earn them heroic recognition. Military journalists were sent to combat units to identify soldiers who fought with particular valor and dedication and then to report on these heroic deeds. Later in 1979, the *PLA Daily* carried a series of reports on Chinese soldiers who had sacrificed their lives for their motherland in the war.[79] Party committees and political organs set standards and requirements for granting merit awards to personnel and units. Individuals were cited for first- to third-class meritorious service. Individual companies received red silk banners inscribed "Shock Hero Company" or "Hero Blocking Company" if they had fought valorously in offensive or defensive operations.[80]

According to Mao's teachings, "The party member must be the first to bear hardship and the last to enjoy comforts." Party members were expected to be in the thick of the fight, wherever there were dangers and difficulties. Unit leaders lived up to the party's requirements during the operation. They were the first to charge forward and the last to withdraw. For example, the 122nd Division reported that cadres and party members had played an exemplary role, enabling the unit's soldiers to fight vigorously. On 20 February, after all officers of his company had been killed or severely wounded, a squad leader who was also a party member took over the leadership of the company on two separate occasions, continuing to fight until reinforced.[81]

From a PLA perspective, whether party members acted bravely depended on the effectiveness of the leadership of the party branch committees at the company level. 39th Division's combat experiences confirmed this assertion. The company branch committees, which had performed well in combat, had often called party branch committee meetings to study operational orders and directives from higher authorities so that the entire company could act in concert. One notable achievement of the party branch was preparing a sequential list of all officer positions to ensure uninterrupted leadership on the battlefield. During combat, the party branch actively engaged in political and ideological work to enable the rank and file to maintain their will to fight. To overcome fear and decline in morale as a consequence of the loss of close comrades, the party branch emphasized getting back at the enemy, promoting slogans such as "Seeking revenge on the enemy for the fallen comrades, and making the enemy pay back with his own blood," to boost the troops' morale.[82]

Nonetheless, political work was regarded as neither omnipotent nor a substitute for military professionalism, and the PLA's review of political experiences in the 1979 war occasionally cited failures. For example, one battalion of the 484th Regiment (a total of 212 troops) was ambushed by a Vietnamese sapper team in a rice field at Ban Mau, north of Cao Bang. The leading officers panicked, made no effort to organize defenses or withdraw, and simply told troops to flee for their lives, leaving them on their own. Consequently, by the end of the fight, half of their men were either killed or wounded. In its post-combat summary, the 162nd Division bluntly ascribed this defeat to the unit leaders' cowardice.[83]

Other such incidents occurred, demonstrating that political work did not guarantee victory. The most notable involved the 150th Division, which entered Vietnam at the end of the invasion to cover the 41st Army's return from the Cao Bang area. The 150th lacked preparation, training, and experience, and most of its veteran soldiers had transferred to reinforce other combat units. As a result, the division was mainly composed of new recruits, and company leaders did not know their soldiers. A three-person team headed by a deputy army commander was sent to help strengthen the 150th Division's leadership but only created confusion, setting the stage for disaster.[84] Their fatal mistake was deciding to follow mountain trails instead of the main highway back into China. The unit was ambushed, broken up, and defeated piecemeal. If its officers and soldiers had been veteran fighters, the unit would not have been defeated so easily.[85]

In sum, in 1979, the PLA was far from being a professional army. New recruits accounted for 48 percent of the troops, and 25 percent of officers had been newly promoted, compromising the force's capability for a large-scale military operation. Most Chinese soldiers came from poor rural families with little education. Raised in a culture that stressed obedience, loyalty, and sacrifice, these soldiers as a group feared neither hardship nor death.[86] They hoped that a few years of military service could help them achieve a better living standard, either through promotion into the ranks of the officer cadre or by training them for nonfarming jobs after leaving military service. Few of them prepared themselves mentally or received adequate training for combat. Thus, political work played a critical role in generating unit cohesion and keeping soldiers focused on performing their mission.[87] Even though the 1979 war was incredibly bloody and savage, in the end, the PLA pulled through to victory, though at a significant cost.

Vietnamese Strategy and Tactics

Prior to the late 1970s, the PLA paid scant attention to the combat doctrine and tactics of the PAVN and had never thought that their two communist countries would engage in an armed conflict against one another. As a result, the PLA underestimated the PAVN's fighting abilities. After the 1979 war, PLA leaders conducted a thorough assessment of the PAVN's strategy, strength, military objectives, and operational tactics.[88] According to Zhou Deli, chief of staff of the Guangzhou Military Region, Vietnam's military thought and combat principles emphasized "the national defense by all the people" (*quanmin guofang*) and "carrying out the people's war" (*shixing renmin zhanzheng*), consisting of four basic approaches.[89]

1. *Tenaciously defending the border and seeking to win victory on the first line of defense*.[90] The Hanoi leadership opposed the strategy of luring the enemy deep into Vietnamese territory given the fact that the area between Hanoi and Lang Son was the heartland of Vietnamese industry. Instead, a military fortress strategy was adopted, turning villages, towns, and cities into strongholds against the invasion. Regular and local forces were employed to defend key positions along the highways and railroads, paramilitary troops were respon-

sible for the first line of defense, and villagers were encouraged to take up arms to help defend areas where military forces were weak.[91]

2. *Aggressive defense.* Vietnamese defenders needed actively and aggressively to engage the enemy at long range using offensive methods to defeat enemy attacks. Preferred defense tactics included the division of a company-sized force into three- to five-soldier squads and using platoon-size groupings of squads to defend strong points. When positions were lost, defenders would stage successive counterattacks with small groups ranging in strength from a squad to a platoon or a full company. (The PLA nevertheless concluded that the PAVN had too few troops overall and was inferior in combat power and that as a result, few Vietnamese counterattacks broke into Chinese defensive positions).[92]

3. *The use of small force to defeat a bigger enemy force.*[93] Surprisingly, given the traditionally strong centralized control pursued by Soviet-style forces, the PAVN (likely reflecting its guerrilla heritage back to the anti-Japanese days of the Second World War) fought using both decentralized control and decentralized execution. The Chinese discovered that Vietnamese defenders fought each engagement on their own and did not contact or support each other. While this structure made it difficult to get inside their command and control (their "decision loop"), it also generated problems for the PAVN that were exacerbated by Hanoi's decision making and thus created opportunities that the PLA exploited. For example, throughout the fighting, Hanoi made no attempts to send reinforcements to help the badly battered PAVN divisions in the Cao Bang, Lang Son, and Lao Cai areas, determined to hold its strategic reserves to engage the Chinese if they invaded the Red River Delta. The Vietnamese defensive strategy—taking no action, failing to send reinforcements, and refusing to run away—made it easy for Chinese forces to encircle and annihilate them piecemeal.[94]

4. *Relying on guerrilla warfare tactics to conduct positional defense and counterattacks.* According to the Chinese assessment, when Vietnamese troops (both PAVN and militia) were unable to hold their fighting positions, they always dispersed into small groups and then used complex terrain (such as mountain saddles, high growths of grass, small clumps of trees, and limestone caves) to organize guerrilla defense along the roads, trails, and routes PLA troops were likely to traverse. The guerrilla-type attacks inflicted significant casualties on Chinese forces, and PAVN sapper teams effectively sabotaged Chinese rear echelons and rear area supply lines.[95]

It is difficult to know to what extent the PLA's assessment of the Vietnamese forces' tactical characteristics is objective when Vietnam's own assessment remains absent. In retrospect, the Chinese military leadership found itself in a contradictory position when conducting such an assessment. While claiming victory, China nevertheless had to acknowledge the heavy toll the PAVN and Vietnamese militia units had inflicted. In the view of the PLA's leadership, an impartial evaluation of PLA deficiencies was imperative. However, at the same time, they worried about overestimating Vietnamese military capabilities and performance.[96] In the end, national pride and cultural prejudice prevented the PLA from making truly objective assessments about the Vietnamese military and its tactics. Moreover, for fear of giving too much credit to the Vietnamese military, the PLA assessment concluded that the PAVN's regular forces lacked persistence in offense and defense and had few coordinated operations. The PLA was also particularly critical of Hanoi's response to Chinese campaign objectives. It believed that the PLA's multidirectional attacks on Vietnam had confused Vietnamese leaders, preventing them from recognizing in a timely fashion the main thrust of the Chinese invasion. Facing multipronged attacks, the Vietnamese military command appeared befuddled and frequently changed the mission and location of their reinforcement forces.[97] For the Chinese, the Vietnamese military leadership's hesitation created favorable conditions for the PLA to concentrate a large number of forces to overpower the PAVN.[98] The PLA's tactic of pushing its infantrymen into close mass combat against the PAVN and its acceptance of high human losses may help explain why the PLA overwhelmed the PAVN and why the PLA subsequently proclaimed the PAVN incapable of defending against China's attacks.[99]

PLA literature certainly conceded that the PAVN's guerrilla-type tactics, its sappers, and its local militias were surprisingly successful in keeping the Chinese forces off balance as they anxiously sought to engage the PAVN in decisive battles during the lightning war. One Chinese frustration was distinguishing civilian refugees from defeated PAVN soldiers, who would shed their uniforms and blend in. These disguised PAVN soldiers would then coerce Vietnamese civilians to instigate attacks on Chinese forces.[100]

The PLA assessment also recognized the effectiveness of Vietnamese defense tactics such as placing mortars and heavy antiaircraft machine guns on the top of hills to suppress PLA infantry movement. The long-range and heavy-hitting multiple 12.7mm antiaircraft machine guns were extremely deadly, particularly because none of the PLA's infantry soldier weapons had sufficient range to engage them in counterfire.[101] As an American officer once noted, it was impossible "to penetrate, flank, or envelop" the Vietnamese fortified positions "without taking extremely heavy casualties."[102]

Some Vietnamese accounts supported the PLA's interpretation of both the performance and the perceived weaknesses of the PAVN. Interviews with senior Vietnamese officers led Henry Kenny to conclude that although the Vietnamese army would have preferred to exploit mobile rather than positional tactics against the Chinese advance, the employment of "mines, mortar attack, and direct-fire ambushes from dominating terrain features" by dug-in Vietnamese defenders had proven an effective means of inflicting heavy losses on PLA forces and delaying their advance.[103] The Vietnamese claimed that three PLA regiments and eighteen battalions had been either destroyed or suffered heavy attrition, while 550 vehicles, including 280 tanks and armored vehicles, and 115 artillery pieces had been destroyed or damaged.[104] The Vietnamese have consistently asserted that they fought a "people's war," relying heavily on an armed peasantry and crediting these militias for defending the key border towns of Dong Dang, Cao Bang, and Lao Kai. Hanoi has never publicly admitted the extensive involvement of its regular forces in the conflict.[105] Uncritically accepting Vietnamese accounts—in fact, Vietnamese propaganda—otherwise informed Western observers have stated incorrectly that the PLA failed to achieve its intervention objectives and "did not account itself well in the fighting."[106] Any honest evaluation of Vietnamese performance in the 1979 war remains dependent on the opening of Vietnamese records, however.

Lessons Learned

Today, notwithstanding the PLA's persistent assertions of military victory, several critical questions remain to be addressed. How did the PLA perceive its performance in Vietnam in terms of planning, command and control, fighting, and combat tactics? What lessons did it learn from the campaign? And to what degree did this experience affect PLA thinking about its future? Although the PLA's tradition placed importance on writing summaries of combat experience, Chinese national pride and cultural prejudice prevented the PLA from making candid conclusions about the war. Nonetheless, the PLA synthesized the lessons learned from the war into six themes.

The first theme was in keeping with a traditional PLA maxim that any correct military decision and strategy must involve thoroughly comprehending the situation. But the 1979 war showed that the PLA's reconnaissance capability and battlefield situational awareness and intelligence were limited. The lack of human intelligence severely hampered the PLA throughout the military campaign. One leading reason was that most of the PLA's reconnaissance units lacked adequate training before the invasion. During the operation, they were often taken off intelligence duties and simply assigned as replacement forces

Militiamen bring ammunition to the front in the midst of fighting, 1979. Courtesy Wang Huazhang.

or adjuncts to assault strongpoints and defend key points along with infantry units.[107] The political officers who were responsible for the POW work had no training in interrogation techniques, further hampering intelligence collection.[108] During the campaign, lower-level units constantly complained that leadership at higher levels did not provide with detailed information about the enemy but failed to conduct any reconnaissance missions to obtain information. This problem was further aggravated by the fact that the PLA's assessment of the geography and terrain of northern Vietnam often relied on outdated maps and geographic information. In addition, PLA forces generally had poor map-reading skills.[109] As a result of all these deficiencies, the PLA's postaction report admitted that its forces engaged in many muddle-headed actions in the 1979 war.

The unexpected operational difficulties posed by Vietnam's surprisingly active militia units led to a second lesson, one involving conflict planning. A key PLA combat principle stressed the concentration of superior forces to ensure annihilation of an enemy. One major deficiency of the Vietnam operation was that planners failed to consider the large number of militia forces in their calculation of Vietnamese military strength. Indeed, in retrospect, the PLA believed that the militia put up a more relentless resistance and launched more surprise attacks than the PAVN's vaunted regulars. PLA planners thought they had an overwhelming 8:1 force disparity over the Vietnamese. But the Cao Bang area alone had 40,000 to 50,000 militia members, altering the force ratio to 2:1. During the campaign, the PLA thus never possessed sufficient forces to deliver the knockout strike that its doctrine advocated and its leaders sought, seriously slowing PLA combat operations.[110] The Battle of Cao Bang took ten days rather than the planned five, requiring the deployment of additional troops. In response to these difficulties, the PLA had to adapt quickly to the "objective reality" of the battlefield, doing so in time to engage in a mopping-up campaign against the dispersed Vietnamese forces. Analysts concluded that this adaptation helped the PLA secure its victory, but it was a very close call.[111]

The third lesson involved combined arms operations. The 1979 incursion marked the first time that the PLA leadership conducted combined arms operations with tank, artillery, and engineering elements in support of infantry attacks while assembling an air and naval force to provide cover (even though the latter did not enter combat). But backwardness in doctrine and tactics prevented Chinese forces from carrying out the kind of coordinated operation that could be undertaken at that time by, for example, NATO or the Warsaw Pact. While Beijing's political constraints and outdated military thinking proscribed the commitment of air forces to support ground operations, ground forces also demonstrated poor coordination between infantry, tank, and artillery units, limiting the PLA's ability to execute full combined arms tactics. For example, infantry units had never trained sufficiently with tank units and thus could not adequately maneuver with them. Such were the crudities of operational art that PLA infantry soldiers fastened themselves to the top of tanks with ropes so that they would not fall off. Accordingly, when they came under enemy fire, they were effectively bound in place.[112] Conversely, tank units, which often operated without infantry support or direct communication with infantry units, suffered many unexpected losses and damage because they exposed themselves to Vietnamese tank-killing teams.[113] Although the artillery forces performed better than tank units, they also often failed to provide timely support for coordinated infantry-armor assaults, and basic command and control architectures and procedures were clearly lacking. For example, during the PLA's 1 March drive on Lang Son, the misreading of operational orders caused artillery batteries (under regimental infantry command) to fail to lay down suppressing fire against Vietnamese strongpoints before the infantry assault, which consequently failed, with heavy losses.[114]

The fourth lesson was the general issue of command and control, and it, too, derived largely from the PLA's traditions and culture. Personal relationships between commanding officers and troops, which had been cultivated in the past, still mattered to the PLA. Because interpersonal relationships were more important than institutional ones, it is not surprising that the leaders of the Guangzhou Military Region later acknowledged that they felt uncomfortable commanding troops transferred from the Wuhan and Chengdu Military Regions.[115] These leaders also received many complaints from rank and filers about Xu's leadership style because he had not previously commanded them. Even Xu acknowledged that he (and his subordinates as well as most PLA troops) had little knowledge of the challenges of fighting in a tropical, wooded mountain environment. They quickly realized that their combat experience in northern China did not apply to the battleground in Vietnam.[116] The lack of combat-experienced officers further compounded the PLA's command problems. Despite sending higher-ranking officers who were also war veterans to lower-level troop units to help with command, the PLA's operations remained frustrated by most lower-ranking officers' inability to make independent judgments and coordinate operations at critical moments.[117] Instead of radios, the PLA's squads and platoons received hand flags and horns, and soldiers were instructed in the use of hand signals for communication. But the heavy vegetation covering the hilly terrain prevented the effective use of the signals, forcing troops to stay in close and vulnerable formations lest communication be lost. This lack of radio equipment severely hampered battlefield communication and coordination between squads, platoons, and their company command.

Fifth, logistics posed another serious challenge and thus was a major area in which the PLA could draw lessons. The PLA lacked a modern logistics supply system and structure to support a fast-moving, distant, offensive action in which the average daily consumption included 700 tons of ammunition and another 700 tons of fuel.[118] Instead, a makeshift supply system required every unit to be self-sufficient in "retail logistics," the supply system employed on the battlefield. Up to 36 percent of supplies were carried into Vietnam by human and animal labor.[119] Without adequate storage and transportation facilities, both the Guangzhou and Kunming Military Regions had to scramble to put together a supply system, and it never functioned smoothly and efficiently. The combination of poor PLA management and Vietnamese attacks caused the loss of considerable quantities of supplies. In one incident, PAVN artillery destroyed a column of thirty-seven trucks along with their loads. Some PLA troops carrying out deep-penetration tasks did not receive food supplies for seven days.[120] As the forces advanced deeper into Vietnamese territory, the PLA's logisticians had increasing difficulty keeping communication lines open without diverting a large number of forces to protect them.[121] Based on this experience, the PLA concluded it needed a dedicated transportation command.[122] In 2002, when the former vice commander of the PLA National Defense University spoke at a military symposium, he stressed the importance of "control of communication."[123]

Finally, China's experience in Vietnam in 1979 caused the PLA to reconsider its thinking about "people's war" as applied to conflicts beyond China's borders. The traditional principle of people's war stressed the importance of mobilizing the citizenry to support the war effort. The 1979 war experience reemphasized this but also took it further, showing that it was almost impossible for huge PLA forces to operate outside the country without popular support for the war at home. Beijing's propaganda machines had aroused great public patriotism and pride in Chinese soldiers. These strong expressions of patriotism helped the PLA get direct support from the people living in the two border provinces fronting Vietnam. Tens of thousands of local residents served as stretcher bearers, security guards, and porters, and militia soldiers from the border region were involved in direct combat activities. Local governments made things easy for troops by simplifying requisition procedures, thereby helping them receive adequate material and fresh food in the shortest possible time. Such experiences persuaded the PLA leadership that mobilization of local governments and civilians to support a war remained an enduring—and essential—key to victory.[124]

Conclusion

The 1979 war with Vietnam baptized a young generation of army cadres on the battlefield, and many of them later rose to high PLA positions, carrying the experiences and lessons of the war into their subsequent careers. From a Western perspective, the lessons learned from the 1979 war with Vietnam may not seem coherent, comprehensive, or even fully objective, because the PLA evaluates its success in military operations not from the traditional perspective of operational "battlefield" outcomes but rather on the basis of the impact of the conflict on the overall geopolitical-military strategic situation. Deeply influenced by Mao's teaching that war is fundamentally a political undertaking, as long as China could claim to achieve its strategic and military objectives, the PLA would consider any problems resulting from perceived tactical failures secondary. The PLA's assessments are also colored by the belief that warfare can be learned through the experience of fighting and that knowledge can be gained rapidly enough to employ it even in the context of very brief conflicts. For example, the PLA was convinced that its forces performed much better during the second stage of the 1979 campaign than they did during the first stage. Overall, the PLA's self-assessment of lessons learned in the 1979 conflict with Vietnam is comprehensive but varies significantly from those found in Western studies. While some of the Western studies are informative and correct to some extent, they share common failings in attempting to make overarching conclusions based on very limited sources. This approach, never satisfactory, is even less so when applied to an extremely complicated and nuanced subject such as the PLA, its structure, doctrine, culture, operational thought, and combat behavior.[125]

Perhaps most significantly, PLA studies conclude that the infamous Cultural Revolution constituted the single most detrimental factor undermining the PLA's previously successful—in its eyes—combat tradition. The "battlefield" lessons the PLA may have learned in this war overemphasize operation (command and control, coordination between troops, force structure and weaponry) at the expense of strategy and doctrine.[126]

During its evaluation of the 1979 war, the PLA appeared to make no attempt to hide or overlook its own deficiencies and problems. The PLA nevertheless failed to take into account its flawed military thinking and traditions. If there is any one issue about which the PLA still seems disingenuous, it is airpower—specifically, the importance of air superiority and battlefield air support. PLA literature and textbooks continue to cite the PLAAF's alleged "deterrent capability" as the primary reason the Vietnamese Air Force did not become more directly involved in the conflict.[127] Marshal Ye Jianying even ridiculously commented that China's show-of-force air operations in the war against Vietnam were an "ingenious way of employing the air force."[128] Such a remark demonstrates that China's military leadership continues to fail to appreciate the critical and complex role of airpower in modern warfare.

While significant differences exist between the Western and Chinese perspectives on the 1979 conflict, the two are nevertheless consistent in some aspects of their review of how Chinese leaders approached matters of war and strategy.[129] First, Chinese leaders were deliberative and calculating about when and how military power was to be used but did not hesitate to go to war once they decided that China's national interests were at stake. Second, the PLA demonstrated a preference for seizing and maintaining operational initiatives by deploying superior and more powerful forces. Third, the Chinese sense of military victory lay more in their evaluation of the geopolitical outcomes than in their judgment of operational performance on the battlefield. Fourth, political work remains a unique PLA approach to ensure the effectiveness of its forces on the battlefield. This distinct set of Chinese characteristics deserves further scholarly attention and should be considered in any study of Chinese military doctrine, policy, and capabilities.

The war was designed not to pose a substantial threat to Hanoi but merely to erode Hanoi's will to occupy Cambodia. The Khmer Rouge hoped that the PLA could strike deeply into Vietnamese territory, but China's invasion was short and limited to the border area. Nonetheless, China's "symbolic" attack helped the Khmer Rouge escape total annihilation and enabled them to sustain their resistance against the Vietnamese occupation forces. Was the punitive nature of the war a true objective, or was it just rhetoric and a reflection of Beijing's anger toward Hanoi and the invasion of Cambodia? If teaching a lesson was China's main objective, the PLA should have struck hard to achieve significant military results. But speaking to Japanese journalists in the middle of the war, Deng asserted that he did not "need military achievements."[130] He later explained, "Teaching Vietnam a lesson was not based on a consideration of what was happening between China and Vietnam or in Indochina but was based on a contemplation of the matter from the angle of Asia and the Pacific—in other words, from the high plane of global strategy."[131] His calculus was ultimately dominated by two priorities: improving China's external security environment and reforming China's economy and opening up the country.

6 A Decadelong Continued Border Conflict, 1980–1990

The withdrawal of Chinese troops from Vietnam did not bring an end to hostilities between the two countries; instead, military confrontation continued as the Chinese and Vietnamese regular forces competed for control of mountainous positions along the border, with attacks and counterattacks throughout the 1980s. The conflict peaked in 1984 with both sides sending a significant number of troops into battles over hills in the Laoshan area (in the Vi Xuyen District of Vietnam). China claimed that the battles were fought in defense of Chinese territory; accordingly, the conflict was called "Defensive Operations against Vietnam in the Laoshan Area."[1] Because the exchange of artillery fire was one of the features of the conflict, one Western study characterized the border clashes as China's "artillery diplomacy" that was intended to oust Vietnam from Cambodia but failed to achieve this strategic objective.[2]

China indeed engineered the border conflict to coerce Hanoi to withdraw from Cambodia. The Chinese leadership did not expect that military action to have an immediate effect but was convinced that over time, Vietnam would accede to China's wishes. China's policy toward Vietnam was persistent and rigid throughout the 1980s. Hanoi, conversely, adopted a tit-for-tat approach in response to China's military pressure, changing the nature of the conflict, which occurred over the isolated, strategically insignificant hills on the Sino-Vietnamese border. The conflict was significantly larger, longer, and more costly than expected. Drawing from Chinese sources, this chapter explores the intent, nature, course, and implications of the 1980s border conflict, during which Vietnam was outmaneuvered and eventually worn down more by China's persistence in pursuing a military pressure policy than by the PLA's battlefield performance. However, the use of force against Vietnam along the border offered China a way to express its support for the countries opposing Vietnam's aggression during the last stage of the Cold War.

MAP 4 PLA Operations along the Sino-Vietnamese Border, 1981–1984

The 1980s border conflict between China and Vietnam can be divided into four phases. During the first phase (April 1979–November 1980), both sides sought to reconfigure their border defenses and to harass each other on a small scale. The second phase (May 1981–November 1984) saw the PLA forces take more offensive actions against Vietnamese-occupied mountain ranges along the border. The third phase (December 1984–October 1987) featured intensified fighting in the Laoshan area, with both sides committing a large number of forces to offensive and counteroffensive operations. The last phase (November 1987–March 1990) was a stalemate, with the PLA forces conducting special operations until the withdrawal of the last field army unit from the border region.

Keeping Up the Military Pressure on Vietnam

From the end of the 1979 incursion through the 1980s, the PRC remained firmly opposed to the SRV and its regional hegemonic ambitions. One manifestation of this policy was China's commitment to maintaining military pressure as an expression of its opposition to Vietnam's aggression against Cambodia and later Thailand. The Chinese leadership understood that it would be unrealistic either to launch a second attack, despite repeated threats, or to maintain a large number of forces in the border regions for a long period of time.[3] The Chinese leadership may well never have truly intended to launch a "second lesson" strike.[4] Chinese leaders believed they could eventually outlast Vietnam on the Cambodia issue through prolonged pressure—and hence pain—against the Hanoi regime. According to Deng Xiaoping, in three to five years, political and economic pressure would inflict substantial hardship on Vietnam and would add to the Soviet Union's burden. The Chinese leader predicted a change in the Vietnamese leadership by that time as well.[5]

China initially beefed up its border defense forces. In Guangxi, several field army units were transferred to formulate new border defense divisions (nine infantry regiments and three artillery regiments), and the total number of border defense regiments in Yunnan increased from twelve to seventeen.[6] Telecommunication lines and roads were built to connect villages. Villagers and militias were encouraged to fortify their settlements.[7] By the end of 1979, the Chinese border with Vietnam had been heavily fortified, significantly reducing its previous vulnerabilities.

At the same time, China returned to negotiations with the Vietnamese on the border issue, which had been suspended in July 1978. Beijing did not believe that negotiations could resolve the problems between the two countries but treated the talks as a continuation of China's battlefield struggle against Vietnam moved to the political, diplomatic, and propaganda arenas.[8] From April to December 1979, fifteen meetings were held alternately in Hanoi and Beijing. The two sides remained too far apart to reach any understanding. Beijing wanted to discuss all the issues responsible for the deteriorating relationship between the two countries, including Vietnam's invasion of Cambodia, territorial disputes, and ethnic Chinese problems in Vietnam. Hanoi did not want to engage in dialogue with China about topics that had nothing to do with border tensions. The talks ran into a dead end, and on 8 March 1980, China called off the negotiations indefinitely.[9]

Hanoi was not fooled by China's initiative on border talks. The recent Chinese invasion had confirmed Hanoi's perception of a Chinese threat. The Vietnamese leadership henceforth had to assume, for planning purposes, that the Chinese could suddenly invade Vietnam again. Following a general mobilization order issued in early March 1979, Vietnam began to shore up its military presence along its northern border, matching China's buildup. The 5th, 6th, and 8th Army Corps were established, bringing the Vietnamese regular and local forces in Hoang Lien Son, Gao Bang, and Lang Son Provinces under a single regional command. The coastal defense to the east was also consolidated and reinforced by creating the Guang Ninh Special Zone, with three PAVN infantry divisions (the 323rd, 328th, and 395th) and one coastal defense division (the 242nd).[10]

The Vietnamese forces in Military District 2 were increased from two to seven infantry divisions. The 313th and 314th deployed to areas adjacent to the so-called Laoshan battle zone, where both the Chinese and Vietnamese forces later engaged in offensive and counteroffensive operations for almost ten years. The 345th, 355th, and 316th were stationed in a triangle formation opposite the Chinese town of Hekou, in Yunnan Province.[11] In Military District 1, seven PAVN infantry divisions (the 3rd, 311th, 322nd, 327th, 337th, 346th, and 347th) deployed to the border region facing China's Guangxi Province. In Thai Nguyen and Bac Giang Provinces, the 2nd and 3rd Army Corps, totaling another six PAVN infantry divisions (the 31st, 304th, 306th, 312th, 320th, and 325th), served as backup and reserve forces.[12] A total of 220,000 Vietnamese troops were deployed to the border area. All this buildup confirmed that Hanoi did not wish to risk another Chinese invasion, especially since it might not halt in the border regions.

In addition, Vietnam moved aggressively to occupy key mountain ranges and ridgelines crossing the border between the two countries. By the end of 1980, Vietnamese forces occupied twenty-two hills that straddled the border. China reported that more than 1,500 Vietnamese provocations occurred that year, posing serious threats to Chinese lives and properties in the border region.[13] (Chinese reports may well have exaggerated the total number and degree of seriousness of these incidents.) The deployment of a large number of armed forces by the two countries on their common mountainous borders provided a potential battle zone in any future conflict.

Border clashes increased significantly after the CMC ordered PLA forces to seize the initiative in the border struggle against Vietnam. Late in 1980, Beijing ordered Chinese forces along the Vietnam border to respond to Vietnamese provocations with a tit-for-tat strategy, "fighting against all intrusions and winning every battle." Realistically, China could not afford another large-scale cross-border operation—another campaign would not only be too costly but also jeopardize the PRC's ongoing economic reforms. Accordingly, the CMC urged the Guangzhou and Kunming Military Regions "to display China's national strength and military might by winning big at low cost."[14] Guided by these principles, the PLA border units initiated provocative attacks on Vietnamese border posts and patrol teams.[15]

China's military actions along the border closely corresponded to Vietnam's occupation of Cambodia. From Hanoi's perspective, the only way to delegitimize Chinese support for the Khmer Rouge was to completely wipe out its resistance, thereby giving Vietnam de facto control of Cambodia. Accordingly, from 1980 to mid-1985, Vietnam conducted a series of dry-season offensives against anti-Vietnamese enclaves along the Thai-Cambodian border. The Vietnamese offensives culminated in the seizure of the last of the Khmer Rouge strongholds in the Phnom Malai Mountains in February 1984. Each of the Vietnamese offensives in Cambodia seemed to echo China's harsh military actions along their northern border.[16]

In the early 1980s, Deng Xiaoping's further consolidation of power ensured that China's policy toward Vietnam became even more rigid. Deng's inflexible views—he perceived Vietnam's occupation of Cambodia as more a global security problem than a regional one—worked to ensure that Beijing's Vietnam policy was cast in stone. Moreover, the Chinese leader still faced a credibility issue: even though he believed that China had taught Vietnam lesson after lesson in 1979, Vietnam still had not stopped its aggression against Cambodia—and had moved against Thailand as well. China remained intransigent toward Vietnam, especially its invasion of Cambodia, a posture exacerbated by Deng's increasingly dominant position within the government. In June 1981, at the CCP's Sixth Plenum, he replaced Hua Guofeng as chair of the CMC, the actual chief in command of the Chinese armed forces. This promotion gave Deng a solidly authoritarian leadership position fully equivalent to that of Mao.[17]

Deng's policy toward Vietnam reflected his larger perception of a continuing Soviet threat. He continued to associate closely what Vietnam did in Southeast Asia with Soviet hegemonic desire, insisting that Vietnam's occupation of Cambodia was part of Moscow's concerted effort to encircle China from the south. Considering Cambodia from a global strategic perspective despite the Khmer Rouge's notorious reputation, the Chinese leader did not support any international effort to resolve the Cambodia issue without the Khmer Rouge's participation. For Beijing, the Khmer Rouge was the only force actively fighting Vietnam's invasion at a time when other Cambodian groups were weak. While promising that China would not sit still if Vietnam invaded other Southeast Asian countries, Deng encouraged Cambodians to form an anti-Vietnamese coalition.[18] Beginning in late 1979, Beijing persistently attempted to develop an anti-invasion, anti-Vietnamese coalition in the region.[19]

At home, Deng redefined China's defense policy, *jiji fangyu* (active defense), applying it to conflicts not only inside but also beyond China's borders.[20] While urging the PLA to value professional military education and training, Deng also sought to rejuvenate and indeed rehabilitate the PLA's legendary fighting prowess and allow more troops to acquire war experience.[21] According to General Zhang Youxia, a rising star who emerged out of the border conflict, the 1979 invasion using massed forces was not Deng Xiaoping's preferred way of war; instead, he advocated using capable and highly trained forces under the command of talented generals to defeat an enemy by surprise attack. In 1979, Deng resorted to Korean War–style massed assault because the disastrous Cultural Revolution had severely depreciated the PLA's capabilities, giving Deng no other choice but to conduct the 1979 war on a massive scale. (Those military leaders who had long been associated with Deng regretted that the quality of PLA forces prevented more imaginative and effective combat at the time.) The ongoing border conflict, however, provided another opportunity for the PLA to explore the tactics of modern war as Chinese military modernization was ongoing. Zhang later recalled that the border conflict (during which his infantry regiment decisively defeated the PAVN at Laoshan) allowed him to achieve his dream of waging modern war with modern methods.[22]

Seizing Vietnamese Strongholds on the Border, 1980–1983

In the PLA history, taking military action against the Vietnamese occupied positions along the border during this period is known as "Offensive Operations against the Enemy's Controlled Points" (*badian zuozhan*). The first major action, in October 1980, was to recapture the Luojiaping mountain range on the Yunnan-Vietnam border. The mountain range consists of several hills, with its highest peak at an elevation of 2,002 meters on the China side of the boundary near the village of Jinchang. On 25 September, the PLA border unit received a report that Vietnamese troops had occupied the hills of Luojiaping, were fortifying their positions, and were laying mines. More seriously, a few days later, a PLA patrol clashed with Vietnamese troops: 5 Chinese soldiers, including a company commander, were killed or missing in action. Thus provoked, local military authorities decided to retaliate.[23]

On 15 October, the PLA attacked the Vietnamese positions on the Luojiaping range. In a 3.5-hour fight they killed 42 enemy troops and captured 3.[24] On 9 November, the PLA attacked another Vietnamese-defended mountain, Ma'anshan (Hill 1175.4). At its foot was a highway connecting Malipo in the north and the Vietnamese border town of Thanh Thuy in the south. Further southwest, the 1,700-meter peak of Koulinshan Mountain dominated the horizon, signaling its dubious distinction as objective of the next Chinese offensive.[25]

In light of Beijing's decision to maintain military pressure on Vietnam, PLA forces in Guangxi and Yunnan selected Fakashan (near the city of Pingxiang) and Kuolinshan for attack. The military action, initially scheduled for New

Year's Day 1981, was ostensibly postponed by mountain floods in the region. Perhaps the real but unspoken reason for the postponement was that these attacks would be the first major operations by the PLA since 1979 and the PLA's military leadership had no desire to oversee a disappointing PLA performance on the battlefield: they recognized that more planning and training were needed to ensure success. Thus, the military action did not take place until early May.[26]

Both Fakashan and Koulinshan comprise several peaks, with each occupying an area of less than 10 square kilometers. They were defended by troops from the PAVN 327th and 313th Divisions, respectively. To confront them, the CMC ordered deployment of seven PLA infantry regiments and four artillery regiments to the Guangxi–Lang Son border; in addition, the 42nd Division from the PLA's 14th Army was deployed to the Yunnan–Ha Tuyen (now Ha Giang) border.[27] The PLA deployed these robust forces to counter Vietnamese forces, which had fortified their positions with trenches, firing points, and mines. The main thrust of attack in Guangxi was assigned to the 9th Regiment of the 3rd Border Defense Division; in Yunnan, it was assigned to the 126th Regiment of the 42nd Division.[28]

The assault began on 5 May 1981 in Guangxi and two days later in Yunnan. Each attack followed a massive preparatory artillery barrage. One PLA company captured Vietnamese positions at three separate heights (two of them on the Vietnam side of the border) on Fakashan in less than an hour, with 26 PAVN soldiers killed and 43 wounded. But the battles at Koulinshan were fought on a much larger scale. The PLA forces, operating at regimental strength, attacked Hill 1705.2 and Hill 1862.3 simultaneously, securing control of them after bitterly fighting for almost ten hours. In the ensuing days, the 42nd Division troops continued to attack other hills held by Vietnamese forces, and at the end, they claimed to have killed 430 enemy troops at the cost of 273 of their own personnel.[29]

Despite this bloodletting, Vietnam had no desire to show any white flag. Beginning on 10 May, the PAVN launched a series of vicious counterattacks, the likes of which had not been seen since 1979. Like their Chinese counterparts, the Vietnamese staged human-wave counterattacks, with groupings of troops ranging from company- to battalion-size. Artillery fire also played a significant role in these assaults. More than 20,000 rockets and artillery shells were lobbed at the hilltops of Fakashan. The most vicious battles (known to the Vietnamese as the Battles of Hill 400) were fought on 10, 16, and 19 May and 7 June. The PLA defenders repulsed the Vietnamese assaults, claiming to have inflicted 1,200 casualties (705 dead and 513 wounded) on the enemy. The PLA unit later received the honorific title "Fakashan Hero Battalion."[30] After the last Vietnamese counterattack failed, both sides continued to exchange artillery fire until the end of the month.

Contemporary foreign observers always linked China's military action on the border to the ongoing situation in Cambodia.[31] But although the PLA's 1981 attacks on Vietnamese positions along the border undoubtedly marked an initial effort to maintain military pressure on Vietnam, they were not a true response to the Cambodian situation. While the border conflict had been initiated by China, Vietnam had most significantly influenced the scale and duration of the fight. Relentless counterattacks by PAVN troops dragged out and intensified the fighting. Ironically, doing so played into the PLA's overarching policy, for the heavy commitment of PAVN forces and their plunge into intense war furthered China's goal of "bleeding Vietnam."

During 1982–83, tensions along the Sino-Vietnamese border simmered, erupting into a boil with occasional Chinese artillery bombardments but otherwise remaining markedly less intense than during the preceding year.[32] Why did China maintain only limited pressure on Vietnam during these two years? Some observers argue that Beijing's effort to improve the Sino-Soviet relationship accounted for this lull.[33] A recent study speculates that domestic politics—particularly the strained relationship between Deng and strong supporters of Mao's policies and the subsequent replacement of many of Mao's old generals with younger generals who supported Deng's reform policy—constituted a major factor in PLA and Chinese leaders' distraction from the border conflict.[34]

Both of these arguments overlook Deng Xiaoping's absolute leadership position and his decisive role in directing and enforcing China's foreign policy. More important, both explanations fail to recognize that the Chinese leadership did not expect that military pressure on Vietnam would bring any immediate change to Hanoi's Cambodia policy but believed that military pressure would nevertheless work in China's favor in the long run. Further, the Chinese leadership was unwilling to express its support for the Cambodian resistance movement only in rhetorical terms, believing that action constituted the best evidence of its commitment. Particularly at a time when Vietnam increased its intrusions against Thailand, China's reputation and credibility as a regional power were at stake.[35] Artillery shelling and ground assaults on Vietnamese border positions offered China options for responding to the situation in Cambodia and Thailand that also enhanced its regional and global reputation. In this light, it is easy to see that the relative tranquility along the Sino-Vietnamese border was fated to end all too soon.

The Laoshan Offensive Operations, 1984

Border tensions and fighting culminated with the Laoshan Offensive of 1984, which constituted China's response to the 1984 Vietnamese dry season offensive against Cambodian resistance forces. The Laoshan Offensive unexpectedly locked the China and Vietnam into a deadlier border confrontation for the remainder of the decade. China divided the Battle of Laoshan into two phases: (1) the PLA initiated an offensive operation to seize Vietnamese positions along the Yunnan-Vietnam border in April, and the PAVN responded with counterattacks until the end of the year; and (2) China rotated the PLA forces from other military regions through Laoshan from 1985 to 1989.[36]

On 24 December 1983, Deng Xiaoping met Prince Norodom Sihanouk, head of a delegation from the coalition government of Democratic Cambodia to Beijing. Sihanouk's visit complemented efforts by the three main Cambodian resistance factions (Sihanouk's group, Son Sann's conservative nationalist group, and the Khmer Rouge) to formulate an anti-Vietnamese united front.[37] The Cambodian leader urgently requested help because Vietnamese forces were engaged in an aggressive military campaign against the resistance groups at Phnom Malai and the Cardamom Mountains and the PAVN had blockaded Cambodia's border with Thailand, cutting off Cambodia's only access to outside assistance. His plea coincided with deployment of PLA forces to confront the PAVN. Early in the month, the CMC had ordered the 11th and 14th Armies from the Kunming Military Region to prepare for offensive operations against Vietnam in the Laoshan area. This planned military action appeared more deliberate than timed and might have been born from a realization that China's military pressures along the border had not in fact worked well enough to deter Vietnam's aggressions in Cambodia.[38] Indeed, during the subsequent fight for Laoshan, China invited General Arthit Kamlang-ek, commander in chief of the Royal Thai Army, to visit the battlefield and discuss with PLA officers their fight against the PAVN.[39]

Twenty-six hills bestride the Sino-Vietnamese border between Yunnan and Ha Tuyen Provinces.[40] Laoshan, the main battleground, is situated between boundary markers 12 and 13 on the right bank of the Song Lo (Panlong) River. A road ran along the river through the valley connecting the Chinese village of Chuantou with Vietnam's Thanh Thuy. Laoshan consists of three ridges, radiating from its main peak (1,422 meters high) to the northeast, northwest, and south. It is covered with dense grass, bamboo groves, and bushes, and the slopes on the Chinese side are steeper than those on the Vietnam side.[41]

The second battlefield was located at Dongshan, a range of hills five kilo-

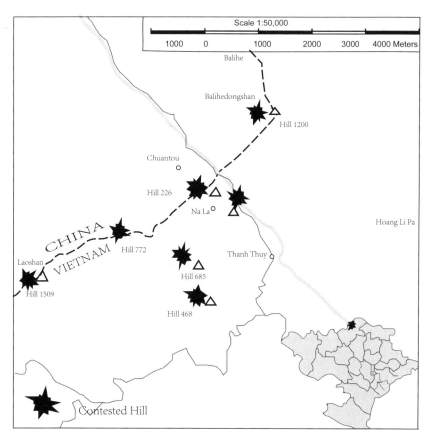

Scale 1:50,000

1000   0   1000   2000   3000   4000 Meters

Balihe

Balihedongshan

Hill 1200

Chuantou

Hill 226

Na La

Hoang Li Pa

CHINA

VIETNAM

Hill 772

Laoshan

Thanh Thuy

Hill 1509

Hill 685

Hill 468

Contested Hill

MAP 5 The Battles of Laoshan and Bailihedongshan, 1984–1987

meters east of Laoshan, near the Yao hamlet of Balihe on the left bank of the Song Lo River. The Dongshan Hills run south to north for about 1,300 meters and are about 400 meters wide; they are crowned to the south by a hill that is 1,175 meters high.[42] The other primary battle zone was Zheyinshan, located at boundary marker 9, near the town of Yangwan on the China border and adjacent to the Yen Minh district of Ha Giang on the Vietnam side.[43]

It is still unclear why China chose these areas for its offensive operations in 1984. The Laoshan area was mountainous, remote, and difficult to reach from any Chinese and Vietnamese capital cities other than Ha Giang. Chinese attacks in these areas certainly did not pose a serious threat to the Vietnamese heartland. Deng Xiaoping likely ordered the PLA to attack these hills because this action sent an important signal to the Thais that China would not tolerate any loss of its territory, even in a remote area, and would force Vietnam to break its concentration on its military invasion of Cambodia and Thailand.[44]

Laoshan and Dongshan, 1984. Courtesy Wang Huazhang.

The battles over these hills played an important role in China's foreign policy in the mid-1980s. Furthermore, Laoshan could constitute an ideal testing ground for the PLA to assess the training and organizational reforms introduced following the 1979 border war.

In mid-February, the 40th and 31st PLA divisions plus one infantry regiment from the 42nd Division were ordered to attack Laoshan and Zheyinshan. An overwhelming artillery force, consisting of the 4th Artillery Division, the artillery regiment of the 14th Army, and the artillery regiment of the 41st Division, was assembled to provide fire support for these infantry units.[45] Defending Laoshan were the 122nd Infantry Regiment of the 313th Infantry Division, supported by three other infantry regiments from the rear. The Vietnamese artillery firepower in the area included eleven battalions and twenty-three rocket artillery companies.[46] The Chinese offensive had two components, Project 14, a ground assault; and Project 17, a ferocious artillery bombardment.[47]

From 2 to 27 April, 256 Chinese artillery pieces bombarded Vietnamese territory every day, allegedly hitting 414 targets, including command posts, artillery emplacements, troop assemblies, and fortifications. Decoy ground attacks attempted to lure Vietnamese troops away from their fortified positions so that the Chinese artillery could target them in the open. Simultaneously, deception operations were conducted along the Hoang Lien Son border to conceal preparations for the ground assaults of Laoshan and Zheyinshan (Project 14).[48] The official history of Vietnamese Military District 2 confirms that China conducted almost one month of sustained and savage shelling against PAVN positions before launching ground assaults in the Vi Xuyen and Yen Minh Districts of Ha Tuyen Province.[49] Studies based on foreign journalists' reports incorrectly claimed that Chinese battalion-sized attacks occurred simultaneously in four Vietnamese border provinces.[50] Both countries engaged in public diplomacy at the time. Vietnam wanted to be seen as a victim, while China did not want to be viewed as a provocateur. Exaggerations and false information characterized both sides' pronouncements and positions.

On 28 April, the Chinese forces opened up their ground attacks on Laoshan. Troops from five different regiments participated. The 118th Regiment assaulted the main peak of Laoshan, whose buttressing heights were defended by two dug-in and fortified Vietnamese companies. One company element of the PLA's 119th Regiment launched concurrent attacks on Hill 662.6 (known to the Chinese as Songmaoling), which guarded a road between Thanh Thuy and Laoshan. The same fire-maneuver tactics were used as in 1979, including concealed movements to close the enemy's position, penetration maneuvers to encircle the enemy from behind, and simultaneous attacks from the enemy's lateral and rear positions. Along with these primitive (if standard) tactics, several soldiers sacrificed themselves to clear paths through minefields.[51]

Over several hours of bitter fighting, the PLA soldiers secured each hilltop one by one. They reportedly killed 220 PAVN troops and captured only 5 while losing 71 of their own, along with 200 wounded.[52] The victory had been hard-won. The battalion undertaking the penetration task had failed to reach its staging position on time. Consequently, by the time the fighting started, most of its troops remained trapped in jungles, exhausted and disorientated after four hours of traversing heavy vegetation and steep mountain terrains as rain pelted down. Next came Vietnamese artillery. Those who survived then engaged in unorganized assaults against the two heights that screened Laoshan's main peak from the south. The PLA troops nevertheless persisted in the attack. The battalion lost two-thirds of its men, and only after receiving reinforcements did it finally seize the enemy positions the next day.[53]

This courageous if poor performance brought criticism against the army and division leadership, who had failed to make decisions with a clear understanding of local conditions such as how the combination of high mountains, steep slope, thick forests, and bad weather would constrain the assault: the penetration unit needed more than four hours to complete a march that had been estimated to take two. Even worse, leaders refused to accept changes suggested by subordinates who noted that the operation plan lacked a full consideration of terrain conditions.[54] A few years later, Chen Zhijian, deputy commander of the 40th Division, commented that "the leader [of the 14th Army] arrogated to himself some importance, acting in [autocratic] parental leadership style, while showing no trust in his subordinates. After the fighting, he blamed his subordinates for mistakes and then wrongly punished them."[55]

What happened at Laoshan likely did not truly represent the PLA's operational abilities, for at Zheyinshan the situation differed greatly. There, PLA units experienced the same difficulties as their comrades at Laoshan, but at Zheyinshan they responded with flexibility and ingenuity. Two infantry regiments of the 31st Division were assigned to seize Zheyinshan, with the army's artillery regiment providing fire support. The Vietnamese defenders were the independent battalion of Yen Minh District. Heavy rain prevented Chinese troops from arriving at their starting points as scheduled. The division commander twice postponed the attack time for almost an hour, allowing the exhausted troops to take a short break before launching.[56] The Chinese offensive lasted for a few hours and claimed to have killed 550 Vietnamese troops, including the battalion's commander (a senior captain) and captured 18.[57] This battle became a textbook example of PLA operations in the Sino-Vietnamese border region. The division's commander, Liao Xilong, was soon promoted to commander of the 11th Army, another rising star general launched through the Laoshan operations.[58]

Vietnam's Response: The MB-84 Campaign Plan

After the seizure of Dongshan's six heights on 15 May, the Laoshan offensive operation ended with the Chinese in a much-improved defensive posture on the left flank of the Chuantou area. Chinese forces then shifted to defensive operations, while Vietnam attempted to recover the lost heights in Vi Xuyen and Yen Minh. Western studies ignored the changing nature of the fight over the remainder of the year.[59] Pursuant to a policy of not initiating any provocations on the border, the Vietnamese military did not take action against China's "land-grabbing" at Luojiaping and Koulinshan. At Fakashan, Vietnam responded with only limited counterattacks. Later events at Laoshan apparently convinced Hanoi that Vietnam's restraints would not stop China from attacking deeper as long as Vietnamese troops remained in Cambodia, so Vietnamese leaders changed their strategy. They decided to engage in active, offensive action against the PLA, pointedly choosing Laoshan as their battleground to avoid giving the impression that Vietnam was weak.[60]

The loss of Laoshan, known to the Vietnamese as Hill 1509, brought several senior Vietnamese military leaders to Ha Giang to discuss countermeasures. That group included General Le Trong Tan, chief of the General Staff; Lieutenant General Le Ngoc Hien, deputy chief of the General Staff; and Lieutenant General Vu Lap, commander of Military District 2. Assisted by Soviet advisers, they allegedly came up with a campaign plan, MB-84, aimed at destroying Chinese strongpoints and then recovering the hills that the Chinese had captured in Ha Tuyen Province.[61] Military District 2 set up an artillery command post at Ha Giang, brought the 313th Division up to full strength, and sent large numbers of reinforcements to the Thanh Thuy area, including the 356th Division (the 149th and 153rd Infantry Regiments and the 150th Artillery Regiment) from Hoang Lien Son, four battalions from the 168th and 368th Artillery Brigades, and the main force of the 821st Sapper Regiment. Engineering units worked to construct roads and command and control systems. By early June, Vietnam had assembled substantially stronger forces (eight infantry regiments and eighteen artillery battalions) than the Chinese forces (five infantry regiments and twelve artillery battalions) in the region.[62]

The first PAVN counteroffensive operation occurred on 11 June 1984. Prior to dawn, the Vietnamese 313th Division sent out two battalions of the 14th Regiment, supported by elements of the 821st Sapper Regiment, attempting to retake some strongpoints near hamlet Na La. From there, they could secure the road along the Song Lo River Valley through Thanh Thuy to Ha Giang. Chinese troops from the 119th Regiment held their positions, repulsing several Vietnamese assaults over two hours. In the late afternoon, the 313th made a second attempt against the Chinese positions at Na La and Dongshan, using battalion-sized attacks. Accurate and timely Chinese artillery fire played a major role in disrupting PAVN attacks. The recently imported Cymbeline artillery-locating radar from Great Britain gave Chinese artillery forces an advantage over their Vietnamese counterparts. Having suffered heavy casualties, the Vietnamese forces ended their fruitless attacks shortly after sunset.[63]

The Chinese perceived the 11 June counterattacks as a Vietnamese probe of China's defensive system in the Laoshan area and speculated that the Vietnamese would concentrate their attacks on hills at Na La and Dongshan because these two locations were essential to the defense of Chinese positions. Divided by the Panlong (Song Lo) River, the Chinese forces were situated between Laoshan to the east and Dongshan to the west. The 41st Division was ordered to join the fight to defend the hills on the east side of the river, while the 40th Division concentrated on defending the western area.[64] The total strength of the Chinese defensive forces increased to eighteen infantry battalions and fourteen artillery battalions. Artillery firepower was expected to play a pivotal role, and each artillery gun received three times the base number of shells. (For example, the 122mm howitzer base number is 80 shells, so 240 shells were supplied.) The Chinese defensive positions were arranged with fewer troops in several key sectors on the front lines and a large number of troops kept behind to provide timely replenishment as needed. The Chinese front command urged troops to prepare for a long tenacious fight and to use both defensive and offensive tactics to win at low cost.[65]

On 19 June, the Vietnamese military leadership decided to send more troops to implement the MB-84 Offensive in the Ha Giang area. The fresh troops included the 316th Division's 174th Regiment, the 312th Division's 141st Regiment, and the 10th Division's 66th Regiment as well as three artillery battalions and one sapper battalion from Military District 1. The total number of Vietnamese forces reached ten infantry regiments, two sapper regiments, and fourteen artillery battalions, for a total of 40,000 troops. From 12 to 22 June, more than 30,000 artillery shells and 2,000,000 bullets were delivered to the Vietnamese frontline troops.[66] The Vietnamese offensive plan called for an attack first on Na La to split Chinese forces between Laoshan and Dongshan. Then, the newly acquired positions at Na La would serve as a springboard for further attacks on the Chinese positions along the border, one by one. Ha Giang was selected as the Vietnamese military headquarters, with Lieutenant Generals Le Ngoc Hien and Vu Lap in charge. Their deputies, Major General Le Uy Mat and Senior Colonel Bui Van Thang, set up a forward command post at Coc Nie, while division commanders directed operations at Nam Cat, Thanh Thuy, and Pa-li-ho (Balihe).[67]

On the early morning of 12 July, the Vietnamese counteroffensive began. Five infantry regiments along with two sapper regiments launched battalion-sized attacks on Heights 142 and 149 at Na La, Height 662.5 at Songmaoling, Height 1072 at Laoshan, and the hills at Dongshan in what represented the largest Vietnamese offensive operation since the beginning of the military confrontation between China and Vietnam in 1979. The Vietnamese troops raced up the slopes in waves. According to one Chinese soldier stationed at a forward observation post, "The Vietnamese made forward charges without stopping. Many of them were killed by our artillery firepower. Those who followed turned their backs, not to run away but to drop to their knees and kowtow to the rear, perhaps saying good-bye to their family members and homeland. They then held their guns to charge again . . . until they were killed."[68]

The Vietnamese assaults lasted for more than eighteen hours. When the guns fell silent over the hills of Laoshan, hundreds of dead PAVN soldiers lay strewn on hillsides in front of Chinese positions. Official Chinese records initially estimated that 1,080 Vietnamese troops had been killed and wounded that day, but a Chinese intercept of Vietnamese communications traffic led officials to revise that number upward to 3,000.[69] Moreover, when Vietnam finally reclaimed the hills to the south of Laoshan during a 2001 boundary settlement between the two countries, the Vietnamese excavated the remains of a large number of PAVN soldiers and brought them back home.[70]

Online discussions among Vietnamese veterans questioned the Chinese accounts but supported the Chinese side of the story to some extent. The Chinese noted that new technologies such as night-vision devices and ground-target-indicator radars helped them win.[71] One Vietnamese veteran observed that many soldiers were killed or wounded by Chinese artillery firepower while eating rice balls and waiting for attack orders under the cover of darkness in the staging area.[72] The Chinese also concluded that the time-effective logistics—the "rear service"—was crucial in defeating Vietnamese counteroffensive operations. The Chinese rear service shipped more than 120,000 shells to the frontline forces. Artillery firepower played a major role in destroying the enemy's effective strength. One artillery commander recalled that for the first time in his career, he could fire at enemy positions as many times as he wished without worrying about the cost or availability of shells.[73] On the Vietnamese side, heavy casualties as well as ammunition shortages led Vietnamese commanders to call off the attack.

Rotation of Troops through Laoshan, 1985–1989

Following the collapse of Vietnamese counteroffensives in July 1984, Beijing also changed its strategy, directing the Chinese forces "to fight tenaciously, to hold fast their positions over a long period, to kill a large number of the enemy, and not to lose an inch of land."[74] The 11th Army had replaced the 14th Army at Laoshan by the end of July, and the PLA General Staff began to mull over a rotation of the PLA field armies from different military regions through the battlefields of Laoshan—as Deng Xiaoping allegedly said, "Let our field armies touch the buttocks of a tiger" (*rang women de yezhanjun momo laohu pigu*).[75] As Thailand faced increasing incursions and shelling from Vietnamese forces in 1984–85, the Chinese leader became convinced that Hanoi had not been constrained and was continuing to use all of Vietnam's armed might to indulge in wars of aggression. This thinking led Beijing to rotate the PLA units through Laoshan, and the CMC subsequently named the strategy "holding fast in defensive operations against Vietnam."[76]

On 10 February 1985, CCP secretary-general Hu Yaobang visited Laoshan, exhorting Chinese soldiers that the fight would continue for "three to five more years" and would stop only when Vietnam no longer pursued a policy of regional hegemony and withdrew its forces from Cambodia. Hu then urged his troops to "achieve victory in offensive battles and to be impregnable in defensive battles" (*gongbike, shoubigu*). Hu continued that while their primary mission was defensive, they needed to take offensive action to hit Vietnam hard and win greater victories at a minimum cost so that Vietnam "would not look down on us."[77] After Hu's speech, the PLA adopted a strategy known as "maintaining appropriate military pressure on Vietnam" (*baochi shidu junshi yali*) and "avoiding losses, not showing weakness" (*buchikui, bushiruo*).[78] The guiding principle for military action was redefined as winning big with small losses.[79] Beijing allowed the PLA forces at Laoshan to decide when and how to put military pressure on Vietnam, although those decisions needed to remain in line with China's foreign policy.[80] However, stressing the primacy of the political over the military did not appear practical for the PLA's leaders at Laoshan.

Thus, starting in late 1984, the use of force against Vietnam became a routine activity for PLA border forces. Observers have speculated that China's position regarding Vietnam became less hard at this time, even though "minor military skirmishes" continued.[81] On the contrary, however, China remained both consistent and persistent in pursuing a policy aimed at creating an adverse situation for Vietnam politically, economically, and militarily. While military action on the Vietnam border was closely connected with this strategic objective, the PLA also showed an increasing interest in using Laoshan as training ground where Chinese troops could gain combat experience. By the end of 1989, a total of five rotations had occurred, involving units from seven field armies, including infantry, artillery, antiaircraft, engineering, antichemical-warfare, and electronic warfare troops, with each unit sent for a six-month to one-year deployment.[82]

The PLA's defensive operations at Laoshan covered an area 23 kilometers long and 35 kilometers wide with some 120 defensive positions.[83] Preparing to fight in the Laoshan area, Chinese troops dug more than 47,000 meters of trenches and 36 tunnels (911 meters long) and built almost 10,600 fortifications, which allegedly could sustain attacks by 122mm artillery guns.[84] Laoshan symbolized animosity between China and Vietnam throughout the 1980s and served as a battleground on which the two countries' military forces contested their will and capability.

The first troop assigned to rotation was the 1st Army, from the Nanjing

The reconnaissance company of the 138th Division prior to attacking a Vietnamese position at Dongshan, September 1985. Courtesy Wang Huazhang.

Military Region, along with some engineering regiments from other military regions and an electronics-countermeasure battalion from the General Staff Department. After spending five months acclimating and training in a reserve area around Wenshan, Yunnan Province, the 1st Army replaced the 11th Army at Laoshan. The 1st Army's order of battle included two infantry divisions (the 1st Division and the 12th Army's 36th Division), plus two artillery divisions (the 3rd and 9th), amounting to more than 26,600 men. In addition, five engineering regiments, two automobile regiments, and one antiaircraft artillery regiment from other military regions provided support.[85] From early December 1984 through May 1985, the 1st Army fought six major defensive and counteroffensive battles, reportedly holding its ground against nine battalion- to regimental- sized attacks and more than 100 platoon- to company-sized attacks. The 1st Army claimed to have destroyed twenty-eight Vietnamese strongpoints and killed 5,007 Vietnamese soldiers while losing only 404 men.[86]

On 30 May 1985, the 67th Army from the Jinan Military Region, comprised of two infantry divisions (the 119th and the 46th Army's 138th) and one artillery division (the 12th) plus one regiment (the 46th) from the 8th Artillery Division, was deployed to the border. For a year, the units of the 67th Army prided themselves on their combat success. However, they suffered more ca-

PLA troops attack
Height 211, 1 June 1985.
Courtesy Wang Huazhang.

sualties than any other field armies at Laoshan.[87] The third and fourth groups were the 47th Group Army from the Lanzhou Military Region and the 27th Group Army from the Beijing Military Region. (In 1985, the PLA's field armies were renamed group armies.) The 47th Group Army had 37,351 troops, while the 27th had 33,700.[88]

From May 1986 to April 1988, the Vietnamese offensives changed from heavy attacks to raiding tactics along with artillery bombardments. The 47th Group Army reported that over a year, the Vietnamese forces fired more than 18,000 artillery shells on Chinese positions and initiated more than 800 raids. In response, the Chinese forces launched four company-sized counterattacks along with more than 100 small-unit sabotages and ambushes.[89] The 27th Group Army recorded 600 or more Vietnamese raids and 8 major artillery exchanges between April 1987 and April 1988.[90] The last unit rotated to the Laoshan front was the 13th Group Army from the Chengdu Military Region, which arrived in May 1988. However, the size of the Chinese forces was reduced to an infantry division along with some support units. Reconnaissance and counterreconnaissance operations characterized the last period of military conflict at Laoshan.[91] Both countries began to withdraw their forces from the border as the communist world was shrinking.[92] By October 1989, the last of the 13th Group Army's units had returned to their service area in Chengdu. The defense of Laoshan was turned over to the border defense units of the Yunnan Provincial Military District.[93]

During the rotation period, the PLA also deployed a significant number of reconnaissance units—the equivalent of the U.S. Special Forces—to carry out infiltration and raiding missions along the border. Traditionally, PLA reconnaissance units were responsible for collecting intelligence information on the battlefield. From the beginning of the conflict between China and Vietnam, Vietnamese sapper (*dac cong*) units actively brought the war to the Chinese rear area. On 5 July 1984, a team from the Vietnamese 821st Sapper Regiment destroyed the Cymbeline artillery-locating radar system that had proven so devastatingly effective against PAVN troops. Deng Xiaoping supposedly was startled by this incident, questioning the chief of the General Staff why the Chinese reconnaissance forces could not carry out similar activities against Vietnam. The General Staff then ordered all of China's military regions to organize reconnaissance brigades and deployed them to Laoshan for between six months and one year.[94]

A total of fifteen reconnaissance brigades were created. They ranged in size from three to five companies—between 500 and 700 troops.[95] Three to five brigades at a time were deployed to the border between Laoshan and Zheyinshan. They engaged enemy sapper forces, collected intelligence information, and raided enemy barracks, depots, and artillery emplacements deeper in Vietnamese territory. Between September 1985 and October 1986, the 10th Reconnaissance Brigade of the 21st Group Army reported carrying out eighteen raids and destroying twenty-five troop stations, fifty-nine barracks, sixteen artillery pieces, two ammo depots, one warehouse, and one bridge; 258 enemy troops were wounded or killed, while seven others were captured.[96] The combat experience gained by these reconnaissance units later inspired the PLA to create special operations forces.

The PLAAF also rotated its units to pressure Vietnam from the air. As in 1979, large formations of fighters flew over the border region. Hanoi voiced concerns about Chinese escalation of the conflict after the PLAAF intensified its activities along the border.[97] The air force's most significant contribution was reconnaissance. PLAAF recce pilots flew a total of ninety-seven sorties between 1984 and 1986, typically flying deep along National Highway 2 from Thanh Thuy to Ha Giang and then Bac Me, from there turning eastward toward Muong Cha, and then traveling through Quan Ba back to China. These flights reportedly provided Chinese ground forces with photo images of more than 1,000 Vietnamese military objects.[98]

The Vietnamese air force also used its Soviet made MiG-21 Fishbeds to fly over China's airspace. Between May 1979 and May 1986, Chinese radar tracked twelve incursions, usually lasting between a few seconds and a few minutes. These incidents may have had no military value other than constituting a psychological tit for tat. The PLAAF also rotated SA-2 Guideline surface-to-air missile units—a total of twenty-five SAM battalions—through the Sino-Vietnamese border.[99] Most of the time, the missiles failed to intercept the intruders. However, on 28 March 1984, the PLAAF claimed that one Vietnamese MiG-21 was damaged by a surface-to-air missile, and on 5 October 1987, the missiles finally brought down one Vietnamese MiG-21 reconnaissance aircraft. Its pilot was captured.[100]

Western studies characterized the military situation along the Vietnamese-Chinese border as a "phony war" or "minor military skirmishes."[101] But the scope, ferocity, and intensity of the conflict belied such facile, dismissive judgments. The violence and persistence of the conflict far surpassed the 1960s clashes along the Sino-Indian and Sino-Soviet borders. Between 1984 and 1989, a total of 180,000 Chinese troops were sent to fight at Laoshan. To them, the days and nights were imbued with blood and fire. Caves (used as shelters) were dark and musty, filled with hordes of voracious gnats and mosquitoes as well as rats and snakes. Supplies were scarce and for days at a time nonexistent. Enemy shelling came daily and hourly. Soldiers' nerves were constantly on edge, mirroring the experiences of trench warfare on the Western Front in the First World War. From 1985 to 1989, PLA forces claimed to have inflicted more than 33,500 casualties on the Vietnamese, destroying or damaging approximately 840 kinds of artillery pieces and some 180 trucks. The Chinese admitted to suffering 4,100 casualties, about half of them deaths.[102]

The Chinese View on Vietnamese Operations

Accounts from both sides in the conflict must be considered with caution and carefully scrutinized. Chinese accounts can be biased. Similarly, Vietnamese accounts are often exaggerated to suit propaganda purposes.[103] Vietnam was neither a victim nor a passive actor in the border conflict. From a Chinese perspective, the upsurge in attacks was closely associated with Hanoi's strategic interests. Vietnam's attacks on Chinese positions at Laoshan on 18 November 1984 were perceived as occurring in concert with Hanoi's dry-season offensives in Cambodia. Because of its dependence on Soviet aid, a mainstay of Vietnam's economy and military, Hanoi was concerned about any improvement of Sino-Soviet relations at the time. The Chinese considered the 20 December 1984 attacks a deliberate attempt to sabotage Soviet deputy premier Mikhail

Arkhipov's visit to Beijing in late December. Vietnam attempted to deceive the world, proposing a New Year's cease-fire shortly before launching regiment-sized attacks against Chinese positions at Na La on 15 January 1985.[104]

For its part, in response to Chinese actions, Vietnam adopted a new strategy, "active defense"—that is, the use of offensive tactics to achieve defensive ends. Initially, the Vietnamese forces were restrained from provoking China. But beginning in 1984, Hanoi ordered its forces to counterattack Chinese encroachments on Vietnam's border territories. Vietnam's tactical approach also shifted from "adhocracy" guerrilla tactics to large, regularized mass-and-maneuver operations following scripted and detailed action plans. The Vietnamese forces concentrated their large-scale offensive operations during the dry season. For the rest of the year, they preferred to conduct small-unit raids, wearing down the Chinese defenders.[105] The Vietnamese also returned to the kind of trench warfare the Viet Minh had used against French forces at Dien Bien Phu in 1954. More than 50 kilometers of trenches were constructed as the Vietnamese attempted to separate Chinese forward positions from each other.[106]

The PAVN's increasing reliance on heavy artillery bombardments likewise reflected the experience of Dien Bien Phu over the previous three decades. The Chinese also discovered better coordination between Vietnamese artillery and infantry forces. Artillery focused on hitting deep against Chinese artillery emplacements. Between 15 and 18 January 1985, the Chinese detected that the Vietnamese fired approximately 10,200 shells, more than 85 percent of them at Chinese infantry.[107] With 60 to 85 percent of its forward defensive positions destroyed by artillery fire, the PLA's 1st Army reported that the accuracy of Vietnamese artillery forces had improved. The Vietnamese not only employed the Soviet BM-21 multiple rocket launcher system at Laoshan but also used more mortar and direct artillery fire, which counted for 73 percent of enemy artillery firepower, against the Chinese frontline infantries, which often found themselves with no place to hide except between rocks.[108]

From the second half of 1984, China was no longer the dominant driver in the conflict. Vietnam fought back determinedly with consistent small-unit attacks and occasionally massive counteroffensives. The Chinese observed some notable features of the Vietnamese offensive operation: (1) the use of strong forces to concentrate attacks on key locations for quick victory; (2) a preference for offensive attacks in waves, in different sizes, and from multiple approaches; and (3) a predilection for a nipping approach by seizing one position first and launching more attacks from there. The Chinese acknowledged that these characteristics were by no means exhaustive or all-inclusive.[109]

Vietnam also brought forces from other military districts to Vi Xuyen, though it remains difficult to identify which forces participated. According to one Vietnamese Internet blogger, the units came from all five military districts north of Hanoi.[110] One Western study estimates the total number of Vietnamese troops in the area at between 56,000 and 70,000.[111] Given the unhealthy state of Vietnam's economy, the remoteness of the area, and its poor transportation conditions, the Vietnamese military had difficulties in meeting the troops' need for provisions. Throughout the campaign in Vi Xuyen, the forward command of Military District 2 frequently reported that it could not guarantee troops minimum rations—mostly rice balls and dried fish. One Vietnamese veteran recalled that morale deteriorated and desertion occurred.[112]

Based on Vietnamese accounts, one Western scholar reports that the most ferocious Chinese attacks against Vietnamese positions in the Laoshan area took place in June, September, and December 1985 and October 1986, with an involvement of PLA forces from companies to regiments and even divisions.[113] Recently available Chinese documentation reveals Vietnamese counterattacks by battalion- to regimental-sized forces along with numerous squad- and platoon-sized attacks in May and July 1985, January 1986, and April 1987.[114] The disparity between Vietnamese and Chinese accounts also colors each side's interpretations of the scale of each fight. All these engagements were conducted by elements not larger than a company. Vietnamese accounts are rarely available for comparison with Chinese records, so it is difficult to judge Vietnamese performance during the border conflicts fairly.

However, some exceptions exist. For example, a 1985 article published in a Vietnamese military journal, *Quan Doi Nhan Dan* (People's Army), by Senior General Chu Huy Man, director of the PAVN political bureau, may offer insights about the problems that Vietnamese troops experienced in the border conflict with China. Like his Chinese counterparts, the Vietnamese general wrote the article using political jargon and propaganda rhetoric while offering little detailed information. Nevertheless, the article reveals some startling problems that correspond to Chinese observations.[115] General Chu presented problems covering the areas of training, combat efficiency, discipline and morale, preparation, logistical support, and leadership. Vietnamese troops' shortcomings included inefficient use of weapons and disorderly and scared responses to battlefield situations. In addition, Vietnamese troops failed to follow orders and to correctly estimate the enemy's strategy and offensive plan, leading Vietnamese forces to lose initiative and to be incapable of executing their war plans. Shortages of food supplies and wasting of ammunition were exacerbated by corruption, as some supplies were diverted before reaching the troops. And many of these problems could be attributed to poor leadership. Officers were unable to make correct decisions in difficult situations and failed to act as role models. These problems are far from a complete account of how Vietnamese forces performed in the border conflict, and General Chu admitted that false reports were made by officers at lower levels.[116] The Vietnamese side of the story will not be complete until Hanoi's records become available.

Chinese Assessments of Their Operations

The 1980s border conflict between China and Vietnam was defined by the Chinese as special, limited warfare conducted under modern conditions. They continued to emphasize the intimate connection between fighting and politics. According to Fu Quanyou, commander of the 1st Army, the PLA's military action at Laoshao was determined by political rather than military considerations and served political and diplomatic needs.[117] He gave no specific evidence. One of his subordinates indirectly noted that the large-caliber and rocket artilleries were used in a tightly controlled manner because of their long range and large destruction scale.[118] Other sources suggested that some scheduled offensive operations were either postponed or called off by Beijing as a result of political considerations.[119] Because troops sent to Laoshan came from different branches of the services, coordination was regarded as a major feature of the PLA's operations at Laoshan. Other unique characteristics included (1) frequent shifts from offensive to defensive operations because troops on both sides not only positioned themselves so close to each other but also interlocked their positions; (2) mountainous terrain and harsh climate that aggravated the complexity of the battlefield environment; and (3) fighting under arduous conditions accompanied by supply difficulties.[120]

Laoshan raised another challenge for the PLA—that is, the changing appeal of the military in a China that was rapidly modernizing. In the mid-1980s, the better life and greater economic opportunity brought about by Deng's economic reforms triggered a motivational crisis among PLA troops. The emphasis on education as a criterion for promotion tarnished many less-educated rural youth's hopes for social mobility via military service.[121] "Why me?" or "Why us?" was the first question that the conscripts would ask military leaders after received orders to go to Laoshan.

Soldiers also wanted to know why they had to fight for hills on the Vietnamese side of the border in "self-defense."[122] The PLA again resorted to studying the CMC's directives and party secretary-general Hu Yaobang's speech, urging troops to give full play to the Five Revolutionary Spirits advocated by Deng Xiaoping: doing whatever one can for the revolution, strictly observing discipline and making self-sacrifices, giving no thought to the individual and putting the interests of others first, defeating all enemies and overcoming all difficulties, and maintaining revolutionary enthusiasm and striving for victory.[123]

Western studies always question the effectiveness of the PLA's political motivation program on the modern battlefield.[124] The Chinese leadership was firmly convinced that not fearing death was the most important quality for troops to possess in a war. Political motivation was the most effective strategy for making Chinese troops feel brave and willing to sacrifice themselves in combat. The 1st Army reported that Deng Xiaoping's Five Revolutionary Spirits inspired many officers and soldiers to give up opportunities to stay behind to take care of sick family members or attend funerals or to attend universities. Those suspicious of China's justifications for military action at Laoshan were told that limited offensives against the Vietnamese positions inside Vietnam fell under the new "active defense" policy.[125]

Unlike the units from the Guangzhou and Kunming Military Regions, the PLA forces rotated to Laoshan from other military regions had not experienced combat for more than thirty years. The political work system was necessary to motivate the troops and ensure their compliance with orders. A defensive engagement by a non-battle-tested unit was considered a confidence-building measure. Such units later proved more successful in offensive operations than non-battle-tested units that had suffered fewer casualties.[126] PLA units appeared more skilled in fire-and-movement and fire-and-maneuver tactics at Laoshan, in which a group of three to four soldiers would rush the enemy, take cover, and fire to support each other in offensive operations.[127]

The PLA's artillery doctrine changed after 1984. Zhang Youxia, commander of the 118th Regiment, complained that one major problem in 1979 was the failure to apply artillery firepower to break up the enemy's frontline positions while employing raiding tactics against Vietnamese defenders skilled in guerrilla tactics.[128] At the beginning of the Battle of Laoshan in April 1984, the older generation of army leaders refused to employ artillery firepower to support infantry operations as a result of concerns about the cost of shells. Not until the early summer of that year were all restrictions removed. Fire-and-movement and fire-and-maneuver tactics were widely used to coordinate infantry and artillery operations, which featured artillery firepower effective enough to break the enemy's attacks and inflict heavy casualties.[129] Another significant change was that the Chinese forces no longer carried out penetra-

Soldiers on the front lines drink rainwater after running out of supplies, 1986. Courtesy Wang Huazhang.

tion and outflanking maneuvers because artillery firepower played more of an interception role in the fight against Vietnamese retreat and reinforcement.[130]

The border conflict saw more coordination between different army branches at regimental and divisional levels than did the 1979 war. Officers at these two levels took command of not only infantry but also artillery, tank, air defense, engineering, communications, and chemical warfare units. They worked more collaboratively than before. Both wire and wireless networks ensured communications not only from the top down but also between varying levels of the force. More important, for the first time, frontline infantries could directly call for artillery fire support. Radar and electronic listening technology strengthened the artillery force's ability to monitor enemy movements and increased artillery precision.[131]

The 1979 campaign revealed many logistics problems within the PLA. Throughout the 1980s, the scale of border operations was smaller, but logistics nevertheless remained a challenge. Chinese forces still depended on local communities for fresh food, and civilian support remained indispensable. In the summer of 1984, more than 800 civilian trucks were called to convey artillery shells to the front.[132] The army's logistics department had been a headquarters organization with no real function to provide logistics services. Because the Kunming Military Region's logistics department could not provide for the units who came from other military regions, the army sent to Laoshan had to expand its logistics department.[133] The biggest challenge to the PLA logistics system was providing food, water, and ammunition for troops at the forward positions and bringing back the wounded. Troops with no combat assignments were organized into transshipment teams to transport war supplies manually to the front positions. During the heat of the fight, transshipment teams needed to carry twenty tons of supplies to the front positions and evacuate ten wounded personnel per day.[134]

The Chinese understood that lessons learned from the border conflict were limited. The 1st Army's after-action report noted that several issues deserved further attention. First, both divisions under the command of the 1st Army were troops engaged in year-round training and on combat duty.[135] They responded to the deployment order swiftly and efficiently but still found themselves undermanned and their equipment inadequately maintained. Second, the border conflict was fought primarily by small units such as companies and battalions. Officers at these two levels often appeared incapable of independently organizing and conducting operations. Third, training in real combat conditions was deficient, especially because fighting conditions in mountain and jungle terrain differed from those in the troops' home environment.[136] The PLA's experience at Laoshan convinced its leaders to build modern bases that could simulate training among different army branches in all kinds of environments.[137]

The PLA's experience again demonstrated that individual skills were essential to the troops' combat ability and efficiency. The Chinese acknowledged that their forces did not perform well when they fought individually. One reason was that they trained only in a single skill, making them ill equipped to handle more complex battlefield situations. The PLA leadership found that the officers and enlisted soldiers who had received higher education could always find solutions to the problems that arose in the midst of combat, while less educated soldiers often failed to respond well and suffered more casualties.[138] Although the border conflict was limited in scope, it revealed that the PLA urgently needed to improve itself in terms of force structure and organization, training, equipment, and logistical support systems.

Conclusion

During the 1980s, the Chinese leadership regarded the border conflict as an extension of the political and diplomatic struggle against regional and global hegemony. Laoshan served two strategic purposes for Beijing, forcing changes in Vietnamese policy toward Cambodia and demonstrating China's support for those countries that resisted Vietnamese aggression in Indochina. The Chinese leadership did not anticipate this approach would bring about an immediate resolution of the Cambodia issue but persisted in believing that keeping up military pressure on the Sino-Vietnamese border would help create more of a burden on Vietnam. The success of China's strategy depended not on battle-field victories but rather on creating a situation detrimental to Vietnam that would facilitate a leadership change in Hanoi, as Deng once suggested.[139] In the end, only in 1990, after Vietnam's withdrawal from Cambodia, did the PLA pull its forces back from the occupied Vietnamese hills.[140]

Vietnam's national pride and domestic politics made Hanoi's leadership unable to tolerate Chinese occupation of any Vietnamese territory, even hills in the remote border region, and it therefore responded to Chinese military pressure with a tit-for-tat strategy. After 1984, Vietnam vigorously resisted Chinese military encroachments, initiating attacks and counterattacks with huge forces even when its economy was weak. Although the fighting took place far from Vietnam's political and industrial heartland, the conflict encumbered the country's economy for a long period of time. For China, battlefield costs were fractional at a time of economic prosperity. In this way, China strategically out-maneuvered Vietnam. Since the Hanoi leadership played into Beijing's hands, China's military pressure appears to have worked.

On the battlefield, it is difficult to say who won. The PLA forces were bet-ter equipped with artillery pieces and ammunition. They were in transition from a rudimentary army to a modern one (for example, they possessed early night vision systems and artillery-controlling radar) and tried to correct the many shortcomings exposed in the 1979 campaign. However, they maintained traditional concepts and characteristics of warfare, outdated organizational structures, and inadequate training. As a result, they both won and lost battles. Laoshan became a learning ground for the PLA to improve its fighting capabil-ity and efficiency. The fighting over those remote mountainous ranges sym-bolized a very bloody and savage relationship between two Asian communist countries during the Cold War.

7 In the Shadow of the Border Conflict

The history of China in the 1980s is commonly reduced to simply a discussion of Deng Xiaoping's reform movement and his policy of opening China to the West. Journalists, diplomatic observers, and historians alike have concentrated on these two themes and their related political and social developments. Consequently, not enough attention has been paid to the border conflict with Vietnam and particularly to its impact on the home front within the PRC, its influence on China's military modernization, and its lasting cultural legacy.[1] Given that thousands of servicemen and civilians fought in the border conflict, their experiences deserve documentation and study, especially since those experiences differed so dramatically from the lives of Chinese citizens from the conflict. Two border provinces, Guangxi and Yunnan, not only were intensely involved in supporting the war but endured many repercussions long afterward. The conflict offered an opportunity for the PLA to evaluate itself, providing a major impetus for military modernization. In addition, the military's wartime exploits were trumpeted to restore the PLA's reputation, damaged during the Cultural Revolution by highly publicized abuses of power.

In his study of China under Mao during the Cold War, Chen Jian documents Beijing's linkage of its foreign and domestic policies, finding that the Mao regime had a proclivity to use force against foreign enemies as "the best means" of mobilizing the whole nation to achieve its domestic agendas.[2] Deng Xiaoping followed this practice during his tenure at the helm of the Chinese state. He showed no concern for maintaining ideological orthodoxy per se in the wake of his reform or for opening China to the West. He was, however, determined to prevent political relaxation from leading the country to "bourgeois liberalization." Such relaxation, he feared, would erode socialism's strength within society and consequently would undermine the party's authority over the people. In this spirit, he used the border war with Vietnam to promote his "socialist spiritual civilization" and to maintain China's communist heritage while pursuing needed economic reforms.

A string of opuses were produced to manipulate public opinion throughout the 1980s, and a generation of Chinese grew up under this cultural influence, which even now continues to serve as a convenient catalyst for China's increasingly strident nationalism. Socially and culturally, the war with Vietnam generated literature, songs, and motion pictures that extolled PLA soldiers who had sacrificed themselves. This chapter examines the local contributions to the war with Vietnam (and vice versa), the conflict's impact on local economic reform and development, the PLA's efforts to modernize itself and to restore its prestige in traditional terms, and the media's coverage of the conflict, including literature, movies, and music, and its influence on Chinese society in the 1980s. Through such examination, the chapter provides a better understanding of China and its development during Deng Xiaoping's reform era in the context of the border conflict with Vietnam.

Local Contributions, Sacrifices, and Legacies

Throughout the 1980s, economic reform was a dominant theme in government policies and people's lives in most parts of China. The military conflict with Vietnam diverted Guangxi and Yunnan Provinces from concentrating their efforts on economic reform. Their sacrifice ensured what Deng Xiaoping once called "a safe and stable" environment for other parts of China to pursue economic development. Moreover, the "people's war" doctrine required mobilizing local government and society to support the war, and China's border conflict with Vietnam was no exception. Prior to the invasion, each province established an office headed by a party secretary and a deputy governor charged with "aiding-the-front" work (*zhiqian gongzuo*). Its responsibilities included construction of roads, supplying troops with food and water, organizing locals to serve as stretcher bearers, and mobilizing militias to participate in the fight.

During the ten years of the border conflict with Vietnam, Guangxi and especially Yunnan played significant roles in mobilizing civilian support. In 1979, Guangxi drafted 2,700 local people from Napo, Jingxi, and Longzhou Counties to build a 52-kilometer road for military use. More than 40,000 people were called to help transport more than 150 tons of materials for the front.[3] Guangxi witnessed two major military operations (at Fakashan in 1981 and a 1984 artillery bombardment) along its border with Vietnam. Despite their limited scale, these two operations forced the removal of 27,000 border residents from their home villages and towns.[4] Each time the PLA prepared for military action on the border, the local governments were responsible for setting up service

Stretcher bearers carry wounded soldiers at Laoshan, 1985. Courtesy Wang Huazhang

stations (*gongyingzhan*) along the railroads and highways to supply the troops with food, water, and other materials.[5] The costs were borne by the local governments. Beginning in 1979, the Guangxi government spent more than $6.5 million for this purpose.[6] In 1984 alone, more than one hundred service stations were set up, providing about 8,000 tons of provisions for military forces.[7]

Yunnan differed from Guangxi in that it had a far longer involvement in the border war, supporting the front for more than a decade. Yunnan's experience evolved over three stages: the 1979 cross-border operations, territorial reclamation operations from 1980 to 1984, and border defensive operations from 1984 to 1989. Yunnan faced four challenges during these operations.[8] First, since military action was determined by what the central government in Beijing felt needed to be done along the Sino-Vietnamese border, local governments often had inadequate time to mobilize local support for the PLA's operations after Beijing had issued its orders. Second, Yunnan, a multiethnic frontier province, was economically and socially backward. Two of its border prefectures, Wenshan and Honghe, lacked both human and material resources. Third, military operations in the region's tropical jungle and mountainous terrain demanded the greatest dependency on local communities for support. For example, bringing one day's worth of supplies to the front for a single PLA soldier at the front required the work of 2.5 civilians. Eight to ten stretcher bearers were needed to bring one wounded soldier down through mountainous and jungle terrain, which was so thick and convoluted that progress averaged at most 200 meters per hour, which equates to just 11 feet per minute. Fourth, more than 1,000,000 troops deployed to Yunnan over the period, with a peak of more than 200,000 troops at one time. Such numbers severely taxed local governments' ability to provide fresh food, water, fuel, construction materials, and other daily necessities. To do so, more than a quarter million of Yunnan's border residents had to put aside their normal lives to participate in aid-the-front work.

Guangxi and Yunnan had previously served as the immediate rear for support to North Vietnam during the Vietnam War. At that time, for China's national defense, these two provinces had been designated not only as the front line but also as the "big third line" (*dasanxian*) and "big rear area" (*dahoufang*) in national development strategy.[9] This contradictory overlay of defensive structures placed Yunnan in an awkward situation. On the one hand, it had to concentrate resources to provide supplies for Vietnam. On the other hand, it had to develop itself into an industrial base to serve as a strategic reserve in the event that China became drawn into war. But by 1979, Yunnan's economy ranked among the lowest in China on the basis of per capita industrial output.[10] Despite Beijing's optimistic hopes, the third-line industrial enterprises in Yunnan (like most of their counterparts across the country), were unprofitable and inefficient precisely because they were located in remote regions, virtually ensuring that they would confront problems such as ever-increasing costs and (far more seriously) a lack of skilled workers and managers.[11]

At the beginning of the 1980s, the Chinese government readjusted its investment from concentration on third-line construction programs in the southwest to imported technology projects in the more highly developed and urbanized coastal areas. The war with Vietnam continued to force Yunnan's provincial government to devote its efforts to supporting military action along the border—this time, ironically, against rather than for Vietnam. In comparison, Guangxi's role in the aid-the-front work significantly declined after 1984, since most fighting occurred along the Yunnan-Vietnam border.[12]

In December 1978, the Yunnan provincial government established a special committee headed by a provincial party secretary in Kunming to lead local aid-the-front work. While the border conflict blazed up in 1984, Beijing launched a series of new policies to expand reforms in the areas of industry, commerce, science, and education. The Yunnan provincial government was required to form a joint group comprising members of party, government, and military officials to enhance Yunnan's aid-the-front efforts.[13] Beijing defined its mission as "fighting a long war [*changqi zuozhan*], providing support for the front for a long period of time [*changqi ziqian*], and ensuring supplies for [troops] over a long period of time [*changqi baozhang*]." The provincial government adopted a corresponding policy, the "Use of War to Promote [Economic] Development [*yizhan cujian*] and the Use of [Economic] Development to Support the War [*yijian baozhan*]."[14]

Under this policy, Yunnan's government continued to focus on providing support for military operations against Vietnam. The third-line ordnance enterprises went into accelerated production of various light weapons, including semiautomatic rifles, machine guns, antiaircraft machine guns, bullets, mortar shells, rocket-propelled grenades, hand grenades, and mines.[15] This military output allegedly had a significant influence on the PLA's conduct in the 1979 campaign against Vietnam. However, by 1985, these products were outdated and suffered from quality problems, requiring repairs and replacement parts.[16]

Because the battleground occupied a formidable terrain in the remote border region, transport posed a special challenge, threatening to prevent the flow of supplies to the front. The construction of highway networks was a high priority for local government authorities. Thousands of rural residents mobilized to build roads alongside troops and civil engineering technicians. A total of seventy-three roads with a length of 3,071 kilometers were built, including 330 kilometers of paved roads connecting the front with the rear. Water supply was a major problem for the troops at Laoshan, Zheyinshan, and Koulinshan, even near the city of Wenshan. Consequently, more than 70,000 meters of water supply pipes were laid and forty-nine water supply projects furnished water for the troops.[17]

Little information has been published to assess the repercussions of such activities on the local economy and life of Yunnan residents. Still, glimpses can be seen of the cascading effects and costs that Yunnan's devotion to Beijing's directives generated. For two years beginning in early 1979, Yunnan experienced a drought. The central government allotted Yunnan 1,000 tons of steel pipes from northern China to help local people secure water, but no rail transport was available to ship them to Yunnan because military trains had top priority.[18] When the crops failed as a result of the lack of water, food shortages in rural Yunnan ensued.[19]

Yunnan had been an economically backward province. With a large number of troops massing on its border with Vietnam throughout the 1980s, the local government at all levels faced soaring difficulties in supplying fresh vegetables and livestock for the military as well as for local residents. The provincial government adopted a food policy, "military first, civilian after" (also known as "the front first, the rear after").[20] Though farmers in the two border prefectures grew rice rather than vegetables, the provincial government requested in De-

A slaughtered pig being delivered to the troops at the Laoshan front, 1986. Courtesy Wang Huazhang.

cember 1981 that they switch to vegetables for the troops, offering subsidies of two hundred yuan per mu (Chinese acre).[21] Farmers who converted their rice paddies into vegetable plots were also exempted from state taxes on the sales of their grains. For Wenshan Prefecture, vegetable plots expanded from 282 acres in 1979 to 1,321 acres in 1988, but 60 percent of local vegetable consumption needs remained unsatisfied.[22]

Farmers also faced problems with cash shortages and a lack of knowledge about how to improve yields, forcing local governments to import food from other provinces and to institute a rationing program limited urban residents to 40 percent of their 1979 consumption levels.[23] Throughout the 1980s, Yunnan's urban dwellers lived on a per-person monthly quota of 12.5 kilos of staple food and .5 kilo of meat.[24] At the time of the emergency, the local government asked border villagers to "voluntarily" donate their rice, meat, and vegetables, often leaving them with corn as their main grain ration.[25] Because the local government could only provide 2.5 kilos of meat per soldier per month, PLA units had to grow vegetables and raise hogs to consume even during their tours of duty at the front, taking them away from military-related duties.[26]

Civilian sacrifice during the decadelong border conflict was enormous. Wenshan Prefecture alone suffered war-related economic losses amounting to almost $356 million, not including indirect costs.[27] Infrastructure development such as roads, reservoirs, and communication facilities did not help bring the border populations out of poverty.

Even worse, millions of land mines laid down by both sides took a huge toll among border civilians. (Artificial limbs and walking sticks reportedly are common in border villages.) From 1992 to 2007, the PLA conducted three major operations to sweep land mines along the border. More than 2.5 million mines and explosive devices have been removed, but because of the disturbing longevity of mines—a problem seen in other crisis regions such as the Falkland Islands and the Mideast—the danger to humans and livestock will continue for some time.[28]

The border region remains China's poorest locale.[29] In 1992, a reconstruction plan for the Wenshan war zone was adopted with the promise of a $360 million investment from the central and provincial governments. But only a little over one-third of this funding had arrived by 2002.[30] According to a 2007 study, three border counties—Maguan, Malipo, and Hekou—remained among China's most impoverished, with hundreds of thousands of dwellers living below the poverty line. Lack of water supply, electricity, and transportation remain major drawbacks in their lives. Residents even lacked access to Chinese television. People in the border region have always wondered why the government has not helped them cope with the deaths and injuries suffered during the war and why they still live in poverty under a state welfare program furnishing an annual income of just $25–40 per year. Not surprisingly, they repeatedly question whether they would be willing to fight another border war.[31]

Various aspects of history and bad government policies generated the misery that locals experienced both during and after the border war. The use of war to promote the economy (as advocated by both the central and local governments) failed to yield any benefits for the border region. It also meant that the policies of openness and market-based reform that steadily transformed the country did not come to Guangxi and Yunnan until the end of the conflict. Consequently, these two border provinces have lagged the coastal and central parts of China by at least ten years in economic and social development, and the gap not only remains but appears to be widening today.[32]

Border Conflicts and Military Reform

On 16 March 1979, Deng Xiaoping spoke to the CCP Central Committee about China's border war. He appeared gratified at the fact that Chinese troops had fought courageously and did not behave like "ducks" on the battlefield, even after experiencing heavy casualties. Nonetheless, the Chinese leader pointed out that the time had come for the PLA to make changes in matters pertaining to force structure, doctrine for army building, and training.[33] Deng's dissatisfaction with the military dated back to 1975, when he described the PLA as "swollen, slack, arrogant, extravagant, and lazy."[34] Several years later, the overgrown organization remained the PLA's biggest problem.

On 12 March 1980, at an enlarged CMC meeting, Deng expressed concerns about the ability of China's military forces to fight against a more powerful opponent than Vietnam. He warned his generals that a seriously bloated force "would be difficult to deploy and, needless to mention, to command in fighting a real war." Deng saw too many aging senior officers holding high-level positions and urged the generals to retire from their posts and select younger replacements.[35] Indeed, behind this rhetoric lay Deng's desire to select his own officials to command the PLA. First, he resigned as the chief of General Staff and passed the job of managing the PLA's daily affairs to Yang Dezhi, who served in the Second Field Army during the civil war. Deng then replaced all eleven military region commanders, selecting five men who had served under him in the Second Field Army. Finally, he appointed Yang Shangkun, who had worked under Deng from 1956 to 1966, as secretary-general of the CMC after Hua fell from power in December 1980. Two years later, Yang was appointed the CMC's first vice chair, in charge of military matters, freeing Deng to concentrate on other issues.

Deng also pushed to downsize the PLA and supported proposals to reorganize at least some land force armies and divisions into combined-arms forces. Referring to the problems the 1979 campaign had exposed, such as PLA officers unable to read maps or to fight with other support components, the Chinese leader was very critical of PLA training, which required troops only to practice marksmanship, throw grenades, and fight with bayonets. He urged the troops to train in combined arms and especially on air-ground coordination.[36]

The force structure of the PLA's field armies in the late 1970s and early 1980s had overwhelmingly emphasized infantry formations with few fire-support components. Its tank, artillery, and engineering corps were organized as independent arms under the command of the PLA's armor corps, artillery corps, and engineering corps. But shortly after the 1980 CMC meeting, sweeping changes were made in the leadership structures of all military regions, including most field armies and army corps.[37] The PLA downsized by a half million troops in 1980 and reorganized its component branches (tank, artillery, air defense, engineering, anti-chemical-warfare, and so forth) into combined-arms-focused field armies.[38] The demobilization did away with the headquarters organizations of these corps and incorporated their troops into field armies, with some tank and artillery divisions under the direct command of military regions.[39] In 1980, the CMC requested a budget of $27 billion. Vice Premier

Li Xianlian opposed this proposal because of national financial difficulties. To make better use of scarce government military funding after 1980, the CMC decided to reduce the size of the forces and improve the PLA's operational capabilities.[40]

In the early 1980s, Chinese military strategy remained predicated on the assumption of an eventual land war with the Soviet Union. But the PLA's poor performance in the 1979 war with Vietnam raised serious concerns about whether China was actually capable of fighting a war against the Soviet Union. At a senior officer seminar on defensive operations held by the PLA General Staff in October 1980, Marshal Ye Jianying stressed that an enemy invasion would come from land, air, and sea, so the future war would be "unprecedented three-dimensional, combined, and total warfare." "In terms of ground operations," he stated, China "would face a series of attacks by a mass of enemy tanks and have to fend off attacks by air-dropped and air-landed enemy forces." Deng Xiaoping added that these changes required the PLA infantries to train with tank, antiaircraft, and missile units.[41] All these talks prompted the PLA to adopt new requirements and new ways to train troops and carry out combined-arms exercises in the early 1980s.

New training requirements included the rejuvenation of the PLA officer corps, the improvement of education standards for officers, and training with modern concepts and methods that reflected combat lessons learned from the border war with Vietnam. According to the deputy chief of the General Staff, Zhang Zhen, the issue of training PLA troops to operate closely with artillery and tank support brooked no delay.[42] Beginning in 1980, military training took 70 percent of troops' time, with the remainder dedicated to political and cultural education. A series of exercises were conducted in a simulated battlefield environment with many features of modern warfare. For example, the first exercise, held near Luoyang in Henan in November, involved an infantry division (just returned from the border region) supported by air, artillery, and paratroop components as it trained to break through an enemy's defenses. This exercise could have been a reaction to the PLA's invasion of Vietnam, during which the air force did not provide support for infantry attacks and artillery and tanks had been relatively ineffective.[43]

The largest and most highly publicized exercise integrating forces from more than one service occurred northwest of Beijing near Zhangjiakou in September 1981. The scenario envisioned a possible Soviet invasion, and the PLA mobilized more than 100,000 to participate. War gamers simulated a tactical nuclear attack in accordance with the PLA's preparation for fighting "early war, major war, and nuclear war."[44] The exercise involved troops from different services, with each conducting separate tasks in close proximity to the others. Thus, the PLA began combined-arms warfare training.

After 1982, new training programs were developed and new training manuals were issued on such topics as "military training outlines for ground forces," "the decree of tactical exercises by combined arms," "provisions for troops' evaluation," and "operational support for infantry elements."[45] The General Staff also proposed eight large-scale exercises simulating the kind of defensive-offensive fight the Soviet Union had waged in the Second World War. The limited budget available to the military, however, forced the PLA to cancel or reschedule these exercises.[46] Under the new guidelines, PLA units trained themselves, emphasizing missions assigned to them in conjunction with the distinctive features of their designated combat areas.

According to a 1984 report by General Zhang Zhen, the training reforms featured several notable departures from previous practice: combined-arms campaigns; training under the rubric of the "three attacks, three defenses" ("attack tanks, attack aircraft, attack paratroops; defend against air strikes, defend against artillery fire, defend against nuclear and biochemical weapons"); and use of simulators and computer modeling. However, the PLA's traditionalist-minded troops did not seem enthusiastic about simulator training and expressed their dissatisfaction by storing these devices in warehouses. Not until 1989 did the use of simulators became universal in Chinese military training, far later than the world's other leading military forces.[47]

In his memoirs, Zhang Zhen mentioned that the border conflicts allowed the PLA to evaluate the quality of its training with results gained in actual combat, though he gave no other details.[48] The PLA 1st Division reported that the statistics from its operations at Laoshan demonstrated some continuing problems, including the failure to train individual soldiers with adequate basic combat skills. First, Chinese soldiers did not know how to defend themselves against the enemy's artillery fire, which inflicted more casualties than any other weapon on the Chinese forces, accounting for more than 80 percent of combat casualties. Second, they did not know how to conduct demining operations in a combat situation where both sides had laid more than 100,000 mines near and around their positions. As a result, mines constituted the second leading cause of PLA casualties. Third, Chinese soldiers exhibited potent marksmanship on the shooting range but had not been adequately trained to fire their weapons under complex and difficult combat conditions. Indeed, fire from light weapons accounted for only 2 percent of the PLA's total ammunition consumption in the war.[49]

According to a report, the Soviet-focused training program did not prepare the 1st Division troops for the rigors of a mountain and jungle fight amid a chain of undulating hills. It also revealed that despite the strong emphasis on combined-arms training, coordination was still lacking between attack groups, between different arms and services, and between combat and support teams. This problem highlighted the fact, as the report acknowledged, that the 1st Division's infantry units had never carried out any really meaningful combined-arms training against specialized aggressor forces (as with the U.S. Army at the National Training Center at Fort Irwin, California, or the U.S. Air Force's "Red Flags" held at Nellis Air Force Base in Nevada), instead simply using their own infantry units to play the role of other services.[50]

All these troubles indicated that the PLA's early reform efforts suffered from numerous constraints and obstacles that reflected both China's strategic outlook and the PLA's institutional culture. The assumption about an inevitable world war that would provoke China into an armed conflict against the Soviet Union remained dominant in China's strategic thinking throughout the first half of the 1980s. Military reform continued to center on the enhancement of the PLA's ability to conduct a limited, conventional war against the USSR. Deng Xiaoping had been displeased about the slow pace of reform, but he became a victim of this strategic calculus.[51]

Not until June 1985 did the Chinese leader began to accept that the danger of a Sino-Soviet war had receded.[52] In the face of stubborn and persistent opposition to any major changes inside the military, he then embarked on efforts to persuade the PLA to make the "strategic shift" from planning for "early war, major war, and nuclear war" to "army building in peacetime."[53] In retrospect, the real challenges faced by the PLA in its early reform were traditional concepts, older ways of doing things, and outdated organizational structures, all of which prevented the PLA from effectively addressing the problems that the 1979 campaign had exposed. For example, the PLA's draft and retirement cycle did not permit troops to learn the use of weapons other than their own, and insufficient time was allocated for coordinated unit training. The PLA's institutional culture had never encouraged individual initiative, exchange of information, and confidence in subordinates, so that few lower-level unit leaders demonstrated the ability to organize and conduct independent operations.[54]

Though the 1979 war with Vietnam was seen as the catalyst for the PLA's reform and modernization, the PLA was a long-established and tightly controlled institution, and any substantial changes and progress toward reform would require time. Not until 1985 did the CCP leadership officially decided to cut its overall strength by one million troops and reorganize land force armies into combined-arms-group armies. Eleven military regions merged into seven military regions, while thirty-five field armies were reduced to twenty-four.[55] The performance of each army and division in the 1979 campaign was examined to determine whether it should be demobilized or maintained.[56] Four armies that had seen combat in 1979 were on the list of troop reduction but survived thanks to the combat performance of some of their subordinate formations.[57] The ongoing border conflict did not spare the Kunming Military Region from the military cuts of the 1980s. On 30 June 1985, it deactivated and transferred its operational command to the Chengdu Military Region.[58]

Western scholarship has associated the PLA's Vietnam lessons with the Chinese leadership's 1985 reevaluation of the nature of modern war and the threats China faced and with efforts to streamline and professionalize the PLA throughout the 1980s.[59] At best, this characterization is only partially accurate. The PLA's Vietnam lessons and the continuing flare-ups on the Sino-Vietnamese border might have helped the Chinese leadership shift from an emphasis on preparing to fight total war to an emphasis on preparing for limited and local war.[60] But in reality, few efforts were made to correct China's flawed military thinking. Although the Chinese military became smaller and more streamlined, it contended with many of the same traditional constraints and obstacles for many years to come.[61] Not until the 1991 Gulf War shocked the PLA with a vision of a new air-driven, high-tech, precision-weapon, combined-arms war of rapid mobility did the Chinese military take seriously the challenge of readdressing the PLA's many shortfalls, beginning with the frank realization that China had fallen far behind in military modernization. Most of the lessons that it had learned from the border conflict with Vietnam were irrelevant, because the border battles had been fought with no air power and with few high-tech weapons systems. What the PLA had found most useful, as Zhang Zhen recalled, was employing reconnaissance brigades, establishing a precedent for the creation of PLA special operations forces later.[62]

Rebuilding the PLA's Public Image

On 3 March 1979, the PLA Daily newspaper carried a field report on its first page about the 43rd Army in the war against Vietnam. The article concluded, "Our border defense troops have not let the people's expectation down. Acting like the Chinese Volunteer Army in Korea, they are the most beloved people of the new generation of us" (women xinyidai zui ke'ai de ren).[63] The phrase "The most beloved people" first appeared in a famous essay written during the

Korean War to promote the Chinese military's public image. After Korea, it had become synonymous with the PLA.[64]

But popular attitudes toward the PLA underwent significant changes in the 1970s. During the Cultural Revolution, PLA forces were ordered to engage in the "three supports and two militaries" (*sanzhi liangjun*) task to stabilize political and social order across the country. As a result, thousands of PLA soldiers were brought into key administrative positions at all levels of government, including schools, factories, companies, villages, and farms. Abuses of power by military men became common and even included terrorizing civilians.[65] Civilian resentment of the PLA's political influence and high-handed behavior grew exponentially. By the eve of China's invasion of Vietnam, the PLA's reputation had been severely damaged. Part of Deng's motivation for sending in Chinese forces had been using war exploits to restore the PLA's reputation in the eyes of the Chinese people.[66]

According to Andrew Scobell, the Chinese people had little enthusiasm for the war, in part because of the PLA's unpopularity.[67] A series of efforts were made to mobilize public support. Military and civilian correspondents were sent to Guangxi and Yunnan to track down and report heroic deeds of Chinese soldiers; newspapers carried detailed and vivid descriptions of how Chinese soldiers sacrificed themselves in combat and defeated the enemies. When PLA forces returned from Vietnam, Beijing sent delegations headed by high-ranking CCP and government officials to convey greetings and official appreciation to troops in Guangxi and Yunnan. They distributed care packages and commemorative badges to the troops and arranged for entertainment by song-and-dance ensembles. In the two provinces' capital cities, local governments and military regions held rallies celebrating victories and conferring merit awards on more than 123,000 individual soldiers. Forty-four units and seventy-nine individual servicemen received the highest possible awards from the CMC.[68] Deng Xiaoping and other leaders in Beijing were closely involved in promoting the PLA's war exploits, personally calling on the party, the military, and the country to learn from the troops and militias who participated in combat. They invited PLA and militia heroes to Beijing to tell their stories and then sent them to other parts of the country to give the same reports to more than 4.35 million listeners.[69]

In the early 1980s, further efforts were made to restore the PLA's public image. One was the release of military resources to support economic construction. A number of airfields, ports, rail lines, communication lines, warehouses, and barracks were subsequently made available for civilian or joint military-civilian use. Thousands of PLA soldiers also took part in the construction of key economic projects, including airports, railroads, highways, oil fields, coal mines, power plants, dams, reservoirs, and water supply systems.[70] In Ellis Joffe's words, these undertakings sought primarily to "restore the PLA to its traditional role of assisting the population in times of need rather than ruling over it."[71] The PLA's involvement in the "socialist spiritual civilization" program constituted another effort to play a positive role in society. Worrying about China's reform and about the insertion of "decadent" ideas from the outside world that would work against communist ideology and socialist morality, Deng endorsed "economic construction as the 'core' and spiritual civilization as an 'important guarantee' of China's socialist modernization."[72] The PLA actively involved itself in a joint effort with local governments and communities to build civilized "factories, villages, towns."[73]

The official history of the PLA recorded impressive achievements in improving civil-military relations, yet the impact of these efforts on the military's public image remained ambiguous.[74] Under the influence of traditional culture, military service was often ridiculed as inferior in Chinese society, a view evident in a popular proverb: "Good iron never turns into nails; good men never enlist as soldiers" (*haotie bu dading; haonan bu dangbing*).[75] Since the founding of the People's Republic, the PLA had been a social channel for peasant youth to move out of rural poverty by taking up other professions and eventually becoming urban residents. One Chinese American scholar observes that after the mid-1980s, PLA recruiting officers faced unprecedented obstacles in convincing young peasants to join the military because economic reforms opened up new opportunities.[76] Indeed, the population's attitude toward the military changed significantly under the influence of the market economy, which enriched many individuals overnight.[77] Many people considered joining the army unthinkable and began to call PLA soldiers "*dabing*" (big soldier), a derogatory slur used to refer to military service, which no longer enjoyed public favor.[78]

In response, officials renewed the emphasis on propaganda about the PLA's heroic exploits in the recent border conflict with Vietnam as a means of inspiring patriotism and revolutionary heroism and promoting a better understanding of the military among the populace. Again, PLA heroes and model soldiers were invited to Beijing to speak about their heroic deeds in the Great Hall of the People, where only important party and state events were held. Yang Shangkun, the CMC's vice chair, complimented the troops and their exemplary deeds on the battlefield as the best manifestation of Deng Xiaoping's Five Revolutionary Spirits.

College students at Xi'an rail station welcome troops returned from Laoshan, 1986.
Courtesy Wang Huazhang.

In 1985, the CCP's propaganda department and the PLA's political department intensified the campaign by sending war heroes and model soldiers selected from the entire armed forces to lecture around the country.[79] Unlike in the past, audience members included primarily young people and college students, who were considered increasingly "cynical, materialistic, and hedonistic" and significantly "less idealistic" than previous generations, making them "targets" for a traditionalist reeducation by exposure to China's military heroes.[80] The stories of honorees were presented in very powerful terms to evoke emotional responses. Students were encouraged to show their appreciation for the role of the Chinese military; in one case, the students from Shenyang Music College performed a series of songs dedicated to the soldiers from the southern border as an expression of their gratitude. In another instance, student representatives of Shandong University presented a military delegation with a silk banner inscribed, "Long Live Soldiers."[81]

One well-known story highlighting the effects of the campaign involves a college student from Xi'an Music College, Xu Liang. He had been selected to be a member of a delegation sent to Laoshan to express appreciation to the troops in late 1985. There, he requested to join the military to stay at the front. On the evening of 2 May 1986, Vietnamese troops launched a surprise attack on his unit's positions. He and his squad were sent to reinforce the front positions, and he was involved in a firefight with three Vietnamese soldiers, losing one of his legs. As a first-class war hero, he was sent to tour the country and tell stories about how he had "matured" from a college student into a war hero. Central television invited Xu Liang to be a special guest at its 1987 New Year's gala, during which he sang "Blood-Stained Valor," written to commemorate those who died in the war with Vietnam. He became a well-known figure, and his compelling story and singing struck a deep chord with many people, generating a new round of public admiration for soldiers.[82]

But this wave of adulation for the military as a model worthy of emulation by the nation did not last very long. The attractiveness and cohesiveness of the armed forces steadily eroded under the impact of the market economy. Fewer soldiers joined the PLA during the 1980s than at any previous time. Outright dissention appeared in the ranks. In one case, after receiving orders to go to Laoshan, the 27th Group Army (one of the best forces in the PLA's history), experienced unprecedented morale and disciplinary problems. A number of soldiers went AWOL, giving such excuses as they needed to see their parents or wanted to get married before being killed or wounded in combat. Traditionally, they would have been punished as deserters, but not this time: no serious disciplinary actions were taken against them. Some soldiers also wrote letters to their hometown governments requesting specific help resolving their families' difficulties. To them, their sacrifice on the battlefield made them deserving of special care from local governments, particularly since other people were living in peace and happiness and becoming prosperous while the soldiers were risking life and limb at the front.[83]

One PLA writer commented that it was inevitable that soldiers sent to Laoshan saw the great disparity of individual destiny between those who shed their blood at the front and those who lived in peace and prosperity in the rear. During the Korean War and the 1962 border conflict with India, PLA soldiers had been driven by a strong political consciousness that regarded the defense of the motherland as their sacred duty. The introduction of the commodity economy significantly undermined soldiers' faith in this PLA tradition.[84] The deterioration of the PLA tradition became increasingly apparent. On one occasion, a regiment of the 67th Army rotating out of the border fighting requested that an incoming regiment from the 47th Army pay $1,500 for all intelligence information pertaining to the enemy's firepower sites, artillery positions, and sapper activities.[85] On another occasion, an armor unit did not receive care packages sent from the rear and dispatched armored vehicles to surround an infantry division headquarters post, demanding their fair share.[86]

Corruption further undermined troops' confidence in leadership and morale as war-weariness grew. According to one 1987 report to the CMC, a young PLA officer, the son-in-law of President Li Xiannian, reported that morale had not been a problem in the 1979 military campaign but was a major problem in Laoshan. According to his report, in 1984–85, only officers above regimental level wanted to fight because they faced fewer hazards than officers at battalion and company levels. In 1987, the whole group army, from the bottom to the top, was not enthusiastic about continuing the fight.[87] After returning to its home barracks in northern China, the 27th Group Army surveyed 186 veterans from Laoshan, asking questions such as, "What issues are you most concerned about? What do you want from the army? What suggestions can you give to the military?" Respondents' answers indicated that they wanted to leave the service.[88]

By the late 1980s, whatever efforts had been made to restore the PLA's image in the eyes of the public appeared insufficient to turn the tide of negative public opinion. Economic reform had created a new social ethos that not only championed the idea that "to get rich is glorious" but also legitimized and promoted "self-serving behavior."[89] As a result, the traditional propaganda efforts of the past seemed inadequate to provide solutions for boosting the PLA's morale and public image as they had during the Mao era. The author of a 1988 report discovered that public sentiment regarding servicemen was completely different when the troops departed for Laoshan and when they returned to their home base. College students and young people were eager to get better jobs and earn extra income, not serve in the military. Local government officials reneged on promises of jobs for soldiers who received merit awards, telling them that the rapid economic reforms prevented them from honoring those commitments. After returning from Laoshan to their home barracks, many soldiers found that those who had not joined the service or who had left the service earlier enjoyed much better economic and living conditions.[90] The use of the expression "soldier of Laoshan" to promote PLA personnel as the "most beloved people of the new generation" never caught on as a patriotic crusade.[91] The public image of the PLA deteriorated even further after troops were sent to stop the Tiananmen protests of 1989, and media—including Chinese internal media—showed pictures of tanks confronting peaceful demonstrators.

Literature, Movies, and Songs on "Self-Defense Counterattack"

The CCP had a tradition of using cultural artifacts, including novels, stories, films, and songs, to help shape the minds and hearts of the people and evoke the war as a convenient wellspring of nationalism and patriotism. The 1980s saw the rise of literature, movies, and songs about the border conflict with Vietnam, with themes depicting the sacrifice of PLA soldiers and their heroic battles with the enemy. Writers, especially military writers, were embedded with troops on the front lines in Guangxi and Yunnan and conducted extensive interviews with soldiers to learn their personal stories. Like anywhere else in the world where war literature serves as propaganda, such stories were used to manipulate public opinion about China's war with Vietnam.

LITERATURE

The first novel of the "self-defense counterattack" was Xu Huaizhong's *Xixian yishi* (*Anecdotes of the Western Front*, 1980), which appeared in the first issue of *Renmin wenxue* (*People's Literature*). The story is not about battles or heroes but about six female telephone soldiers and their own and their family's responses to the war. The best-known literature on the 1979 war is Li Cunbao's *Gaoshan xia de huahuan* (*Wreaths of Flowers at the Foot of the Mountains*, 1982), which first appeared in a bimonthly literary journal in Beijing and was then reprinted in more than fifty other periodicals and magazines across the country.[92] The author illustrates the war through personal accounts, an approach that counteracted the growing apathy toward the stereotypical hero character in communist literature and meshed with the increased interest in characters with individual personalities. The story involves one PLA company in the 1979 war, and the protagonists are ordinary soldiers shaped by the social and economic conditions of the time rather than superheroes. The plot resonated with Chinese readers as if it was their own life story.

Li's works touched on corrupt social tendencies among those who had power to use the back door (*kaihoumen*) for their personal interests. The mother of the company's political instructor, a high-ranking cadre's wife, attempts to use her personal connections with the military to get her son transferred before he is sent to war. Another aspect of Li's novel was the sad reality that the military was an unappreciated profession at the time. The author revealed that Chinese servicemen were underpaid and often found themselves buried deep in debt and unable to support their families. When the company leader is killed in combat, he leaves his mother, wife, and baby son one frock, two sets of used uniforms, and a bloodstained note showing that a debt of more than $380—ten times his monthly salary.

Li also indirectly criticizes the arbitrary organizational culture of the Chinese military. The deputy company leader grumbles and criticizes his superiors. He fights bravely in the war but is killed in a mine blast on his way back from fetching a bundle of sugarcane to help slake his soldiers' thirst. The violation of the "Three Main Rules of Discipline and Eight Points for Attention" plus his unpleasant personality cost him his merit award even though his company recommends him for the honor.[93]

Subsequent novels about the 1979 war failed to achieve the same popularity as Li Cunbao's works. Despite the popularity of *Wreaths of Flowers*, the PLA's 1 August Movie Studio, which specializes in military films, refused to make it into a movie because producers worried that the novel exposed too many dark aspects of the Chinese society and military as well as poverty in rural areas—in short, that such a film could "discredit" the Communist Party and socialism.[94] A subsequent movie version of *Wreaths of Flowers* by a nonmilitary filmmaker exploited the emotions of cinemagoers across China.[95]

Concerns about war literature's unsuitability for propaganda purposes soon became reality. Chinese leaders voiced increasing criticism of authors who were "eager to write their works gloomily and pessimistically." According to Deng, such writings "recklessly concocted the history of revolution" and contained false versions of "what really happened." The danger of these writings, the Chinese leader continued, was that they cast doubts on the future of socialism, thereby sowing confusion in people's minds and preventing them from correctly understanding many problems in socialist society.[96] He therefore labeled such phenomena "spiritual pollution" and called for a vigorous ideological campaign "to overcome weakness, laxity, and liberal attitudes."[97]

At the same time, the Chinese leader expressed his gratitude to those who engaged in "literary reportage" (*baogao wenxue*), which informed "the new life of socialism," "inspired the revolutionary spirit of our youth and the people," and thus "motivated them to courageously devote themselves to the construction and struggle of the fatherland in all spheres."[98] Literary reportage is the "writing of real people and real events directly drawn from actual life . . . reported quickly and in time with proper artistic processing to serve the current political purposes."[99] The first publication that resembled literary reportage on the 1979 war was *Yingxiong zan* (*Ode to the Heroes*, 1979) compiled by the political department of the Guangzhou Military Region. A collection of stories about individuals and units that fought "heroically" against Vietnam, it constitutes more of a propaganda piece than a literary work.[100] Not until the late 1980s and early 1990s did literary reportage on the border war become available publicly. The representative works are *Yibaishuan yanjing* (*Hundred Eyes*, 1989), an account of the 14th Army's involvement in the Laoshan battles; *ZhongYue zhanzheng milu* (*A Secret Record of the Sino-Vietnamese War*, 1990); and *Keyi gongkai de conglin mizhan* (*A Secret Jungle War That Can Be Publicized*, 1991), concerning the 27th Group Army's involvement in the border conflict in 1987–88.[101]

On the one hand, these works of literary reportage take a patriotic tone, using political and ideological vocabularies to glorify the PLA's performance and emphasize its connections to its revolutionary tradition. On the other, they reveal the cruelty and viciousness of armed conflict and the fear, confusion, and loneliness experienced by soldiers in caves on Laoshan. Information in these accounts comes from personal memoirs as well as from Chinese military archives. Many Chinese find these works novel and informative.

The 1980s witnessed a marked increase in literature by military writers with access to military records. They, like their civilian counterparts, wrote more freely because of China's gradual political relaxation and opening-up policy. They were very critical about the "doing everything for money" phenomenon and its impact on military service.[102] One shocking disclosure was the surge in prostitution in the Laoshan war zone and the failure of the PLA's traditional iron discipline to control soldiers' sexual desire in the face of death.[103] China's war with Vietnam remains a sensitive subject for Chinese authorities. In an effort to keep this history from being forgotten, reportage continues to serve as a platform that enables participants in the 1979 war to offer their side of the story.[104] Unfortunately, their impact remains limited, and they are unlikely to create the same level of enthusiasm as did the writing from the Korean War.

CINEMA

China's war with Vietnam provided a golden opportunity for moviemakers to promote the party-advocated spirit of revolutionary heroism to a wider audience. By 1989, nearly twenty films had been produced, about half of them centering on the theme of revolutionary heroism, much like other PRC war films. Some simply duplicated popular Korean War movies such as *Yingxiong ernü* (*The Heroic Sons and Daughters*), attesting that the young people in the 1980s, like their predecessors thirty years earlier, unhesitatingly devoted their lives to their country.[105] These movies, however, failed to excite audiences and draw mass attraction.

One film deserving of attention is an educational movie by the PLA, *Changpaishan zhi zhan* (*The Battle of Changpaishan*, 1981), based on the operations of the 41st Army's 122nd Division against the PAVN's 246th Regiment in the Troung Bach Son Mountain region (around Soc Giang, a strategic position that screens Cao Bang from the north). It is unclear why such an operation was selected as a textbook case for military education purposes, but it might reveal the PLA's perception that the war against Vietnam was a small-unit operation despite the involvement of a large number of PLA forces.

The mid-1980s saw a trend toward free expression in literature and the arts, and humanism became the main theme of the self-defense counterattack movies. The movie *Wreaths of Flowers at the Foot of the Mountains* differed from the traditional Chinese military genre in that Chinese soldiers were portrayed not as transcendent heroes but rather as real humans with passion and compassion. After 1986, war movies began to emphasize humanity, especially human nature and human feelings in peace and war, death and life, and honor and dishonor. The archetypical new-genre war film is *Leichang xiangsishu* (*The Lives They Left Behind*, 1988), in which five military academy cadets are sent to Laoshan, where they confront the issue of how people should live and act when they are subject to imminent death. Despite the movie's positive aspects, it is still a propaganda film that served the party's call for promoting the "Laoshan spirit"—"to sacrifice oneself to bring happiness to one billion people" (*xisheng woyige xingfu shiyi ren*).[106]

The boldest new cinematic works on the war with Vietnam are *Gezhi shu* (*Tree of Pigeons*, 1985) and *Tamen zheng nianqing* (*They Are Young*, 1986), neither of which passed the communist censors to be shown in theaters. Both movies were criticized for undermining the PLA's glorious image and questioning the just nature of the war. *Tree of Pigeons* features a Vietnamese female soldier who encounters three PLA soldiers on the battlefield. She saves the lives of two wounded PLA soldiers but is killed by the third. They later bury her with grief and respect. *They Are Young* tells the story of nine Chinese soldiers defending a frontline position. For three months, they live in a limestone cave with no sunlight, suffering from malnutrition and lack of sleep. Fatigue makes them slow on the draw, and their faces look dull and lifeless, even hysterical. The use of aesthetic evocations to underline soldiers' humanity and the cruelty of war apparently was deemed inconsistent with official propaganda (a positive theme of correctness in the party's policy and social development).

MUSIC AND SONGS

The genres of music and song reached a wider audience than written literature and movies, particularly among young Chinese. More than one hundred songs have featured lyrics extolling PLA border defense troops and their victories over the enemy and expressing hatred toward the Vietnamese aggressors.[107] Most of these songs are overburdened with standardized, repetitive rhetoric, making them predictable and ultimately uninteresting. A few exceptions offer rich, robust folk melodies delivered with passion and a spontaneous playfulness. The most popular songs are "The Moon on the Fifteenth" (*Shiwu de yueliang*, 1984) and "The Blood-Stained Valor" (*Xueran de fengcai*, 1987), which focus on the inner world of the PLA soldiers rather than on stereotyped heroes and fallen soldiers.[108] "The Moon on the Fifteenth" expresses soldiers' longing for spouses. The songwriter was inspired by Sung Dynasty poet Su Shi's

"Though miles apart, could men but live forever dreaming they shared this moonlight endlessly."[109] This sentimental song affectionately portrays the agony of separation in strong nationalistic tones:[110]

> The moon on the fifteenth of every month sheds light
>> on the home and the border;
> We are missing each other on the tranquil night.
> You are sitting on the side of baby's cradle,
> I am patrolling along the borderline of the motherland.
> You are plowing the fields at home,
> I am on guard duty at the border.
> Ah, the fruits of your labor, while making you feel sweet,
>> also make me feel sweet.
> Ah, the medal of honor I received, while belonging to me,
>> also belongs to you.[111]

Economic reform brought strong commercial consciousness to Chinese society while severely weakening the communist political tradition, which always highlighted contributions and sacrifices. Fighting on Laoshan, PLA soldiers faced a sharp contrast between their difficult and lonely lives on the front lines and the colorful, contented lives and economic prosperity enjoyed at home. "The Blood-Stained Valor," which puts forth a particularly positive message, uses an elegiac approach to help audiences understand why soldiers fought against Vietnam:[112]

> Perhaps I will bid farewell, never to return,
> Can you comprehend? Do you understand?
> Perhaps I will fall, never to rise again,
> Do you still want to wait forever?
> If it is to be like this,
> Do not be sad; the flag of the republic has our
>> blood-stained valor.[113]

In traditional communist music, war was a description of "a series of abstractions: loyalty, devotion, courage, and sacrifice."[114] The songwriter of "The Blood-Stained Valor" used questions and what-ifs to manipulate images and words to sway public sentiment in favor of China's ongoing war effort.[115] In the 1980s, young Chinese people were interested in music from Hong Kong and Taiwan, but this song somehow became a favorite, with emotional resonance for thousands of Chinese people.[116]

Today, the war with Vietnam is forgotten history in China. Chinese intellectuals are prohibited from writing about the subject, and official media have not disseminated literature and movies about the war. Nonetheless, people still enjoy the music, which not only reminds them of this particular time in history and its political implications but also evokes a sense of nationalism with contemporary meaning. Indeed, today's communist propaganda machine continues to use many of these songs for political purposes, and the phrase "blood-stained valor" frequently appears as an ongoing characterization of heroic and patriotic deeds.[117]

Conclusion

China's invasion of Vietnam triggered an enduring and malicious border conflict between the two countries. Its influence on the home front, its interaction with military modernization, and its cultural legacy cannot be neglected. While most of China was engaged in economic reforms, the border war with Vietnam forced Guangxi and especially Yunnan Provinces to commit enormous human and material resources to support military operations. Although the reasons for the region's backwardness were multifaceted, the border conflict certainly took a huge toll on its economic and social development. The government policy was truly questionable. Throughout the border conflict, the central and local governments invested billions of Chinese yuan in military action along the border. However, funding for postconflict reconstruction was tardy and unsatisfactory.

The flaws in the PLA's force structure and training exposed in the 1979 war served as motivations for military reforms in the 1980s. Two factors hampered military changes, which initially seemed slow and ineffective. The strategic outlook of Chinese leaders, which focused on potential conflict with the USSR, was misleading, leading the PLA to continue to prepare for a conflict resembling the Second World War. Such an outlook had little utility for troops deployed to the border. The PLA's institutional culture was most comfortable doing things in traditional ways and mustered little enthusiasm for innovation. The border conflict allowed Deng Xiaoping to gain full control of the PLA so that he could convince the military leadership accept significant reductions in military expenditures to support economic reform. The Chinese military also used the border conflict to train troops in real combat conditions. Numerous constraints and obstacles confronted the PLA's efforts in all aspects of military modernization, but the Gulf War demonstrated that post–Cold War armed conflict was most likely to be local war and that technology and information would play critical roles.[118] Most of the lessons learned by the PLA from the border conflict became extraneous because they represented war in an increasingly bygone era.

The war with Vietnam offered an opportunity to rebuild the PLA's reputation, which had been severely damaged during the Cultural Revolution. The military's wartime exploits were deliberately used to rejuvenate public affection for the PLA. The lamentable and increasing tendency to "worship money" brought ideological indifference and a decline in patriotism, which doomed the public love for and interest in the "most beloved people of a new generation." The deleterious effects of economic reform also seriously eroded morale and discipline. Soldiers and their families perceived their lives in the 1980s as a tale of two different worlds, one filled with fear, uncertainty, confusion, and the anguish of separation, the other featuring peace and prosperity.

Even sadder, the 12,192 dead buried in the Sino-Vietnamese War cemeteries in Guangxi and Yunnan have no place in official Chinese history, and their stories (despite widespread propaganda efforts at the time) are rarely mentioned in public media today. Most of them came from poor rural families and died before their twentieth birthdays. When they devoted their lives to the war with Vietnam, they were convinced that their sacrifice was equivalent to those who gave their lives in the anti-Japanese war, the liberation war against the Nationalists, and the war assisting North Korea against America and its UN allies. Today's China continues to commemorate those wars on every anniversary, but not its border war against Vietnam. Once popular literary works on the self-defense counterattack against Vietnam have never been reprinted; official media never show movies that at one time were widely distributed. From Beijing's perspective, the Sino-Vietnamese conflict has turned into a political taboo, and any discussion of the conflict is perceived as having an unhealthy influence on today's Sino-Vietnamese relations. Many Chinese continue to wonder whether the conflict was worthwhile. The answer to that sobering question still awaits a verdict. But at the time, the Chinese leadership was certainly convinced that the war against Vietnam was commendable and, above all, just.

8 The Road to Conflict Termination

China's decision to use military force to counter Vietnam's "hegemony" was largely based on the Chinese leadership's calculation of a serious evolving Soviet threat to its geopolitical interests. Vietnam's invasion of Cambodia was regarded as a key component of a broader Soviet scheme to encircle China. Such concerns continued to drive China's hostile policy toward Vietnam after 1979.

Although Beijing ended its invasion of Vietnam the same year that it began, China became bogged down in an enervating border conflict for more than a decade, mainly as a consequence of Vietnam's continuing occupation of Cambodia. Although China enjoyed a military advantage over Vietnam along the border, military means alone were not sufficient to resolve the differences between the two communist nations. The smoldering conflict inevitably degenerated into a stalemate on the battlefield, costing lives and resources far beyond the battlefield and affecting regional food production, industrialization, and even public health and sanitation.

Because the war was fought for political rather than military objectives, both belligerents ultimately had to return to diplomacy. The road to terminating hostilities between Beijing and Hanoi proved long and tortuous, and progress was slow. One contributing factor was China's unwavering insistence on Vietnam's withdrawal from Cambodia as a prerequisite for the resumption of Sino-Vietnamese relations. The process of Vietnam's withdrawal began with renewed attempts by Beijing and Moscow to improve their relations. Only under that larger umbrella did termination of Sino-Vietnamese hostility become possible. Although Deng Xiaoping slowly revised his view of an imminent Soviet threat, he did not change his position on Cambodia throughout the 1980s. Not until a new Hanoi leadership withdrew its forces from Cambodia and then accepted Deng's regional security model/framework—a neutral Southeast Asia—did the PRC agree to normalize its relations with the SRV.

Then came 1989, when the Warsaw Pact shattered and the Soviet threat to Western Europe ended. New evidence from China supports an argument that the collapse of the communist bloc in Eastern Europe played a decisive role in motivating Hanoi to change its policy, thus smoothing the road to a conclusion of the Cold War between the two Asian communist countries. Although both sides claimed victory following the resumption of Sino-Vietnamese relations after thirteen years of hostility, Vietnamese leaders' 1990 trip to China encouraged their Chinese counterparts to believe that they had triumphed. China's national priority—economic development—did not depend on either Vietnam or Cambodia. Beijing was in a most advantageous position to demand political concessions from Hanoi. Nonetheless, the termination of hostilities likewise served Hanoi's long-term strategic interests—Vietnam's own economic reform.

Deng Xiaoping and the PRC Play the Soviet Card

Sino-Vietnamese hostility to a large extent arose out of China's perception of an imminent Soviet threat to the PRC. The Soviet-Vietnamese alliance in the late 1970s strengthened this fear. From Beijing's perspective, the Soviet Union encouraged Hanoi's aggression in the region—the most important cause of China's determined opposition to Vietnam. Thus, any effort to terminate Sino-Vietnamese hostility had to start with improving Sino-Soviet relations, which "were mired in a quagmire."[1] Some officials from the ministry of foreign affairs saw an opportunity to reduce tensions between China and the Soviet Union when the 1950 Sino-Soviet treaty expired in the spring of 1979. But Deng found this view naive given that the Soviet Union had turned itself into the most hostile force faced by China, surpassing even the United States.[2] Deng thus directed the foreign ministry not to extend the treaty after it expired, but he also approved ministry plans to engage in a new round of talks with the Soviets.[3]

At a 29 August 1979 Politburo meeting, Deng set forth principles to guide China's future negotiations with the Soviet Union. China should not agree to normalize relations until the Soviet Union withdrew its forces from Mongolia and ended its support of Vietnam's invasion of Cambodia. Furthermore, the PRC and USSR should agree not to send threatening military forces to or set up military bases in neighboring countries. Deng concluded that he did not believe a deal could be reached via negotiation; rather, any agreement would have to come from a realistic appreciation of China's strategic perspective and needs. The Chinese chief negotiator must stick to principles rooted in strategic considerations.[4]

Sino-Soviet talks began in October 1979, but no progress occurred, and talks were suspended indefinitely after the Soviet invasion of Afghanistan the following December.[5] China accused the Soviet Union of stalling by refusing to discuss the removal of Soviet forces from Mongolia and Vietnamese forces from Cambodia. In light of the perception that the Soviet Union was China's primary enemy, negotiations between the two countries may have been doomed to failure.

Even so, a start had been made, and Qian Qichen, former minister of foreign affairs, rightly asserts that the 1979 Sino-Soviet talks marked the beginning of a new phase in relations between the two countries.[6] Based on the recollections of ex-diplomats, Chinese scholar Niu Jun concludes that the abolition of the Sino-Soviet alliance treaty offered an opportunity for both countries to seek détente.[7] But this perception greatly annoyed Deng Xiaoping. In 1980, he criticized such "silly" notions, reminding listeners that he understood the Soviet Union better than others because he had visited Moscow seven times to debate Soviet "revisionists" since 1956. The Soviet invasion of Afghanistan reinforced Deng's belief that the Soviet Union would start a war against China in 1985. By that time, he believed, the Soviet Union's domestic problems would become increasingly acute, Soviet military expansion would be complete, and the Soviet state would be ready to go to war to alleviate its growing domestic crisis. Deng believed that Moscow lacked any sincere desire to improve bilateral relations between the two countries, as evidenced by the more than one million Soviet troops stationed on the Chinese border.[8] Given Deng's intense feelings, China's initial effort to negotiate with the Soviet Union may have been window dressing, designed more to counter accusations that Beijing was not taking steps to resolve tensions than to reach a lasting resolution.[9]

In late 1980, Beijing felt that Moscow had to remedy three obstacles hindering improved Sino-Soviet relations: (1) the pullback of the Soviet military presence from the Chinese border, (2) the removal of Soviet forces from Mongolia, and (3) the cessation of Soviet support for Vietnam's occupation of Cambodia. On 11 February 1981, Deng Xiaoping stated that China could not improve relations with the Soviet Union until these obstacles were addressed.[10] In 1982, China added the Soviet invasion of Afghanistan as a new obstacle to negotiations with the Soviets while combining the first two original obstacles into one.

The same year, Soviet leader Leonid Brezhnev delivered a conciliatory speech at Tashkent, prompting Beijing to make corresponding conciliatory responses. China's adjustments in its policy toward the Soviet Union came as Beijing was becoming increasingly frustrated about the one-China policy pursued by the United States. After attempting to forge a strategic relationship with the United States, Beijing was disappointed that Washington continued to sell sophisticated weapons systems to Taiwan during the early years of the Reagan administration.[11] Early in the summer of 1981, Washington informed Beijing of its continued intention to treat China as "a friendly nation with which the United States is not allied but with which it shares many interests," but Chinese leaders remained determined to improve Sino-Soviet relations as a counterbalance to what they perceived as the unfavorable direction of Sino-American relations in the Reagan era.[12]

Some Chinese leaders, including Hu Yaobang, secretary-general of the party, became increasingly suspicious that the prevalent PRC conception of the Soviet threat was wrong. Having swung away from the anti-Americanism of the 1950s and early 1960s, they now swung back to a more suspicious view of Washington, recognizing that the United States could pose a threat to China should American leaders pursue a hegemonic policy in Asia.[13] Even more crucial, the Beijing leadership no longer defined the global strategic posture as bound on one hand by Soviet aggression and on the other by U.S. retrenchment.[14] Thus, in a changing security environment, Beijing decided to shift China's foreign policy toward a more balanced approach that included Sino-Soviet détente.[15]

Accordingly, Chinese leaders embarked on a new round of talks with the Soviet Union to be held in Moscow between 5 and 21 October 1982. Understanding that three obstacles (Cambodia, border forces, and Afghanistan) could not be resolved at the same time, the Chinese special envoy proposed that both sides first try to tackle Vietnam's occupation of Cambodia. From a Chinese point of view, the Soviet Union had no vital interest in Cambodia but could use its influence to stop the occupation, ending the Cambodian people's suffering. The Soviets maintained that their country posed no threat to China and that the talks should not proceed with a prerequisite that harmed the interests of a third party. The Soviet chief negotiator then suggested that the two countries concentrate on the draft of a framework document to guide Sino-Soviet relations. No further progress occurred on the three obstacle issues over the next four years, though negotiations were periodically held in both capital cities.[16]

China attributed the deadlock to the frequent change in Kremlin leadership: the deaths of so many aging Soviet leaders during these years became an international joke.[17] This leadership instability prevented the Soviet Union from making policy changes.[18] China also stood firm in negotiations because its leaders believed that the Soviet geostrategic position had become less favorable and that the PRC thus had no need to make concessions. According to Deng Xiaoping, Moscow's weakness became evident when the Soviet Union failed to respond strongly to Israel's invasion of Lebanon in 1983. He construed that this weaker position made the Soviet Union eager to improve its relations with China.[19] The Chinese leader held a strong stance against the Soviet Union because he believed that China's economic development did not require anything from Moscow; therefore, concessions at the negotiating table were the only thing the Soviets could offer China.[20]

More important, while others might be changing their thinking, Deng had not changed his mind about the Soviet threat to China. On 18 April 1985, the Chinese leader told former British prime minister Edward Heath that Moscow's strategic posture remained the biggest menace to China and that liquidation of the "three obstacles" would free China from such a hazard. Deng maintained that the easiest way for Moscow to tackle the obstacles was to persuade Vietnam to withdraw from Cambodia.[21] By the fall of 1985, Deng's unfaltering view was quite evident—the resolution of the Indochina problem was China's priority in the ongoing negotiations with the Soviets.[22] On 9 October, Deng asked Romanian President Nicolai Ceauşescu to tell the new Soviet leader, Mikhail Gorbachev, that either Deng or secretary-general Hu Yaobang was available to attend a Sino-Soviet summit, provided that the Soviet Union could come to an agreement with China on Vietnam's withdrawal from Cambodia.[23] This position represented a major change in China's Soviet policy, which was no longer focused on "three obstacles" but instead primarily interested in resolving the Indochina issue.

What could explain this change in China's attitude? The ongoing military conflict in the region evidently did not serve China's strategic interests, constituting a serious distraction at a time when the PRC was devoting every effort to achieve Deng's Four Modernizations. As one Chinese diplomat later recalled, "Who wanted to go to war over Cambodia again?"[24] Other pressures came from the ASEAN countries, which refused to include the "egregious" Khmer Rouge as part of the post-Vietnamese-occupation political process in Cambodia.[25] However, Beijing remained uncompromising on the Cambodia issue and particularly on the Khmer Rouge. Deng Xiaoping had never thought highly of the Khmer Rouge, and its "procrustean" policies often reminded him of his suffering during the Cultural Revolution.[26] But this feeling was tempered by the idea of Hanoi's regional hegemony. He did not believe that other resistance groups could defeat the Vietnamese occupiers. Any approach to resolving the Cambodia issue without the Khmer Rouge, which had the largest and best organized forces, would weaken the resisting groups.[27] Deng nevertheless would not object if the Khmer Rouge were defeated in a free election.[28]

Despite remaining steadfast on Cambodia, the Chinese leadership increasingly believed that Soviet expansion had ceased. This view was evident in Moscow's failure to score successes with an offensive global strategy as a consequence of strong U.S. resistance as well as in Soviet leaders' exploration of policy options that could enable it to extricate itself from an increasingly disadvantageous position. The Cambodia issue was less important to the USSR but central to China's security concerns. Thus, Deng established Vietnamese withdrawal from Cambodia as a condition for a meeting with the new Soviet leader; such a prerequisite would test the sincerity of Moscow's pronounced desire to improve Sino-Soviet relations.[29] (It was unclear whether the Soviet Union was truly in control of Vietnam's policy regarding Cambodia, but Chinese leaders certainly believed that Moscow had significant leverage in the continuing Indochina crisis.)[30]

The Soviets found it much easier to make concessions with regard to Soviet border forces and the invasion of Afghanistan. During a speech at Vladivostok on 28 July 1986, Gorbachev declared that the Soviet Union would begin both withdrawing troops from Afghanistan and reducing its military presence along the Sino-Soviet and Sino-Mongolian frontiers. Regarding Vietnam's occupation of Cambodia, the Soviet leader simply noted that resolution of the Cambodia problem would hinge on "the normalization of Sino-Vietnamese relations," with no other indication that Moscow wanted to pressure Vietnam into leaving Cambodia.[31]

Why did the Soviets make concessions on the other two obstacles but not on Vietnam? On one hand, Gorbachev recognized the complexity of the Cambodia problem and the limitations of the Soviets' ability to resolve it (whatever China perceived the USSR's influence over Vietnam to be). On the other, he spoke frankly about what was foremost in his mind—that is, the withdrawal of Soviet troops from Afghanistan was more imminently important to the USSR than was a resolution in Cambodia.[32]

Following such strategic calculations, the Soviet Union began pulling troops out of Afghanistan and Mongolia—as well as Vietnam. From 15 May 1988 to 15 February 1989, Moscow completely withdrew Soviet troops (including three motorized infantry divisions, one airborne division, and three independent motorized infantry brigades) from Afghanistan. On 7 December 1988, Gorbachev promised that the Soviet Union would redeploy three-quarters of Soviet forces (including three army divisions and all air and air defense units, a total of more than 50,000 troops) from Mongolia. The Soviet Union also removed most of its MiG-23 Flogger fighters and Tu-16 Badger bombers from Vietnam and significantly cut back its naval activities at Cam Ranh Bay.[33] All these developments eased relations between Beijing and Moscow. The security environment around China substantially improved, placing Beijing in a better position to settle the Cambodia problem and eventually to patch up Sino-Vietnamese relations.

Vietnam after Le Duan

Shortly after Vietnamese Communist Party secretary-general Le Duan's visit to Moscow in late June 1985, the Soviet foreign ministry made it known that Soviet and Vietnamese leaders had discussed the issue of Sino-Soviet relations and agreed that normalization of Soviet-Chinese and Vietnamese-Chinese relations would "help enhance peace in Asia and international security."[34] It is still unknown to what extent the two sides touched on Vietnam's occupation of Cambodia. During the summer of 1985, the Vietnamese leadership expressed its intention to seek a political solution to the Cambodia issue. On 16 August, at the eleventh meeting of the Indochinese Foreign Ministers Conference in Phnom Penh, the Vietnamese delegation announced that Hanoi would withdraw Vietnamese forces from Cambodia by 1990 without any conditions. Given the fact that Hanoi's previous position had been that Vietnam would not consider a pullout of Vietnamese troops as long as the threat from China continued, the promise of a unilateral withdrawal by 1990 was a major—even stunning—turnabout in Vietnam's policy. Brantly Womack points out that such a change marked the beginning of the SRV's "two-track policy." While promising to withdraw from Cambodia, Hanoi reserved "its option of reoccupation if its security demanded it."[35] At the time, the border conflict between Vietnam and China at Laoshan remained intense. Responding to Western journalists' questions regarding Vietnamese-Chinese relations, Vietnamese foreign minister Nguyen Co Thach maintained that "both doors were open to" Vietnam and China, "with one leading to peace and the other leading to war."[36]

A major transformation in Hanoi's policy toward China occurred after the July 1986 death of Le Duan. At the Sixth Party Congress in December, several of Le Duan's associates "retired from political life or fell from power." Younger leaders now assumed leadership positions.[37] The new leaders readily admitted that life in Vietnam was difficult.[38] The SRV's economy had plummeted into stagnation and hyperinflation, and aid from the USSR—itself in the first throes of its decline—began decreasing. Nguyen Van Linh, the new Vietnamese Communist Party secretary-general, visited Moscow in May 1987 in a fruitless attempt to secure additional support from the Soviet Union.[39] Hanoi consequently embarked on a new foreign policy course, departing from an almost exclusive dependence on the Soviet Union to a new strategy of "making friends with all countries in the world." Accordingly, mending relations with China became the new Vietnamese leadership's top priority. Anti-China rhetoric disappeared from party and state pronouncements, and Hanoi pointedly reaffirmed its appreciation for China's earlier assistance and support.[40] At the end of 1988, Hanoi unilaterally reopened its border with China to promote economic and trading activities and withdrew its troops from the border.[41]

However, the withdrawal of Vietnamese troops from Cambodia—not from the border region with China—had been the PRC's precondition for ending hostilities. In May 1987, Beijing informed Moscow and Hanoi that China would support a Cambodian joint government headed by Prince Sihanouk and including the Khmer Rouge and did not support the return of the Khmer Rouge regime after the Vietnamese departure. Chinese officials also reaffirmed that the Cambodia problem had to be resolved before Sino-Vietnamese relations could be normalized.[42]

Within Vietnamese higher circles, dissension reigned. Nguyen Van Linh allegedly did not have absolute control over Vietnam's foreign policy, so he could not prevent Foreign Minister Nguyen Co Trach (a crony of Le Duan and a member of the Politburo of the Vietnamese Communist Party), from continuing to take a hard line on the Cambodia issue.[43] Accordingly, Hanoi insisted that any withdrawal from Cambodia must be accompanied by a rejection of Khmer Rouge participation in the future Cambodian government. While concurring—also for the first time—that Cambodia should be a topic in Soviet-Chinese negotiations for normalization, Soviet leaders also wanted to exclude the Khmer Rouge from any post-Vietnam government. More important, the Soviet Union identified Afghanistan rather than Cambodia as Moscow's top foreign policy priority.

Whatever else it might have wished, by 1988, Moscow could no longer sit on the sidelines of the Cambodia issue. Accordingly, on 23 May, while meeting with Vietnamese foreign minister Nguyen Co Trach, Soviet foreign minister Eduard Shevardnadze indicated that the Soviet Union was ready to work with all parties to resolve the Cambodia situation. Two days later, the Hanoi leadership announced that Vietnam would withdraw 50,000 troops from Cambodia beginning in June and that all its troops would depart by the end of 1990.[44] In August, Soviet deputy foreign minister Igor Alexyevitch Rogachev conceded to the Chinese for the first time that Vietnamese withdrawal was necessary to resolve the Cambodia issue and stated that he expected Vietnam to pull out all of its troops in 1989.[45]

Both Eastern Europe and the Soviet Union reduced their aid to Vietnam, another major change in the Soviet-Vietnamese alliance during this period. Even more significant, on 14 March 1988, a maritime clash erupted between China and Vietnam over the Spratly Islands, resulting in the destruction of three Vietnamese naval vessels.[46] The Soviet Union, however, offered only tepid support to Vietnam at the time, sending an important signal that the

Soviet-Vietnamese alliance was in decline despite the ongoing threat Vietnam faced from China. If nothing else, Moscow's actions made it clear that Sino-Soviet normalization required that Vietnam exit Cambodia.

At the 1988 annual meeting of the UN General Assembly, China and the Soviet Union accepted a compromise establishing a provisional "mechanism" (not a government) under the leadership of Prince Sihanouk once Vietnam departed from Cambodia. This arrangement would allow the continuation of the regime Vietnam sought to maintain while leaving a door open for the Khmer Rouge to participate in some future Cambodian government.[47] During Foreign Minister Qian Qichen's visit to Moscow in early December 1988, China and the Soviet Union drew up a memorandum of agreement promising an "early, fair, and reasonable" political resolution to the situation in Cambodia that was predicated on the completion of Vietnam's withdrawal over the next year.[48]

Shortly thereafter, on 14 December, the Vietnamese Foreign Ministry informed the Chinese embassy in Hanoi that Deputy Minister Dinh Nho Liem proposed a meeting with the Chinese ambassador to discuss Vietnamese-Chinese relations. Beijing accepted the proposal, and talks between Chinese and Vietnamese officials began the next day at the Vietnamese Foreign Ministry. The Vietnamese deputy minister handed the Chinese envoy a letter from Nguyen Co Thach to Qian Qichen requesting a visit to Beijing.[49] The Chinese countered that Hanoi should first send a deputy minister to Beijing to resolve the Cambodia problem. The Chinese assumed that the Soviet Union was behind Vietnam's diplomatic move. In any case, China's strategy—making the normalization of Sino-Soviet relations contingent on Soviets pressure on the Vietnamese to withdraw from Cambodia—finally worked.[50]

From China's standpoint, a quick normalization of Sino-Vietnamese relations would allow Guangxi and Yunnan Provinces to join the rest of China in pursuing economic reform. But Beijing was not in such haste that it abandoned its military posture to achieve a quick settlement. Instead, the PRC continued to maintain military pressure on the Vietnam border while engaging in dialogue with the Vietnamese regarding a political resolution to the Cambodia problem.[51] In January 1989, Vietnamese deputy foreign minister Dinh Nho Liem traveled to Beijing to meet with Chinese deputy foreign minister Liu Shuqing. Discussions centered on the Cambodia issue and the resumption of a peaceful Sino-Vietnamese relationship. While the Vietnamese were much interested in the issue of normalization, the Chinese wanted to discuss only Cambodia. The major difference separating the two sides was that China favored an interventionist approach after Vietnam's withdrawal, insisting that both countries should continue to help establish a transitional government headed by Prince Sihanouk with the participation of all political factions, while Vietnam contended that the Cambodia problem would then become an internal issue to be resolved by Cambodians without the intervention of either Hanoi or Beijing.[52] At the final meeting, Chinese foreign minister Qian Qichen told his Vietnamese visitor that normalization of relations between China and Vietnam would come naturally—after the Cambodia issue was settled.[53]

China's Vietnam policy remained firmly under the control of Deng Xiaoping, chief architect of the Sino-Vietnamese conflict. He welcomed the long-awaited change in Hanoi's leadership but did not appear interested in modifying Chinese policy toward Vietnam until Vietnamese troops had completely departed from Cambodia. On 7 October 1989, he met Laotian communist leader Kaysone Phomvihane, who brought a letter from Vietnamese leader Nguyen Van Linh expressing a desire to visit China. Deng responded that he was delighted to learn that the Vietnamese leader wanted to improve relations with China but emphatically reiterated the principles of China's policy: "The crux of the matter is that Vietnam must completely and thoroughly withdraw troops from Cambodia. Only after the settlement of the Cambodia problem will the relationship between China and Vietnam be restored, and we can put the past behind us and look into the future."[54]

Despite ten years of conflict between China and Vietnam, Deng clearly had not yet changed his position on the issue of Cambodia. He also urged Vietnam to end its military presence in Cambodia before his retirement. Doing so would mean to the Chinese leader that China had won the political and military struggle against Vietnam. On 26 August 1989, Hanoi declared that Vietnam had withdrawn its last unit from Cambodia.[55] But the wary Chinese leadership hesitated to accept the announcement as fact given the Vietnamese track record of misleading other countries.[56] Deng particularly felt that Nguyen Co Thach was personally dishonest and that the UN presence in Cambodia was an important safeguard to prevent the Vietnamese from playing "little tricks" (*xiaodongzuo*).[57]

The 1990 Chengdu Meeting

In June 1990 (when Eastern Europe was free from communism for the first time in more than forty years), Vietnamese leaders made another plea for a visit to China. During his meeting with the Chinese ambassador in Hanoi, Nguyen Van Linh recalled his trips to China before the border dispute and his meetings with Mao, Zhou, and Deng. Nguyen Van Linh claimed to have been a student of Mao's revolutionary theory and stated his great appreciation for China's aid during Vietnam's struggles against the French and Americans. He then admitted that Vietnam had wronged China and was willing to correct its mistakes. With respect to Cambodia, the Vietnamese leader expressed confidence that the situation would be resolved peacefully but urged both Vietnam and China to work together to prevent the West and the UN from meddling in Cambodia in the future. The exclusion of the Khmer Rouge from a future Cambodian government, Nguyen Van Linh admitted, was impractical. Somewhat echoing Deng, he finally expressed a desire to meet Chinese leaders to resolve the Cambodia issue and the Vietnamese-Chinese relations issue before his retirement.[58] Chinese leaders nevertheless apparently remained indifferent to the Vietnamese leader's views on Cambodia and were annoyed by what they perceived as Vietnamese foreign minister Nguyen Co Thach's aggressive posturing during his meeting with the Chinese deputy foreign minister in Hanoi.[59] The Chinese leadership may no longer have been satisfied with the withdrawal of Vietnamese military forces from Cambodia, but now expected more from Hanoi. In a swift reply to Nguyen Van Linh, China insisted that a summit between the two countries could come only after the resolution of the Cambodia issue: Vietnam still needed to complete its withdrawal and then help with Cambodian national reconciliation.[60]

The Vietnamese reaction to this disappointing response remains unknown. Some progress had been made between January and August 1990. First, the five permanent members of the UN Security Council had already reached an agreement on the framework for a political settlement on the Cambodia problem: all external aid to the competing factions would be halted, the United Nations Transitional Authority in Cambodia would be created, and Cambodian sovereignty would be respected.[61] Second, all Cambodian political factions had accepted this agreement, and a new round of talks with Hanoi had been scheduled for September in Jakarta. On 16 August, the Chinese embassy in Hanoi received an oral message from Nguyen Van Linh via the son of former Vietnamese leader Hoang Van Hoan, who had defected to China in 1979. The Vietnamese leader made yet another conciliatory appeal, blaming his foreign minister for endless haggling between Vietnam and China over Cambodia and maintaining that such a difficult situation could be overcome only by a summit between the two countries' top leaders.[62]

Because this message did not come directly from the Vietnamese leader, Beijing ordered Zhang Dewei, the Chinese ambassador to Vietnam, to seek personal contact with Nguyen Van Linh to find out his real intentions with regard to Sino-Vietnamese relations. The decade of hostility between the two countries kept contact between Chinese diplomats and Vietnamese officials to the bare minimum necessary for communication. Chinese diplomats had great difficulty identifying the best person to contact the top Vietnamese leader after many years of limited dialogue between the two sides. Because Nguyen Co Thach controlled the Ministry of Foreign Affairs, the Chinese ambassador decided to ask General Le Duc Anh, the minister of national defense, who had echoed many of Nguyen Van Linh's points at an earlier meeting with the Chinese ambassador, to help arrange a meeting with his superior.

This approach worked. On 22 August, Nguyen Van Linh received Zhang Dewei at the Ministry of National Defense. The Vietnamese official acknowledged that he had sent an oral message to the Chinese ambassador and reiterated his intention to visit China. He specifically noted that his meeting with Chinese leaders would help silence those who still opposed his desire to resolve the Cambodia issue.[63] Under such circumstances, Beijing had to make a concession. On 27 August, Premier Li Peng went to the home of the now semiretired Deng Xiaoping to report his successors' decision to invite the Vietnamese leader to visit China. Li then suggested that for security reasons related to the 1990 Asian Games, which would be held in Beijing, the meeting would take place in Chengdu, the capital of Sichuan Province. Deng approved.[64]

On 3 September, the summit was convened. In attendance were China's party secretary-general, Jiang Zemin, and premier, Li Peng, and Vietnam's party secretary-general, Nguyen Van Linh; premier, Do Muoi; and party adviser Pham Van Dong. Jiang Zemin candidly stated that both sides must come to terms with what had been right and wrong between the two countries since the late 1970s. According to the Chinese leader, China wanted not to settle old scores but rather to get to the root of the problem and break fresh ground for the future. He welcomed the new Vietnamese leadership's initiative to improve relations but pointed out yet again that Cambodia remained the major obstacle to normalization. The Chinese leader then urged his Vietnamese counterparts to accept the UN's plan. Nguyen Van Linh confessed that Vietnam had pursued a wrong policy for the past twelve years and explained that the current Vietnamese leadership wanted to make corrections to resume the friendship between the two countries and parties established by Ho Chi Minh. He promised to support a political settlement of the Cambodia issue based on the UN's framework documents.[65]

Even so, the Vietnamese still resisted Beijing's plan for a Cambodian Transitional Authority under the leadership of Prince Sihanouk, though Pham Van Dong was the only strong opponent of China's proposal.[66] Beijing proposed that the Hanoi-supported Phnom Penh government would occupy six seats in the Cambodian Transitional Authority, while each of the three resistance factions would take two seats. Because Sihanouk also belonged to the resistance side, Vietnam felt that this arrangement was unfair and unreasonable. The first day of talks lasted until eight o'clock in the evening without reaching agreement. Later in the evening at the welcome banquet table, Chinese leaders allegedly continued to try to persuade the Vietnamese leaders to accept China's proposal. After another lengthy meeting the following day, Vietnamese leaders capitulated. They also promised to persuade the Phnom Penh regime to accept China's plan. The two sides subsequently reached agreement on the principles for the political settlement of the Cambodia issue and the resumption of relations.[67]

On 6 September, Chinese foreign affairs officials rushed to Jakarta to inform all parties of the new agreement between China and Vietnam on Cambodia and to urge them to reach an accord. Another year of infighting among the Cambodians would pass before a peace agreement was signed. The Chengdu summit denoted the end of China's twelve years of hostility toward Vietnam. Jiang Zemin concluded the meeting by quoting a Qing poem: "Disasters are never powerful enough to separate true brothers; a smile is all they need to eliminate ingratitude and resentment" (*Dujin jiebo xiongdi zai; xiangfeng yixiao min enchou*).[68] The new Chinese leader waxed sentimental in recollecting the brotherly relationship between China and Vietnam from 1950 to 1970, though he later admitted that the decadelong mutual hostility had made it impossible for the two countries to return to the kind of close and cordial relationship they enjoyed during the 1950s and 1960s.[69] For their part, the Chinese people remained bitterly aware that their earlier sacrifices for Vietnam had not brought permanent friendship and gratitude and became even more annoyed with Vietnam's unreliable behavior. They reproved Hanoi's ingratitude by recalling an old Chinese expression, "Whoever suckles me is my mother" (*younai bianshi niang*).

Nicholas Khoo is correct that "the decrease in Sino-Soviet conflict" was the inevitable corollary of opening "the door for Sino-Vietnamese rapprochement."[70] In retrospect, as Hanoi reached out to Beijing in 1989 and 1990, the communist world was on the cusp of dramatic and profound changes. Political storms raged through Eastern Europe. The Soviet Union was on the verge of disintegration. In the midst of the collapsing of communism, many Vietnamese party members and supporters began to worry about what would happen to their nation, one of the youngest communist countries. China's success in economic reform and openness to the world offered hope. According to Nguyen Van Linh, because the SRV was a small nation and the Vietnamese

Communist Party was a small party, they needed to count on the PRC and the CCP to carry forward the socialist flag. The Vietnamese leader further pointed out that the SRV and the Vietnamese Communist Party needed their socialist neighbors' support.[71] Again, from Vietnam's point of view, shared political and ideological interests should be enough to bring these two socialist countries back into a close alliance. For China, however, this ideologically guided tradition was outdated: in the current international environment, each socialist country should pursue policies that served its own national interests. At the time, China's national priorities were economic reform and openness. Despite Vietnam's eagerness to improve its relationship with China, Beijing appeared unmoved and continued to insist on a final settlement of the Cambodia problem before normalizing their bilateral relationship.[72]

A Tentative Interpretation

The passage from hostility to normalization was a slow and sometimes complicated journey. China firmly upheld its position that Sino-Vietnamese normalization would occur only after the final resolution of the Cambodia issue. On 23 October 1991, all four Cambodian political factions and eighteen countries signed a peace agreement at the Paris Peace Conference. Two weeks later, newly elected Vietnamese party leader Do Muoi and premier Vo Van Kiet traveled to Beijing for an official visit, symbolizing the resumption of normal relations between China and Vietnam. During the visit, the Vietnamese leaders asked China to provide financial assistance for economic development. The Chinese leadership agreed.[73] The Sino-Vietnamese relationship now reflected the terms on which both sides had previously agreed: "The past is gone, and the future is beginning."[74]

However, the status quo did not return to the Yunnan border until early 1993. Even during the normalization negotiations, the PLA continued the policy of maintaining military pressure on Vietnam at Laoshan. In March 1992, the PLA responded to Vietnamese farming and construction activities in the disputed territories with force.[75] Not until 10 February 1993, in response to the Chengdu Military Region's request, did the CMC finally terminate the PLA's combat missions along the border. The Yunnan Military District thereafter dismantled its forward combat command post and other supporting systems, and the PLAAF suspended the rotation of aviation and AAA units to the border region.[76] Nine days later, Beijing ordered the Guangzhou and Chengdu Military Regions to conduct minesweeping operations to "open our door to [Vietnam], prosper and enrich the border region" (*dakai guomen, xinbian zhifu*).[77]

In examining both China's and Vietnam's efforts to terminate hostility between the two countries from the mid-1980s to the early 1990s, Sophie Richardson ascribes Beijing's failure to bring the conflict to a quick end to Chinese irrationality, noting that it "not only rendered the principles but also common sense irrelevant." This irrationality, she continues, resulted from "a fury" that saw "Vietnam's invasion of Cambodia as a deep betrayal." She further criticizes China's rejection of "quicker and more efficient ways of settling" the Cambodia problem even after the Vietnamese occupation was no longer perceived as part of a Soviet effort to encircle China.[78]

In his analysis of asymmetry in the power relations between China and Vietnam, Womack expounds on why China took a no-hurry stance on ending the Sino-Vietnamese conflict. He concludes that China's priority at the time was domestic stability and economic development, and Vietnam offered little to China in this respect. With "the luxury of moving more slowly," China could adhere firmly on its position, since "the general success of its reform and openness policies did not depend on" the normalization of relations with Vietnam.[79]

Almost three decades ago, in his study of the causes of wars, Michael Howard explicitly stated, "The conflicts between states which have usually led to war have normally arisen, not from any irrational and emotive drives, but from an almost superabundance of analytic rationality."[80] Dan Reiter provides a rational theory of war termination focusing on "how states seek to maximize benefits and minimize costs."[81] To what extent was China's approach toward ending the conflict with Vietnam rational? The answer lies in Beijing's calculation of what it could gain from a conflict-ending bargain. China's behavior in negotiating with Vietnam fit into the bargaining model of war termination, in which "the side seeing itself as stronger demands more."[82]

Beijing's decision to wage a war against Vietnam hinged mainly on the Chinese leadership's assessment of the country's strategic situation at the time when Soviet expansion was perceived as a major threat. To Chinese leaders, Vietnam's invasion of Cambodia formed part of the Soviet scheme for global expansion; more specifically, Vietnam's dominance over Indochina threatened to China's security interests in the region. China felt it needed to act to improve China's geopolitical situation. The attempt to "teach Vietnam a lesson" also constituted a Chinese response to Vietnam's betrayal of the traditional party and national relationship established by Mao and Ho. China also sought to punish Vietnamese ingratitude for China's help against France and the United States. By the time Hanoi attempted to repair relations with Beijing in the late 1980s, Chinese leaders had abandoned their perception of an imminent Soviet threat as well as the idea of Vietnam's occupation of Cambodia as part of a larger Soviet effort to encircle China. Nevertheless, China's strategic objective in the region remained the promotion of a neutral Southeast Asia—a region not dominated by Vietnam but friendly to China. Beijing's use of force in 1979 and thereafter was never designed to seek the absolute defeat of Vietnam; instead, it was aimed at coercing Hanoi into making critical concessions: accepting China's strategic interests in the region and acknowledging China's traditional stances on Sino-Vietnamese relations. In addition, many years of hostility with Vietnam increased Beijing's skepticism about a compromise settlement.

Furthermore, when the Vietnamese leadership began to improve relations, Chinese leaders believed that their country's strategic situation was much more advantageous. China had already established a good strategic relationship with the United States and Japan. An influx of Western capital and technology had satisfied China's economic development. In response to the Soviet attempts to improve relations with China, Deng had been very practical if not snobbish, asking what Moscow could offer to China. His answer was simple: nothing. One Chinese diplomat identified this as the guiding principle for Chinese negotiations with both the Soviets and the Vietnamese.[83] Obtaining political concessions from the antagonist side was the driving force behind China's insistence on placing the Cambodia problem at the center of the resumption of relations with both the Soviet Union and Vietnam.

Another factor possibly affecting Chinese behavior in terminating hostility with Vietnam was concern for maintaining and bolstering China's international credibility. The Vietnamese invasion of Cambodia was one of many issues/factors that prompted the Chinese leadership to use force to counter Vietnam's expansion in the region. Afterward, Vietnam's occupation of Cambodia not only directly threatened China's own security but also affected its relations with ASEAN countries. The Chinese leadership had long promised to support ASEAN countries' efforts toward peace and neutrality. Maintaining a strong position on Cambodia would show that China was not only a reliable friend and partner but also a credible one, thus boosting its worldwide reputation. In early 1979, Deng Xiaoping told the U.S. president that "the Chinese mean what they say" about the Indochina crisis.[84] After settling its Cambodian problem—long a principal policy objective—Beijing could not accept any resolution short of what had been demanded. Deng could dismiss the other obstacles but kept his demand on Cambodia intact during negotiations to improve relations with the Soviet Union and Vietnam. Moreover, no one other than Deng could make changes in China's foreign policy. Chinese leaders saw Vietnam's ultimate acceptance of China's plan to settle the Cambodia problem as proof to the international and particularly regional audiences that China would keep its word. Perhaps more important, the Vietnamese leadership's acknowledgment of policy mistakes indicated that China had been correct in its views and handling of the Sino-Vietnamese dispute. The whole episode happened precisely as the Chinese leadership's reputation hit rock bottom after the 1989 Tiananmen crackdown. When the Hanoi leadership indicated that the Vietnamese Communist Party would again follow the CCP's lead, Beijing may have thought that the former relationship between the two parties and countries had returned.

Terminating unsuccessful military ventures in Cambodia and a stalemated conflict with China was painful for Vietnamese statesmen, especially those who clung to the position that Vietnam must achieve a "peace with honor." When Hanoi withdrew all troops from Cambodia, it portrayed the move as the PAVN ending its "internationalist duties" there and triumphantly emerging from the Cold War. Yet one major barricade along Hanoi's road to peace was Beijing's persistent stance regarding Cambodia: the Chinese leadership wanted to minimize Vietnam's influence on Phnom Penh. Any effort by Hanoi to rejoin the world community would be of little avail should hostility between China and Vietnam continue. Vietnam was a proud nation with a history of resisting foreign interference and pressure while refusing to let anyone outside the country know its weaknesses. Perhaps more important was the idea that "Le Duan's legacy lives on,"[85] since many of his cronies became Politburo members. While promising to withdraw from Cambodia, Hanoi maintained its occupation policy until 1989, when international openness took priority. Longtime associates of the deceased leader and his policies believed that concessions would signal Vietnam's weakness to the outside world. As yet, there remains no way to know whether Nguyen Van Linh was sincere when he pronounced his willingness to correct mistakes in Hanoi's foreign policies or make concessions to China at the beginning of his reign. His understanding of Vietnam's strategic problem could have evolved in response to the difficulties facing Hanoi at home and abroad. The internal political struggle, especially the divergence between Nguyen Van Linh and Nguyen Co Thach over Vietnam's foreign policy, inhibited Hanoi's negotiations with China. The new party secretary often found himself outmaneuvered by his foreign minister on the Cambodia issue when China persistently demanded a settlement as a prerequisite for normalizing relations.

Hanoi could claim victory after thirteen years of hostility by arguing that it had held out against Chinese pressure and had diminished the Khmer Rouge threat.[86] However, Hanoi's decision to prioritize the normalization of relations with China over maintaining control in Cambodia was based on its calculation of how to extricate itself from a strategic predicament. The new Vietnamese leaders recognized that their country was in a much weaker position than it had previously occupied. The communist world had crumbled, and the Soviet Union, Hanoi's patron, was disintegrating. The decadelong confrontation between Vietnam and China, as a Vietnamese diplomat admitted to his Chinese counterparts, had inflicted heavy losses that Vietnam could no longer afford.[87] The continuation of the deadlock over Cambodia became too much of a liability for Vietnamese national interests when the country had already decided that economic reform would be a major part of its strategic plan for the future. At the same time, China was perceived as a model for surviving communist states and as a desperately needed partner for Vietnam's economic development. A debate over grand strategy probably ensued as the new Hanoi leadership came to see the rational expediency of admitting policy mistakes in front of the Chinese leadership and then making concessions to the Chinese plan for Cambodia.

A secret deal may have been made regarding how to address the unpleasant thirteen years so that the interlude would not imperil future Sino-Vietnamese relations. The two sides allegedly reached a tacit agreement that prohibited the media from publishing stories and scholars from conducting studies about the border conflict in hopes that the recent hostility would then fade from memory on both sides of the border. Both countries could then concentrate on rejuvenating their relationship. Once again, Vietnam looked to China for direction and guidance, and the relationship was described officially as "good neighbors, good friends, good comrades, good partners" (*haolinju, haopengyou, haotongzhi, haohuoban*).[88]

Even though the new Sino-Vietnamese relations have been characterized in these terms, in practice, China has displayed an occasional firmness against Vietnam. For example, after the border was settled three meters away from the PLA's main battle position at Laoshan, a Vietnamese regiment commander asked to step on the main peak of Laoshan to take a look, but the local Chinese commander turned down the request.[89] Because "memories and resentment of the recent hostility" remained, Womack concludes that this new relationship between China and Vietnam will simply enter "a new cycle of endless series of misunderstandings" and misperceptions.[90] Normalization concluded the Cold War between the two communist nations and ended the abnormal state-to-state relations that had existed between the two countries since the founding of the People's Republic in 1949. The knowledge and experience gained from the Sino-Vietnamese conflict would undisputedly have indelible, lingering effects on both China and Vietnam and their relations.

Conclusion

A Personal Retrospective on China's Border War,
Rapprochement with Vietnam, and Implications for
East Asian Affairs

In his classic study of war, noted historian Michael Howard comments that "an understanding of the causes and the nature of war is a necessary characteristic of the educated citizen; and . . . that the deeper such understanding is, the less likely is war to occur."[1] Howard also implies that this understanding will reduce the likelihood of mistakes that set a nation on the path to conflict.

After years of research and writing about the Sino-Vietnamese conflict of the 1970s and 1980s, I feel confident in assessing what *Deng Xiaoping's Long War* provides in terms of knowledge, insight, and analysis for those seeking to understand the essence of East Asian international affairs in the twenty-first century.

The Sino-Vietnamese conflict was the longest sustained war the PRC ever experienced and constituted one of the pivotal developments in the Cold War, in the Sino-Soviet conflict, and in Chinese foreign policy. However, given the conflict's significance to the nation, it is extraordinary that it has not received greater attention from East Asian specialists. In 1979, more than 500,000 Chinese troops participated in the short incursion into Vietnam; after 1984, more than 180,000 PLA soldiers rotated through the border conflict. The thirteen years of fighting with Vietnam—the most violent episode in Cold War history among communist countries—cost more than 12,000 Chinese lives and resulted in another 20,000 wounded soldiers and militia members. Vietnam has never revealed the PAVN's casualty figures, but analysis of the fighting suggests that they would be at least equal to and likely greater than those experienced by the PLA. Ironically, given how highly trumpeted the war was at the time, it is the least commemorated and memorialized of all conflicts in modern Chinese history, mentioned only in terms of the bloodshed, loss, and suffering that it caused. The popular perception of the conflict has been well captured by historian Chen Jian, who damningly concluded that the Chinese-Vietnamese border war must be considered "one of the most meaningless wars in world history."[2]

Nevertheless, the Sino-Vietnamese split and the ensuing long period of conflict between the two communist countries constituted a major event in the Cold War, with implications that went far beyond East Asia, and thus is worthy of detailed study and analysis. With people focused primarily on the ideological struggle between democracy and communism since the end of World War II, the 1979 Sino-Vietnamese war, in Odd Arne Westad's words, "created shock-waves within the international system of states." It not only marked the first time that "countries led by Communist parties had been at war with each other" but also "happened in the immediate aftermath of the Second Indochina War" between Vietnam and its proxies and the United States.[3] After the Iron Curtain fell in the late 1940s, communist countries aligned together and locked themselves in a global struggle against "Western imperialism." The eruption of the Sino-Vietnamese conflict in 1979, on the heels of the Sino-Soviet split a decade earlier, further divided the communist world, driving socialist countries to align themselves in coalitions ready to go to war against each other. The rift between China and Vietnam was so deep and wide that armed conflict resulted. However, no one foresaw that the Sino-Vietnamese conflict would dramatically change the balance of power between the two principal Cold War belligerents—the United States and the Soviet Union—setting the stage for the eventual collapse of the Soviet empire.

Scholars have addressed how and why China and Vietnam became foes at the end of the long anti-U.S. war in Indochina. This study of China's 1979 war with Vietnam is consistent with the claim by many scholars—at least in hindsight—that the Sino-Vietnamese conflict probably could not have been averted. A wide array of factors (playing subtle and major roles) pushed both sides to war—mutual history, frustration, dissatisfaction, disappointment, skepticism, and even hatred. As a result, war was virtually inevitable. Close scrutiny of Chinese decision making in 1978 and 1979 raises the question not whether the two countries would come to blows but why "brother plus comrade" communist nations would do so.

An analysis of China's involvement in Vietnam after the founding of the People's Republic in 1949 indicates that the root of the Sino-Vietnamese conflict lay in the failure of both Chinese and Vietnamese leaders to properly manage their countries' relations. As ideological communists, they emphasized their commitment to proletarian internationalism (the concept that the global proletariat share common desires and goals) rooted in doctrinal Marxist-Leninist ideology—the foundational rational system driving national organization and political policy. This ideology encouraged leaders to place individual national interests above other concerns, but doing so was far easier theorized than put into practice. China and Vietnam shared a common enemy, the United States, and took the politically expedient position that their relations were fraternal, with no divergence (much like Sino-Vietnamese relations under Mao and Ho). Yet China and Vietnam steered gradually differing courses, leading to friction that hastened the steady decline of Sino-Vietnamese relations.

Since the early 1960s, the deteriorating Sino-Soviet relationship caused Beijing to perceive—and hence to manage—its relations with Hanoi through the prism of Mao's (and later Deng's) anti-Soviet revisionism. Chinese leaders increasingly pressured their Vietnamese counterparts to endorse China's anti-Soviet position as a condition for continued PRC support. Hanoi was first annoyed and disappointed, but as the pressure persisted, those feelings transformed into outright anger and then hostility toward China. When relations between the two countries deteriorated after a shift in Chinese security concerns from the south to the north, Beijing and Hanoi were disposed to violence even deadly armed conflict (as under Deng and Le Duan.)

Beijing's ideological dispute with the Soviet Union thus brought China a new and daunting security concern that went far beyond just its relationship with Vietnam. Chinese leaders found themselves in an awkward position. Their support for national liberation movements in Asia, evidenced by the PRC's close ties with all Indochinese communists, conflicted with their latest national security interests. When China's Indochina policy had to defer to this reality, Hanoi saw a huge gap between China's words and deeds despite China's continued military and material support to the Vietnamese Communist Party. After many years of committing resources to Hanoi's war effort, the Chinese had created a new enemy.

Over time, the ideological rivalry between Beijing and Moscow evolved into essentially a competition for leadership of the communist world. The PRC's leadership was more doctrinaire and traditionalist in its pursuit of Marxist-Leninist orthodoxy than were Soviet leaders. Beijing's criticism of Soviet "revisionism" challenged Moscow's ideological position in terms of and in ways that were analogous to the struggle between the Protestant Reformation and the Papacy for leadership of Christianity in the late Middle Ages. In a practical geopolitical sense, China also challenged the Soviet Union's claims to communist world leadership, with other communist states expected to take sides. Only those who held high the Marxist-Leninist banner, Mao and his followers believed, were entitled to claim legitimate leadership of the international communist movement.

Ideological rivalry thus made the two communist countries sworn enemies, with no possibility for reconciliation. After Beijing's security interests had shifted, the Chinese leadership's perceptions of a Soviet threat became even more magnified and exaggerated, with fears of "Soviet encirclement" ultimately prompting China's violent response to Vietnam's invasion of Cambodia and anti-China policy in the late 1970s. The military clashes along the Sino-Vietnamese border extended the Sino-Soviet conflict into Southeast Asia, becoming China's longest conflict since the Korean War and the most violent episode of communist-bloc dissension and difference in Cold War history.

Sino-Soviet hostility during Mao's years originated in ideological competition, giving rise to the Chinese leadership's inability to seek compromise to avoid conflict. The post-Mao Chinese leaders, especially Deng Xiaoping, acted much less rigidly along the lines of communist ideology but still remained prisoners of their own worldview, simplistically seeing the steady deterioration of Sino-Vietnamese relations as further evidence of a perfidious, intractable, menacing, and growing Soviet threat. Deng Xiaoping's return to the apex of Chinese leadership in 1978 thus brought no changes in China's foreign policy. Indeed, Beijing's leadership cadre subsequently even more vigorously pursued Mao's strategy of allying with the United States against the Soviet Union.

Deng played a crucial role in China's conflict with Vietnam. For him, the Soviet threat did not connote an imminent invasion of China. The Chinese leader, however, was extremely concerned about Soviet expansion into Southeast Asia, perceiving it as the encirclement of China from the south. Nonetheless, this factor alone did not motivate Deng to go to war. Rather, his decision resulted from the convergence of many factors: Soviet hegemony, Hanoi's anti-China policy, Vietnam's invasion of Cambodia, and the Soviet-Vietnamese alliance. All blended together into a perfect picture of an increasing Soviet threat. In addition, Deng turned westward, again in keeping with Mao's wishes. Deng was convinced that China could achieve economic and industrial reform only by following a policy of openness to the outside world that would bring Western capital and technology.

Deng perceived a causal logic between these two otherwise uncorrelated matters. The war with Vietnam constituted a response to the Soviet threat. In turn, he believed, it would help promote a pro-Chinese international alliance that joined together the United States, Japan, and Europe in a united front against Soviet expansionism. The result would be a safer and more stable environment conducive to China's Four Modernizations, which would be achieved in great measure because, Deng believed, Western countries would be generous with their money and technology, both badly needed for China's transformation. Further, China's credibility was at stake. Deng had repeatedly criticized the West, especially the United States, for being too soft in confronting Cuba's invasion of Angola. For him, China could not afford to ignore Vietnam—"East Cuba"—right under China's nose. Moreover, he believed that military action against Vietnam would not only punish an arrogant country that had proclaimed itself "the world's third-strongest military power" but also send a stern and not-to-be-ignored message—indeed, a warning—to both the USSR and the SRV to stop meddling in China's sphere of interest. Likewise, Beijing's decision to go to war with Vietnam would demonstrate to the West that China was a reliable and vital partner in the ongoing struggle to prevent Soviet global hegemony.

However, other motivations for China's intervention cannot be ignored. Deng detested Hanoi's arrogance and especially its ingratitude for Chinese sacrifices in the Second Indochina War. His talk about "teaching Vietnam a lesson" sounded a serious warning to the Vietnamese about the consequences of continuing to ignore China's concerns. When the time came, he had virtually no misgivings about launching the war. Perhaps more important, the ongoing power struggle inside the party leadership coupled with factionalism within the PLA to motivate Deng to employ military action against Vietnam. Believing that only a stable domestic environment would attract foreign support for China's modernization, Deng saw the war as offering an opportunity to consolidate his control over the party and the military. Indeed, the military was in its worst shape since the founding of the People's Republic and badly needed reform and modernization. The invasion of Vietnam thus gave the PLA an opportunity to gain war-fighting experience and thereby polish its badly tarnished reputation among the Chinese people.

The 1979 war was probably unavoidable most because of Deng's dictatorial leadership style, which prevented any serious high-level discussion or debate about going to war. A highly centralized Chinese political system plus personal prestige and authority freed Deng of internal constraints on his wishes. As supreme commander of the PLA, he had the power unilaterally to mobilize PLA forces against Vietnam even before the Politburo had discussed the decision. In retrospect, the question of whether the Chinese leadership's rationale for war was sound remains unanswered.

Deng Xiaoping's temperament and personality also played roles in his decision to attack Vietnam. As a dictatorial leader, he believed that admitting mistakes could weaken his authority and credibility, particularly after he had formulated a decision. Therefore, he was not only decisive but also inflexible. For Deng, the hostile relationship between China and Vietnam resulted from

Hanoi's "hate-China" policy and its invasion of Cambodia.[4] In response, he determined not only to expel Vietnam from Cambodia but also to bleed it white by providing endless assistance to the Cambodian resistance forces and by placing military pressure on Vietnam's northern border throughout the 1980s. As China's supreme leader and ultimate policymaker from the late 1970s through the early 1990s, Deng was a most formidable figure whom almost no one dared to challenge.

The centrality of Deng Xiaoping to the Sino-Vietnamese border conflict raises a set of questions: Would the conflict still have occurred had Deng not been in such a dominant and influential position? Or could Chinese leaders, especially Deng, have achieved the same strategic objectives without resorting to military force against Vietnam? There is no way to conclusively determine either that war could have been avoided or that the military conflict represented the natural course of Cold War Sino-Vietnamese relations no matter who was in charge. However, Deng Xiaoping's importance as China's paramount leader shaped the course of both the Sino-Vietnamese military conflict and Cold War history. Any answers to these hypothetical questions cannot neglect the fact that Deng was not only a witness to but also a participant in the roller-coaster relations between China and the Soviet Union and between China and Vietnam in the 1960s and 1970s. One conclusion is that Deng was simply unable to avoid the role that he was supposed (or that he believed it was reasonable) to play at the time—that, in effect, he was a hostage to history. Beijing's decision to invade the border regions of Vietnam could be seen as both inevitable and sound as long as Deng believed that he needed to react to a very real Soviet threat and desired Western support for China's economic modernization.

Deng Xiaoping's role aside, the members of the PRC's leadership cadre were deliberative and calculating as they pondered their decision to go to war. They were inclined to calculate China's strategic interests from a broad and long-term geopolitical and economic perspective to balance any short-term repercussions. As long as China's use of force could be justified on the basis of countering Vietnam's aggression, Chinese leaders reckoned that any repercussions would be limited and short-lived. Likewise, any short-term gains from military action—for example, Vietnam's withdrawal from Cambodia or PLA battlefield victories—would be desirable. The most important goal was a better strategic environment for China, resulting in stability conducive to both the PRC's security and economic development. Therefore, the Chinese sense of what constituted military "victory" lay more in anticipated geopolitical outcomes than in the PLA's operational battlefield performance.

The post-Mao Chinese leadership, like its predecessors, certainly responded to international events and adjusted China's policy accordingly. China's early 1980s decision to negotiate with the Soviet Union offers a clear example. At the center of this leadership ring, Deng's position on Vietnam was critical, and it never seemed to change over his tenure. Such constancy may have resulted from his distaste for (or perhaps his distrust of) the various Vietnamese leaders he encountered. In the end, however, he rationally calculated the nation's gains and losses and acted based on the result.

Over the 1980s, the Soviet threat to China significantly declined and with it Vietnam's significance to China's security. China's (and Deng's) highest national priority, economic development, did not depend on improved Sino-Vietnamese relations, as desirable as they might otherwise be. As the power and prestige of the Soviet Union waned and with it Vietnam's international position, China demanded more of Vietnam: Hanoi needed to confess its mistaken policy toward China and withdraw from Cambodia before Sino-Vietnamese relations would improve. Deng remained adamant on this point. When Hanoi sought rapprochement with Beijing in 1989, the new Chinese leadership continued Deng's policy, even asking his endorsement for their negotiations with the Vietnamese leadership. Consequently, after more than ten years of conflict and the loss of many Vietnamese lives and resources, Hanoi had to agree to terms that were virtually dictated by Deng Xiaoping. The Vietnamese leadership's capitulation obviously came as a relief to Deng.[5]

The Sino-Vietnamese conflict confirms the findings of previous studies suggesting that repressive states generally display little or no concern for the legitimacy of both domestic opposition to governmental decisions to use force to settle international disputes and subsequent popular discontent once the nation is at war. Instead, repressive states silence opposition and dissent and manipulate public opinion to support the leaders' cause. In the case of the Sino-Vietnamese border dispute, the Chinese government resorted to propaganda and mass mobilization to suppress opposition views and to stir up war sentiment. Both strategies were highly effective at the time. As a result, the 1979 invasion of Vietnam became itself a useful means to unite the country behind the drive for the Four Modernizations as well as to squash the liberal Democracy Wall movement.[6]

The 1980s military conflict along the Vietnamese border provided Beijing authorities with a convenient means of controlling the minds of people, especially young people. The era featured a campaign against "spiritual pollution" launched when it appeared that Western values ("imported" by Deng Xiaoping's openness policy) had begun to encroach alarmingly on socialist traditions and the PRC's strict ideological system. The maintenance of military pressure on Vietnam's northern border sacrificed the local interests of Guangxi and Yunnan Provinces in favor of a broader Chinese strategic intent. Otherwise, the border war had only a limited impact on China as a whole. Indeed, the Sino-Vietnamese conflict suggested that China could afford to continue low-intensity local conflicts, even in remote isolated areas, for long periods. Vietnam's situation differed substantially, since it had to both resist China's pressure from the north and continue to fight rebels in Cambodia to the west.

Vietnam's leaders never adequately met the challenge of mustering their nation's limited forces and abilities against China. Hanoi's real problem lay in Cambodia, where, despite the PAVN's combat successes, the Khmer Rouge proved surprisingly resilient. Le Duan's decision to send forces into Cambodia is widely considered to have been at best thoughtless, with no plan for ending the conflict and little attention paid to the invasion's political goals. Vietnam's inability to end its Cambodian occupation precluded a negotiated peace for the Sino-Vietnamese conflict. Vietnam's rationale for hostile policies toward China involved continuous Soviet support. Once the balance of power tilted in favor of China against the Soviet Union during the last years of the Cold War, Vietnamese leaders found themselves in a situation they could never have foreseen: China had new sources of international support, and Vietnam was tied to an older and increasingly decrepit partner. Thus, Hanoi's venture against China came to a bad end. In the Vietnamese-Chinese relationship, size did matter, and whatever deprivations and problems China faced were exacerbated for Vietnam by its much smaller size. By any measure and particularly by those governing today's international relationships in the Asia-Pacific region, Vietnam's reckless intervention in Cambodia, together with its provocation of China, was ill-advised.

Studying the China-Vietnam border conflict greatly enhances an understanding of the PLA and its evolution from the time of Mao to the present day. Having not fought a major war for nearly thirty years, China geared up for military action against Vietnam in 1979 with an army whose thinking, strategy, operational traditions, and combat capabilities were rooted firmly in its past practices, including detailed planning and preparation, the linkage between fighting and political mobilization, operational design, and combat tactics and performance.

The planning for the invasion of Vietnam was remarkable for its duration and comprehensive nature. Beijing's decision to fight a war in limited time and space by assembling a large number of resources and troops who lacked combat experience meant more complex preparations than the PLA had undertaken at any time since the Korean War. China's careful, almost obsessive, war plan not only involved a precise schedule but also was mapped out down to the deployments and maneuvers of the smallest units. The PLA's operational design demonstrated a preference for annihilating the enemy force through deep penetrations and encirclements and through deploying superior forces to seize and maintain the operational initiative. The most important and consistent characteristic of the Chinese way of war displayed in the border conflict remained the primacy of political control over military action. Because the CCP controlled the armed forces, the PLA was fully aware of the importance of the economic, political, and psychological elements of national power. The propaganda machine ran at full steam, concurrent with war preparations and fighting. Throughout the emerging crisis and the war that followed, the PLA's political work program continued to serve as a useful tool for the improvement of its combat effectiveness.

Since the 1979 war and the 1980s border conflicts with Vietnam, the PLA has undertaken sweeping revisions in defense doctrine, command and control, operational tactics, and force structure. The world of military operations transformed significantly after the 1991 Gulf War. The new emphasis on long-range and precision joint strikes drove the PLA's transformation even further. As the PLA continues to evolve, few expect China's armed forces to repeat their performance in the border war with Vietnam. But lingering remnants of that earlier and now-unpopular conflict remain, not least at the human level: for the short-term future, Sino-Vietnamese war veterans will continue to be promoted into top PLA leadership positions.[7] Many lessons learned from the Sino-Vietnamese military conflict are already outdated in light of today's high-tech-dominated modern warfare. But these leaders are the last generation of battle-tested PLA generals, and they experienced the PLA's post-1990 modernization. From a historical perspective, the distinctive Chinese way of fighting revealed by the Sino-Vietnamese military conflict may thus remain relevant both to China's military institutions and to observers seeking to understand the Chinese approach to employing military power—past, present, and future.

Notes

ABBREVIATIONS

Deng junshi wenji   CCP Central Documentary Research Department and PLA Military Science Academy, ed., *Deng Xiaoping junshi wenji* (Collected Military Works of Deng Xiaoping) vol. 3 (Beijing: Junshi kexue and Zhongyang wenxian, 2004)

Deng nianpu   Leng Rong and Wang Zuoling, chief eds., *Deng Xiaoping nianpu* (Chronicle of Deng Xiaoping's Life), 2 vols. (Beijing: Zhongyang wenxian, 2004)

FPA   Fujian Provincial Archives, Fuzhou

GGZH   Guangzhou Military Region Forward Command Political Department Cadre Section, ed., *ZhongYue bianjing ziwei huanji zuozhan ganbu gongzuo ziliao huibian* (Compilation of Materials on Cadre Work during the Counterattack in Self-Defense on the Sino-Vietnamese Border) (Guangzhou: Guangzhou junqu qianzhi zhengzhibu, 1979)

JCPL   Jimmy Carter Presidential Library, Atlanta

Mao junshi wenji   CCP Central Documentary Research Department, *Mao Zedong junshi wenji* (Collected Military Papers of Mao Zedong), vol. 2 (Beijing: Junshi kexue and Zhongyang wenxian, 1993)

Mao wengao   CCP Central Documentary Research Department, *Jianguo yilai Mao Zedong wengao* (Mao Zedong's Manuscripts since the Founding of the Country), 13 vols. (Beijing: Zhongyang wenxian, 1988–98).

77 Conversations   Odd Arne Westad, Chen Jian, Stein Tonnesson, Nguyen Vu Tung, and James G. Hershberg, eds., *77 Conversations between Chinese and Foreign Leaders on the War in Indochina, 1964–1977*, Cold War International History Project Working Paper no. 22 (Washington, D.C.: Woodrow Wilson International Center for Scholars, 1998)

YXFB   War Preparation and Aiding-the-Front Leading Group of Yunnan Province and Propaganda Department of the CCP Committee of Yunnan Province, eds., *Yingxiong de fengbei: Yunnan renmin shinian zhiqian jishi* (Heroic Monument: True Record of the Ten-Year Aiding-the-Front Work by the Yunnan People) (Kunming: Yunnan renmin, 1991)

ZGJX   General Office of the General Political Department, ed., *ZhongYue bianjing ziwei huanji zuozhan zhengzhi gongzuo jingyan xuanbian* (Compilation of Experiences of Political Work during the Counterattack in Self-Defense on the Sino-Vietnamese Border), 2 vols. (Beijing: Zongzhengzhibu, 1980).

Zhanlie   Headquarters of the PLA 55th Army, ed., *ZhongYue bianjing ziwei fanji zuozhan zhanlie xuanbian* (Selected Battle Cases from the Counterattack in Self-Defense on the Sino-Vietnamese border) (n.p.: n.p., 1980).

221

INTRODUCTION

1 See, for example, Xu Yan, *Diyici jiaoliang*; Department of Military History Studies, *Zhongguo Renmin Zhiyuanjun kangMei yuanChao zhanshi*; Qi, *Chaoxian zhanzheng*; Shen Zhihua, *Mao Zedong*.

2 Department of Military History Studies, *Zhongguo Renmin Jiefangjun qishinian*, 409.

3 Westad, "Introduction," 1–2.

4 *Renmin ribao*, 19 March 1979. For an English version, see *Peking Review*, 23 March 1979.

5 Jencks, "China's 'Punitive' War," 802–3; Hood, *Dragons Entangled*, 50–57; O'Dowd, *Chinese Military Strategy*, 6; Ross, *Indochina Tangle*, 285. For Deng's role in China's foreign policy beginning in the second half of the 1970s, see Ross, *Chinese Security Policy*, 213–30.

6 Segal, *Defending China*, 211, 213–15.

7 King C. Chen, *China's War with Vietnam*, 112–16, 152–53.

8 Ross, *Indochina Tangle*, 199–235.

9 Duiker, *China and Vietnam*, 90, 93.

10 Scobell, *China's Use of Military Force*, chapter 6; Lewis and Xue, *Imagined Enemies*, 127–33; Xiaobing Li, *History*, 250–64.

11 O'Dowd, *Chinese Military Strategy*, 160–61, 166.

12 Womack, *China and Vietnam*; Richardson, *China, Cambodia, and the Five Principles*; Khoo, *Collateral Damage*.

13 Womack, *China and Vietnam*, 1, 6–7.

14 Richardson, *China, Cambodia, and the Five Principles*, 111, 152–53.

15 Shu Guang Zhang illustrates the similar problem that the PLA confronted in the Korean War (*Mao's Military Romanticism*, 1).

16 See, for example, Baum, *Burying Mao*, 80; Evans, *Deng Xiaoping and the Making*, 226, 228; Benjamin Yang, *Deng*, 206–7. One exception is the recent publication of Vogel's *Deng Xiaoping*.

17 Marti, *China and the Legacy*, ii, argues that Deng and the military struck a "grand compromise" that allowed economic reform to go forward in exchange for larger military budgets.

18 Mao Mao, *Wo de fuqin Deng Xiaoping*, 292.

19 43rd Army, *DuiYue ziwei fanji zuozhan zongjie xuanbian*; Headquarters of the Kunming Military Region Artillery, *ZhongYue bianjing ziwei fanji zuozhan paobing zhuanti xuanbian*.

20 *Chinese Law and Government*, September–October 2009, 3–100; November–December 2009, 3–113.

21 Li Qianyuan and Song Ke, *Conglin qilue* (intended for internal use and classified as secret). The 1st Army was deployed to Laoshan between July 1984 and May 1985.

22 To pass PLA censors, Zhou acknowledged that he had to sanitize sensitive military information from manuscripts and obscure the unit's identity in his books.

23 Zhang Zhen, *Zhang Zhen huiyilu*.

24 Jiang Feng, Ma, and Dou, *Yangyong jiangjun zhuan*; Yang Qiliang, *Wang Shangrong jiangjun*.

25 Liu Jixian, *Ye Jianying nianpu*; Zhu, *Chen Yun nianpu*; Zhou Junlun, *Nie Rongzhen nianpu*; Wang Weicheng, *Li Xiannian nianpu*.

26 This website was available at http://bwl.top81.cn/war79/index.html.

27 See, for example, Zhang Yun, *Yunnansheng dang'an zhinan*.

CHAPTER 1

1 Vietnam, Ministry of Foreign Affairs, *Truth about Vietnam-China Relations*.

2 Duiker, *China and Vietnam*, 1.

3 For early studies, see Chen Jian, "China's Involvement"; Chen Jian, "China and the First Indochina War"; Zhai, "China and the Geneva Conference"; Xiaoming Zhang, "Vietnam War."

4 A recent study pinpoints 1970 as the year during which the breakdown of Vietnamese-Chinese relations began (Lien-Hang T. Nguyen, *Hanoi's War*, 193).

5 Shen Zhihua, "Dissolution of the Sino-Soviet Alliance," 36.

6 Walt, *Origins of Alliances*, 36.
7 Christensen, *Worse Than a Monolith*, 22.
8 Zhai, "Transplanting the Chinese Model," 694–96.
9 Vo, *Road to Dien Bien Phu*, 14–15.
10 Chen Jian, *China's Road to the Korean War*, 112.
11 Duiker, *Ho Chi Minh*, 420–22, 430.
12 For details of Chinese assistance to the Viet Minh during the First Indochina War, see Zhai, *China and the Vietnam Wars*, chapters 1, 2.
13 Mao to Wang Jianxiang, 27 May 1953, in CCP Central Documentary Research Department, *Mao wengao*, 4:240; Mao to Chinese Military Advisory Group, June 1953, quoted in Han Huaizhi and Tan, *Dangdai Zhongguo jundui de junshi gongzuo*, 536.
14 Diary entry, 6 September 1950, in Chen Geng, *Chen Geng riji (xu)*, 22. In a reprinted edition in 2003, Chen's criticism of Vietnamese leaders has been deleted.
15 In addition, of course, self-centered generals frequently make little mention of their coalition comrades and even those of their own armies, as was the case with such famous rivalries as Zhukov and Koniev or Montgomery and Patton.
16 Le Duan, "Comrade B."
17 Ibid., 280.
18 Li Danhui, "Issues."
19 According to Le Duan's account, this exchange of views took place between Le Duan and Zhang Wentian, deputy minister of foreign affairs, and then the latter reported it to Mao, who made such a comment in his cable to Zhang. Le Duan, "Comrade B." *Biography of Zhang Wentian* indicates that Zhang visited North Vietnam in early March 1959. See also Cheng, *Zhang Wentian zhuan*, 722.
20 Chen Jian, *Mao's China*, 131–32.
21 Le Duan, "Comrade B."
22 *Victory in Vietnam*, 49–50, 56.
23 Le Duan, "Comrade B." The proscription on using forces larger than platoon size might as well have reflected China's traditional emphasis on small, mobile, lightly armed guerrilla forces as well as a recognition that whenever Giap's Viet Minh had massed in large formations waging war in the open (right up to Dien Bien Phu), they had generally been overwhelmed by firepower-dominant opponents.
24 Hoang, *YueZhong zhandou de youyi*, 7–8; Guo Min et al., *ZhongYue guanxi*, 65–66.
25 Zhai, *China and the Vietnam Wars*, 77–81.
26 Shen Zhihua, "Dissolution of the Sino-Soviet Alliance," 30, 32.
27 Zhai, *China and the Vietnam Wars*, 82.
28 Ye Fei, *Ye Fei huiyilu*, 666.
29 Li Danhui, "Issues."
30 For the abandonment/entrapment dilemma in alliance theory, see Walt, "Alliances in a Unipolar World," 90.
31 Li Danhui, "Issues."
32 Wang Taiping, *Zhonghua Renmin Gongheguo waijiaoshi*, 2:35; Guo Min et al., *ZhongYue guanxi*, 67.
33 Xu Zehao, *Wang Jiaxiang zhuan*, 563, 565, 567.
34 Yang Kuisong, "Mao Zedong," 38.
35 In a meeting with General Chen Shiqu, commander of the Engineering Corps, and other officers in mid-June 1965, Zhou Enlai stressed this concern, saying that American imperialists wanted to encircle China but had failed in their conspiracy to do so in Korea: "They now come back again from Vietnam. Our assistance to Vietnam is to break the ring of encirclement and defend the country" (Wang Xiangen, *Zhongguo mimi dafabing*, 161).
36 Cong, *Quzhe qianjin*, 465; Liao, Li, and Xu, *Mao Zedong junshi sixiang*, 338–39.
37 Li Ke and Hao, *Wenhua dageming zhong de Jiefangjun*, 89–90.
38 Han Huaizhi and Tan, *Dangdai Zhongguo jundui de junshi gongzuo*, 539–40.
39 Ibid., 556–57.

40 Le Duan, "Comrade B." He made this strange charge in the emotional aftermath of the 1979 Chinese invasion.

41 Zhou Enlai, Deng Xiaoping, Kang Sheng, Le Duan, and Nguyen Duy Trinh, 13 April 1966, in *77 Conversations*, 94–96.

42 Le Duan, "Comrade B."

43 Wu Xiuquan, *Huiyi yu huainian*, 367–73.

44 Mao to Ho, 17 December 1963, in CCP Central Documentary Research Department, *Mao wengao*, 10:465–67.

45 "Matters Requiring Explanation for Foreign Inquiries Regarding Vietnam and Other Issues," 19 March 1963, CCP Central Committee. I received a copy of this document from a Chinese scholar who found it in the Jilin Provincial Archives.

46 Olsen, *Soviet-Vietnam Relations*, 121–25.

47 "Issues Pertaining to China's Aid to Vietnam," Yang Chengwu, deputy chief of the General Staff, to Luo Ruiqing, chief of the General Staff, Zhou Enlai, and Deng Xiaoping, 16 June 1965, in Li Danhui, "Issues."

48 "Report on the Negotiations between PRC Foreign Economic Commission/Ministry of Foreign Trade and DRV Economic Delegation," 10 July 1965, in ibid.

49 Zhou Enlai and Ho Chi Minh, 8 November 1965, in *77 Conversations*," 88n135.

50 Zhou Enlai and Pham Van Dong, 9 October 1965, Zhou Enlai and Le Duan, 23 March 1966, in ibid., 89–90, 93–94.

51 Zhou Enlai, Deng Xiaoping, Kang Sheng, Le Duan, and Nguyen Duy Trinh, 13 April 1966, in ibid., 96–97.

52 Ibid., 195.

53 "Revisionist-U.S. Conspiracy," *Peking Review*, 7 January 1966, 18.

54 Li Ke and Hao, *Wenhua dageming zhong de Renmin Jiefangjun*, 414.

55 On 17 November 1968, during an interview with Pham Van Dong, Mao asked North Vietnamese leaders to consider the possible withdrawal of Chinese troops since Washington had stopped bombing. To assure Hanoi's leaders of China's continuing support, Mao said that they could keep some Chinese troops there. The Chinese withdrawal did not end until July 1970. See *Mao Zedong waijiao wenxuan*, ed. PRC Ministry of Foreign Affairs and CCP Central Documentary Research Department, 582–83.

56 Khoo, "Breaking the Ring," 29–37.

57 Gaiduk, *Soviet Union and the Vietnam War*, 216–17.

58 Xiaoming Zhang, "Communist Powers Divided," 90–92.

59 Hoang, *Canghai yisu*, 307.

60 Hoang, *YueZhong zhandou de youyi*, 25. See also *New York Times*, 7 March 1966.

61 Political letter of the Soviet embassy in the DRV, "Report of the Workers' Party of Vietnam's Indochina Policy from Soviet Ambassador to Vietnam," 21 May 1971, in Li Danhui, "Issues."

62 Wang Xiangen, *YuanYue kangMei shilu*, 229–35.

63 Guo Min et al., *ZhongYue guanxi*, 102.

64 Wang Xiangen, *YuanYue kangMei shilu*, 60–68.

65 Li Danhui, "Issues."

66 Truong, Chanoff, and Doan, *Viet Cong Memoir*, 248.

67 Minutes of conversation between Zhou Enlai and Le Duc Tho, 18 June 1972, Ministry of Railroad. I received a copy of this document from a Chinese scholar.

68 After Czechoslovakia, Mao no longer perceived China's dispute with the Soviet Union as an ideological issue but rather saw it as a struggle against Soviet "socialist imperialism." See Niu, "Outline," 81.

69 Ostermann, "New Evidence," 186–87; Li Danhui, "Debut," 157–58.

70 Xiong Xianghui, *Lishi de zhujiao*, 173–74.

71 CCP Party History Research Office, *Zhonggong dangshi dashi nianbiao*, 371; Li Ke and Hao, *Wenhua dageming zhong de Renmin Jiefangjun*, 255–59.

72 Xiong Xianghui, *Lishi de zhujiao*, 194; Li Danhui, "Debut," 162.

73 On 23 November 1969, Zhou talked with Vietnamese Politburo members Le Thanh Nghi

and Hoang Van Hoan about the ongoing Sino-Soviet border negotiations (Foreign Ministry, Diplomatic History Research Office, *Zhou Enlai waijiao huodong dashiji*, 546).

74 Li Ke and Hao, *Wenhua dageming zhong de Renmin Jiefangjun*, 412.

75 Zhai, *China and the Vietnam Wars*, 198.

76 According to Hoang Van Hoan, Zhou Enlai promised the Hanoi leadership that "the Vietnam and Indochina problem must be resolved prior to the normalization of Sino-U.S. relations to ease tensions in the Far East. We [the Chinese] do not seek the settlement of the Taiwan issue first and will do it next" (*YueZhong zhandou de youyi*, 26).

77 On 3 March 1972, Le Duan told Zhou, "Nixon has met with you already, comrade. Soon they [the US] will attack me even harder" (Le Duan, "Comrade B"). See also Li Qi, *Zhou Enlai nianpu*, 515.

78 Zhai, *China and the Vietnam Wars*, 204–5.

79 Han Nianlong, *Dangdai Zhongguo waijiao*, 162.

80 According to one Chinese source, between 1971 and 1972, the direct transfer of PLA arms and equipment to North Vietnam included 14 planes, 3 surface-to-air missile systems and 180 missiles, 2 warning radar systems, 20 amphibious tanks, 2 sets of pontoon bridge equipment, and 204 large-caliber field guns along with 45,000 shells (Li Ke and Hao, *Wenhua dageming zhong de Renmin Jiefangjun*, 412).

81 On 9 May 1972, Hanoi's ambassador in Beijing asked the Chinese leadership to help sweep mines in Haiphong Harbor. Zhou realized China's weakness in this regard and thus responded by asking why the North Vietnamese did not ask the Soviets for assistance inasmuch as their navy was much better equipped and advanced. The Vietnamese side never responded, instead reiterating the request (Lai, "Premier Zhou's Management," 297; Lai was the PLA navy's deputy chief of staff at the time).

82 Guo Min et al., *ZhongYue guanxi*, 102.

83 Le Duan, "Comrade B."

84 Zhai, *China and the Vietnam Wars*, 207.

85 Morris, *Soviet-Chinese-Vietnamese Triangle*, 20.

86 Zhou Enlai, Kang Sheng, and Pham Van Dong, 29 April 1968, in *77 Conversations*, 130.

87 Zhai, *China and the Vietnam Wars*, 214.

88 Deng Xiaoping and Le Duan, 29 September 1975, in *77 Conversations*, 194–95.

89 Morris, *Why Vietnam Invaded Cambodia*, 181.

90 Tonnesson, "Le Duan," 275.

91 Morris, *Why Vietnam Invaded Cambodia*, 180–81.

92 Pang and Jin, *Mao Zedong zhuan*, 1650–52, 1674–77.

93 Mao Mao, *Wo de fuqin Deng Xiaoping*, 292–93.

94 Han Huaizhi and Tan, *Dangdai Zhongguo jundui de junshi gongzuo*, 648–57.

95 Khoo, *Collateral Damage*, 94.

96 Li Qi, *Zhou Enlai nianpu*, 689–90; Evans, *Deng Xiaoping zhuan*, 98.

97 Ministry of Foreign Affairs Archives, *Weiren de zuji*, 86–87.

98 Gong, *Deng Xiaoping yu Meiguo*, 137.

99 See, for example, Deng's talk with Gerald Ford, 21, 22 December 1975, in *Weiren de zuji*, ed. Ministry of Foreign Affairs Archives, 151–52.

100 Tonnesson, "Le Duan," 275.

101 On 4 September 1958, the Chinese government issued twelve-mile territorial sea claims that included the Dongsha (Pratas), Xisha (Paracels), Zhongsha (Macclesfield Bank), and Nansha (Spratlys) Islands as Chinese territories. On 14 September, Phan Van Dong wrote to Zhou Enlai that the Vietnamese government agreed with China's sea territorial claims (http://blog.sina.com.cn/s/blog_6f4257280100sie3.html; 10 December 2011).

102 Wang Taiping, *Zhonghua Renmin Gongheguo waijiaoshi*, 3:62; Zhai, *China and the Vietnam Wars*, 209–10.

103 Han Huaizhi and Tan, *Dangdai Zhongguo jundui de junshi gongzuo*, 659.

104 Lien-Hang T. Nguyen, "Sino-Vietnamese Split," 26.

105 Li Qi, *Zhou Enlai nianpu*, 717.

106 Mao and Le Duan, 24 September 1975, in + *Conversations*, 194.
107 Deng and Le Duan, 29 September 1975, in ibid., 194–95.
108 Goscha, "Vietnam," 152.
109 Zhai, *China and the Vietnam Wars*, 265n100; Goscha, "Vietnam," 173–74.
110 Ministry of Foreign Affairs Archives, *Weiren de zuji*, 132–36, 140–44, 149–50.
111 Vogel, *Deng Xiaoping*, 273.
112 According to a Ministry of Foreign Affairs document, Vietnam's cleansing efforts against ethnic Chinese began in early 1977 and intensified in early 1978. "How to Answer the Questions by Foreigners about Sino-Vietnamese Relations," 13 May 1978, Ministry of Foreign Affairs, Sichuan Provincial Archives, Chengdu.
113 Editorial Group, *Li Xiannian zhuan*, 917–18.
114 Wang Taiping, *Zhonghua Renmin Gongheguo waijiaoshi*, 64–67.
115 Hua Guofeng and Pol Pot, 29 September 1977, in *77 Conversations*, 196.
116 Khoo, *Collateral Damage*, 122.
117 Goscha, "Vietnam," 174.
118 Ross, *Indochina Tangle*, 160.
119 Richardson, *China, Cambodia, and the Five Principles*, 98–99.
120 Vogel, *Deng Xiaoping*, 273.
121 Di, "Most Respected Enemy"; Chen Jian, "China's Involvement."
122 Chen Jian, *Mao's China*, 237.
123 Xiaoming Zhang, "China's Involvement."

CHAPTER 2

1 Ross, *Indochina Tangle*, 118–23, 127–28. The Chinese claimed that they could not maintain the same level of assistance for Vietnam as they had during the war because China's economy was facing great difficulties at the time. See Guo Min et al., *Zhong Yue guanxi*, 114.
2 King C. Chen, *China's War with Vietnam*, 35–36.
3 Luo, *Baizhan jiangxing Wang Shangrong*, 375–77; Yang Qiliang, *Wang Shangrong jiangjun*, 626.
4 Vasquez and Henehan, "Territorial Disputes."
5 Guo Min et al., *Zhong Yue guanxi*, 169; Zhou Deli, *Yige gaoji canmouzhang de zishu*, 241–42.
6 Han Huaizhi and Tan, *Dangdai Zhongguo jundui de junshi gongzuo*, 659.
7 Zhou Deli, *Yige gaoji canmouzhang de zishu*, 239–40.
8 Han Nianlong, *Dangdai Zhongguo waijiao*, 285–86.
9 Military History Institute, *Yuenan Renminjun wushinian*, 267–68.
10 Womack, *China and Vietnam*, 199.
11 Since 1949, China has been involved in twenty-three territorial disputes with its neighbors on land and at sea but has used force in only six of those incidents (Fravel, *Strong Borders, Secure Nation*, 1–2).
12 Zhou Deli, *Yige gaoji canmouzhang de zishu*, 242–43.
13 This information comes from a source that credited it to *Guangzhou junqu dashi ji*.
14 "Zhongguo Renmin Jiefangjun Tongjian" Editorial Committee, *Zhongguo Renmin Jiefangjun tongjian*, 2173.
15 Zhang Zhen, *Zhang Zhen huiyilu*, 165–66.
16 Unless otherwise noted, all detailed information about China's invasion plan was provided by Cai Pengcen, a history graduate student at Southwest University in China.
17 Zhou Deli, *Yige gaoji canmouzhang de zishu*, 244–45; Zhang Zhen, *Zhang Zhen junshi wenxuan*, 298; Wang Hancheng, *Wang Hancheng huiyilu*, 535. Both Zhang and Wang mention that the troops from the Wuhan and Chengdu Military Regions were regarded as constituting the PLA's strategic reserves.
18 Jin Ye, Hu, and Hu, *Baizhan jiangxing Xu Shiyou*, 329–31.
19 Geng, "Secret Report," 150–52.
20 King C. Chen, *China's War with Vietnam*, 87.

21 Ye Yonglie, *Cong Hua Guofeng dao Deng Xiaoping*, 526–27; Sun, "Historical Turning Point," 498; Xiao, *Xiao Jinguang huiyilu xuji*, 361–63.

22 The Third Plenum of the Tenth Central Party Committee, which was held between 16 and 21 July 1977, designated Hua, as CCP chair, to maintain overall control of party, state, and military affairs while Ye remained in charge of the military. Wang, who was promoted to vice chair of the party one month later, was responsible for party organization, propaganda, and public security (Ye Yonglie, *Cong Hua Guofeng dao Deng Xiaoping*, 222, 227, 235–36, 240).

23 CCP Central Documentary Editorial Committee, *Deng Xiaoping wenxuan*, 2:65.

24 Ye Yonglie, *Cong Hua guofeng dao Deng Xiaoping*, 222–26; Sun, "Historical Turning Point," 478–80.

25 Lee, *From Third World to First*, 601–2.

26 The most authoritative account of the 1978 Central Work Conference is Yu Guangyuan, *1978*. Yu was a participant in the conference.

27 King C. Chen, *China's War with Vietnam*, 85.

28 Although Wang remained as one vice chair of the party, he was no longer in control either of the party's general office or of the PLA's central guard unit (Yu Guangyuan, *1978*, 156–68). See also Ye Yonglie, *Cong Hua Guofeng dao Deng Xiaoping*, 463–528.

29 CCP Central Documentary Editorial Committee, *Deng Xiaoping wenxuan*, 3:269.

30 Li Shenzi, *Li Shenzhi Wenji*, 334.

31 Qian Jiang, *Deng Xiaoping yu ZhongMei jianjiao*, 153; Gong, *Deng Xiaoping yu Meiguo*, 236.

32 Howard, *Causes of War*, 13.

33 Aron, *Peace and War*, 19.

34 Zhai, *China and the Vietnam Wars*, 214.

35 Zhou Enlai, Deng Xiaoping, Kang Sheng, Le Duan, and Nguyen Duy Trinh, 13 April 1966, Deng Xiaoping and Le Duan, 29 September 1975, both in *77 Conversations*, 94–96, 193–94.

36 Le Duan, "Comrade B." See also Nguyen Vu Tung, "Interpreting Beijing and Hanoi," 57.

37 Vogel, *Deng Xiaoping*, 274.

38 These are Chinese official statistics, though it is difficult to determine how the Chinese calculated their aid. According to an authoritative Chinese source, China provided North Vietnam with a total of 4.26 billion RMB in military assistance between 1950 and 1974 (Li Ke and Hao, *Wenhua dageming zhong de Renmin Jiefangjun*, 409).

39 More than 40,000 ethnic Chinese living in Vietnam had been repatriated by April 1978. All their belongings were confiscated before they crossed the border ("How to Answer the Questions by Foreigners about Sino-Vietnamese Relations," 13 May 1978, Ministry of Foreign Affairs, Sichuan Provincial Archives, Chengdu).

40 Guo Min et al., *ZhongYue guanxi*, 106.

41 Luo, *Baizhan jiangxing Wang Shangrong*, 377.

42 Lee, *From Third World to First*, 595.

43 Vogel, *Deng Xiaoping*, 528.

44 Khoo, *Collateral Damage*, 106–7.

45 Ross, *Indochina Tangle*, 189.

46 Zhai, *China and the Vietnam Wars*, 214.

47 For example, in March 1978, the leader of the Supreme Soviet sent a message to the Standing Committee of the Chinese National People's Congress proposing a joint statement on principles guiding state relations. The Chinese publicly turned down this proposal.

48 For Deng's views on the Soviet Union, see Memcon, Brzezinski-Deng, 21 May 1978, China Vertical File, JCPL. See also Wang Zhongchun, "Soviet Factor," 165–66.

49 Wang Zhongchun, "Soviet Factor," 158–64.

50 Ministry of Foreign Affairs Archives, *Weiren de zuji*, 158.

51 Memcon, Brzezinski-Deng, 21 May 1978, China Vertical File, JCPL.

52 *Kyodo*, 26 February 1979, in Foreign Broadcast Information Service, PRC, 26 February 1979, A6.

53 Deng Xiaoping believed that the war against Vietnam would show the international com-

munity that "China will not be bullied" (*buxinxie*) and "will show that a tiger whose backside can be touched." (*laohu pigu keyi mo*) *Deng junshi wenji*, 177.

54 Memorandum, Stansfield Turner to Brzezinski, 21 November 1978, NLC-26-57-1-6-4, JCPL.
55 Nathan and Ross, *Great Wall*, 44–45.
56 Wang Zhongchun, "Soviet Factor," 166. The existing Western scholarship reveals no evidence of any Soviet role in support for Vietnam's decision to invade Cambodia. See Morris, *Why Vietnam Invaded Cambodia*, 215–17.
57 *Deng nianpu*, 1:411.
58 Xie Yixian, *Zhongguo waijiao shi*, 78.
59 Deng Xiaoping's meeting with Vice President Walter Mondale, 27 August 1979, Ministry of Foreign Affairs, FPA.
60 Min, *ZhongYue zhanzheng shinian*, 15.
61 "Deng Xiaoping's Speech, 16 March 1979."
62 Deng Xiaoping's meeting with Hassan Tuhami, vice premier, Egyptian president Anwar Sadat's representative, 28 February 1979, Ministry of Foreign Affairs, FPA.
63 Zhou Deli, *Yige gaoji canmouzhang de zishu*, 246.
64 Qian Jiang, *Deng Xiaoping yu ZhongMei jianjiao*, 151.
65 Zhong Wen and Lu, *Bainian Deng Xiaoping*, 160. See also Gong, "Difficult Path," 315.
66 Gong, "Difficult Path," 140.
67 *Deng nianpu*, 1:417.
68 Tyler, *Great Wall*, 260.
69 Wang Taiping, *Zhonghua Renmin Gongheguo waijiaoshi*, 3:378.
70 Qian Jiang, *Deng Xiaoping yu ZhongMei jianjiao*, 156.
71 Memcon, Carter-Chai, 19 September 1978, China Vertical File, JCPL.
72 Memorandum, Brzezinski to Carter, 5 December 1978, China, Box 9, Brzezinski File, JCPL.
73 On 5, 9, and 11 December, Deng spent half days working with his speechwriters on his final address at the Central Work Conference, which was scheduled for the afternoon of 13 December (*Deng nianpu*, 1:448–49).
74 Min, *ZhongYue zhanzheng shinian*, 18.
75 Woodcock to Vance and Brzezinski, 13, 14 December 1978, China Vertical File, JCPL.
76 Woodcock to Brzezinski, 15 December 1978, China Vertical File, JCPL.
77 Li Jie, "China's Domestic Politics," 87.
78 Li Shenzhi, *Li Shenzhi wenji*, 335.
79 Geng, "Secret Report," 149.
80 King C. Chen, *China's War with Vietnam*, 85–87; Ross, *Indochina Tangle*, 23–31; Scobell, *China's Use of Military Force*, 130–32.
81 See, for example, Liu Jixian, *Ye Jianying nianpu*; Fan Shuo, *Ye Jianying zhuan*; Zhou Junlun, *Nie Rongzhen nianpu*; Editorial Group, *Li Xiannian zhuan*.
82 China News Agency International Information Group, *Woguo duiYue ziwei huanjizhan ziliao ji*, 16–17.
83 Liu Zhi and Zhang, *Xu Xiangqian zhuan*, 549, 553–54.
84 My source learned of Ye's opposition to the war against Vietnam from one of Ye's family members.
85 Liu Jixian, *Ye Jianying nianpu*, 1165.
86 When Deng's picture was projected on a big screen at the evening celebration of the 1977 PLA Day, all participants cheered and applauded. The central leadership considered this response a serious political incident because Deng was not the commander in chief and subsequently criticized the action for ignoring the party's rules and discipline. However, the General Political Department allegedly refused to let the incident become a serious issue (Zhang Sheng, *Cong zhanzheng zhong zoulai*, 412–13).
87 Ye Yonglie, *Cong Hua Guofeng dao Deng Xiaoping*, 212.
88 Liu Jixian, *Ye Jianying nianpu*, 1158, 1165.
89 "Wang Shangrong's Speech, 16 March 1979."

90 Liu Huaqing recalls that when he served as assistant chief of the General Staff in early 1979, important documents were always sent to Deng for approval (*Liu Huaqing huiyilu*, 394).

91 "Deng Xiaoping's Speech, 16 March 1979."

92 Ibid.

93 Zuo Yi, "Diplomats from China." The author, a reporter with the China News Agency, was assigned to Cambodia during Vietnam's invasion.

94 Xing Heping, a railway adviser in Cambodia in 1978, posted his diaries on the Internet under the pseudonym Zhong Li, "Xing Heping Diary," 26 December 1978.

95 Zhang Zhen, *Zhang Zhen huiyilu*, 166; Xie Hainan, Yang, and Yang, *Yang Dezhi yisheng*, 302.

96 These two armies were the 50th from the Chengdu Military Region and the 54th from the Wuhan Military Region, which received their mobilization orders on 5 January 1979 (Cai Pengcen, "Events").

97 "Wang Shangrong's Speech, 16 March 1979."

98 Ye Jianying was on vacation in Shanghai from late December 1978 to 1 January 1979 and did not participate this meeting (Liu Jixian, *Ye Jianying nianpu*, 1165). Also there is no record that Li Xiannian attended the meeting (Wang Weicheng, *Li Xiannian nianpu*, 691).

99 Jin Ye, Hu, and Hu, *Baizhan jiangxing Xu Shiyou*, 332; Wang Xuan, *Mao Zedong zhi jian*, 132; Xie Hainan, Yang, and Yang, *Yang Dezhi yisheng*, 302.

100 Solinger, "Politics in Yunnan Province," 657.

101 The two generals had bickered over whose unit had won a combat victory over a Nationalist elite unit during the civil war period. In addition, as a deputy commander in the Nanjing Military Region, Wang had openly supported a local political faction against Xu during the Cultural Revolution in 1966.

102 Xie Hainan, Yang, and Yang, *Yang Dezhi yisheng*, 302.

103 According to Deng, many of the Gang of Four's supporters continued to hold their positions inside the PLA in 1978. See Deng Xiaoping's talk with the leadership of PLA General Political Department, 11 April 1978, in *Deng junshi wenji*, 99–100.

104 After receiving the oral report about the conference from Xu, Wei Guoqing (director of the General Political Department), and Yang Yong, Deng made four points: first, the members of the leading group must be united; second, the problem of factionalism within the leadership must be eliminated; third, all issues must be handled by the CMC at meetings; and fourth, the policies for rehabilitation must be implemented (*Deng nianpu*, 1:459–60).

105 Zhang Sheng, *Cong zhanzheng zhong zoulai*, 415.

106 Yu Guangyuan, *1978*, 241–42.

107 *Deng junshi wenji*, 148.

108 "Deng Xiaoping's Speech, 16 March 1979."

109 *Deng nianpu*, 1:492.

110 "Lecture Notes." This item has been published anonymously, but it appears accurate.

111 Jiang Feng, Ma, and Dou, *Yangyong jiangjun zhuan*, 495; Luo, *Baizhan jiangxing Wang Shangrong*, 377.

112 Zhou Deli, *Xu Shiyou*, 16.

113 Zhu, *Chen Yun nianpu*, 235–36.

114 Zhang Zhen, *Zhang Zhen huiyilu*, 166.

115 Iklé, *Every War Must End*, 8.

116 Min, *ZhongYue zhanzheng shinian*, 17; Jin Hui, Zhang, and Zhang, *ZhongYue zhanzheng milu*, 27–28.

117 Segal, *Defending China*, 214.

118 Zhou Deli, *Yige gaoji canmouzhang de zishu*, 246.

119 *ZGJX*, 1:2–19.

120 Zhang Zhen, *Zhang Zhen huiyilu*, 170–71.

121 Jiang Feng, Ma, and Dou, *Yangyong jiangjun zhuan*, 495.

122 Zhou Deli, *Yige gaoji canmouzhang de zishu*, 257–58; Zhang Zhen, *Zhang Zhen huiyilu*, 171.

123 Qian Jiang, *Deng Xiaoping yu ZhongMei jianjiao*, 211.

124 Deng made it clear that he was continuing Mao's strategy ("Deng Xiaoping's Speech, 16 March 1979").

125 Gong, *Deng Xiaoping yu Meiguo*, 255; Tao, "Deng Xiaoping"; Li Xiangqian, "Establishment."

126 Geng, "Secret Report," 156.

127 Memorandum, Brzezinski to Carter, n.d. 1979, China, Box 9, Brzezinski File, JCPL.

128 Memorandum, Michel Oksenberg to Brzezinski, 29 January 1979, China, Box 9, Brzezinski File, JCPL.

129 Memocon, Carter-Deng, 29 January 1979, China Vertical File, JCPL.

130 Brzezinski, *Power and Principle*, 409.

131 Carter to Deng, 30 January 1979, China, Box 9, Brzezinski File, JCPL.

132 Brzezinski, *Power and Principle*, 410.

133 Many of his subordinates have recalled that Deng would not change his mind once he had thought a situation through and made his decision. See, for example, Chen Zaidao, *Chen Zaidao huiyilu*, 462.

134 Brzezinski, *Power and Principle*, 410.

135 In his memoirs, Robert Gates recollects that Carter and Deng had reached an agreement for technical intelligence cooperation against the Soviet Union, and in 1980, Gates and CIA director Stansfield Turner traveled to Beijing to implement this agreement (*Duty*, 413).

136 Chen Jian, *Mao's China*, 73–74.

137 Tyler, *Great Wall*, 276–78.

138 "Deng Xiaoping's Speech, 16 March 1979."

139 Deng even invited some of his escorts to play bridge with him on the plane (Qian Jiang, *Deng Xiaoping yu ZhongMei jianjiao*, 291).

140 Geng, "Secret Report," 158.

141 According to Mann, during China's invasion of Vietnam, Brzezinski met with Chinese ambassador Chai Zemin every night, turning over American intelligence on Soviet military deployments on their Chinese border (*About Face*, 100).

142 "Deng Xiaoping's Speech, 16 March 1979."

143 Zhou Deli, *Yige gaoji canmouzhang de zishu*, 259–60; Jiang Feng, Ma, and Dou, *Yangyong jiangjun zhuan*, 496–97.

144 A copy of this document appears in Min, *ZhongYue zhanzheng shinian*, 34.

145 Jencks, "China's 'Punitive' War," 804–5; Yee, "Sino-Vietnamese Border War, 22. Segal, *Defending China*, 214.

146 Gong, "Triangular Relationship"; Wang Zhongchun, "Soviet Factor," 173.

147 Wang Zhongchun argues that China overstated the Soviet military threat to prevent the PRC from falling into "a strategically weak position" ("Soviet Factor," 173).

148 Gong Li mistakenly states that Deng notified Carter of China's war decision at an official meeting on 29 January 1979, thereby misleading his readers into believing that the notification took place during a normal discussion between the leaders as they exchanged their views of the world ("Triangular Relationship," 68).

149 Deng Xiaoping's speech at the Fifth Meeting of Diplomats, 7 July 1979, Ministry of Foreign Affairs, FPA.

150 Deng Xiaoping's meeting with Guinean president Ahmed Sékou Touré, 5 May 1980, Ministry of Foreign Affairs, FPA.

151 Niu, "Returning to Asia," 65.

152 "Deng Xiaoping's Speech, 16 March 1979."

153 Foot points out that no one actually expected the Taiwan arms sales issue to remain "a central point of tension in U.S.-China relations to today" ("Prizes Won, Opportunities Lost," 109).

154 "Deng Xiaoping's Speech, 16 March 1979."

CHAPTER 3

1 Zhou Deli, *Yige gaoji canmouzhang de zishu*, 246.

2 Department of General Staff, *Mao Zedong junshi wenxuan*, 197–200, 218, 225–34.

3 Ibid., 75.
4 Ibid., 327–28.
5 Ibid., 18–20.
6 Ibid., 261.
7 Zhou Keyu, *Dangdai Zhongguo jundui de zhengzhi gongzuo*, 234–37.
8 CCP Central Documentary Research Department, *Mao junshi wenji*, 2:106–7.
9 Department of Military History Studies, *Zhongguo Renmin Jiefangjun qishinian*, 224.
10 The three armies of the North China Field Army were never reorganized, as some Western literature has claimed, into a fifth field army. Instead, they were initially under the direct control of the CMC, and a few months later, two of the three armies were reassigned to the First Field Army. Ibid.
11 Segal, *Defending China*, 213–17.
12 Ross, *Indochina Tangle*, 224.
13 Cai Pengcen, "Events."
14 Ibid.
15 "Lecture Notes."
16 Zhou Deli, *Xu Shiyou*, 123–24.
17 Xiang Zhonghua, political commissar of the Guangzhou Military Region, was absent due to his attendance at the Central Work Conference in Beijing (Zhou Deli, *Yige gaoji canmouzhang de zishu*, 247).
18 The forces in Guangdong Province were the 42nd Army at Huiyang, the 55th Army at Shantou, the 1st Artillery Division at Shaoguan, and the 70th Antiaircraft Artillery Division at Shantou (ibid., 254).
19 Ibid., 248–49.
20 Zhou Deli, *Xu Shiyou*, 43–44.
21 Jin Ye, Hu, and Hu, *Xu Shiyou zhuan*, 87, 435.
22 Zhou Deli, *Yige gaoji canmouzhang de zishu*, 249–50.
23 For details about the Lin Biao incident, see Qiu Jin, *Culture of Power*.
24 Fan Junchang, *Tiexue zhanjiang Liu Changyi*, 458–59.
25 For example, the commander of the 54th Army was apprehensive about the way Xu assigned each of his divisions to support the three armies of the Guangzhou Military Region during the invasion (Chaoshui, "1979").
26 Zhou Deli, *Yige gaoji canmouzhang de zishu*, 252–53.
27 Ibid., 257–59.
28 Wang purportedly left Kunming indignantly and requested that two of his children serving in Yunnan be allowed to participate in the war.
29 Xie Hainan, Yang, and Yang, *Yang Dezhi yisheng*, 304.
30 Ni, *Shinian ZhongYue zhanzheng*, 1:85–86.
31 King C. Chen, *China's War with Vietnam*, 152.
32 "Lecture Notes."
33 Cai Pengcen, "Events." See also Financial Department of Kunming Military Region Logistics, "Basic Summary of Financial Support Work in Yunnan," in *Yunnan fangxiang ZhongYue bianjing ziwei huanji zuozhan houqin caiwu baozhang gongzuo ziliao xuanbian*, ed. Financial Department of Kunming Military Region Logistics, 10.
34 Local History Compilation Committee of Guangdong, *Guangdong shengzhi junshi zhi*, 751.
35 "Combat History."
36 Zhou Deli, *Yige gaoji canmouzhang de zishu*, 251, 254.
37 Ibid., 251.
38 "Lecture Notes."
39 Wang Dinglie, *Dangdai Zhongguo kongjun*, 637.
40 Zhang Zhizhi, "Air Force Troops," 350–52.
41 South Sea Fleet, Political Department, "Personal Experiences of the '217' Task Force on Launching Political Work while Coordinating Efforts during the War of Self-Defense against Vietnam," in *ZGJX*, 1:359–66.

42 Zhou Deli, *Yige gaoji canmouzhang de zishu*, 269–71.

43 Zhou Deli, *Xu Shiyou*, 66.

44 Local History Compilation Committee of Guangdong, *Guangdong shengzhi junshi zhi*, 751, 797–98; Local History Compilation Committee of Guangxi, *Guangxi tongzhi junshi zhi*, 425.

45 Local History Compilation Committee of Guangdong, *Guangdong shengzhi junshi zhi*, 797.

46 "Circular from the Military Region Forward Command Political Department and Logistics Department on Retention of Technically Skilled Cadres," 12 December 1978, in *GGZH*, 26–27.

47 "Summary of 42nd Army Cadre Wartime Work," and "Summary of 55th Army Wartime Cadre Work," both in ibid., 83, 93.

48 "Summary of 42nd Army Cadre Wartime Work," in *GGZH*, 83.

49 "Combat History."

50 Zhou Deli, *Xu Shiyou*, 68.

51 Department of Military History Studies, *Zhongguo Renmin Jiefangjun qishinian*, 425.

52 Wang Dinglie, *Dangdai Zhongguo kongjun*, 511.

53 Zhang Zhen, *Zhang Zhen huiyilu*, 170–71.

54 Zhou Deli, *Xu Shiyou*, 67.

55 Ibid., 67–68.

56 Ibid.

57 The unit history of the PAVN forces suggests that many of the divisions in Vietnam's northern border region had just shifted from working on economic construction projects to preparing for possible combat missions prior to China's invasion. See, for example, see Dang Van Nhung, *Su Doan 338*; Nguyen Huu Bo, *Su Doan Bo Binh*. Copies of translated texts provided by Merle Pribbenow.

58 *Deng junshi wenji*, 20–25.

59 Zhang Zhen, *Zhang Zhen huiyilu*, 166–68.

60 Ibid., 167.

61 Yunnan Provincial Military District, *Junshi zhi*, 595.

62 Zhang Zhen, *Zhang Zhen huiyilu*, 167.

63 Shu Guang Zhang, *Mao's Military Romanticism*, 13.

64 "CMC's Political Order for Protecting the Border in the Counterattack in Self-Defense, 12 February 1979," in *ZhongYue bianjing ziwei huanji zuozhan zhengzhi gongzuo jingyan xuanbian*, ed. Training Department of PLA Political College, 1–2.

65 O'Dowd, *Chinese Military Strategy*, 165.

66 Mo Wenhua's speech at the armored force work conference, in *DuiYue ziwei huanjizhan zhuangjiabing zhengzhi gongzuo jingyan*, ed. Armored Force Political Department, 1, 7–8, 10.

67 Unit 33720 (43rd Army's 127th Division) Political Department, "Launching Thorough Education Programs on Patriotism and Revolutionary Heroism," in *ZGJX*, 1:137.

68 Unit 39530 (Air Force Kunming Command), Political Department, Propaganda Office, "Launching Tactical Research Programs and Utilizing Our Current Equipment to Win the War," in *ZGJX*, 1:391.

69 Mo Wenhua's speech at the armored force work conference, in *DuiYue ziwei huanjizhan zhuangjiabing zhengzhi gongzuo jingyan*, ed. Armored Force Political Department, 7–8.

70 Office of the General Political Department, "Experiences of Political Work in the Counterattack in Self-Defense against Vietnam," in *ZGJX*, 1:2–3.

71 Zhou Keyu, *Dangdai Zhongguo jundui de Zhengzhi gongzuo*, 152.

72 This information is based on reports from the 43rd Army, the 41st Division of the 14th Army, the 3rd Border Guard Division of the Guangxi Military District, the 124th Regiment of the 42nd Division of the 14th Army, and the 22nd Automobile Regiment of the Guangzhou Military Region. See *ZGJX*, 1:132–60.

73 Unit 33720 (43rd Army's 127th Division) Political Department, "Launching Thorough Education Programs on Patriotism and Revolutionary Heroism," in *ZGJX*, 1:138–39.

74 In Yunnan Province alone, local county governments sent border residents and Chinese who had returned from living in Vietnam to help military forces to conduct these educational activities. "Report by Yunnan Provincial Military District," in *YXFB*, 533.

75 Unit 54257 (3rd Border Division of Guangxi Military District), Political Department, "Conducting Widespread and Thorough Education Centering on Denunciation to Achieve Political Mobilization," and Unit 35208 (14th Army's 41st Division), Political Department, "Arousing Hatred for the Enemy through the Effective Use of Denunciation," both in *ZGJX*, 1:146–55.

76 Cai Pengcen, "Events."

77 Unit 33720 (43rd Army's 127th Division) Political Department, "Launching Thorough Education Programs on Patriotism and Revolutionary Heroism," in *ZGJX*, 1:140.

78 "Circular from the Military Region Forward Command Political Department Cadre Division," 28 December 1978, in *DuiYue ziwei huanjizhan zhuangjiabing zhengzhi gongzuo jingyan*, ed. Armored Force Political Department, 28–30.

79 Zhou Deli, *Xu Shiyou*, 39–44; Office of the General Political Department, "Experiences of Political Work in the Counterattack in Self-Defense against Vietnam," in *ZGJX*, 1:8.

80 South Sea Fleet, Political Department, "Personal Experiences of the '217' Task Force on Launching Political Work while Coordinating Efforts during the War of Self-Defense against Vietnam," in *ZGJX*, 1:361–62.

81 Unit 39530 (Air Force Kunming Command), Political Department, Propaganda Office, "Launching Tactical Research Programs and Utilizing Our Current Equipment to Win the War," in *ZGJX*, 1:390–93. An important aspect of the Pakistani air force's success against the MiG-21 was the addition of American heat-seeking AIM-9 Sidewinder air-to-air missiles.

82 Jiang Hao and Lin, "Recollections."

83 "Directives from the General Political Department on Political Work Conducted by Troop Units during Military Operations," 12 December 1978, and "Circular from the General Political Department on Deployment of Military Cadres during Wartime," 14 December 1978, both in *GGZH*, 1–3.

84 "Circular from the CMC on the Appointment and Removal of Division-Level Cadres," 1 February 1979, in *GGZH*, 4.

85 "Directive from the Military Region Forward Command Political Department on the Effective Execution of Political Work during Military Operations," 26 December 1978, "Circular from the Military Region Forward Command Political Department on Effectively Handling Problems with Political Work during Combat," 10 January 1978, and "Circular from the Military Region Forward Command Political Department on Cadre Promotion on the Firing Line," 21 February 1979, all in *GGZH*, 22–23, 31.

86 Office of the General Political Department, "Experiences of Political Work in the Counterattack in Self-Defense against Vietnam," in *ZGJX*, 1:15–17.

87 See, for example, Chen Jian, *China's Road to the Korean War*, 139–41, which details how the CCP used political mobilization to consolidate its control of China during the Korean War.

88 Chanda, *Brother Enemy*, 361–62; Scobell, *China's Use of Military Force*, 140; Diamant, *Embattled Glory*, 374.

89 The information in this section comes mainly from *YXFB*, which is a government publication, but it contains fascinating statistics that shed light on how local communities were mobilized to support the border war with Vietnam.

90 Chao, "Influence of Specific Geopolitical Environment," 86–89.

91 Local History Compilation Committee of Guangxi, *Guangxi tongzhi junshi zhi*, 322.

92 Chengdu Military Region, Political Department, "The Army Needs Support from the People to Be Victorious," in *YXFB*, 531.

93 Ibid., 535.

94 War Preparation and Aiding-the-Front Leading Group, "Summary of Ten-Year Work in Aiding the Front by Yunnan Province," in *YXFB*, 18–23.

95 Zhou Deli, *Yige gaoji canmouzhang de zishu*, 305; War Preparation and Aiding-the-Front Leading Group, "Summary of Ten-Year Work in Aiding the Front by Yunnan Province," in *YXFB*, 1–2.

96 Zhang Zhen, *Zhang Zhen junshi wenxuan*, 183.

97 Hekou County, "Providing Support for the Front for Ten Years," in *YXFB*, 57.

98 Pingbian Miao Ethnic Autonomous County, CCP Party Committee, "Providing Support for the Front," in *YXFB*, 73–87.

99 Yunnan Province Commerce Department, "Providing Supplies for the Front," in *YXFB*, 331–36.

100 Local History Compilation Committee of Guangxi, *Guangxi tongzhi junshi zhi*, 471.

101 Yunnan Province Grain Department, "Food and Fodder Should Go Ahead of Troops and Horses," in *YXFB*, 320–30.

102 Chao, "Influence of Specific Geopolitical Environment," 89.

103 Zhou Deli, *Yige gaoji canmouzhang de zishu*, 301.

104 Chengdu Military Region, Political Department, "The Army Needs Support from the People to Be Victorious," in *YXFB*, 536.

105 Qujing Prefecture, CCP Committee, "Mobilizing Militias to Support the Front," in *YXFB*, 191–95.

106 More than 20,000 of Hekou County's roughly 50,000 residents were mobilized (Hekou County, "Providing Support for the Front for Ten Years," in *YXFB*, 57).

107 War Preparation and Aiding-the-Front Leading Group, "Summary of Ten-Year Work in Aiding the Front by Yunnan Province," in *YXFB*, 13.

108 "Summary of the 121st Division's Deep-Thrust Operations."

109 Zhou Deli, *Yige gaoji canmouzhang de zishu*, 301, Local History Compilation Committee of Guangxi, *Guangxi tongzhi junshi zhi*, 326.

110 Yunnan Provincial Military District, *Junshi zhi*, 697–98; Local History Compilation Committee of Guangxi, *Guangxi tongzhi junshi zhi*, 464.

111 "War Preparation and Aiding the Front during the Counterattack in Self-Defense against Vietnam," 6 September 1979, Yunnan Province Revolution Committee, Yunnan Provincial Archives, Kunming.

112 Yunnan Province People's Air Defense Office, "People's Air Defense Work," in *YXFB*, 505; Zhou Deli, *Yige gaoji canmouzhang de zishu*, 301.

113 George, *Chinese Communist Army in Action*, viii–ix; Whitson and Huang, *Chinese High Command*, 462.

114 King C. Chen, *China's War with Vietnam*, xiii.

CHAPTER 4

1 "Wang Shangrong's Speech, 16 March 1979."

2 Li Peng, "Remembering 1979, Part 1." See also *Zhanlie*, 63–136; "Summary of the 121st Division's Deep-Thrust Operations."

3 Existing studies basically provide inaccurate descriptions of Chinese operations. For example, see King C. Chen, *China's War with Vietnam*, 105–6; O'Dowd, *Chinese Military Strategy*, 58–59.

4 Luong Thuong Quyen et al., *Lich Su Su Doan Bo Binh 346*. Copies of translated texts provided by Merle Pribbenow.

5 Zhou Deli, *Xu Shiyou*, 131, 155. See also "43rd Army in the 1979 Counterattack."

6 Luong Thuong Quyen et al., *Lich Su Su Doan Bo Binh 346*.

7 "41st Army's Operations." See also Luong Thuong Quyen et al., *Lich Su Su Doan Bo Binh 346*.

8 Zhou Deli, *Xu Shiyou*, 94; Zhou Deli, *Yige gaoji canmouzhang de zishu*, 294–95. According to the Guangzhou Military Region Forward Command's intelligence, the Cao Bang area had 8,500 troops with the 346th Division, some 3,000 in three independent regiments, about 2,000 in five independent battalions of the border counties and one special operations battalion, and about 1,000 at the public security stations.

9 King C. Chen, *China's War with Vietnam*, 103.

10 Yang Liufan, *Yongzhe wuwei*, 117–18.

11 Information from Cai Pengcen.

12 Zhou Deli, *Xu Shiyou*, 135.

13 Qu, *Wu Zhong shaojiang*, 444–46.

14 Zhou Deli, *Yige gaoji canmouzhang de zishu*, 279–80.

15 The 1st Battalion of the 43rd Army tank regiment lost more than ten tanks, while the two battalions of the 126th Division suffered some 80 casualties at one point during the combat maneuver. "43rd Army's Tank Regiment"; Cai Pengcen, "Events."

16 Zhou Deli, *Xu Shiyou*, 155–58.

17 According to this recollection, the 54th Army did not depart for Guangxi until 9 February, and arrived at its staging area on the border four days later. Hao, "Fighting against Vietnam."

18 Zhou Deli, *Xu Shiyou*, 176–77.

19 Luong Thuong Quyen et al., *Lich Su Su Doan Bo Binh 346*.

20 Nguyen Tri Huan et al., *Su Doan Sao Van*, 412. A Chinese version is available on the website: http://blog.wenxuecity.com/blogarticle.php?date=200709&postID=14300. Copies of translated texts provided by Merle Pribbenow.

21 *Zhanlie*, 27, 63–64.

22 Nguyen Tri Huan et al., *Su Doan Sao Van*, 413.

23 *Zhanlie*, 27.

24 Nguyen Tri Huan et al., *Su Doan Sao Van*, 476.

25 Zhou Deli, *Xu Shiyou*, 182; Zhou Deli, *Yige gaoji canmouzhang de zishu*, 259.

26 *Zhanlie*, 29.

27 Zhou Deli, *Xu Shiyou*, 182–83.

28 *Zhanlie*, 31–32.

29 The U.S. Army and PAVN fought at Hamburger Hill on 10–20 May 1969. It was the last major U.S. ground assault of the Vietnam War, and both sides suffered high casualties. See Zaffiri, *Hamburger Hill*.

30 For the latest English account, see O'Dowd, *Chinese Military Strategy*, chapter 5.

31 For example, see Nguyen Tri Huan et al., *Su Doan Sao Van*.

32 "No Regret," authored by an anonymous squad leader from the 163rd Division's 487th Regiment, provides a detailed account of the battles fought by the 163rd Division in the 1979 war.

33 Zou, "Battles Fought."

34 Unit 53505 (488th Regiment), "Personal Experiences of Conducting Political Work during Combat in Dong Dang and Lang Son," in *ZGJX*, 1:30.

35 *Zhanlie*, 32–33.

36 Nguyen Tri Huan et al., *Su Doan Sao Van*, 421–68.

37 Zhou Deli, *Xu Shiyou*, 189–90; "Main Experiences" describes the combat experience of the 163rd Division in the Lang Son area.

38 "Main Experiences," 57.

39 Information from Cai Pengcen.

40 *Zhanlie*, 34.

41 Unit 53513 (165th Division), Political Department, "Earnestly Conducting Educational and Ideological Work of Cadres Who Participated in the War," in *ZGJX*, 1:195.

42 Nguyen Tri Huan et al., *Su Doan Sao Van*, 439. This Vietnamese account is disputed. PLA reports indicate that Vietnamese counterattacks involved only a small number of troops whose combat power was relatively weak. Among the eleven counterattacks on the positions of the 488th Regiment's 7th Company, only once did a total of seven enemy troops break into the position ("Main Experiences," 57).

43 Zhou Deli, *Xu Shiyou*, 193–94; see also *Zhanlie*, 36–37.

44 O'Dowd, *Chinese Military Strategy*, 81.

45 Zhou Deli, *Xu Shiyou*, 194.

46 Nguyen Tri Huan et al., *Su Doan Sao Van*, 451.

47 *Zhanlie*, 91–94.

48 Zhou Deli, *Xu Shiyou*, 194–98; for the Vietnamese account, see Nguyen Tri Huan et al., *Su Doan Sao Van*, 449, 454.

49 "Main Experiences," 59. The unit history of the PAVN 3rd Division admitted civilians were killed inside the French Fort. See Nguyen Tri Huan et al., *Su Doan Sao Van*, 455.

50 Nguyen Tri Huan et al., *Su Doan Sao Van*, 443.

51 *Zhanlie*, 93–95. "Attacks on Tham Mo," http://bwl.top81.cn/war79/index.html.

52 Nguyen Tri Huan et al., *Su Doan Sao Van*, 446–47.

53 According to the 3rd Division history, artillery batteries of the 166th Regiment were emplaced on a number of hills around Dong Dang, including one antiaircraft artillery battalion at Tham Mo.

54 *Zhanlie*, 37.

55 For example, O'Dowd's *Chinese Military Strategy*, 61–65, was published in 2007, but it continues to use Foreign Broadcast Information Service and a 1981 Hong Kong publication to analyze the Chinese attacks on Lao Cai.

56 Vu, *Su Doan 316 Tap Hai*, cited in O'Dowd, *Chinese Military Strategy*, 183.

57 Nguyen Tien Hung, *Lich Su Luc Luong Vu Trang Quan Khu 2*. Copies of translated texts provided by Merle Pribbenow.

58 "Lecture Notes."

59 Nguyen Tien Hung, *Lich Su Luc Luong Vu Trang Quan Khu 2*.

60 Ni, *Shinian ZhongYue zhanzheng*, 1:487–504.

61 Li Peng, "Remembering 1979, Part 2."

62 "Combat History."

63 "Defending Height 300" (an online article by a Vietnamese veteran).

64 Li Peng, "Remembering 1979, Part 2," 45.

65 One company of the 40th Division launched twelve attacks to take one height at Tieu Tao, five kilometers east of Lao Cai (Unit 35207 [118th Regiment], Political Office, "Personal Experiences of Political Work during the 1st Battalion's Attack on Lao Cai," in *ZGJX*, 2:25–26).

66 Li Peng, "Remembering 1979, Part 2," 45.

67 Nguyen Tien Hung, *Lich Su Luc Luong Vu Trang Quan Khu 2*.

68 Unit 56017 (13th Army's 39th Division), Political Department, "Political Work Conducted during the Repulse at Thay Nai," in *ZGJX*, 1:54.

69 "Combat History."

70 Li Peng, "Remembering 1979, Part 2," 46.

71 Cai Pengcen, "Events."

72 Ni, *Shinian ZhongYue zhanzheng*, 2:513–16.

73 "Pictorial Illustration."

74 Nguyen Tien Hung, *Lich Su Luc Luong Vu Trang Quan Khu 2*.

75 "Pictorial Illustration."

76 China News Agency, "Bulletin."

77 O'Dowd, *Chinese Military Strategy*, 63.

78 Li Peng, "Remembering 1979, Part 2," 47.

79 Zhou Deli, *Yige gaoji canmouzhang de zishu*, 281–82.

80 "Lecture Notes."

81 Zhou Deli, *Yige gaoji canmouzhang de zishu*, 282.

82 Zhou Deli, *Xu Shiyou*, 209–13.

83 *Zhanlie*, 39–40.

84 Zhou Deli, *Xu Shiyou*, 214.

85 "No Regret."

86 Zhou Deli, *Yige gaoji canmouzhang de zishu*, 282.

87 *Zhanlie*, 97, 109–111. See also Zhou Deli, *Xu Shiyou*, 215–16; Wang Zhijun, *1979 duiYue zhanzheng qinlin ji*, 199; Li Peng, "Remembering 1979, Part 2," 43.

88 Zhou Deli, *Xu Shiyou*, 219–21. See also *Zhanlie*, 40–42.

89 Nguyen Tri Huan et al., *Su Doan Sao Van*, 473.

90 According to information from the captured Vietnamese soldiers, Than Thanh Dong housed a Vietnamese battalion command post and ammunition depot along with more than 100 troops (Wang Zhijun, *1979 duiYue zhanzheng qinlin ji*, 199).

91 *Zhanlie*, 112.

92 Military Science Academy, "Case Study."

93 Military History Institute, *Yuenan Renminjun wushinian*, 411.

94 Zhang Zhenyang et al., "Taking Luc Binh."

95 Zhou Deli, *Xu Shiyou*, 224–28.

96 O'Dowd, *Chinese Military Strategy*, 88.

97 *Zhanlie*, 44.

98 Zhou Deli, *Xu Shiyou*, 228–29.

99 Military History Institute, *Yuenan Renminjun wushinian*, 272.

100 Wang Taiping, *Zhonghua Renmin Gongheguo waijiaoshi*, 3:68.

101 Duong, "In Retrospect." Duong served as the first secretary at the Vietnamese embassy in Beijing beginning in 1977.

102 Zhou Deli, *Xu Shiyou*, 95.

103 Nguyen Tri Huan et al., *Su Doan Sao Van*, 413–14.

104 Kenny, "Vietnamese Perceptions," 227–28.

105 Military History Institute, *Yuenan Renminjun wushinian*, 271.

106 A copy of the memorandum is available in China News Agency International Information Group, *Woguo duiYue ziwei huanjizhan ziliao ji*, 37–41.

107 Kenny, "Vietnamese Perceptions," 228.

108 Nguyen Tri Huan et al., *Su Doan Sao Van*, 426, 431.

109 Duong, "In Retrospect." See also Kenny, "Vietnamese Perceptions," 221, 228.

110 Nguyen Tri Huan et al., *Su Doan Sao Van*, 432.

111 Ibid., 436. This assessment was supported by the Soviet view. See "Welcome by Vietnam with Flowers," which originally appeared in the Russian Ministry of Defense *Red Star Daily*, 16 January 2001. It has also been published as "Soviet Military Advisers in Vietnam."

112 Pike, *PAVN*, 264.

113 "Soviet Military Advisers in Vietnam."

114 Pham, *Lich Su Quan Doan 2*, 386. Copies of translated texts provided by Merle Pribbenow.

115 "Soviet Military Advisers in Vietnam." Ironically, the PLA captured examples of the BM-21 Grad, then reverse-engineered it and produced it as the Type 81 SPRL (now designated PHZ81) in a much improved and more useful form than its Soviet predecessor.

116 Le Trong Tan, *Binh Doan Quyet Thang*, 135–36. Copies of translated texts provided by Merle Pribbenow. O'Dowd includes the PAVN 320th Division in defense of Hanoi. *Chinese Military Strategy*, 84. Other sources indicate that this division did not return to Hanoi from Cambodia in July 1979 ("Summarized Accounts of PANV's Fifty-One Divisions"). According to the following source, Le Nong, commander of the 320th Division's 59th Regiment, made a tour of Cambodia in 1979. Yunnan Provincial Military District, *Yuenan Renminjun jiangxiao junguan minglu*, 402.

117 This is based on my conversations with Vietnamese students. For the information about the PAVN 2nd Corps, see Military History Institute, *Yuenan Renminjun wushinian*, 395–96; Pham, *Lich Su Quan Doan 2*.

118 China News Agency International Information Group, *Woguo duiYue ziwei huanjizhan ziliao ji*, 83–85.

119 Military History Institute, *Yuenan Renminjun wushinian*, 274–75; "Vietnamese Military Deployment."

120 Cai Pengcen, "Events."

121 China News Agency International Group, *Woguo duiYue ziwei huanjizhan ziliao ji*, 17–18.

122 Zhou Deli, *Xu Shiyou*, 235.

123 Quan, "Bodyguard," 43–44.

124 Hao, "Fighting against Vietnam."

125 "Recollections of an Artillery Company Commander."

126 King C. Chen, *China's War with Vietnam*, 114.

127 Zhang Zhen, *Zhang Zhen huiyilu*, 172.

128 Zhou Deli, *Xu Shiyou*, 175–77.

129 Li Peng, "Remembering 1979, Part 2," 47.

130 Zhou Deli, *Xu Shiyou*, 235–36.

131 King C. Chen, *China's War with Vietnam*, 111.

132 On 23 February, the PAVN 460th Regiment's 3rd Battalion attacked one Chinese position in China ("2nd Border Defense Division"). For a Vietnamese account, see Dang Van Nhung, *Su Doan 338*, 124–25.

133 The unit history of the 338th Division offers a different account, giving no mention of the engagement over these two days (Dang Van Nhung, *Su Doan 338*, 130–37).

134 Zhou Deli, *Xu Shiyou*, 236–44.

135 Zhou Deli's *Xu Shiyou* does not provide a balanced, comprehensive account about the 150th Division's disastrous loss during this phase of the war.

136 Wang Zhijun, *1979 dui Yue zhanzheng qinlin ji*, 275–77.

137 Chen Yuanjing, "Recollections."

CHAPTER 5

1 "Deng Xiaoping's Speech, 16 March 1979."

2 *Jiefangjun bao*, 11 April 1979.

3 Christman, "How Beijing Evaluates," 264.

4 Ibid., 265.

5 Jencks, "China's 'Punitive' War."

6 Wortzel, "China's Foreign Conflicts," 283.

7 Jencks, "China's 'Punitive' War," 809, 813.

8 See, for example, Tretiak, "China's Vietnam War," 750–51.

9 Central Intelligence Agency, "China's Vietnam War: Preparations, Combat Performance, and Apparent Lessons," March 1980, NLC-SAFE 17 A-9-18-1-6, JCPL.

10 Ibid.

11 The U.S. side initially thought the talks would cover a broad range of topics including Iran, SALT, Pakistan and India, Indochina, and bilateral relations (Memorandum, Michel Oksenberg to Brzezinski, 28 March, 1979, NSA File, Box 46, JCPL).

12 Ibid.

13 Wang Dinglie, *Dangdai Zhongguo kongjun*, 638.

14 *ZGJX*, 1:363–65. PLAN's only combat action was on 10 April 1979, when it captured three small Vietnamese reconnaissance vessels along with 24 armed personnel near Zhongjian (Triton) Island in the South China Sea. "Modern Ships" Editorial Board, "Interview," 14.

15 Party History and Political Work Department, "Issues on Political Work," 1. Another Guangzhou Military Region document claimed a total of 40,300 Vietnamese casualties. Goods and Materials Office, "Aspects of Logistical Supply," 11.

16 Min, *Zhong Yue zhanzheng shinian*, 65. The Guangzhou Military Region claimed that its forces captured 226 tanks and other vehicles, 457 artillery pieces, 8,298 small weapons, 230,000 rounds of shells, 8,000,000 rounds of small arms ammunition, and 2,635 tons of food (Goods and Materials Office, "Aspects of Logistical Supply," 11–12).

17 Kenny, "Vietnamese Perceptions," 231; King C. Chen, *China's War with Vietnam*, 113.

18 Le Duan, "Comrade B."

19 Radio Hanoi, domestic service, 4 March 1979, Foreign Broadcast Information Service, 5 March 1979, Vietnam, K25.

20 Kenny, "Vietnamese Perceptions," 217–36. The fragmentary accounts of Vietnamese involvement in the conflict were also available at http://www.chinadefense.com/forum/index.php?showtopic=2016&hl=1979+war+with+Vietnam.

21 AFP (Hong Kong), 2 May 1979, Foreign Broadcast Information Service, 3 May 1979, PRC, E1.

22 The casualty numbers in Guangxi are cited from Wang Zhijun, *1979 dui Yue zhanzheng qinlin ji*, 313. The casualty numbers in Yunnan are cited from "Lecture Notes."

23 Based on journalist reports out of Hong Kong, King C. Chen offers this statistic in *China's War*, 113–14.

24 Kenny, "Vietnamese Perceptions," 231.

25 Wang Zhijun, *1979 dui Yue zhanzheng qinlin ji*, 207.

26 During the 1962 Sino-Indian border war, China claimed 4,897 Indian troops killed or

wounded, while Indian records showed 1,383 Indian soldiers killed, 1,696 missing in action, and 1,047 wounded, totaling 4,126. The Chinese claims were a few hundred higher than the Indian figures. Cheng Feng and Wortzel, "PLA Operational Principles," 188.

27 Something noted, incidentally, in the many short after-action studies by America's noted analyst of small-unit actions, Brigadier General S. L. A. Marshall, U.S. Army. See *Man against Fire*.

28 "Deng Xiaoping's Speech, 16 March 1979." The classic ground combat ratio for large-scale combat action, at least in American experience, is approximately four wounded for every killed.

29 Ibid.

30 Ross, *Indochina Tangle*, 223–37; Scobell, *China's Use of Military Force*, 135–36.

31 Vice Premier Deng Xiaoping's meeting with Alejandro Orfila, secretary-general, Organization of American States, 19 February 1979, Ministry of Foreign Affairs, FPA.

32 "Deng Xiaoping's Speech, 16 March 1979."

33 Hanoi allegedly planned to use four divisions to launch a counteroffensive at Lang Son on 7 March but never did so because of the PLA's withdrawal.

34 Deng's meeting with Tuhami, 28 February 1979, FPA; Zhou Deli, *Yige gaoji canmouzhang de zishu*, 246.

35 Gilks, *Breakdown*, 233.

36 King C. Chen, *China's War with Vietnam*, 135.

37 As a result, U.S. tariffs on Chinese goods were reduced from 20 percent to around 10.5 percent (Jones and Kevill, *China and the Soviet Union*, 121).

38 Deng Xiaoping's meeting with Vice President Walter Mondale, 27 August 1979, Ministry of Foreign Affairs, FPA.

39 "Deng Xiaoping's Speech, 16 March 1979."

40 "Hua Guofeng's Speech, 16 March 1979."

41 From March to May 1979, more than thirty people were arrested in accordance to Deng's order (Mann, *About Face*, 102).

42 Kenny, "Vietnamese Perceptions," 234–35; Pike, *PAVN*, 265–66.

43 "Suggestions from the Guangzhou Military Region Forward Command Political Department on Cadre Work after Troops Transferring to Normal Combat Training," 27 May 1979, in *GGZH*, 49.

44 More than thirty-one PAVN infantry divisions were deployed in Vietnam's northern and northwestern regions. Each infantry division had 10,000 troops. See map 4.

45 Thayer, *Vietnam People's Army*, 11–12.

46 Iklé, *Every War Must End*, 2.

47 Kenny, "Vietnamese Perceptions," 236.

48 Ryan, Finkelstein, and McDevitt, *Chinese Warfingting*, 9–10.

49 Joffe, *Chinese Army*, 95–97; Tretiak, "China's Vietnam War," 751; O'Dowd, *Chinese Military Strategy*, 67–68; King C. Chen, *China's War with Vietnam*, 101–3.

50 According King C. Chen, the Vietnamese air force had only 70 MiG-19s, 70 MiG-21s, and some U.S.-made F-5s captured in 1975. He wrongly mentioned that the Vietnamese also flew MiG-23s, which actually belonged to the Soviet air units stationed at Cam Ranh Bay (*China's War with Vietnam*, 103).

51 The Chinese-made MiG-21 (J-7) had many technical problems at the time. See Ge, *Feixing zhaji*, 155–60.

52 Toperczer, *MIG-21 and MIG-19 Units*, 82; Boniface, *MiGs over North Vietnam*, 129–31.

53 For example, during Operation Bolo, the Vietnamese MiG-21s launched in individual single-ship sorties to fly up through the weather (they were not proficient at formation flying in clouds) and were picked off one by one by U.S. Air Force Phantoms waiting upstairs as the Vietnamese plans individually emerged from the tops of the clouds (Douglas C. Dildy, a retired air force officer, to author, 14 June 2012; see also Thompson, *To Hanoi and Back*, 55–58).

54 According to Chinese sources, this deployment included three air divisions, three AAA regiments, and two SAM regiments ("Vietnamese Military Deployment").

55 More than ten radars were deployed to track Vietnamese air activities during the war (Zuo Guang, "Development and Growth," 404–5; see also Zhang Zhizhi, "Air Force Troops," 354).

56 "Aviation Units."

57 Zhang Zhizhi, "Air Force Troops," 353–54.

58 These sorties included 43 flown by JZ-6s and 9 flown by HZ-5s (cited from a web article, "Chinese Air Force Conducted Special Operations during the War against Vietnam," but the information comes from the General Staff Intelligence Department, *ZhongYue bianjing zhencha zuozhan jingyan ji*).

59 Jiang Hao and Lin, "Recollections," 30.

60 Zhang Zhizhi, "Air Force Troops," 354.

61 Boniface, *MiGs over North Vietnam*, 133–34.

62 Liu Guoyu, *Zhongguo Renmin Jiefangjun zhanshi jiaocheng*, 235.

63 The PLA came closest to using its air force to support ground operations on the morning of 20 February. After the 124th Division had occupied two hilltops near Cao Bang, the forward command instructed it to stop attacks and mark the targets for the air force. By early afternoon, the air force had not showed up and the division reassumed its ground assaults (information from Cai Pengcen).

64 "Aviation Units."

65 Shu Guang Zhang, *Mao's Military Romanticism*, 23, 27.

66 King C. Chen, *China's War with Vietnam*, 107; Segal, *Defending China*, 219.

67 O'Dowd, *Chinese Military Strategy*, 143–44.

68 Ibid., 145.

69 Zhang Wannian, *Zhang Wannian junshi wenji*, 25–29.

70 Kenny, "Vietnamese Perceptions," 231.

71 For the best analysis of the Lin Biao incident, see Qiu Jin, *Culture of Power*, chapter 7.

72 Wang Zhijun, *1979 duiYue zhanzheng qinlin ji*, 256.

73 Jiang Feng, Ma, and Dou, *Yangyong jiangjun zhuan*, 497; Zhang Zhizhi, "Air Force Troops," 355.

74 O'Dowd, *Chinese Military Strategy*, 143, 146.

75 Ibid., 154–55.

76 *Deng junshi wenji*, 168.

77 Office of the General Political Department, "Experiences of Political Work in the Counterattack in Self-Defense against Vietnam," in *ZGJX*, 1:1–23.

78 Unit 53505 (488th Regiment), "Personal Experiences of Conducting Political Work during Combat in Dong Dang and Lang Son," 25–33. See also Wang Zhijun, *1979 duiYue zhanzheng qinlin ji*, 142–44.

79 *Jiefangjun bao*, 3 March 1979.

80 Unit 33720 (43rd Army's 127th Division) Political Department, "Launching Thorough Education Programs on Patriotism and Revolutionary Heroism," 137–45.

81 Unit 53019 (364th Regiment), "Political Work Conducted during the Assault on Fortified Positions at Soc Giang," 47–53.

82 Unit 56017, "Political Work Conducted during the Repulse at Thay Nia," in *ZGJX*, 1:54–59.

83 Unit 33990 (162nd Division), Party Committee, "Personal Experiences of Conducting Political Work during Mobile Operations," in ibid., 76–84.

84 This group consisted of two deputy army commanders and one deputy army political commissar. As a consequence of the loss of the 448th Regiment, one deputy army commander was removed from office, the other one was demoted, and the deputy political commissar received intraparty disciplinary punishment.

85 Wang Zhijun, *1979 duiYue zhanzheng qinlin ji*, 275–76.

86 Shu Guang Zhang, *Mao's Military Romanticism*, 215.

87 "Brief Account."

88 Zhou Deli, *Yige gaoji canmouzhang de zishu*, 288–89.

89 For the discussion of Vietnamese postwar strategic thinking, see Pike, *PAVN*, 267–77.

90 These four approaches were cited from Zhou Deli, *Yige gaoji canmouzhang de zishu*, 290.

91 Wang Zhijun, *1979 duiYue zhanzheng qinlin ji*, 96–97.

92 Ibid., 97. Vietnamese sources supported this observation, candidly noting that each division "did not have sufficient forces to send forward to support and relieve" the badly depleted front-line troops (Dang Van Nhung, *Su Doan 338*, 118).

93 For example, Hanoi held its reserves near Chi Lang, south of Lang Son, with no engagement with Chinese forces until the Lang Son defense line collapsed (O'Dowd, *Chinese Military Strategy*, 65).

94 Information from Cai Pengcen. The PAVN unit history shows no organized battles fought by division or regiment (Nguyen Huu Bo, *Su Doan Bo Binh*; copies of translated texts provided by Merle Pribbenow).

95 Wang Zhijun, *1979 duiYue zhanzheng qinlin ji*, 97–98.

96 Luo, *Baizhan jiangxing Wang Shangrong*, 382.

97 Nguyen Huu Bo, *Su Doan Bo Binh*.

98 Zhou Deli, *Yige gaoji canmouzhang de zishu*, 291.

99 Western analysts initially believed that these units of the PAVN, comprised of veterans of the long war in the south, were both battle-wise and highly skilled in guerrilla war tactics (Kenny, "Vietnamese Perceptions," 217–36). But recent Vietnamese sources indicate that they were new recruits, having only joined the army in June 1978. Fragmentary accounts of Vietnamese involvement in the conflict were available at http://www.chinadefense.com/forum/index .php?showtopic_2016&hl_1979_war_with_Vietnam.

100 Political Department of Unit 33760 (129th Division), "How We Effectively Disintegrated the Enemy Army and Leniently Treated POWs," in *ZGJX*, 1:291.

101 Ibid., 294.

102 Lanning and Cragg, *Inside the VC and the NVA*, 208.

103 Kenny, "Vietnamese Perceptions," 230.

104 Military History Institute, *Yuenan Renminjun wushinian*, 272.

105 Kenny, "Vietnamese Perceptions," 230.

106 Ibid., 231.

107 Information from Cai Pengcen.

108 Unit 33700 (43rd Army), Political Department, Public Affairs Office, "Personal Experiences of Effective Use of Interrogation," in *ZGJX*, 1:300–303.

109 The maps the PLA used were 1:100,000 scale, printed in 1965 on the basis of a 1938 French map of questionable accuracy. As a result, PLA forces often got lost in the northern Vietnamese hills.

110 Zhou Deli, *Yige gaoji canmouzhang de zishu*, 294–95.

111 Unit 53024 (367th Regiment of the 123rd Division), "Personal Experiences of Conducting Political Work during Mop-Up Operations," in *ZGJX*, 1:69–75.

112 Zhou Deli, *Yige gaoji canmouzhang de zishu*, 292.

113 According to Chinese sources, 87 percent of PLA tank units' losses occurred in the first four days of combat, but most were repairable. At the end of the war, only forty-four tanks and armored vehicles were deemed total losses ("Chinese Armored Forces").

114 Wang Zhijun, *1979 duiYue zhanzheng qinlin ji*, 195–96.

115 Zhou Deli, *Yige gaoji canmouzhang de zishu*, 287–88.

116 Wang Zhijun, *1979 duiYue zhanzheng qinlin ji*, 98–99.

117 Zhou Deli, *Yige gaoji canmouzhang de zishu*, 289.

118 Ibid., 298.

119 Xu Guangyi, *Dangdai Zhongguo jundui de houqin gongzuo*, 177.

120 Information from Cai Pengcen.

121 For example, two engineering battalions, one antichemical company, and one militia battalion were employed to protect the traffic and flow of supplies between Yai Tien and Loc Binh, which are thirteen kilometers apart (Xu Guangyi, *Dangdai Zhongguo jundui de houqin gongzuo*, 178).

122 Zhou Deli, *Yige gaoji canmouzhang de zishu*, 300.

123 Chen Zuhua and Liu, "Summary."

124 Zhou Deli, *Yige gaoji canmouzhang de zishu*, 301.
125 For example, O'Dowd and Corbett, "1979 Chinese Campaign," study the PLA based on only two sources: a summary of the role played by the students of the Guangzhou Military Region's infantry school in the war, and a brief analysis of the 1979 campaign by the researchers from the Military Science Academy.
126 Department of Military History Studies, *Zhongguo Renmin Jiefangjun de qishi nian*, 613.
127 Liu Guoyu, *Zhongguo Renmin Jiefangjun zhanshi jiaocheng*, 235.
128 Zhang Zhizhi, "Air Force Troops," 355–56.
129 See Elleman, *Modern Chinese Warfare*; Scobell, *China's Use of Military Force*; Ryan, Finkelstein, and McDevitt, *Chinese Warfighting*; Burless and Shulsky, *Patterns in China's Use of Force*; Whiting, "China's Use of Force."
130 Kyodo, 26 February 1979, Foreign Broadcast Information Service, PRC, 26 February 1979, A5.
131 Deng Xiaoping's meeting with members of U.S. Senate Committee on Foreign Relations in Beijing, 19 April 1979, in Gong, "Triangular Relationship," 70.

CHAPTER 6

1 Order from the Central Military Commission, 7 June 1985, in *Conglin qilue*, ed. Li Qianyuan and Song Ke, 1–2.
2 O'Dowd, *Chinese Military Strategy*, 89.
3 War spending in Yunnan by the Kunming Military Region alone amounted to 74.28 million RMB ($47.77 million) during the 1979 invasion (Financial Department of Kunming Military Region Logistics. "Basic Summary of Financial Support Work in Yunnan," in *Yunnan fangxiang ZhongYue bianjing ziwei huanji zuozhan houqin caiwu baozhang gongzuo ziliao xuanbian*, ed. Financial Department of Kunming Military Region Logistics, 14).
4 For Western analysts slow to reach this realization, see Nations, "Great Leap Sideways," 15–16.
5 Deng Xiaoping's meeting with Vice President Walter Mondale, 27 August 1979, Ministry of Foreign Affairs, FPA.
6 Local History Compilation Committee of Guangxi, *Guangxi tongzhi junshi zhi*, 247; "Organizational Changes."
7 Local History Compilation Committee of Guangxi, *Guangxi tongzhi junshi zhi*, 413–14.
8 "Circular on Negotiation Talks between Chinese and Vietnamese Deputy Foreign Ministers," 16 April 1979, Ministry of Foreign Affairs, FPA.
9 Xie Yixian, *Zhongguo waijiao shi*, 268–78.
10 Military History Institute, *Yuenan Renminjun wushinian*, 274–75.
11 "Vietnamese Military Deployment."
12 "Illustrations of Vietnamese Military Deployment."
13 Han Huaizhi and Tan, *Dangdai Zhongguo jundui de junshi gongzuo*, 678–81.
14 "Summary of Chengdu Military Region."
15 "Initial Analysis."
16 Wang Kangsheng, "Basic Tactics," 631–32.
17 *Deng nianpu*, 2:643, 752.
18 Deng Xiaoping's meeting with Vice President Walter Mondale, 27 August 1979, Ministry of Foreign Affairs, FPA.
19 "Circular on Cambodia's Situation," 25 December 1979, Ministry of Foreign Affairs, FPA.
20 *Deng junshi wenji*, 186.
21 Ibid., 178. See also "Deng Xiaoping's Speech, 16 March 1979."
22 Zhang Youxia, "Pondering How to Shape," 308–10. Zhang was deputy commander of the 40th Division at the time.
23 Yunnan Provincial Military District, *Junshi zhi*, 424.
24 Ibid.
25 "Summary of Chengdu Military Region."
26 Chan, "Offensive and Defensive Battles."

27 Ibid.
28 Ni, *Shinian ZhongYue zhanzheng*, 2:638, 649.
29 The history of Vietnamese Military District 2 offers no details about these Chinese attacks (Nguyen Tien Hung, *Lich Su Luc Luong Vu Trang Quan Khu 2*).
30 Chan, "Offensive and Defensive Battles."
31 Thayer, "Security Issues," 11.
32 *General History of Guangxi* records that in 1983, Chinese artillery forces shelled three Vietnamese heights across the border (Local History Compilation Committee of Guangxi, *Guangxi tongzhi junshi zhi*, 541; see also He Zhongjun's memoirs, published online under the pen name Qiuye Junxue, "Red Cotton Trees").
33 Thayer, "Security Issues," 11–12.
34 O'Dowd, *Chinese Military Strategy*, 95.
35 Thayer, "Security Issues," 8, 15.
36 Ni, *Shinian ZhongYue zhanzheng*, 2:668–69, 751.
37 *Deng nianpu*, 2:951.
38 Ni, *Shinian ZhongYue zhanzheng*, 2:674.
39 Cai Pengcen, "Events."
40 Chen Zhijian, "Trust," 315. Chen was the deputy commander of the 40th Division.
41 Ni, *Shinian ZhongYue zhanzheng*, 2:670.
42 Ibid., 698.
43 Ibid., 739.
44 Thayer, "Security Issues," 20.
45 Ni, *Shinian ZhongYue zhanzheng*, 2:672–74.
46 Vietnamese sources indicate that the Ha Tuyen sector was defended by the 313th Division, Ha Tuyen Province Regiment, nine district local-force battalions, and one local force artillery battalion (Nguyen Tien Hung, *Lich Su Luc Luong Vu Trang Quan Khu 2*).
47 "Short History."
48 Ibid.
49 Nguyen Tien Hung, *Lich Su Luc Luong Vu Trang Quan Khu 2*.
50 Thayer, "Security Issues," 17–18; O'Dowd, *Chinese Military Strategy*, 98; for journalist reports, for example, see Quinn-Judge, "Peking's Tit for Tat," 14.
51 Ni, *Shinian ZhongYue zhanzheng*, 2:676.
52 Shen Tingxue, "Bloody Road of Laoshan."
53 Ouyang, *Baizhan jiangxing Xie Zhenghua*, 362; Li Jianguo, "Losses Incurred."
54 Ding Longyan, *Yibaishuan yanjing*, 240–43.
55 Chen Zhijian, "Trust," 313.
56 Tian, *ZhongYue zhanzheng jishilu*, 223–27.
57 Ouyang, *Baizhan jiangxing Xie Zhenghua*, 365–71; Yunnan Provincial Military District, *Junshi zhi*, 429–30; Ding Longyan, *Yibaishuan yanjing*, 89–92.
58 Han Qing, "Legendary Liao Xilong."
59 O'Dowd, *Chinese Military Strategy*, 101. See also Thayer, "Security Issues," 18.
60 Wang Kangsheng, "Basic Tactics," 632.
61 Nguyen Tien Hung, *Lich Su Luc Luong Vu Trang Quan Khu 2*.
62 Ni, *Shinian ZhongYue zhanzheng*, 2:706–7.
63 Ouyang, *Baizhan jiangxing Xie Zhenghua*, 373. See also "Battalion Political Instructor's Experience."
64 Ouyang, *Baizhan jiangxing Xie Zhenghua*, 374.
65 Ni, *Shinian ZhongYue zhanzheng*, 2:710–12.
66 Information from Cai Pengcen.
67 Cai Pengcen, "Big Victory." See also Yunnan Provincial Military District, *Junshi zhi*, 431–32.
68 Ding Longyan, *Yibaishuan yanjin*, 223.
69 Yunnan Provincial Military District, *Junshi zhi*, 432. Vietnamese casualty figures remain inaccessible. According to one Vietnamese netizen, few soldiers who participated in the battles

survived. A veteran of the 314th Division agreed, mentioning that 1,680 soldiers killed at Laoshan between 1984 and 1986 were buried at a newly built cemetery in Vi Xuyen and pointing out that this number did not include the dead bodies that either had been taken away by their families or had never been found ("Debates by Vietnamese Netizens").

70 Li Jianguo, *Qinli Laoshan zhizhan*, 410.
71 Cai Pengcen, "Big Victory."
72 "Debates by Vietnamese Netizens."
73 Ding Longyan, *Yibaishuan yanjing*, 219, 310.
74 Zou, "Wartime Reminiscences."
75 Tian, *ZhongYue zhanzheng jishilu*, 55.
76 "Summary of Chengdu Military Region."
77 "Hu Yaobang's Speech."
78 Ni, *Shinian ZhongYue zhanzheng*, 2:828. See also Cai Pengcen, "Events."
79 Fu Quanyou, "Unique War," 4.
80 "Inside Story on Planning."
81 Richardson, *China, Cambodia, and the Five Principles*, 134–36.
82 "Units from Different Military Regions."
83 Ni, *Shinian ZhongYue zhanzheng*, 2:751–52.
84 Fu Quanyou, "Unique War," 4.
85 Ni, *Shinian ZhongYue zhanzheng*, 2:751–52.
86 Fu Quanyou, "Unique War," 3.
87 Ni, *Shinian ZhongYue zhanzheng*, 2:768–85.
88 "Summarized Accounts of Units."
89 Ni, *Shinian ZhongYue zhanzheng*, 2:805.
90 Ibid., 822.
91 "Summary of Chengdu Military Region."
92 Zheng Yu, "Collapse," 49.
93 "Summarized Accounts of Units."
94 "Understanding the Conduct."
95 These reconnaissance groups came from the 13th, 16th, 19th, 20th, 21st, 24th, 26th, 38th, 40th, 43rd, 46th, 50th, 54th, and 64th Armies; the 15th Airborne Army; the Xinjiang Military Region, and the Beijing and Tianjin Garrisons (Li Jianguo, *Qinli Laoshan zhizhan*, 389–94).
96 Ni, *Shinian ZhongYue zhanzheng*, 2:857–58.
97 Wang Kangsheng, "Basic Tactics," 631–32.
98 "Air Reconnaissance Operations."
99 Wang Futian, "Shooting Down," 572.
100 "Precious Photos."
101 Thayer, ""Security Issues." 28; Richardson, *China, Cambodia, and the Five Principles*, 135.
102 Ni, *Shinian ZhongYue zhanzheng*, 2:751–830.
103 See, for example, Thayer, "Security Issues," 20–29; O'Dowd, *Chinese Military Strategy*, 104–6 (borrowing Thayer's thesis).
104 Wang Kangsheng, "Basic Tactics," 632.
105 Ibid., 632–34; Fu Quanyou, "Unique War," 8.
106 Li Qianyuan, "Using Active Defense," 25; Gu and Hu, "Measures," 77.
107 Zhang Xuezhao and Song, "Operational Characteristics," 645–47.
108 Fu Quanyou, "Unique War," 8.
109 Shen Weiguang and Hu, "Response to Enemy's Changes," 65–66.
110 "Debates by Vietnamese Netizens."
111 O'Dowd, *Chinese Military Strategy*, 101.
112 "Vietnamese Veteran's 1984."
113 Thayer, "Security Issues," 22–23, 26, 28.
114 "Units Rotated in the Defensive War at Laoshan," http://bwl.top81.cn/war79/index.html.

115 Chu Huy Man, "Problems in Political Work during Training and Combat," in *Yuenan wenti ziliao xuanbian*, ed. Chengdu Military Region, 207–17.

116 Ibid., 209.

117 Fu Quanyou, "Unique War," 3.

118 Feng Jinmao, "Fighting Effectively," 39.

119 Ni, *Shinian ZhongYue zhanzheng*, 2:751–822.

120 Fu Quanyou, "Unique War," 3.

121 Xiaobing Li, *History*, 250.

122 Zhang Youxia, "Pondering," 312.

123 CCP Central Documentary Editorial Committee, *Deng Xiaoping wenxuan*, 2:327.

124 O'Dowd, *Chinese Military Strategy*, 24.

125 Shi, "Political Work," 177–78.

126 Fu Quanyou, "Unique War," 5–7.

127 Jiang Wenyu, "Counterattacks," 53–56.

128 Zhang Youxia, "Pondering," 309.

129 Chen Zhijian, "Trust," 314.

130 Jiang Wenyu, "Counterattacks," 56.

131 Zhang Caixing, "Coordination Problems," 86–87.

132 Li Jianguo, *Qinli Laoshan zhizhan*, 277.

133 Gao and Cao, "Discussions."

134 Zheng Jianmin, "Using Manpower."

135 Army Logistics Department, "Things We Learned," 624.

136 Li Qianyuan, "Pondering Future Force Development."

137 The PLA's combat experience at Laoshan may have helped the Chinese leadership to decide to establish a realistic joint combat training base at Sanjian in Anhui Province in April 1986 (Zhang Zhen, *Zhang Zhen huiyilu*, 247–48).

138 Guo Peigong, "Issues Learned," 597–99.

139 Deng Xiaoping's meeting with Vice President Walter Mondale, 27 August 1979, Ministry of Foreign Affairs, FPA.

140 Ni, *Shinian ZhongYue zhanzheng*, 2:826.

CHAPTER 7

1 See, for example, Lieberthal, *Governing China*; Marti, *China and the Legacy*; Baum, *Burying Mao*.

2 Chen Jian, *Mao's China*, 11, 14.

3 Local History Compilation Committee of Guangxi, *Guangxi tongzhi junshi zhi*, 327.

4 Ibid., 329.

5 Since the PRC's founding, supply depots have traditionally been established by civil affairs officers in response to military needs. See "Implementation of the General Staff's Request for Establishing Food and Water Supply Depots," 11 August 1968, Yunnan Province People's Congress File, vol. 103/2/161, Yunnan Provincial Archives, Kunming.

6 Yunnan Province Civil Affairs Bureau, "Ensuring Close Coordination between the Rear to the Fighting Front," in *YXFB*, 379.

7 Local History Compilation Committee of Guangxi, *Guangxi tongzhi junshi zhi*, 327.

8 War Preparation and Aiding-the-Front Leading Group, "Summary of Ten-Year Work in Aiding the Front by Yunnan Province," in *YXFB*, 7–8.

9 See Naughton, "Third Front."

10 Dali Yang, "Pattern," 239.

11 Chao, "Particulars of the 'War Preparation' Economy," 105–7.

12 Chao, "Influence of Specific Geopolitical Environment," 88.

13 Chengdu Military Region, Political Department, "The Army Needs Support from the People to Be Victorious," in *YXFB*, 535–36.

14 War Preparation and Aiding-the-Front Leading Group, "Summary of Ten-Year Work in Aiding the Front by Yunnan Province," in *YXFB*, 9–12.

15 Chao, "Influence of Specific Geopolitical Environment," 87. For an English account of the local defense industry, see Bachman, "Defense Industrialization."

16 PLA soldiers in the 1979 war commonly complained that their Type 56 semiautomatic rifles were no match for the Vietnamese AK-47s. Ironically, American troops had lodged similar complaints a decade earlier, comparing their M-16s to the ubiquitous and rugged Kalashnikovs (Wang Zhijun, "New Stage"). See also Lian, "Small Arms"; Yunnan Province Defense Science and Industry Office, Political Department, "Doing Everything to Win the War during the Counterattack in Self-Defense," in *YXFB*, 417–19; Wang Zhiguo, *Sanxian jianshe*, 85.

17 War Preparation and Aiding-the-Front Leading Group, "Summary of Ten-Year Work in Aiding the Front by Yunnan Province," Chengdu Military Region, Political Department, "The Army Needs Support from the People to Be Victorious," both in *YXFB*, 12, 539.

18 "Brief Report on Agriculture and Forest Situation," no. 2, 10 March 1979, Yunnan Provincial Agriculture and Forest Office, Political Department, File 70, vol. 250, Yunnan Provincial Archives, Kunming.

19 "Brief Report on Agriculture and Forest Situation," no. 24, 11 April 1979, Yunnan Provincial Agriculture and Forest Office, Political Department, File 70, vol. 251, Yunnan Provincial Archives, Kunming.

20 Chengdu Military Region, Political Department, "The Army Needs Support from the People to Be Victorious," in *YXFB*, 536.

21 Yunnan Province Supply and Marketing Cooperative, "Aiding-the-Front Is the Most Sacred Obligation," in *YXFB*, 356.

22 Yunnan Province Commerce Bureau, "Ensuring Commercial Supplies to the Front," in *YXFB*, 336.

23 Yunnan Province Grain Bureau, "Food and Fodder Should Go Ahead of Troops and Horses," in *YXFB*, 321.

24 This information is based on interviews with local people by one Chinese graduate student from Yunnan.

25 The CCP Committee of Wenshan Zhuang/Miao Autonomous Prefecture and People's Government of Wenshan Zhuang/Miao Autonomous Prefecture, "The People of Laoshan, the Spirit of Laoshan," in *YXFB*, 128.

26 Chengdu Military Region, Political Department, "The Army Needs Support from the People to Be Victorious," in *YXFB*, 538; Zhang Cuiju, "New Ideas and Directions," 428.

27 Ni, *Shinian ZhongYue zhanzheng*, 2:955.

28 Ibid., 2:950–62.

29 Ding Ming, Li, and Wang, "Important Task," 22.

30 Ni, *Shinian ZhongYue zhanzheng*, 2:955.

31 Wang Kongjing, "Vietnam's Policy," 48–49.

32 Ding Ming, Li, and Wang, "Important Task," 22.

33 "Deng Xiaoping's Speech, 16 March 1979."

34 Deng Xiaoping's speech at an enlarged meeting of the CMC, 14 July 1975, *Deng junshi wenji*, 28–32.

35 Deng Xiaoping's speech at an enlarged meeting of the Standing Committee of the CMC, 12 March 1980; Deng Xiaoping's talk with CMC leaders, 9 July 1981, both in ibid., 168–79, 197–98.

36 Deng Xiaoping's speech, 12 March 1980, in ibid., 168–79.

37 The change affected eleven military regions, twenty-four field armies, and twenty-seven army corps organizations (Liao Feng, "Commanders").

38 Liu Zhi and Zhang, *Xu Xiangqian zhuan*, 550.

39 Ibid., 557.

40 Zhang Zhen, *Zhang Zhen huiyilu*, 264.

41 Ibid., 201–2.

42 Zhang Zhen, *Zhang Zhen junshi wenxuan*, 195–96.

43 Zhang Zhen, *Zhang Zhen huiyilu*, 233.

44 Zhang Weiming, "Perspectives."

45 Zhang Zhen, *Zhang Zhen huiyilu*, 245.

46 According to Zhang Sheng, these exercises were coded as 803 to 807 (*Cong zhanzheng zhong zoulai*, 456).

47 Zhang Zhen, *Junshi wenxuan*, 316–18; Zhang Zhen, *Zhang Zhen huiyilu*, 246–47.

48 Zhang Zhen, *Zhang Zhen huiyilu*, 243.

49 This remarkable statistic runs generally counter to the practices of Western armies (America's in particular), which have emphasized a doctrine of "firepower dominance." High consumption rates of cartridges and shells reflect widespread firing, even if much of it is unaimed.

50 Guo Peigong, "Issues Learned," 597–601.

51 See, for example, Deng speeches, 4 July 1982, 1 November 1984, in *Deng junshi wenji*, 215, 263.

52 *Deng nianpu*, 3:1050–52.

53 According to Zhang Sheng, the CMC leadership was reluctant to accept this language in its resolution at the enlarged CMC meeting in June 1985 (*Cong zhanzheng zhong zoulai*, 456–59).

54 Li Qianyuan, "Pondering Future Force Development," 569–71.

55 Yang Guihua and Chen, *Gongheguo jundui huimou*, 311–28.

56 Xiang, *Xiang Shouzhi huiyilu*, 428–29.

57 For example, the 55th Army's 163rd Division transferred to the 42nd Group Army; the 43rd Army's 127th and 128th Divisions merged into the 20th and 54th Group Armies, respectively; the 50th Army's 149th Division joined the 13th Group Army; and the 11th Army's 31st Division moved to the 14th Group Army.

58 Yang Guihua and Chen, *Gongheguo jundui huimou*, 327.

59 Shambaugh, "China's Military in Transition," 279.

60 Nan Li, "PLA's Evolving Warfighting Doctrine"; Godwin, "From Continent to Periphery."

61 Blasko, Klapakis, and Corbett, "Training Tomorrow's PLA," 491–94.

62 Zhang Zhen, *Zhang Zhen huiyilu*, :243.

63 *Jiefangjun bao*, 3 March 1979.

64 West, Levine, and Hiltz, *America's Wars*, 195.

65 Xiaobing Li, *History*, 236.

66 "Deng Xiaoping's Speech, 16 March 1979."

67 Scobell, *China's Use of Military Force*, 140.

68 "Zhongguo Renmin Jiefangjun Tongjian" Editorial Committee, *Zhongguo Renmin Jiefangjun tongjian*, 2185–86, 2188, 2197; Zhou Keyu, *Dangdai Zhongguo jundui de zhengzhi gongzuo*, 151.

69 "Zhongguo Renmin Jiefangjun Tongjian" Editorial Committee, *Zhongguo Renmin Jiefangjun tongjian*, 2196.

70 Department of Military History Studies, *Zhongguo Renmin Jiefangjun de qishi nian*, 450–51.

71 Joffe, *Chinese Army*, 154.

72 Baum, *Burying Mao*, 144.

73 Department of Military History Studies, *Zhongguo Renmin Jiefangjun de qishi nian*, 437–38.

74 Ibid.

75 Under the influence of Confucian philosophy, Chinese tradition placed the importance of the civil (*wen*) far above the military (*wu*). The four categories of the people—gentry scholars, peasant farmers, artisans and craftsmen, and merchants and traders—were reckoned as a central part of the social structure. Soldiers did not belong to any of ancient China's respectable social groups. See Fairbank, "Introduction"; Lei, *Zhongguo wenhua yu zhongguo de bing*, 3–53. Moreover, since the Qin and Han dynasties (221 B.C.–A.D. 24), inmates and refugees were conscripted for military service, tarnishing it as unwanted duty. One Chinese scholar has argued that "good men" did not join the army not only because they were unwilling to be with outcasts but also because they were heavily influenced by traditional Confucian family and moral values, which distained the military profession (Xiong Zhiyong, *Cong bianyuan zouxiang zhongxing*, 21; Chinese Military History Editorial Group, *Wujing qishu zhushi*, 169).

76 Xiaobing Li, *History*, 248–50.

77 Diamant attributes the lack of public interest in military service to a long-standing government policy that refused to allow rural veterans to settle in cities after their service (*Embattled Glory*, 376). For the policy of returning veterans to their hometowns, see Diamant, *Embattled Glory*, chapter 2.

78 General Chi Haotian was especially displeased that civilians used such a slur against the PLA's soldiers (Kong et al., *Chi Haotian zhuan*, 292).

79 Ji, *Xin Zhongguo guofang jiaoyu lilun*.

80 Baum, *Burying Mao*, 192.

81 Ji, *Xin Zhongguo guofang jiaoyu lilun*.

82 Xu Jingyao and Liu, "Blood-Stained Valor," 23; Chen Lei, "Laurels of Heroism," 28–30.

83 Fu Jianren, *Keyi gongkai de conglin mizhan*, 3–10.

84 Ibid., 7.

85 Liu Yazhou to Yang Shangkun 10 April 1987, in Liu Yazhou, *Liu Yazhou zhanlue wenxuan*, 329–32.

86 Fu Jianren, *Keyi gongkai de conglin mizhan*, 60–61.

87 Liu Yazhou to Yang Shangkun, 10 April 1987, in Liu Yazhou, *Liu Yazhou zhanlue wenxuan*, 331.

88 Fu Jianren, *Keyi gongkai de conglin mizhan*, 83.

89 Mulvenon, *Soldiers of Fortune*, 140.

90 Ibid., 86.

91 For a detailed description of PLA veterans' fate since 1978, see Diamant, *Embattled Glory*, chapter 8.

92 Liu Hong, "Interview with Li Cunbao."

93 Li Baocun, "Wreaths of Flowers."

94 Zheng Yunxin, "Inside Story."

95 "Inside Story about 'Wreaths of Flowers.'"

96 CCP Central Documentary Editorial Committee, *Deng Xiaoping wenxuan*, 3:39–48.

97 For detailed discussion of Deng's views on "spiritual pollution," see Baum, *Burying Mao*, 156–61.

98 CCP Central Documentary Editorial Committee, *Deng Xiaoping wenxuan*, 3:42.

99 Xia, *Cihai*, 768.

100 Political Department of the Guangzhou Military Region, *Yingxiong zan*.

101 Jin, Zhang, and Zhang, *ZhongYue zhanzheng milu*.

102 Guo Zhongshi and Lu, "'Extracting Facts.'"

103 Fu Jianren, *Keyi gongkai de conglin mizhan*, 21–25.

104 Some veterans published their recollections of the 1979 war at their own expense, without ISBN numbers. See, for example, Yang Liufan, *Yongzhe wuwei*.

105 In this Korean War film, the main character blows himself up along with the enemy, his selfless heroism exemplifying for the audience the sacrifice of the PLA soldiers lost in the war.

106 Fu Xiao, "For Commemorating the Forgotten," 89.

107 Xie Ailing, "Blood-Stained Valor."

108 Yu Ji, "Perspectives," 27, 31.

109 Liang and Yan, "Story," 46.

110 Tang and Su, "Shine on the Home," 26; Wu Qiong, "Resolving Contradictions," 189.

111 The lyrics were written by Shi Xiang. The song was available at "ZhongYue zhanzheng beiwanglu," http://bwl.top81.cn/war79/index.html.

112 Wang Weidong, "We Expect the Soldiers."

113 The lyrics were written by Chen Zhe. The song was available at http://bwl.top81.cn/war79/index.html.

114 Hung, "Politics of Songs," 916.

115 Xie Ailing, "Blood-Stained Valor," 7.

116 Zhang Sheng, *Cong zhanzheng zhong zoulai*, 474.

117 Ironically, the song subsequently became a popular form of commemoration for those killed during the 1989 Tiananmen Square protests, which were triggered by overseas prodemocracy activists.

118 Lu, "Emphasizing the Pre-Emptive Strike."

CHAPTER 8

1 Khoo, *Collateral Damage*, 141.
2 "Deng Xiaoping's Talk on the Issue of Soviet Socialist Imperialism," May 1980, Ministry of Foreign Affairs, Sichuan Provincial Archives, Chengdu.
3 Huang, *Qinli yu jianwen*, 209, 232.
4 Ma, "My Personal Experience," 34.
5 Ibid., 35.
6 Qian Qichen categorizes Sino-Soviet relations into three periods: (1) ideological rivalry (1959–69) (2) confrontation (1969–79), and (3) negotiations (1979–89) (*Waijiao shiji*, 2).
7 Niu, "Returning to Asia," 70.
8 "Deng Xiaoping's Talk on the Issue of Soviet Socialist Imperialism," May 1980, Ministry of Foreign Affairs, Sichuan Provincial Archives, Chengdu.
9 "Circular about Not Extending the Sino-Soviet Treaty," 3 April 1979, and "How to Respond to Foreign Inquiries about the Sino-Soviet Negotiations," 23 April 1979, Ministry of Foreign Affairs, FPA.
10 Editorial Group, *Li Xiannian zhuan*, 1231–32.
11 See Cohen, *America's Response to China*, 225–27.
12 Jones and Kevill, *China and the Soviet Union*, 124.
13 Ma, "My Personal Experience," 32–33.
14 Editorial Group, *Li Xiannian zhuan*, 1236.
15 Qian Qichen, *Waijiao shiji*, 7.
16 Ibid., 10–18.
17 For example, President Ronald Reagan was once asked at a press conference why he did not meet more frequently with his Soviet counterpart. He replied that he would like to do so, "but they keep dying on me." Maureen Dowd, "Where's the Rest of Him?" *New York Times*, 18 November 1990.
18 Niu, "Returning to Asia," 73.
19 Deng Xiaoping's Talk with Kim Il Sung, 18 September 1982, in *Deng nianpu*, 2:850–51.
20 Ma, "My Personal Experience," 37.
21 Deng Xiaoping's Talk with Edward Heath, 18 April 1985, in *Deng nianpu*, 2:1040–41.
22 Indeed, Chinese scholars argue that Deng used the normalization of Sino-Soviet relations to serve China's Indochina policy. See, for example, Niu, "Returning to Asia," 72–73.
23 *Deng nianpu*, 2:1085–86.
24 Richardson, *China, Cambodia, and the Five Principles*, 135–36.
25 Khoo, *Collateral Damage*, 147.
26 Richardson, *China, Cambodia, and the Five Principles*, 99.
27 Deng Xiaoping's Meeting with Vice President Walter Mondale, 27 August 1979, Ministry of Foreign Affairs, FPA.
28 Richardson, *China, Cambodia, and the Five Principles*, 122.
29 Deng Xiaoping's Talks with Franz Josef Strauss, 5 October 1985, and with Nicolai Ceaușescu, 9 October 1985, both in *Deng nianpu*, 2:1084–85.
30 Ma, "My Personal Experience," 37.
31 Khoo, *Collateral Damage*, 146.
32 Niu, "Returning to Asia," 76.
33 Zheng Yu, "Collapse," 48.
34 Niu, "Returning to Asia," 74.
35 Womack, *China and Vietnam*, 203.
36 Chengdu Military Region, *Yuenan wenti ziliao xuanbian*, 169.
37 Lien-Hang T. Nguyen, *Hanoi's War*, 302–3.
38 Li Jiazhong, "Inside Story." At the time, Li served as the chief of Indochina office in the Ministry of Foreign Affairs.
39 Zheng Yu, "Collapse," 49; Richardson, *China, Cambodia, and the Five Principles*, 137.
40 Li Jiazhong, "Inside Story," 22, 25.

41 Zheng Yu, "Collapse," 49.

42 Wang Taiping, *Zhonghua Renmin Gongheguo waijiaoshi*, 1:205.

43 Li Jiazhong, "Inside Story," 22.

44 Niu, "Returning to Asia," 78.

45 Qian Qichen, *Waijiao shiji*, 23–24.

46 Hu, *Renmin haijun zhengzhan jishi*, 560–62.

47 Niu, "Returning to Asia," 79.

48 Qian Qichen, *Waijiao shiji*, 26–27.

49 Ibid., 39–40, 43. See also Li Jiazhong, "Consultations."

50 Li Jiazhong, "Personal Experience," 36–37.

51 According to a 14 July 1989 CMC order, the PLA forces under the command of the Yunnan Provincial Military District were to maintain military pressure on Vietnam, showing strength while minimizing losses (Ni, *ZhongYue zhanzheng*, 2:826, 828).

52 Li Jiazhong, "Personal Experience," 38.

53 Qian Qichen, *Waijiao shiji*, 43–44.

54 Zhang Qing, "After Years of Conflict." Zhang was former Chinese ambassador to Vietnam.

55 Diary entry, 26 August 1989, in Li Peng, *Heping Fazhan Hezuo*, 309.

56 Qian Qichen, *Waijiao shiji*, 50.

57 Li Jiazhong, "Inside Story," 23.

58 Ibid., 24.

59 Womack, *China and Vietnam*, 207–8.

60 Li Jiazhong, "Inside Story," 24.

61 Qian Qichen, *Waijiao shiji*, 51.

62 Li Jiazhong, "Inside Story," 24–25.

63 Ibid., 25–26.

64 Diary entries, 6 June, 26, 27, 30 August, 2, 3, 4 September 1990, in Li Peng, *Heping Fazhan Hezuo*, 309–21.

65 Zhang Qing, "Recollections," 39–40.

66 Li Jiazhong, "Inside Story," 26.

67 Qian Qichen, *Waijiao shiji*, 52.

68 Zhang Qing, "After Years of Conflict," 7.

69 Guo Min et al., *ZhongYue guanxi*, 221.

70 Khoo, *Collateral Damage*, 149.

71 Li Jiazhong, "Inside Story," 24.

72 Womack, *China and Vietnam*, 213.

73 Diary entry, 6 November 1991, in Li Peng, *Heping Fazhan Hezuo*, 313.

74 Richardson, *China, Cambodia, and the Five Principles*, 152.

75 Jianguo Li, *Qinli Laoshan zhizhan*, 388–89.

76 Ni, *Shinian ZhongYue zhanzheng*, 2:829.

77 The minesweeping operations ended in September 1994after removing several hundred thousand mines and explosive devices (ibid., 957–58).

78 Richardson, *China, Cambodia, and the Five Principles*, 153.

79 Womack, *China and Vietnam*, 209.

80 Howard, *Causes of Wars*, 14.

81 Reiter, *How Wars End*, 211.

82 Ibid., 15.

83 Ma, "My Personal Experience," 37.

84 "Deng Xiaoping's Speech, 16 March 1979."

85 Lien-Hang T. Nguyen, *Hanoi's War*, 303.

86 Womack, *China and Vietnam*, 209.

87 Li Jiazhong, "Consultations," 37.

88 Li Jiazhong, "Personal Experience," 39.

89 Li Jianguo, *Qinli Laoshan zhizhan*, 410.

90 Womack, *China and Vietnam*, 211.

CONCLUSION

1 Howard, *Causes of Wars*, 35.
2 Chen Jian, "China, the Vietnam War, and the Sino-American Rapprochement," 58.
3 Westad, "Introduction," 1. The threat of conflict already existed between some socialist states, particularly in the early years of the Tito regime in Yugoslavia, and the long-standing tensions between China and the USSR began in the Khrushchev era and lasted for more than two decades.
4 *Deng Junshi wenji*, 164–66.
5 Zhang Qing, "Recollections," 39.
6 Reiter, *How Wars End*, 19–20.
7 Since the end of the Sino-Vietnamese conflict, more than thirty officers have served as military region commanders and chiefs of PLA headquarters departments and even as CMC members and vice chairs (Xu Santong, *Junzhong shaozhuangpai*, 71–75).

Bibliography

ARCHIVES

Fujian Provincial Archives, Fuzhou
Jilin Provincial Archives, Changchun
Jimmy Carter Presidential Library, Atlanta
PRC's Ministry of Foreign Affairs Archives, Beijing
PRC's Ministry of Railroad Archives, Beijing
Sichuan Provincial Archives, Chengdu
Yunnan Provincial Archives, Kunming

DOCUMENTS AND PAPERS

Armored Force Political Department, ed. *Dui Yue ziwei huanjizhan zhuangjiabing zhengzhi gongzuo jingyan* (Political Work Experiences Gained by the Armored Force during the Counterattack in Self-Defense against Vietnam). Beijing: Zhuangjiabing zhengzhibu, 1979.

CCP Central Documentary Editorial Committee, ed. *Deng Xiaoping wenxuan* (Selected Works of Deng Xiaoping). 3 vols. Beijing: Renmin, 1993.

CCP Central Documentary Research Department. *Jianguo yilai Mao Zedong wengao* (Mao Zedong's Manuscripts since the Founding of the Country). 13 vols. Beijing: Zhongyang wenxian, 1988–98.

———. *Mao Zedong junshi wenji* (Collected Military Papers of Mao Zedong). Vol. 2. Beijing: Junshi kexue and Zhongyang wenxian, 1993.

CCP Central Documentary Research Department and PLA Military Science Academy, ed. *Deng Xiaoping junshi wenji* (Collected Military Works of Deng Xiaoping). Vol. 3. Beijing: Junshi kexue and Zhongyang wenxian, 2004.

Chen Geng. Chen Geng riji (Chen Geng's Diary). Beijing: Jiefangjun, 2003.

———. *Chen Geng riji (xu).* (Chen Geng's Diary [Sequel]). Beijing: Jiefangjun, 1984.

Chengdu Military Region, Political Department, Liaison Office, and Southeast Asia Research Institute of Yunnan Province Social Science Academy, eds. *Yuenan wenti ziliao xuanbian* (Selected Materials on the Vietnam Issue). Vol. 2. N.p.: n.p., 1987.

China News Agency International Information Group, ed. *Woguo dui Yue ziwei huanjizhan ziliao ji* (Collections of Materials on Our Country's Counterattack against Vietnam in Self-Defense). Beijing: Xinhuashe, 1979.

"Deng Xiaoping's Speech at the CCP Central Committee Meeting on Counterattack in Self-Defense on the Sino-Vietnamese Border, 16 March 1979." In *Zhongguo wenhua dageming wenku* (Chinese Cultural Revolution Database), comp. Song Youyi. CD-ROM. Hong Kong: Chinese University Press, 2006.

Department of General Staff, ed. *Mao Zedong junshi wenxuan* (Selected Military Works of Mao Zedong). Beijing: Zongcanmoubu, 1961.

Financial Department of Kunming Military Region Logistics, ed. *Yunnan fangxiang Zhong Yue bianjing ziwei huanji zuozhan houqin caiwu baozhang gongzuo ziliao xuanbian* (Selected

Materials on Financial Work during the Counterattack in Self-Defense on the Sino-Vietnamese Border). Kunming: Kunming junqu houqingbu caiwubu, 1979.

43rd Army, ed. *Dui Yue ziwei fanji zuozhan zongjie xuanbian* (Selected Summaries on the Counterattack in Self-Defense against Vietnam). N.p.: n.p., 1979.

General Office of the General Political Department, ed. *Zhong Yue bianjing ziwei huanji zuozhan zhengzhi gongzuo jingyan xuanbian* (Compilation of Selected Experiences of Political Work during the Counterattack in Self-defense on the Sino-Vietnamese Border). 2 vols. Beijing: Zongzhengzhibu, 1980.

Geng Biao. "Secret Report." 16 January 1979. *Studies on Chinese Communism* 166 (15 October 1980): 142–66.

Goods and Materials Office, Guangzhou Military Region Logistics Department. "Aspects of Logistical Supply." *Houqin tongxun* (Logistics Newsletter), 30 June 1979.

Guangzhou junqu dashi ji (Chronicle of Major Events in the Guangzhou Military Region). Guangzhou: n.p., n.d.

Guangzhou Military Region Forward Command Political Department Cadre Section, ed. *Zhong Yue bianjing ziwei huanji zuozhan ganbu gongzuo ziliao huibian* (Compilation of Materials on Cadre Work during the Counterattack in Self-Defense on the Sino-Vietnamese Border). Guangzhou: Guangzhou junqu qianzhi zhengzhibu, 1979.

Headquarters of the Kunming Military Region Artillery, ed. *Zhong Yue bianjing ziwei fanji zuozhan paobing zhuanti xuanbian* (A Collection of Selected Materials on the Special Subject of Artillery Force during the Counterattack in Self-Defense on the Sino-Vietnamese Border). N.p.: n.p., 1979.

Headquarters of the PLA 55th Army, ed. *Zhong Yue bianjing ziwei fanji zuozhan zhanlie xuanbian* (Selected Battle Cases from the Counterattack in Self-Defense on the Sino-Vietnamese Border). N.p.: n.p., 1980.

"Hua Guofeng's Speech at the CCP Central Committee Meeting on Counterattack in Self-Defense on the Sino-Vietnamese Border, 16 March 1979." In *Zhongguo wenhua dageming wenku* (Chinese Cultural Revolution Database), comp. Song Youyi. CD-ROM. Hong Kong: Chinese University Press, 2006.

Le Duan. "Comrade B on the Plot of the Reactionary Chinese Clique against Vietnam." Trans. Christopher E. Goscha. http://digitalarchive.wilsoncenter.org/document/112982. 17 October 2014.

Li Peng. *Heping Fazhan Hezuo—Li Peng waishi riji* (Peace, Development, Cooperation: Li Peng's Diary on Foreign Affairs). Vol. 1. Beijing: Xinhua, 2008.

Liu Yazhou. *Liu Yazhou zhanlue wenji* (Collected Strategic Essays of Liu Yazhou). Xi'an: n.p., 2009.

Logistics Department of the PLA Fiftieth Army, ed. *Zhong Yue bianjing ziwei fanji zuozhan houqin baozhang jingyan xuanbian* (Compilation of Selected Experiences of Logistics Support during the Counterattack in Self-Defense on the Sino-Vietnamese Border). N.p.: Wushijun houqinbu, 1979.

Party History and Political Work Department, Guangzhou Military Region Infantry School, ed. "Issues on Political Work at Company Level during the Counterattack in Self-Defense on the Sino-Vietnamese Border (draft for discussion)." In *Zhong Yue bianjing ziwei fanji zuozhan zhengzhi gongzuo ziliao* (Materials on Political Work during the Counterattack in Self-Defense on the Sino-Vietnamese Border), no. 14. Guilin: Guangzhou junqu bubing xuexiao, 1979.

"People's Liberation Army Documents on the Sino-Vietnamese Conflict, 1979." *Chinese Law and Government* 42 (September–October 2009): 11–100; (November–December 2009): 8–113.

Political Teaching Office of PLA Nanjing Advanced Infantry School. "Zhong Yue bianjing ziwei huanji zuozhan zhengzhi gongzuo jingyan xuanbian" (Selected Experiences of Political Work during the Counterattack in Self-Defense on the Sino-Vietnamese Border). Nanjing: Nanjing junqu gaoji bubing xuexiao, 1979.

PRC Ministry of Foreign Affairs and CCP Central Documentary Research Department, eds. *Mao Zedong waijiao wenxuan* (Selected Diplomatic Works of Mao Zedong). Beijing: Zhongyang wenxian, 1994.

Training Department of Kunming Military Region Headquarters, ed. *Zhong Yue bianjing ziwei fanji zuozhan zhanlie xuanbian: Lian, pai, ban* (Selected Battle Cases from the Counterattack in Self-Defense on the Sino-Vietnamese Border: Company, Platoon, and Squad). No. 14. N.p.: Kunming junqu silingbu xunlianbu, 1979.

Training Department of Kunming Military Region Infantry School, ed. *Zhong Yue bianjing ziwei huanji zuozhan zhanlie xuanbian* (Selected Battle Cases from the Counterattack in Self-Defense on the Sino-Vietnamese Border). No. 1. N.p.: Kunming junqu bubing xuexiao xunlianbu, 1979.

Training Department of PLA Political College, ed. Zhong Yue bianjing ziwei huanji zuozhan zhengzhi gongzuo jingyan xuanbian (Compilation of Selected Experiences of Political Work during the Counterattack in Self-Defense on the Sino-Vietnamese Border). Beijing: Jiefangjun zhengzhi xueyuan, 1979.

Vietnam, Socialist Republic of. Ministry of Foreign Affairs. *The Truth about Vietnam-China Relations over the Last 30 Years*. Hanoi: n.p., 1979.

"Wang Shangrong's Speech at the CCP Central Committee Meeting on Counterattack in Self-Defense on the Sino-Vietnamese Border, 16 March 1979." In *Zhongguo wenhua dageming wenku* (Chinese Cultural Revolution Database), comp. Song Youyi. CD-ROM. Hong Kong: Chinese University Press, 2006.

War Preparation and Aiding-the-Front Leading Group of Yunnan Province and Propaganda Department of the CCP Committee of Yunnan Province, ed. *Yingxiong de fengbei: Yunnan renmin shinian zhiqian jishi* (Heroic Monument: True Record of the Ten-Year Aiding-the-Front Work by Yunnan People). Kunming: Yunnan renmin, 1991.

Westad, Odd Arne, Chen Jian, Stein Tonnesson, Nguyen Vu Tung, and James G. Hershberg, eds. *77 Conversations between Chinese and Foreign Leaders on the War in Indochina, 1964–1977*. Cold War International History Project Working Paper, no. 22. Washington, D.C.: Woodrow Wilson International Center for Scholars, 1998.

Zhang Wannian. *Zhang Wannian junshi wenji* (Collected Military Works of Zhang Wannian). Beijing: Jiefangjun, 2008.

Zhang Zhen. *Zhang Zhen junshi wenxuan* (Selected Military Works of Zhang Zhen). Vol. 2. Beijing: Jiefangjun, 2005.

PERIODICALS AND MEDIA SOURCES AND WEBSITES

Bainianchao (Hundred Year Tide)
Binggong keji (Ordnance Industry Science and Technology)
Bingqi zhishi (Ordnance Knowledge)
China News Agency
Dangshi zongheng (Over the Party History)
Dongnanya zongheng (Around Southeast Asia)
Far Eastern Economic Review
Foreign Broadcast Information Service
Guoji guancha (International Review)
Hanoi Radio
Jiefangjun bao (PLA Daily)
Junshi shilin (Martial Historical Facts)
Kejiao wenhui (Science and Education Magazine)
Liaowang (Outlook Weekly)
Nanfengchuang (South Wind Window)
Nanfang renwu zhoukan (Southern People Weekly)
New York Times
Peking Review

Qingbingqi (Small Arms)
Renmin ribao (People's Daily)
Renmin ribao haiwanban (People's Daily Overseas Edition)
Renmin yinyue (People's Music)
Shehui kexue yanjiu (Social Science Studies)
Shijie zhishi (World Affairs)
Wenjiao ziliao (*chuzhongban*) (Culture and Education, middle school edition)
Xiandai jianchuan (Modern Ships)
Xiandai junshi (Modern Military)
Xiangchao (Hunan Party History Monthly)
Yinyue tansuo (*zengkan* 2) (Music Exploration, supplement 2)
Zhonggong dangshi yanjiu (Journal of the CCP Party History Studies)
Zhongguo minbing (China Militia)
Zhonghua junshi (military.china.com)
Zhong Yue zhanzheng beiwanglu (Memorandums of the Sino-Vietnamese War)
Zhong Yue zhanzheng jilu daquan (Completed Records of the Sino-Vietnamese War)

BOOKS AND ARTICLES

Army Logistics Department. "Things We Learned from Conducting Logistics in the Battle of Defending Laoshan." In *Conglin qilue* (Fighting Jungle Warfare with Unique Strategy), ed. Li Qianyuan and Song Ke, 614–24. Beijing: Guofang daxue, 1986.

Aron, Raymond. *Peace and War: A Theory of International Relations*. Garden City, N.Y.: Anchor, 1973.

Bachman, David. "Defense Industrialization in Guangdong." *China Quarterly* 166 (June 2001): 273–304.

Baum, Richard. *Burying Mao: China's Politics in the Age of Deng Xiaoping*. Princeton: Princeton University Press, 1994.

Bernstein, Richard, and Ross H. Munro. *The Coming Conflict with China*. New York: Knopf, 1997.

Blasko, Dennis J., Philip T. Klapakis, and John F. Corbett Jr. "Training Tomorrow's PLA: A Mixed Bag of Tricks." *China Quarterly* 146 (June 1996): 488–524.

Boniface, Roger. *MiGs over North Vietnam: The Vietnamese People's Air Force in Combat, 1965–1975*. Manchester, Eng.: Hikoki, 2008.

Brzezinski, Zbigniew. *Power and Principle: Memoirs of the National Security Adviser, 1977–1981*. New York: Farrar, Straus, and Giroux, 1983.

Burless, Mark, and Abram Shulsky. *Patterns in China's Use of Force: Evidence from History and Doctrinal Writings*. Santa Monica, Calif.: Rand, 2000.

CCP Party History Research Office. *Zhonggong dangshi dashi nianbiao* (Chronicle of Important Events in the History of the CCP). Beijing: Renmin, 1987.

Chanda, Nayan. *Brother Enemy: The War after the War*. New York: Harcourt Brace Jovanovich, 1986.

Chang, Maria Hsia. *Return of the Dragon: China's Wounded Nationalism*. Boulder, Colo.: Westview, 2001.

Chao Lihua. "The Influence of Specific Geopolitical Environment on Yunnan's Third-Line Construction." *Kunming shifan gaodeng zhuanke xuexiao xuebao* (Journal of Kunming Teachers College) 3 (September 2006): 86–89.

———. "Particulars of the 'War Preparation' Economy: Understanding of the Third-Line Construction History of Yunnan." *Chuxiong shifan xueyuan xuebao* (Journal of Chuxiong Normal University) 1 (January 2007): 103–8.

Chen Jian. "China and the First Indochina War, 1950–1954." *China Quarterly* 133 (March 1993): 85–110.

———. "China, the Vietnam War, and the Sino-American Rapprochement, 1968–1973." In *The Third Indochina War: Conflict between China, Vietnam, and Cambodia, 1972–1979*, ed. Odd Arne Westad and Sophie Quinn-Judge, 33–64. London: Routledge, 2006.

———. "China's Involvement in the Vietnam War, 1964–1969." *China Quarterly* 143 (June 1995): 356–87.

———. *China's Road to the Korean War: The Making of the Sino-American Confrontation.* New York: Columbia University Press, 1994.

———. *Mao's China and the Cold War.* Chapel Hill: University of North Carolina Press, 2001.

Chen, King C. *China's War with Vietnam, 1979.* Stanford, Calif.: Hoover Institution Press, 1987.

Chen Lei. "The Laurels of Heroism in 1987 Weighed Too Heavily upon Xu Liang." *Nanfang renwu zhoukan,* 21 May 2006, 28–30.

Chen Zaidao. *Chen Zaidao huiyilu* (Memoirs of Chen Zaidao). Beijing: Jiefangjun, 1991.

Chen Zhijian. "Trust—The Art of Best Leadership." In *Yibaishuan yanjing li de zhanzheng: Nanjiang jituanjun zai 1979-1987* (War in One Hundred Eyes: A Group Army in the Southern Borderland, 1979-1987), ed. Ding Longyan, 313–17. Chengdu: Sichuan wenyi, 1989.

Chen Zuhua and Liu Changli. "Summary of the Symposium on 'Control of Communication.'" *Zhongguo junshi kexue* (China Military Science) 15 (January 2002): 145–48.

Cheng, Feng, and Larry M. Wortzel. "PLA Operational Principles and Limited War: The Sino-Indian War of 1962." In *Chinese Warfighting: The PLA Experience since 1949,* ed. Mark A. Ryan, David M. Finkelstein, and Michael A. McDevitt, 173–97. Armonk, N.Y.: Sharpe, 2003.

Cheng Zhongyuan. *Zhang Wentian zhuan* (Biography of Zhang Wentian). Beijing: Dangdai Zhongguo, 2000.

Chinese Military History Editorial Group. *Wujing qishu zhushi* (Annotations of Seven Military Classics). Beijing: Jiefangjun, 1986.

Christensen, Thomas J. *Worse Than a Monolith: Alliance Politics and Problems of Coercive Diplomacy in Asia.* Princeton: Princeton University Press, 2011.

Christman, Ron. "How Beijing Evaluates Military Campaigns: An Initial Assessment." In *The Lessons of History: The Chinese People's Liberation Army at 75,* ed. Laurie Burkitt, Andrew Scobell, and Larry M. Wortzel, 235–92. Carlisle, Pa.: Strategic Studies Institute, U.S. Army War College, 2003.

Cohen, Warren I. *America's Response to China: A History of Sino-American Relations.* 5th ed. New York: Columbia University Press, 2010.

Cong Jin. *Quzhe qianjin de shinian* (A Decade of Tortuous Advance). Zhengzhou: Henan Renmin, 1989.

Dang, Van Nhung. *Su Doan 338* (338th Division). Hanoi: People's Army Publishing House, 1991.

Department of Military History Studies, Academy of Military Science. *Zhongguo Renmin Jiefangjun de qishi nian* (Seventy years of the People's Liberation Army of China). Beijing: Junshi kexue, 1997.

———. *Zhongguo Renmin Jiefangjun qishinian* (Seventy Years of the People's Liberation Army). Vol. 1 of *Zhongguo Renmin Jiefangjun quanshi* (A Complete History of the People's Liberation Army). Beijing: Junshi kexue, 2000.

———. *Zhongguo Renmin Jiefangjun quanshi* (The Complete History of the People's Liberation Army). Beijing: Junshi kexue, 1999.

———. *Zhongguo Renmin Zhiyuanjun kangMei yuanChao zhanshi* (A War History of the Chinese People's Volunteers in the War of Resisting U.S. Aggression and Assisting Korea). Beijing: Junshi kexue, 1990.

Diamant, Neil J. *Embattled Glory: Veterans, Military Families, and the Politics of Patriotism in China, 1949-2007.* Lanham, Md.: Rowman and Littlefield, 2010.

Ding Longyan, ed. *Yibaishuan yanjing li de zhanzheng: Nanjiang jituanjun zai 1979-1987* (War in One Hundred Eyes: A Group Army in the Southern Borderland, 1979-1987). Chengdu: Sichuan wenyi, 1989.

Ding Ming, Li Ziliang, and Wang Mian. "An Important Task to Get the Border Regions out of Poverty." *Liaowang,* 30 January 2007, 22.

Duiker, William. *China and Vietnam: The Roots of Conflict.* Berkeley: Institute of East Asian Studies, University of California, 1986.

———. *Ho Chi Minh.* New York: Hyperion, 2000.

———. *Vietnam: Revolution in Transition.* 2nd ed. Boulder, Colo.: Westview, 1995.

Editorial Group of Li Xiannian's Biography. *Li Xiannian zhuan* (Biography of Li Xiannian). Vol. 2. Beijing: Zhongyang wenxian, 2009.

Elleman, Bruce. *Modern Chinese Warfare, 1785–1989.* London: Routledge, 2001.

Evans, Richard. *Deng Xiaoping and the Making of Modern China.* New York: Viking, 1994.

———. *Deng Xiaoping zhuan* (Biography of Deng Xiaoping). Shanghai: Shanghai renmin, 1997.

Fairbank, John K. "Introduction: Varieties of the Chinese Military Experience." In *Chinese Ways in Warfare,* ed. Frank A. Kierman Jr. and John K. Fairbank, 2–9. Cambridge: Harvard University Press, 1974.

Fan Junchang. *Tiexue zhanjiang Liu Changyi* (Blood-Iron General Liu Changyi). Beijing: Jiefangjun, 2005.

Fan Shuo, chief ed. *Ye Jianying zhuan* (Biography of Ye Jianying). Beijing: Dangdai Zhongguo, 1997.

Feng Jinmao. "Fighting Effectively by Understanding the Special Characteristics of Artillery Warfare." In *Conglin qilue* (Fighting Jungle Warfare with Unique Strategy), ed. Li Qianyuan and Song Ke, 34–39. Beijing: Guofang daxue, 1986.

FitzGerald, D. M. *The Vietnam People's Army: Regulization of Command, 1975–1988.* Canberra: Strategic and Defense Studies Center, Research School of Pacific Studies, Australian National University, 1989.

Foot, Rosemary. "Prizes Won, Opportunities Lost: The U.S. Normalization of Relations with China, 1972–1979." In *Normalization of U.S.-China Relations: An International History,* ed. William C. Kirby, Robert S. Ross, and Gong Li, 90–115. Cambridge: Harvard University Asia Center, 2005.

Foreign Ministry, Diplomatic History Research Office. *Zhou Enlai waijiao huodong dashiji, 1949–1975* (Chronicle of Zhou Enlai's Important Diplomatic Activities, 1949–1975). Beijing: Shijie zhishi, 1993.

Fravel, M. Taylor. *Strong Borders, Secure Nation: Cooperation and Conflict in China's Territorial Disputes.* Princeton: Princeton University Press, 2008.

Fu Jianren. *Keyi gongkai de conglin mizhan* (A Secret Jungle War That Can Now Be Publicized). Beijing: Jiefangjun wenyi, 1991.

Fu Quanyou. "A Unique War Fought under Modern Conditions." In *Conglin qilue* (Fighting Jungle Warfare with Unique Strategy), ed. Li Qianyuan and Song Ke, 3–12. Beijing: Guofang daxue, 1986.

Fu Xiao. "For Commemorating the Forgotten." *Wenjiao ziliao* (*chuzhongban*), 15 July 2004, 89–90.

Gaiduk, Ilya V. *The Soviet Union and the Vietnam War.* Chicago: Dee, 1996.

Gao Donghai and Cao Fuguo. "Discussions of Setting-Up an Independent Logistical Support System at Army Level." In *Conglin qilue* (Fighting Jungle Warfare with Unique Strategy), ed. Li Qianyuan and Song Ke, 431–39. Beijing: Guofang daxue, 1986.

Gardner, Lloyd C., and Ted Gittenger, eds. *International Perspectives on Vietnam.* College Station: Texas A&M University Press, 2000.

Gates, Robert M. *Duty: Memoirs of a Secretary at War.* New York: Knopf, 2014.

Ge Wenyong. *Feixing zhaji* (Flying Notes). Beijing: Lantian, 2004.

George, Alexander. *The Chinese Communist Army in Action: The Korean War and Its Aftermath.* New York: Columbia University Press, 1969.

Gilks, Anne. *The Breakdown of the Sino-Vietnamese Alliance, 1970–1979.* Berkeley: Institute of East Asian Studies, University of California, 1992.

Godwin, Paul H. B. "From Continent to Periphery: PLA Doctrine, Strategy, and Capabilities towards 2000." *China Quarterly* 146 (June 1996): 464–87.

Gong Li. *Deng Xiaoping yu Meiguo* (Deng Xiaoping and the United States). Beijing: Zhongyang dangshi, 2004.

———. "The Difficult Path to Diplomatic Relations: China's U.S. Policy, 1972–1978." In *Normalization of U.S.-China Relations: An International History,* ed. William C. Kirby, Robert S. Ross, and Gong Li, 116–46. Cambridge: Harvard University Asia Center, 2005.

————. "A Triangular Relationship of U.S.–China–Soviet Union during the 1979 China-Vietnam Border Conflict." *Guoji guancha* 3 (June 2004): 66–72.

Goscha, Christopher E. "Vietnam, the Third Indochina War, and the Meltdown of Asian Internationalism." In *The Third Indochina War: Conflict between China, Vietnam, and Cambodia, 1972–1979*, ed. Odd Arne Westad and Sophie Quinn-Judge, 152–86. London: Routledge, 2006.

Gu Shoucheng and Hu Ruhua. "Measures Used to Counter Trench Warfare Tactics." In *Conglin qilue* (Fighting Jungle Warfare with Unique Strategy), ed. Li Qianyuan and Song Ke, 77–81. Beijing: Guofang daxue, 1986.

Guo Min et al. *ZhongYue guanxi yanbian sishinian* (Forty-year Evolution of the Sino-Vietnamese Relations). Nanning: Guangxi renmin, 1992.

Guo Peigong. "Issues Learned from Combat for Improving Training in Peacetime." In *Conglin qilue* (Fighting Jungle Warfare with Unique Strategy), ed. Li Qianyuan and Song Ke, 597–602. Beijing: Guofang daxue, 1986.

Guo Zhongshi and Lu Ye. "'Extracting Facts' in the Literature Surrounding the Changing Relationship between Intellectuals and the State across Three Historical Periods." *Chuanbo yu shehui* (Journal of Communication and Society) 6 (2008). http://www.ilf.cn/Theo/110771_2.html. 20 June 2010.

Han Huaizhi and Tan Jingqiao, chief eds. *Dangdai Zhongguo jundui de junshi gongzuo* (Contemporary Military Work of the Chinese Armed Forces). Vol. 1. Beijing: Shehui kexue, 1989.

Han Nianlong, chief ed. *Dangdai Zhongguo waijiao* (Contemporary China's Diplomacy). Beijing: Shehui kexue, 1987.

He, Di. "The Most Respected Enemy: Mao Zedong's Perception of the United States." In *Toward a History of Chinese Communist Foreign Relations, 1920s–1960s: Personalities and Interpretative Approaches*, ed. Michael Hunt and Liu Jun, 27–66. Washington, D.C.: Woodrow Wilson International Center for Scholars Asian Program, 1995.

Hoang, Van Hoan. *Canghai yisu: Hoang Van Hoan geming huiyilu* (A Drop in the Ocean: Hoang Van Hoan's Revolutionary Reminiscences). Beijing: Jiefangjun, 1987.

————. *YueZhong zhandou de youyi shishi burong waiqu* (The Reality of the Sino-Vietnamese Friendship in Fighting Ought Not to Be Distorted). Beijing: Renmin, 1979.

Hood, Steven J. *Dragons Entangled: Indochina and the China-Vietnam War*. Armonk, N.Y.: Sharpe, 1992.

Howard, Michael. *The Causes of Wars: And Other Essays*. Cambridge: Harvard University Press, 1983.

Hu Yanlin, chief ed. *Renmin haijun zhengzhan jishi* (The True War Record of the People's Navy). Beijing: Guofang daxue, 1996.

Huang Hua. *Qinli yu jianwen: Huang Hua huiyilu* (Personal Experience and Knowledge: Memoirs of Huang Hua). Beijing: Shijie zhishi, 2007.

Hung, Chang-Tai. "The Politics of Songs: Myths and Symbols in the Chinese Communist War Music, 1937–1949." *Modern Asian Studies* 30 (October 1996): 901–29.

Iklé, Fred Charles. *Every War Must End*. New York: Columbia University Press, 1991.

Jencks, Harlan W. "China's 'Punitive' War on Vietnam: A Military Assessment." *Asian Survey* 19 (August 1979): 801–15.

Jiang Feng, Ma Xiaochun, and Dou Yishan. *Yangyong jiangjun zhuan* (Biography of General Yang Yong). Beijing: Jiefangjun, 1991.

Jiang Hao and Lin Pi. "Recollections of His Days in the Air Force: An Interview with Zhou Shouxing, Deputy Chief of Staff of the 7th Air Division." *Binggong keji*, 20 September 2006, 27–30.

Jiang Wenyu. "Counterattacks Fought from Defensive Positions." In *Conglin qilue* (Fighting Jungle Warfare with Unique Strategy), ed. Li Qianyuan and Song Ke, 53–57. Beijing: Guofang daxue, 1986.

Jin Hui, Zhang Huisheng, and Zhang Weiming. *ZhongYue zhanzheng milu* (Secret Record of the China-Vietnam War). Beijing: Jiefangjun, 1991.

Jin, Qiu. *The Culture of Power: The Lin Biao Incident in the Cultural Revolution*. Stanford, Calif.: Stanford University Press, 1999.

Jin Ye, Hu Juchen, and Hu Zhaocai. *Baizhan jiangxing Xu Shiyou* (Biography of General Xu Shiyou). Beijing: Jiefangjun wenyi, 1999.

———. *Xu Shiyou zhuan* (Biography of Xu Shiyou). Shanghai: Shanghai renmin, 2000.

Joffe, Ellis. *The Chinese Army after Mao*. Cambridge: Harvard University Press, 1987.

Jones, Peter, and Sian Kevill, eds. *China and the Soviet Union, 1949–84*. New York: Facts on File, 1985.

Kenny, Henry. "Vietnamese Perceptions of the 1979 War with China." In *Chinese Warfighting: The PLA Experience since 1949*, ed. Mark A. Ryan, David M. Finkelstein, and Michael A. McDevitt, 217–340. Armonk, N.Y.: Sharpe, 2003.

Khoo, Nicholas. "Breaking the Ring of Encirclement: The Sino-Soviet Rift and Chinese Policy toward Vietnam, 1964–1968." *Journal of Cold War Studies* 12 (Winter 2010): 3–42.

———. *Collateral Damage: Sino-Soviet Rivalry and the Termination of the Sino-Vietnamese Alliance*. New York: Columbia University Press, 2011.

Kong Fanjun et al. *Chi Haotian zhuan* (Biography of Chi Haotian). Beijing: Jiefangjun, 2009.

Lai Zhuguang. "Primer Zhou's Management of Mine Sweeping Operations in Vietnam." In *YuanYue kangMei: Zhongguo zhiyuan budui zai Yuenan* (Assist Vietnam and Resist America: Chinese Support Troops in Vietnam), ed. Qu Aiguo, Bao Mingrong, and Xiao Zuyao, 206–315. Beijing: Junshi kexue, 1995.

Lanning, Michael Lee, and Dan Cragg. *Inside the VC and the NVA: The Real Story of North Vietnam's Armed Forces*. New York: Ivy, 1992.

Le Trong Tan, chief ed. *Binh Doan Quyet Thang* (The Determined-to-Win Corps). Hanoi: People's Army Publishing House, 1988.

Lee, Kuan Yew. *From Third World to First: The Singapore Story, 1965–2000*. New York: HarperCollins, 2000.

Lei Haizong. *Zhongguo wenhua yu zhongguo de bing* (Chinese Culture and Chinese Soldiers). Beijing: Shangwu, 2001.

Leng Rong and Wang Zuoling, chief eds. *Deng Xiaoping nianpu* (Chronicle of Deng Xiaoping's Life). 2 vols. Beijing: Zhongyang wenxian, 2004.

Lewis, John Wilson, and Xue Litai. *Imagined Enemies: China Prepares for Uncertain War*. Stanford, Calif.: Stanford University Press, 2006.

Li Baocun. "Wreaths of Flowers at the Foot of the Mountains." *Shiyue*. 6 October 1982. http://book.kanunu.org/book4/8777/. 25 May 2010.

Li Danhui. "The Debut of China's Strategy to Ally with the United States against the Soviet Union." In *Lengzhan shiqi de Zhongguo duiwai guanxi* (China's Foreign Relations during the Cold War), ed. Yang Kuisong, 153–79. Beijing: Beijing daxue, 2006.

———. "Issues in Sino-Vietnamese Relations between the 1950s and the 1970s." Unpublished paper presented at the Sino-Japanese symposium on Cold War in Asia, Shanghai, 15–17 March 2010.

———, ed. *Zhongguo yu Yinduzhina zhanzheng* (China and the Indochina Wars). Hong Kong: Tiandi tushu, 2000.

Li Jianguo. *Qinli Laoshan zhizhan: ZhongYue zhanzheng jingdian zhanyi jishi* (Personal Experience in the Battle of Laoshan: The True Record of Classic Battles in the Sino-Vietnamese War). Beijing: Zhongguo zuojia, 2008.

Li Jiazhong. "Consultations between Chinese and Vietnamese Deputy Foreign Ministers Prior to the Normalization of Sino-Vietnamese Relations." *Dongnanya zongheng*, 30 April 2004, 36–39.

———. "Inside Story about the Secret Meeting between Chinese and Vietnamese Leaders in Chengdu." *Dangshi zongheng*, 1 January 2006, 22–26.

———. "Personal Experience on the Normalization of Sino-Vietnamese Relations." *Xiangchao*, 5 April 2010, 36–39.

Li Jie. "China's Domestic Politics and the Normalization of Sino-U.S. Relations, 1969–1979."

In *Normalization of U.S.-China Relations: An International History*, ed. William C. Kirby, Robert S. Ross, and Gong Li, 56–89. Cambridge: Harvard University Asia Center, 2005.

Li Ke and Hao Shengzhang. *Wenhua dageming zhong de Renmin Jiefangjun* (The People's Liberation Army during the Cultural Revolution). Beijing: Zhonggong dangshi ziliao, 1989.

Li, Nan. "The PLA's Evolving Warfighting Doctrine, Strategy, and Tactics, 1985–1995: A Chinese Perspective." *China Quarterly* 146 (June 1996): 443–63.

Li Peng. "Remembering 1979: A True Account of the Counterattack in Self-Defense against Vietnam, Part One." *Bingqi zhishi*, 4 November 2004, 48–53.

———. "Remembering 1979: A True Account of the Counterattack in Self-Defense against Vietnam, Part Two." *Bingqi zhishi*, 4 December 2004, 42–47.

Li Qi, chief ed. *Zhou Enlai nianpu* (Chronicle of Zhou Enlai's Life). Vol. 3. Beijing: Zhongyang wenxian, 1997.

Li Qianyuan. "Pondering Future Force Development from the Real Combat Perspective." In *Conglin qilue* (Fighting Jungle Warfare with Unique Strategy), ed. Li Qianyuan and Song Ke, 567–74. Beijing: Guofang daxue, 1986.

———. "Using Active Defense to Seize Initiative on the Battlefield." In *Conglin qilue* (Fighting Jungle Warfare with Unique Strategy), ed. Li Qianyuan and Song Ke, 25–29. Beijing: Guofang daxue, 1986.

Li Qianyuan and Song Ke, eds. *Conglin qilue* (Fighting Jungle Warfare with Unique Strategy). Beijing: Guofang daxue, 1986.

Li Shenzhi. *Li Shenzhi wenji* (Collected Works of Li Shenzhi). Beijing: n.p., 2004.

Li Xiangqian. "The Establishment of Chinese-U.S. Diplomatic Relations and a Strategic Shift on the Focus of the Party's Work." *Zhonggong dangshi yanjiu*, 25 January 2000, 44–51.

Li, Xiaobing. *A History of the Modern Chinese Army*. Lexington: University Press of Kentucky, 2007.

Lian Jing. "The Small Arms of the Vietnamese Military." *Xiandai junshi*, July 1994, 29–31.

Liang Jianrong and Yan Zhixin. "Story behind 'The Moon on the Fifteenth Day of the Month.'" *Zhongguo minbing*, 15 March 2002, 46.

Liao Feng. "Commanders of Military Regions since the Founding of the Country." *Junshi shilin*, January 2004, 3–7.

Liao Guoliang, Li Shishun, Xu Yan. *Mao Zedong junshi sixiang fazhanshi* (History of Mao Zedong's Military Thought). Beijing: Jiefangjun, 1991.

Lieberthal, Kenneth. *Governing China: From Revolution through Reform*. New York: Norton, 2004.

Liu Guoyu. *Zhongguo Renmin Jiefangjun zhanshi jiaocheng* (Textbook of PLA War History). Beijing: Junshi kexue, 2000.

Liu Hong. "An Interview with Li Cunbao." *Renmin ribao haiwanban*, 27 October 2002.

Liu Huaqing. *Liu Huaqing huiyilu* (Memories of Liu Huaqing). Beijing: Jiefangjun, 2004.

Liu Jixian, chief ed. *Ye Jianying nianpu* (Chronicle of Ye Jianying's Life). Vol. 2. Beijing: Zhongyang wenxian, 2007.

Liu Yazhou zhanlue wenxuan (Selected Works of Liu Yazhou on Strategy). Beijing: n.p., 2007.

Liu Zhi and Zhang Lin, eds. *Xu Xiangqian zhuan* (Biography of Xu Xiangqian). Beijing: Dangdai Zhongguo, 1997.

Local History Compilation Committee of Guangdong Province, ed. *Guangdong shengzhi junshi zhi* (History of Guangdong Province: Military History). Guangzhou: Guangdong renmin, 1999.

Local History Compilation Committee of Guangxi Zhuang Autonomous Region, ed. *Guangxi tongzhi junshi zhi* (General History of Guangxi: Military History). Nanning: Guangxi renmin, 1994.

Lu Linzhi. "Emphasizing the Pre-Emptive Strike." *Jiefangjun bao*, 14 February 1995.

Luo Yuansheng. *Baizhan jiangxing Wang Shangrong* (Biography of General Wang Shangrong). Beijing: Jiefangjun wenyi, 1999.

Luong, Thuong Quyen, et al. *Lich Su Su Doan Bo Binh 346 (1978–2003)* (History of the 346th

Infantry Division [1978–2003]). Hanoi: People's Army Publishing House, 2003. http://www
.quansuvn.net/index.php?topic=7813.0. 4 June 2012.

Ma Shusheng. "My Personal Experience on the Normalization of Sino-Soviet Relations."
Bainianchao, 14 April 1999, 32–38.

"Main Experiences Gained by the No. XXX Division during the Counterattack in Self-Defense
against Vietnam." *Chinese Law and Government* 42 (September–October 2009): 54–70.

Mann, James. *About Face: History of America's Curious Relationship with China, from Nixon to
Clinton.* New York: Knopf, 1999.

Mao Mao. *Wo de fuqin Deng Xiaoping—Wenge suiyue* (My Father Deng Xiaoping during the
Years of Cultural Revolution). Beijing: Zhongyang wenxian, 2000.

Marshall, S. L. A. *Man against Fire: The Problems of Battle Command.* Norman: University of
Oklahoma Press, 2000.

Marti, Michael E. *China and the Legacy of Deng Xiaoping.* Washington, D.C.: Brassey's, 2002.

Military History Institute, Vietnamese National Defense Ministry. *Yuenan Renminjun
wushinian* (Fifty Years of Vietnamese People's Army). Trans. Liu Huanpu et al. Beijing:
Junshi yiwen, 1994.

Min Li. *ZhongYue zhanzheng shinian* (Ten Years of the Sino-Vietnamese War). Chengdu:
Sichuan daxue, 1993.

Ministry of Foreign Affairs Archives. *Weiren de zuji—Deng Xiaoping waijiao huodong dashiji*
(A Great Man's Footprints: Chronicle of Deng Xiaoping's Important Diplomatic Activities).
Beijing: Shijie zhishi, 1998.

"Modern Ships" Editorial Board. "An Interview with General Chen Weiwen." *Xiandai
jianchuan*, October 2011, 10–15.

Morris, Stephen J. *The Soviet-Chinese-Vietnamese Triangle in the 1970s: The View from Moscow.*
Cold War International History Project Working Paper no. 25. Washington, D.C.: Woodrow
Wilson International Center for Scholars, 1999.

———. *Why Vietnam Invaded Cambodia: Political Culture and the Causes of War.* Stanford,
Calif.: Stanford University Press, 1999.

Mulvenon, James. *Soldiers of Fortune: The Rise and Fall of the Chinese Military-Business
Complex, 1978–1998.* Armonk, N.Y.: Sharpe, 2001.

Nathan, Andrew J., and Robert S. Ross. *The Great Wall and the Empty Fortress: China's Search
for Security.* New York: Norton, 1997.

Nations, Richard. "Great Leap Sideways." *Far Eastern Economic Review*, 5 June 1985, 15–16.

Naughton, Barry. "The Third Front: Defense Industrialization in the Chinese Interior." *China
Quarterly* 115 (September 1988): 351–86.

Nguyen, Huu Bo, chief ed. *Su Doan Bo Binh—Doan Kinh Te—Quoc Phong 337 (Doan Khanh
Khe) 1978–2008* (The 337th Infantry Division—337th National Defense Economic Group
[the Khanh Khe Group], 1978–2008). Hanoi: People's Army Publishing House, 2008. http://
www.quansuvn.net/index.php?topic=5058.0. 4 June 2012.

Nguyen, Lien-Hang T. *Hanoi's War: An International History of the War for Peace in Vietnam.*
Chapel Hill: University of North Carolina Press, 2012.

———. "The Sino-Vietnamese Split and the Indochina War, 1968–1975." In *The Third Indochina
War: Conflict between China, Vietnam, and Cambodia, 1972–1979*, ed. Odd Arne Westad and
Sophie Quinn-Judge, 12–31. London: Routledge, 2006.

Nguyen, Tien Hung. *Lich Su Luc Luong Vu Trang Quan Khu 2 (1946–2006)* (History of Military
Region 2 Armed Forces, 1946–2006) Hanoi: People's Army Publishing House, 2006. http://
blog.wenxuecity.com/blogarticle.php?date=200709&postID=14300. 22 October 2007.

Nguyen, Tri Huan, et al. *Su Doan Sao Van* (The Gold Star Division). Hanoi: PAVN Publishers,
1984. http://www.quansuvn.net/index.php?topic=144.0. 22 June 2012.

Nguyen, Vu Tung. "Interpreting Beijing and Hanoi: A View of Sino-Vietnamese Relations,
1965–1970." In "77 Conversations between Chinese and Foreign Leaders on the War in
Indochina, 1964–1977," ed. Odd Arne Westad, Chen Jian, Stein Tonnesson, Nguyen Vu Tung,
and James G. Hershberg, 43–65. Cold War International History Project Working Paper
no. 22. Washington D.C.: Woodrow Wilson International Center for Scholars, 1998.

Ni Chuanghui. *Shinian ZhongYue zhanzheng* (The Ten-Year Sino-Vietnamese War). 2 vols. Hong Kong: Tianxingjian, 2009.

Niu Jun. "An Outline for Studying Mao Zedong's 'Three-World' Theory." In *Wannian Mao Zedong* (Mao Zedong in His Later Years), ed. Xiao Yanzhong, 80–87. Beijing: Chunqiu, 1989.

———. "Returning to Asia: The Normalization of Sino-Soviet Relations and the Evolution of China's Indochina Policy." *Guoji zhengzhi yanjiu* (International Political Quarterly) 2 (Spring 2011): 62–80.

O'Dowd, Edward C. *Chinese Military Strategy in the Third Indochina War: The Last Maoist War.* New York: Routledge, 2007.

O'Dowd, Edward C., and John F. Corbett Jr. "The 1979 Chinese Campaign in Vietnam: Lessons learned." In *The Lessons of History: The Chinese People's Liberation Army at 75*, ed. Laurie Burkitt, Andrew Scobell, and Larry M. Wortzel, 353–71. Carlisle: Strategic Studies Institute, U.S. Army War College, 2003.

Olsen, Mari. *Soviet-Vietnam Relations and the Role of China, 1949–64: Changing Alliances.* New York: Routledge, 2006.

Ostermann, Christian F. "New Evidence on the Sino-Soviet Border Dispute, 1969–71." *Cold War International History Project Bulletin* 6–7 (Winter 1995–96): 186–93.

Ouyang Qing. *Baizhan jiangxing Xie Zhenghua* (Biography of General Xie Zhenghua). Beijing: Jiefangjun wenyi, 2001.

Pang Xianzhi and Jin Chongji, chief eds. *Mao Zedong zhuan* (Biography of Mao Zedong). Vol. 2. Beijing: Zhongyang wenxian, 2003.

Pham, Gia Duc, chief ed. *Lich Su Quan Doan 2 (1974–94)* (History of the 2nd Corps [1974–94]). Hanoi: People's Army Publishing House, 1994.

Pike, Douglas. *PAVN: People's Army of Vietnam.* Novato, Calif.: Presidio, 1986.

Political Department of the Air Force, ed. *Lantian zhilu* (The Road to the Blue Sky). Vol. 2. Beijing: Kongjun zhengzhibu, 1992.

Political Department of the Guangzhou Military Region, ed. *Yingxiong zan* (Ode to the Heroes). Nanning: Renmin, 1979.

Qi Dexue. *Chaoxian zhanzheng juece neimu* (Inside Story of Decision-Making during the Korean War). Shenyang: Liaoning daxue, 1991.

Qian Jiang. *Deng Xiaoping yu ZhongMei jianjiao fengyun* (Deng Xiaoping and the Establishment of Diplomatic Relationship between China and the United States). Beijing: Zhonggong dangshi, 2005.

Qian Qichen. *Waijiao shiji* (Record of Ten Diplomatic Events). Hong Kong: Sanlian shuju, 2004.

Qu Aiguo. *Wu Zhong shaojiang* (Major General Wu Zhong). Beijing: Jiefangjun wenyi, 2005.

Quan Yanchi. "A Bodyguard in Guangzhou Recalls Ten Well-Known People in History, Part 3." *Nanfengchuang*, 27 December 1991, 40–44.

Quinn-Judge, Paul. "Peking's Tit for Tat." *Far Eastern Economic Review*, 19 April 1984, 14–15.

Reiter, Dan. *How Wars End.* Princeton: Princeton University Press, 2009.

Richardson, Sophie. *China, Cambodia, and the Five Principles of Peaceful Coexistence.* New York: Columbia University Press, 2010.

Ross, Robert S. *Chinese Security Policy: Structure, Power, and Politics.* London: Routledge, 2009.

———. *The Indochina Tangle: China's Vietnam Policy, 1975–1979.* New York: Columbia University Press, 1988.

Ryan, Mark A., David M. Finkelstein, and Michael A. McDevitt, eds. *Chinese Warfighting: The PLA Experience since 1949.* Armonk, N.Y.: Sharpe, 2003.

Scobell, Andrew. *China's Use of Military Force: Beyond the Great War and the Long March.* Cambridge: Cambridge University Press, 2003.

Segal, Gerald. *Defending China.* New York: Oxford University Press, 1985.

Shambaugh, David. "China's Military in Transition: Politics, Professionalism, Procurement, and Power Projection." *China Quarterly* 146 (June 1996): 265–98.

Shen Weiguang and Hu Ruhua. "Response to Enemy's Changes with Counters." In *Conglin qilue* (Fighting Jungle Warfare with Unique Strategy), ed. Li Qianyuan and Song Ke, 62–66. Beijing: Guofang daxue, 1986.

Shen Zhihua. "The Dissolution of the Sino-Soviet Alliance: Causes and Consequences." *Zhonggong dangshi yanjiu*, 10 March 2007, 29–42.

———. *Mao Zedong, Sidalin yu Hanzhan* (Mao Zedong, Stalin, and the Korean War). Hong Kong: Tiandi shuju, 1998.

Shi Yuxiao. "Political Work in Defensive Operations against Vietnam in the Laoshan Area." In *Conglin qilue* (Fighting Jungle Warfare with Unique Strategy), ed. Li Qianyuan and Song Ke, 177–84. Beijing: Guofang daxue, 1986.

Solinger, Dorothy J. "Politics in Yunnan Province in the Decade of Disorder: Elite Factional Strategies and Central-Local Relations, 1967–1980." *China Quarterly* 92 (December 1982): 628–62.

Sun Dali. "A Historical Turning Point in China: The Third Plenum of the Eleventh Central Committee." In *Xin Zhongguo yaoshi shuping* (Review of China's Important Events), ed. Lin Zhijian. Beijing: Zhongyang wenxian, 1994.

Tang Fuyan and Su Changyou. "Shine on the Home, Shine on the Border." *Zhongguo minbing*, 15 May 2000, 26.

Tao Wenzhao. "Deng Xiaoping and China-U.S. Relations, 1970–1991." *Shehui kexue yanjiu*, 22 December 2005, 11–18.

Thayer, Carlyle A. "Security Issues in Southeast Asia: The Third Indochina War." Paper presented at Conference on Security and Arms Control in the North Pacific, Canberra, Australia, 12–14 August 1987.

———. *The Vietnam People's Army under Doi Moi*. Singapore: Institute of Southeast Asian Studies, 1994.

Thompson, Wayne. *To Hanoi and Back: The U.S. Air Force and North Vietnam, 1966–1973*. Washington, D.C.: Smithsonian Institution Press, 2000.

Tian Fuzi. *ZhongYue zhanzheng jishilu* (A True Record of the Sino-Vietnamese War). Beijing: Jiefangjun wenyi, 2004.

Tonnesson, Stein. "Le Duan and the Break with China." *Cold War International History Project Bulletin* 12–13 (Fall–Winter 1998): 273–79.

Toperczer, István. *MIG-21 and MIG-19 Units of the Vietnam War*. Oxford: Osprey, 2001.

Tretiak, Daniel. "China's Vietnam War and Its Consequences." *China Quarterly* 80 (December 1979): 740–67.

Truong, Nhu Tang, David Chanoff, and Doan Van Toai. *A Viet Cong Memoir*. New York: Harcourt Brace Jovanovich, 1985.

Tyler, Patrick. *A Great Wall: Six Presidents and China: An Investigative History*. New York: Public Affairs, 1999.

Vasquez, John, and Marie T. Henehan. "Territorial Disputes and the Probability of War, 1816–1992." *Journal of Peace Research* 38 (March 2001): 123–38.

Victory in Vietnam: The Official History of the People's Army of Vietnam, 1954–1975. Trans. Merle L. Pribbenow. Lawrence: University Press of Kansas, 2002.

Vo, Nguyen Giap. *The Road to Dien Bien Phu*. Hanoi: Gioi, 2004.

Vogel, Ezra F. *Deng Xiaoping and the Transformation of China*. Cambridge: Harvard University Press, 2011.

Vu, Lap. *Su Doan 316 Tap Hai* (The 316th Division). Vol. 2. Hanoi: People's Army Publishing House, 1986.

Walt, Stephen M. "Alliance in a Unipolar World." *World Politics* 61 (January 2009): 86–120.

———. *The Origins of Alliances*. Ithaca: Cornell University Press, 1987.

Wang Dinglie. *Dangdai Zhongguo kongjun* (Contemporary China's Air Force). Beijing: Shehui kexue, 1989.

Wang Futian. "Shooting Down Vietnam's Intruding Reconnaissance Aircraft." In *Lantian zhilu*, ed. Political Department of the Air Force, 2:571–78. Beijing: Kongjun zhengzhibu, 1992.

Wang Hancheng. *Wang Hancheng huiyilu* (Memoirs of Wang Hancheng). Beijing: Jiefangjun, 2004.

Wang Kangsheng. "Basic Tactics Used by Vietnamese Forces at Laoshan and Zheyingshan and Future Trends." In *Conglin qilue* (Fighting Jungle Warfare with Unique Strategy), ed. Li Qianyuan and Song Ke, 631–34. Beijing: Guofang daxue, 1986

Wang Kongjing. "Vietnam's Policy toward the Ethnic People on the Vietnamese-Chinese Border." *Dongnanya yanjiu* (Southeast Asia Studies) 4 (May–June 2007): 46–49.

Wang Taiping, chief ed. *Zhonghua Renmin Gongheguo waijiaoshi* (Diplomatic History of the People's Republic of China). 3 vols. Beijing: Shijie zhishi, 1998–99.

Wang Weicheng, chief ed. *Li Xiannian nianpu* (Chronicle of Li Xiannian's Life). Vol. 5. Beijing: Zhongyang wenxian, 2011.

Wang Weidong. "We Expect the Soldiers to Come Back Alive." *Renmin yinyue*, 29 August 1987, 34–35.

Wang Xiangen. *Yuan Yue kangMei shilu* (A Factual Account of Assisting Vietnam and Opposing America). Beijing: Guoji wenhua, 1990.

———. *Zhongguo mimi dafabing: Yuanyue kangMei shilu* (China's Secret Military Deployment: True Record of Aiding Vietnam and Resisting America). Jinan: Jinan, 1992.

Wang Xuan. *Mao Zedong zhi jian—minjiang zhixing Xu Shiyou* (The Sword of Mao Zedong: Star General Xu Shiyou). Nanjing: Jiangsu renmin, 1996.

Wang Zhiguo. *Sanxian jianshe yu xibu dakaifa* (Third-Line Construction and Great Development in the Western Region). Beijing: Dangdai Zhongguo, 2003.

Wang Zhijun. *1979 dui Yue zhanzheng qinli ji* (Personal Experience in the 1979 War against Vietnam). Hong Kong: Thinker, 2008.

———. "A New Stage of the Development of the Rifle in Our Country, Part 1." *Qingbingqi*, 3 May 1999, 12–15.

Wang Zhongchun. "The Soviet Factor in Sino-American Normalization, 1969–1979." In *Normalization of U.S.-China Relations: An International History*, ed. William C. Kirby, Robert S. Ross, and Gong Li, 147–74. Cambridge: Harvard University Asian Center, 2005.

West, Philip, Steven I. Levine, and Jackie Hiltz. *America's Wars in Asia: A Cultural Approach to History and Memory*. Armonk, N.Y.: Sharpe, 1998.

Westad, Odd Arne. "Introduction: From War to Peace to War in Indochina." In *The Third Indochina War: Conflict between China, Vietnam, and Cambodia, 1972–1979*, ed. Odd Arne Westad and Sophie Quinn-Judge, 1–11. London: Routledge, 2006.

Whiting, Allen S. "China's Use of Force, 1950–95, and Taiwan." *International Security* 26 (Autumn 2001): 103–30.

———. "The PLA and China's Threat Perceptions." *China Quarterly* 146 (June 1996): 596–615.

Whitson, William H., and Chen-Hsia Huang. *The Chinese High Command: A History of Communist Military Politics, 1927–1971*. New York: Praeger, 1973.

Womack, Brantly. *China and Vietnam: The Politics of Asymmetry*. Cambridge: Cambridge University Press, 2006.

Wortzel, Larry M. "China's Foreign Conflicts since 1949." In *A Military History of China*, ed. David A. Graff and Robin Higham, 267–84. Boulder, Colo.: Westview, 2002.

Wu Qiong. "Resolving Contradictions between the Concepts of 'Loyalty' and 'Love' in Military Songs of the New Era." *Kejiao wenhui*, 15 February 2007, 189.

Wu Xiuquan. *Huiyi yu huainian* (Recollections and Memories). Beijing: Zhongyang dangxiao, 1991.

Xia Zhengnong, chief ed. *Cihai* (Sea of Words). Shanghai: Shanghai cihai, 1980.

Xiang Shouzhi. *Xiang Shouzhi huiyilu* (Memoirs of Xiang Shouzhi). Beijing: Jiefangjun, 2006.

Xiao Jinguang. *Xiao Jinguang huiyilu xuji* (Memoirs of Xiao Jinguang). Sequel ed. Beijing: Jiefangjun, 1988.

Xie Ailing. "Blood-Stained Valor, Heroic Ode." *Yinyue tansuo* (*zengkan* 2), 31 December 2006, 4–9.

Xie Hainan, Yang Zufa, and Yang Jianhua. *Yang Dezhi yisheng* (The Life of Yang Dezhi). Beijing: Zhonggong dangshi, 2011.

Xie Yixian. *Zhongguo waijiao shi: Zhonghua Renmin Gongheguo shiqi, 1949–1979* (Diplomatic History of China: The Period of the People's Republic of China, 1949–1979). Zhengzhou: Henan renmin, 1988.

Xiong Xianghui. *Lishi de zhujiao—Huiyi Mao Zedong, Zhou Enlai and silaoshuai* (Footnotes of History: Recollections of Mao Zedong, Zhou Enlai, and Four Old Marshals). 2nd ed. Beijing: Zhongyang dangxiao, 1996.

Xiong Zhiyong. *Cong bianyuan zouxiang zhongxing: Wanqing shehui bianqian zhong de junren jituan* (From Edge to Center: The Change of Military Professionals' Social Status in Late Qing). Tianjin: Tianjin renmin, 1998.

Xu Guangyi, chief ed. *Dangdai Zhongguo jundui de houqin gongzuo* (Contemporary China's Military Logistics Work). Beijing: Shehui kexue, 1990.

Xu Jingyao and Liu Lingzhi. "The Blood-Stained Valor Inspires People." *Liaowang*, 4 May 1987, 23.

Xu Santong. *Junzhong shaozhuangpai zhangwo Zhongguo bingquan* (Younger Generation Officers Take Control of the Military in China). Hong Kong: Haye, 2009.

Xu Yan. *Diyici jiaoliang: KangMei yuanChao zhanzheng delishi huigu yu fansi* (First Encounter: Historical Retrospection and Review of the War to Resist U.S. Aggression and Assist Korea). Beijing: Zhongguo guangbo dianshi, 1990.

Xu Zehao. *Wang Jiaxiang zhuan* (Biography of Wang Jiaxiang). Beijing: Dangdai Zhongguo, 1996.

Yang, Benjamin. *Deng: A Political Biography*. Armonk, N.Y.: Sharpe, 1998.

Yang, Dali. "Pattern of China's Regional Development Strategy." *China Quarterly* 122 (June 1990): 230–57.

Yang Guihua and Chen Chuangang. *Gongheguo jundui huimou* (A Retrospective on the Army of the Republic). Beijing: Junshi keque, 1999.

Yang Kuisong. "Mao Zedong and the Indochina Wars." In *Zhongguo yu Yinduzhina zhanzheng* (China and the Indochina Wars), ed. Li Danhui, 22–55. Hong Kong: Tiandi, 2000.

Yang Liufan, *Yongzhe wuwei—Yige duiYue ziwei fanjizhan canzhanzhe de huiku* (Bravery and Fearlessness: A Retrospective on His Participation in the Counterattack in Self-Defense against Vietnam). N.p.: n.p., n.d.

Yang Qiliang, chief ed. *Wang Shangrong jiangjun* (General Wang Shangrong). Beijing: Dangdai Zhongguo, 2000.

Ye Fei. *Ye Fei huiyilu* (Memoirs of Ye Fei). Beijing: Jiefangjun, 1988.

Ye Yonglie. *Cong Hua guofeng dao Deng Xiaoping: Zhongkong shiyijie sanzhong quanhui qianhou* (From Hua Guofeng to Deng Xiaoping: Before and after the Third Plenum of the Eleventh Central Party Committee). Hong Kong: Tiandi tushu, 1998.

Yee, Herbert. "The Sino-Vietnamese Border War: China's Motives, Calculation, and Strategies." *China Report* 16 (January–February 1980): 15–32.

Yu Guangyuan. *1978: Wo jingli de naci lishi dazhuanzhe* (1978: My Experience at the Historical Turning Point). Hong Kong: Tiandi tushu, 2006.

Yu Ji. "Perspectives on the Song 'The Moon on the Fifteenth Day of the Month.'" *Renmin yinyue*, 1 May 1987, 27, 31.

Yunnan Provincial Military District. *Junshi zhi* (Military History). Vol. 49 of *Yunnan shengzhi* (History of Yunnan Province). Kunming: Yunnan renmin, 1997.

Yunnan Provincial Military District, Political Department, Liaison Office. *Yuenan Renminjun jiangxiao junguan minglu* (Directory of PAVN's Senior and Middle-Rank Officers). Beijing: Junyi, 1988.

Zaffiri, Samuel. *Hamburger Hill*. Novato, Calif.: Presidio, 1988.

Zhai, Qiang. "China and the Geneva Conference of 1954." *China Quarterly* 129 (March 1992): 103–22.

———. *China and the Vietnam Wars, 1950–1975*. Chapel Hill: University of North Carolina Press, 2000.

———. "Transplanting the Chinese Model: Chinese Military Advisers and the First Vietnam War, 1950–1954." *Journal of Military History* 57 (October 1993): 685–715.

Zhang Caixing. "Coordination Problems for Conducting Defensive Operations in Tropical Mountain Forests." In *Conglin qilue* (Fighting Jungle Warfare with Unique Strategy), ed. Li Qianyuan and Song Ke, 86–90. Beijing: Guofang daxue, 1986.

Zhang Cuiju. "New Ideas and Directions in Furnishing Frontline Logistics." In *Conglin qilue*

(Fighting Jungle Warfare with Unique Strategy), ed. Li Qianyuan and Song Ke, 425–30. Beijing: Guofang daxue, 1986.

Zhang Qing. "After Years of Conflict, Our Relationship Remains: The Story of Normalizing Sino-Vietnamese Relations." *Dongnanya zongheng*, 29 February 2000, 4–7.

———. "Recollections of the 'Chengdu Meeting' for Normalizing Relations between China and Vietnam." *Shijie zhishi*, 23 January 2000, 38–41.

Zhang Sheng. *Cong zhanzheng zhong zoulai: Liangdai junren de duihua* (Coming from the War: A Dialogue between Two Generations of Soldiers). Beijing: Zhongguo qingnian, 2007.

Zhang, Shu Guang. *Mao's Military Romanticism: China and the Korean War, 1950–53*. Lawrence: University Press of Kansas, 1995.

Zhang Weiming. "The Perspectives of History and the Future." *Jiefangjun bao*, 2 November 2009.

Zhang, Xiaoming. "China's Involvement in Laos during the Vietnam War, 1963–1975." *Journal of Military History* 66 (October 2002): 1141–66.

———. "Communist Powers Divided: China, the Soviet Union, and the Vietnam War." In *International Perspectives on Vietnam*, ed. Lloyd C. Gardner and Ted Gittinger, 77–107. College Station: Texas A&M University Press, 2000.

———. *Red Wing over the Yalu: China, the Soviet Union, and the Air War in Korea*. College Station: Texas A&M University Press, 2002.

———. "The Vietnam War, 1964–1969: A Chinese Perspective." *Journal of Military History* 60 (October 1996): 731–62.

Zhang Xuezhao and Song Hongguang. "Operational Characteristics of Vietnamese Artillery Forces." In *Conglin qilue* (Fighting Jungle Warfare with Unique Strategy), ed. Li Qianyuan and Song Ke, 645–50. Beijing: Guofang daxue, 1986.

Zhang Youxia. "Pondering How to Shape the Army in a New Era." In *Yibaishuan yanjing li de zhanzheng: Nanjiang jituanjun zai 1979–1987* (War in One Hundred Eyes: A Group Army in the Southern Borderland from 1979 to 1987), ed. Ding Longyan, 308–12. Chengdu: Sichuan wenyi, 1989.

Zhang Yun, chief ed. *Yunnansheng dang'an zhinan* (Guide to Yunnan Provincial Archives). Beijing: Zhongguo dang'an, 1997.

Zhang Zhen. *Zhang Zhen huiyilu* (Memoirs of Zhang Zhen). Vol. 2. Beijing: Jiefangjun 2003.

Zhang Zhenyang et al. "Taking Luc Binh by Stratagem." In *Yingxiong zan* (Ode to Heroes), ed. Political Department of the Guangzhou Military Region, 31–37. Nanning: Guangxi renmin, 1979.

Zhang Zhizhi. "Air Force Troops during the Counterattack in Self-Defense against Vietnam." In *Lantian zhi lu*, ed. Political Department of the Air Force, 2:350–56. Beijing: Kongjun zhengzhibu, 1992.

Zheng Jianmin. "Using Manpower to Transport Supplies in Mountain-Forest Warfare," In *Conglin qilue* (Fighting Jungle Warfare with Unique Strategy), ed. Li Qianyuan and Song Ke, 497–502. Beijing: Guofang daxue, 1986.

Zheng Yu. "Collapse of the Soviet Union and the Change of China's Security Environment." *Eluosi zhongya dong'ou yanjiu* (Russian, Central Asian, and East European Studies) 4 (August 2007): 47–54, 96.

Zhong Wen and Lu Haixiao, eds. *Bainian Deng Xiaoping* (A Centenary of Deng Xiaoping). Vol. 2. Beijing: Zhongyang wenxian, 2004.

"Zhongguo Renmin Jiefangjun Tongjian" Editorial Committee. *Zhongguo Renming Jiefangjun tongjian* (A Comprehensive History of the PLA of China, 1927–1996). Vol. 3. Lanzhou: Gansu renmin, 1997.

Zhou Deli. *Xu Shiyou de zuihou yizhan* (The Last Battle of Xu Shiyou). Nanjing: Jiangsu renmin, 1990.

———. *Yige gaoji canmouzhang de zishu* (Personal Recollections of a High-Ranking Chief of Staff). Nanjing: Nanjing, 1992.

Zhou Junlun, chief ed. *Nie Rongzhen nianpu* (Chronicle of Nie Rongzhen's Life). Vol. 2. Beijing: Renmin, 1999.

Zhou Keyu, chief ed. *Dangdai Zhongguo jundui de zhengzhi gongzuo* (Contemporary China's Military Political Work). Vol. 1. Beijing: Shehui kexue, 1994.

Zhu Jiamu. *Chen Yun nianpu* (Chronicle of Chen Yun's Life, 1905–1995). Vol. 2. Beijing: Zhongyang wenxian, 2000.

Zuo Guang. "Development and Growth of the Air Force Radar Troops." In *Lantian zhilu*, ed. Political Department of the Air Force, 2:395–407. Beijing: Kongjun zhengzhibu, 1992.

INTERNET SOURCES

"Air Reconnaissance Operations during the War against Vietnam." http://bwl.top81.cn/war79/index.html. 4 June 2010.

"Aviation Units during the Counterattack in Self-Defense against Vietnam." http://bwl.top81.cn/war79/file1/418.htm. 18 June 2010.

"A Battalion Political Instructor's Experience in the Battles of Recapturing and Defending Laoshan." http://bbs.tiexue.net/post_3402501_1.html. 20 March 2010.

"A Brief Account of the 43rd and 50th Armies during the 1979 Counterattack in Self-Defense." http://bwl.top81.com.cn/war79/file1/408.htm. 15 August 2009.

Cai Pengcen. "Big Victory at Laoshan on 12 July 1984." http://bwl.top81.cn/war79/index.html. 20 September 2008.

———. "The Events That Happened in 1979." http://www.fyjs.cn/viewarticle.php?id=126634&page=10. 26 February 2010.

Chan, Simon. "Offensive and Defensive Battles at Fakashan." http://club.china.com/data/thread/1011/2704/23/52/6_1.html. 22 June 2010.

Chaoshui. "1979: Personal Experience in the Counterattack against Vietnam." http://www.myqueue.net/military/PLAwar/showwar&id=147.htm. 20 December 2009

Chen Yuanjing. "Recollections of the Counterattack in Self-Defense against Vietnam: Battle Fire in Southwestern Guangxi." http://bwl.top81.cn/war79/index.html. 15 June 2009.

China News Agency. "Bulletin on the Situation of the Counterattack in Self-Defense." 7 March 1979. http://736262.134218.3366dns.com/burningblood/zhanli/tongbao/A0002654–1.htm. 10 July 2009.

"Chinese Armored Forces during the Counterattack in Self-Defense against Vietnam." http://blog.sina.com.cn/s/blog_405f35f10100cbqh.html. 25 January 2009.

"Combat History of the 13th Army during the Counterattack in Self-Defense against Vietnam." http://bwl.top81.cn/war79/index.html. 20 May 2007.

"Debates by Vietnamese Netizens on the Battles That Were Fought in Ha Giang." http://blog.sina.com.cn/s/blog_4afac02c010086tb.html. 7 April 2010.

"Defending Height 300 at Hoang Lien Son." http://www.zywl.cn/his/200705/7230.html. 20 May 2010.

Duong, Danh Dy. "In Retrospect: The Evening of 17 February 1979." http://ydxwzm.blog.hexun.com/31094874_d.html. 16 November 2011.

"The 41st Army's Operations in the Cao Bang Area." http://bwl.top81.cn/war79/index.html. 15 June 2009.

"The 43rd Army in the 1979 Counterattack in Self-Defense." http://www.zywl.cn/his/200601/60.html. 10 August 2009.

"The 43rd Army's Tank Regiment in the Battle of Dong Khe." http://bwl.top81.cn/war79/index.html. 22 March 2006.

General Staff Intelligence Department, ed. *ZhongYue bianjing zhencha zuozhan jinyan ji* (Collections of Experiences in Reconnaissance Operations on the Sino-Vietnamese Border). http://military.china.com/zh_cn/dljl/dyzwfjz/01/11043454/20080724/14985919.html. 12 June 2008.

Han Qing. "The Legendary Liao Xilong." http://bwl.top81.cn/war79/index.html. 9 May 2010.

Hao Dongliang. "Fighting against Vietnam—Recollections of One 54th Army Veteran." http://bwl.top81.cn/war79/index.html. 2 May 2009.

He Zhongjun. "Red Cotton Trees of the Southern Frontier: Recollections of the Counterattack in Self-Defense against Vietnam." http://ebook.tianya.cn/menu/36088.aspx. 10 May 2010.

"Hu Yaobang's Speech at the Meeting Attended by Cadres at Divisional Level and above at Laoshan on 10 February 1985." http://blog.sina.com.cn/s/blog_5166e78f0100ah41.html. 12 June 2009.

"Illustrations of Vietnamese Military Deployment along the Sino-Vietnamese Border." http://hi.baidu.com/ilovexjp/blog/item/72099bc251a8ae1a0ff47731.html. 30 April 2010.

"Initial Analysis of Deng Xiaoping's Contributions to Military Affairs." http://bwl.top81.cn/war79/index.html. 15 September 2010.

"Inside Story about 'Wreaths of Flowers at the Foot of the Mountains' by Zhang Zongren." http://blog.sina.com.cn/s/blog_4b3ba3be010094b2.html. 26 May 2010.

"Inside Story on Planning the 'Project C-3' Operation against Vietnam." http://bwl.top81.cn/war79/index.html. 27 May 2010.

Ji Yunfei, chief ed. *Xin Zhongguo guofang jiaoyu lilun yu shijian* (Theories and Practice in New China's National Defense Education). Beijing: Haichao, 2004. http://military.china.com/zh_cn/dljl/dyzwfjz/01/11043454/20090305/15357494.htm l. 5 May 2010.

"Lecture Notes on the 1979 Counterattack in Self-Defense on the Sino-Vietnamese Border." http://bwl.top81.cn/war79/index.html. 20 May 2005.

Li Jianguo. "Losses Incurred by the 40th Division's 118th Regiment's 1st Battalion during Its Deep Penetration behind Enemy Lines at Laoshan." http://bbs.zywl.cn/viewthread.php?tid=99057?. 25 May 2010.

Military Science Academy. "A Case Study of the 55th Army Combat in the Dong Dang-Lang Son Area." http://bwl.top81.cn/war79/index.html. 2 July 2009.

"No Regret When I Was Young in 1979." http://736262.134218.3366 dns.com/burningblood/wenxue/79/55–163/qingchunwuhui/1.htm. 14 June 2010.

"Offense Conducted by the 487th Regiment's 2nd Battalion at Tham Mo." http://bwl.top81.cn/war79/index.html. 16 June 2009.

"Organizational Changes of Border Defense Forces in Yunnan during Five Historical Periods." http://club.xilu.com/zgjsyj/msgview-819697–65440.html. 10 June 2010.

"Pictorial Illustration: The True Record of the PLA 149th Division's 'Red Army No. 2 Company' in the War against Vietnam." http://mil.tiexue.net/content_367020.html. 28 June 2009.

"Precious Photos: Celebration for Shooting Down One MiG-21 Reconnaissance Aircraft." http://bbs.tiexue.net/post_4178243_1.html. 4 June 2010.

"Recollections of an Artillery Company Commander and Two Other War Veterans." http://bwl.top81.cn/war79/index.html. 20 June 2009.

"The 2nd Border Defense Division's 1st Regiment's 5th Company's Offensive Operations against Hill 543." http://bwl.top81.cn/war79/index.html. 15 June 2009.

Shen Tingxue. "The Bloody Road of Laoshan." http://www.fyjs.cn/bbs/htm_data/158/1005/250838.html. 23 May 2010.

"A Short History of the PLA's 14th Army (2)." http://pk75329.bokee.com/viewdiary.43016573.html. 11 May 2010.

"Soviet Military Advisers in Vietnam during the Sino-Vietnamese War." http://bbs.ifeng.com/viewthread.php?tid-1977215. 8 October 2008.

"Summarized Accounts of PAVN's Fifty-One Divisions in History." http://bwl.top81.com.cn/war79/file1/108–2.htm. 18 August 2007.

"Summarized Accounts of Units from Each Military Region That Fought at Laoshan." http://bwl.top81.cn/war79/index.html. 2 June 2010.

"Summary of Chengdu Military Region's 1st Border Defense Division's 2nd Regiment's Ten-Year Military Operations against Vietnam." http://bwl.top81.cn/war79/index.html. 11 July 2010.

"Summary of the 121st Division's Deep-Thrust Operations." http://blog.sina.com.cn/s/blog_445e58c00100o5hi.html. 26 November 2011.

"Understanding the Conduct of China's 1984 Reconnaissance Operations." http://bwl.top81.cn/war79/index.html. 6 October 2010.

"Units from Different Military Regions Rotated during Defensive Operations at Laoshan." http://bwl.top81.cn/war79/index.html. 25 May 2010.

"Vietnamese Military Deployment on the Western Front after the 1979 War and Remarks." http://bwl.top81.com.cn/war79/file1/408.htm. 8 October 2010.

"A Vietnamese Veteran's 1984." http://burningblood.yournet.cn/burningblood/zhanli/vietnam/vietnam 1509/vietnam1509.htm. 31 March 2010.

Zheng Yunxin. "Inside Story about the Film 'Wreaths of Flowers at the Foot of the Mountains.'" http://blog.stnn.cc/StBlogPageMain/Efp_BlogLogKan.aspx?cBlogLog=1002211607. 26 May 2010.

Zhong Li. "Xing Heping Diary." http://blog.sina.com.cn/s/articlelist_1510164421_8_1.html. 10 December 2011.

Zou Ronglu. "Battles Fought by the 55th Army in Dong Dang and Lang Son." http://blog.sina.com.cn/s/blog_4afac02c010009nk.html. 14 June 2010.

———. "Wartime Reminiscences: The True Record of the Battle Fought at Hill 986." http://blog.sina.com.cn/s/blog_4afac02c010006zp.html. 12 May 2009.

Zuo Yi. "Diplomats from China Fought in Cambodia's Jungles." http://wenku.baidu.com/view/8929bbd4240c844769eaee51.html. 30 June 2012.

Index

76–77, 84, 124, 143; PLA operation from, 60, 64, 78, 95, 104, 124, 119, 146–47
Guangzhou Military Region, 42, 43, 44, 59, 71, 72, 75, 100, 113, 137, 238 (n. 16); forward command of, 73, 77, 83, 104, 105, 234 (n. 8); Forward Command Political Department Cadre Session of, 11

Ha Giang, 147, 150, 154, 155, 160
Hainan Island, 60
Hamburger Hill, 96, 235 (n. 29)
Hanoi, 24, 28, 31, 95, 99, 107, 110, 125, 143, 168, 201, 202, 203
Ha Tuyen, 145, 149, 152, 154, 243 (n. 46)
Hekou, 75, 86, 100, 144, 175, 234 (n. 106)
He Long, 70
Henan, 75, 177
Hoa An, 92, 93
Hoang Lien Son, 99, 100, 103, 143, 151, 154
Hoang Van Hoan, 203, 225 (n. 76)
Ho Chi Minh, 15, 16, 17, 23, 24, 29, 204, 207, 213
Honghe, 171
Hou Shujun, 76
Howard, Michael, 46, 207, 211
Hua Guofeng, 37, 44, 56, 145
Huang Hua, 60
Hu Yaobang, 157, 196, 197

Iklé, Fred Richard, 123
India, 2, 42, 57, 83, 184, 238 (n. 11)
Indochina, 167, 207, 212
Indochinese Communist Party, 15. *See also* Vietnamese Communist Party
Indochinese Foreign Ministers Conference, 199

Jencks, Harlan, 116
Jinan Military Region, 158
Jingxi, 170
Joffe, Ellis, 182
Johnson, Lyndon B., 30

Kenny, Henry, 134
Khau Bo Son, 105, 106
Khau Khao Son, 95, 105
Khau Lau Son, 105, 106
Khau Ma Son, 95, 105, 106
Khau Tang Son, 105, 106
Khmer Rouge, 5, 7, 36, 37, 56, 121, 125, 140, 144–45, 149, 197, 200, 201, 203, 209, 218
Khon Pa Bridge, 107
Khoo, Nicholas, 3, 205
Kim Il Sung, 16, 18

Korean War, 1, 19, 57, 68, 90, 114, 118, 184, 214, 219, 233 (n. 87); Le Duan's criticism of China's participation in, 18; literature of, 180–81; movies of, 188, 248 (n. 105); PLA war experience in, 83–84, 125–26, 146
Koulinshan, 146, 147, 153, 173
Kunming Military Region, 11, 56, 71, 74, 76, 101, 103, 125, 149, 180, 242 (n. 3)
Ky Cung River, 106, 107, 111, 112

Lang Son, 56, 58, 59, 71, 72, 74, 90, 91, 95, 96, 97, 98, 99, 100, 104–8, 109, 110, 111, 112, 113, 114, 118, 127, 131, 132, 136, 143, 147, 239 (n. 33), 241 (n. 93)
Lanzhou Military Region, 159
Lao Cai, 56, 71, 75, 86, 90, 99, 100, 101, 104, 108, 111, 114, 127, 132, 236 (nn. 55, 65)
Laos, 21, 29, 36, 41, 56, 59
Laoshan, 149–50, 183, 184–85, 187, 189, 190, 199, 206, 210, 245 (n. 137); civilian support at, 173; PAVN at, 144, 146, 153–55, 161–63; PLA operation at, 141, 142, 149, 151, 152–53, 156–61, 164–68, 178, 188, 222 (n. 21); Vietnamese losses at, 152, 153, 156, 243–44 (n. 69)
Le Duan, 27, 33, 36, 110, 199, 200, 213; blames U.S. bombing on China, 31, 225 (n. 77); on China's aid to DRV, 22–23, 37; on China's protracted war advice, 19; on China's Soviet policy, 25, 37; on China's U.S. policy, 37; and criticism of China's role at Geneva Conference, 17–19, 223 (n. 19); on Deng Xiaoping, 34–35; on Nixon's visit to China, 32, 225 (n. 77)
Le Duc Anh, 204
Lee Kuan Yew, 44
Le Ngoc Hien, 154, 155
Le Thanh Nhgi, 36
Le Trong Tan, 154
Le Uy Mat, 155
Lewis, John Wilson, 3
Liao Xilong, 153
Li Danhui, 20
Lin Biao, 54, 57, 70, 73, 127
Li Peng, 204
Liu Bocheng, 70
Liu Changyi, 73
Li Xiannian, 37, 47, 49, 53, 184, 229 (n. 98)
Longzhou, 170
Luojiaping Mountain, 146, 153
Luoyang, 75, 177

Ma'anshan, 146
Maguan, 175

Malaysia, 36
Malipo, 146, 175
Mao Zedong, 6, 13, 18, 19, 21, 33, 44, 45, 55, 58, 62, 64, 72, 90, 145, 169, 202; China's rapprochement with United States, 33; on China's role at Geneva Conference, 18; and Chinese assistance for DRV, 23, 28, 224 (n. 55); criticism of Soviet détente policy, 19, 20; criticism of Soviet great-nation chauvinism, 38; on Deng Xiaoping, 8, 34; and Ho Chi Minh, 15, 207, 213; and "horizontal line" strategy, 48, 53, 65; meets with Le Duan (1975), 36; meets with Miyamoto Kenji (1966), 28; military thinking of, 68–69, 89, 118, 126; "people's war" doctrine of, 86, 87, 88, 125, 170; on political mobilization, 80; and Sino-Soviet dispute, 24, 224 (n. 68); "Three Worlds" theory, 34–35; on U.S. war escalation in Vietnam, 22; visits Moscow (1950), 15–16
MB-84 Campaign Plan, 153–55
Mengla, 56
Miyamoto Kenji, 28
Mondale, Walter, 60, 121–22
Moscow, 15, 34, 196, 199, 201
Moung Khang, 100
Mo Wenhua, 81

Na La, 154, 155, 162
Nanjing Military Region, 72, 229 (n. 101)
Nanning, 89, 90, 107, 113, 114
Nansha (Spratly) Islands, 200, 225 (n. 101)
Napo, 170
National Liberation Front (NLF), 21, 26
NATO, 51, 136
Nazi Germany, 13
Ngo Dien Diem, 19
Ngoi Bo River, 102
Nguyen, Lien Hang T., 35
Nguyen Co Thach, 199, 201, 202, 204, 209
Nguyen Duy Trinh, 23
Nguyen Van Thieu, 36
Nguyen Vin Linh, 199, 200, 202–4, 205, 209
Nguyen Xuan Khan, 109
Nhi Thanh Dong, 107, 119
Nie Rongzhen, 12, 53, 59
Nixon, Richard, 30, 48; China visit, 31
Novotny, Antonin, 24

Obaturov, Gennadi I., 110
O'Dowd, Edward C., 3, 107, 237 (n. 116), 242 (n. 125)
Operation Bolo, 239 (n. 54)
Operation Bullet Shot, 31

Operation Linebacker, 29, 31
Operation Rolling Thunder, 22, 30

Pa Vai Son, 105, 106
Pakistani air force, 83–84, 233 (n. 81)
Panlong River, 149, 154. *See also* Song Lo River
Paris Peace Conference (1991), 206
Pearl Harbor, 13
Peng Dehuai, 54, 70
People's Army of Vietnam (PANV), 18, 90, 92, 95, 96, 97, 104, 122, 134, 146, 160, 232 (n. 57), 235 (n. 29), 239 (n. 44); in Cambodia, 110, 125, 237 (n. 116); Capital Military Region, 111; casualties claimed by China, 118, 161, 238 (n. 15); doctrine and tactics of, 131–34; General Staff of, 109, 110, 111, 154; Guang Ninh Special Zone of, 143; Military District 1 of, 95, 144, 155; Military District 2 of, 144, 152, 154, 163; militia, 1, 93, 94, 95, 100, 111, 118, 128, 133, 135; politic bureau, 163; in war against China (1979), 94–97, 99, 100–111, 113–14, 137, 237 (n. 116), 238 (n. 132), 241 (n. 99); in war against China (1980s), 147–48, 149, 154, 155–56
—corps units: 8th Army Corps, 143; 5th Army Corps of, 111, 143; 1st Army Corps of, 107; 2nd Army Corps of, 110, 144; 6th Army Corps of, 111, 143; 3rd Army Corps of, 144
—division units: 10th Division, 155; 3rd Division, 95, 97, 99, 106, 107, 108, 109, 110, 111, 235 (n. 49), 236 (n. 53); 308th Division, 110; 311th Division, 144; 355th Division, 111; 356th Division, 111, 154; 345th Division, 100, 101, 102–3, 111, 144; 347th Division, 144; 346th Division, 93, 95, 113, 144, 234 (n. 8); 304th Division, 110, 144; 314th Division, 111, 144; 390th Division, 110; 395th Division, 144; 306th Division, 110, 144; 316th Division, 99, 100–101, 103–4, 111, 144, 155; 313th Division, 111, 144, 147, 151, 154, 243 (n. 46); 337th Division, 96, 144; 338th Division, 96, 113, 238 (n. 133); 312th Division, 110, 114, 155; 320th Division, 144, 237 (n. 116); 328th Division, 144; 325th Division, 110, 144; 327th Division, 96, 106, 107, 108, 110, 144, 147; 326th Division, 111; 323rd Division, 144; 31st Division, 144; 242nd Division, 144
People's Liberation Army (PLA), 1, 2, 4, 7, 17, 19, 251 (n. 7); and aid-the-front work, 87, 115, 129, 172; and border conflict (1980–1983), 121, 142, 144, 146–48, 168; and bud-

get reduction, 176–77; and casualties of, 118–19, 161; and civilian support, 67, 89, 138, 166; combat effectiveness, 5, 9, 57, 119, 167, 219; under Deng Xiaoping, 6, 8, 44, 54–55, 66, 58, 215; doctrines, 68–69; and economic construction, 181–82; factionalism in, 57–58, 66, 70, 215, 229 (nn. 101, 104); First Field Army, 70, 231 (n. 10); Fourth Field Army, 70, 72; General Logistics Department (GLD), 11, 43, 78, 79–80; General Political Department of (GPD), 11, 81, 84–85, 128, 228 (n. 86); General Staff of, 40, 41–43, 74, 103, 156, 160, 177, 178; and Laoshan Offensive Operation (1984), 149, 150, 151–53, 206; and lessons from 1979 war, 134–38, 216; media's coverage of, 186, 188, 189, 190; and minesweeping, 174–75, 250 (n. 77); morale of, 67, 69, 84, 89, 127–28, 130, 164, 184–85, 192; National Defense University of, 138; in 1979 war, 91–109, 112–14, 122, 139, 140, 235 (n. 42), 240 (n. 109), 241 (n. 113), 246 (n. 16); and planning and preparation, 71–72, 73–74, 75–80, 218; and political work, 11, 67, 69–70, 80–85, 89, 115, 127, 128–31, 139–40, 165, 219; public image of, 12, 180–82, 185, 189, 192; reform of, 5, 10, 145, 169, 176, 177–78, 179–80; and rotation of troops through Laoshan, 156, 157, 158–61, 250 (n. 51); Second Field Army, 70, 176; and Sino-Indian border war, 42, 57, 238 (n. 26); tactics of, 10, 126–27; on Soviet military, 50–51; Third Field Army, 70; on Vietnamese tactics, 131–32, 133; and Vietnam's war against America, 22, 23, 26, 28, 31, 32

—army/group army units: 11th Army, 75, 100, 101, 149, 153, 156, 158, 247 (n. 57); 50th Army, 75, 100, 104, 107; 55th Army, 71, 72, 78, 96, 97, 98, 99, 104, 108, 231 (n. 18); 54th Army, 75, 94, 104, 229 (n. 96), 231 (n. 25), 235 (n. 17), 244 (n. 95), 247 (n. 57); 1st Army, 11, 157–58, 162, 164, 165, 167, 222 (n. 21); 41st Army, 71, 72, 78, 91, 92, 93, 94; 42nd Army, 71, 72, 78, 94, 231 (n. 18); 47th Group Army, 159, 184; 46th Army, 158; 43rd Army, 11, 71, 72, 82, 83, 91, 92, 97, 104, 113, 180, 235 (n. 15), 244 (n. 95); 14th Army, 71, 74, 100, 101, 147, 149, 151, 153, 154, 156, 187, 232 (n. 72), 247 (n. 57); 67th Army, 158, 184; 13th Army/Group Army, 71, 74, 75, 78, 82, 100, 101, 102, 103, 159, 244 (n. 95), 247 (n. 57); 12th Army, 158; 20th Army, 113, 244 (n. 95), 247 (n. 57); 27th Group Army, 159, 184, 185, 187

—division units: 58th Division, 113; 1st Division, 158, 178, 179; 40th Division, 101, 153, 154, 236 (n. 65); 41st Division, 151, 154, 232 (n. 72); 44th Air Division, 83; 42nd Division, 147, 151, 232 (n. 72); 9th Artillery Division, 158; 150th Division, 113, 114, 130, 238 (n. 135); 149th Division, 100, 101, 103–4, 154, 247 (n. 57); 119th Division, 158; 165th Division, 96, 97, 105, 106; 161st Division, 104; 164th Division, 96, 97, 106, 111; 162nd Division, 130; 163rd Division, 79, 96, 97, 105, 107, 119, 235 (n. 32), 247 (n. 57); 138th Division, 158; 125th Division, 92, 94; 121st Division, 79, 92, 94; 124th Division, 92, 94, 240 (n. 63); 129th Division, 71, 91, 92; 122nd Division, 92, 93, 130, 188; 127th Division, 107, 126; 126th Division, 92, 94, 235 (n. 15); 123rd Division, 92, 126; 3rd Artillery Division, 158; 38th Division, 102; 31st Division, 153, 247 (n. 57); 39th Division, 101, 130; 37th Division, 102; 36th Division, 158; 12th Artillery Division, 158

People's Liberation Army Air Force (PLAAF), 5, 73, 74, 75, 78, 81, 83–84, 96, 135, 160–61, 177, 206; Kunming Military Region Air Force, 76; in war with Vietnam, 124–26

People's Liberation Army Navy (PLAN), 5, 32, 34, 74, 75, 83, 118, 225 (n. 81); Political Department of South Sea Fleet, 76

Pham Van Dong, 21, 37, 109, 204, 224 (n. 55)

Philippines, 36

Phnom Malai Mountain, 149

Phnom Penh, 37, 56, 109, 199

Phong Tho, 75, 90, 100, 112

Phu Hoa, 92, 94, 95

Pingmeng, 82, 93

Pingxiang, 77, 146

Pol Pot, 5, 36, 37

Qian Qichen, 195, 201–2, 249 (n. 6)

Qujing Prefecture, 88

Reagan, Ronald, 195, 249 (n. 17)

Red Army, 69, 73, 123

Red River, 100, 101

Red River Delta, 132

"Reform and opening up" (*gaige kaifang*), 7

Reiter, Dan, 207

Richardson, Sophie, 3, 37, 207

Rogachev, Igor Alexyevitch, 200

Romania, 112

Ross, Robert, 3

United States Army, 119, 179, 235 (n. 29); National Training Center, 179
United States Navy, 25, 60, 81

Vance, Cyrus, 60
Van Tien Dung, 109
Viet Minh, 17, 18, 113, 162, 223 (n. 23)
Vietnamese air force, 76, 84, 124–25, 139, 160, 239 (n. 50)
Vietnamese Communist Party (VCP), 15, 16, 17, 200, 206, 209, 213; Central Military Commission, 109; Fourth Plenary Session, 42; Politburo of, 37. *See also* Vietnamese Labor Party
Vietnamese Labor Party, 24. *See also* Indochinese Communist Party; Vietnamese Communist Party
Vietnam War, 5, 27, 34, 35, 46, 83, 113, 124, 172, 235 (n. 29). *See also* Second Indochina War
Vi Xuyen, 141, 152, 153, 163, 244–45 (n. 69)
Vogel, Ezra, 36, 47
Vo Nguyen Giap, 16, 17
Vo Van Kiet, 206
Vu Lap, 154, 155

Wang Bicheng, 56, 57, 74, 229 (n. 101), 231 (n. 28)
Wang Dongxing, 44, 45, 53, 227 (nn. 22, 28)
Wang Hai, 76
Wang Shangrong, 58
Warsaw Pact, 51, 136, 193
Wei Guoqing, 59, 229 (n. 103)
Wenshan, 158, 171, 173, 174, 175
Westad, Odd Arne, 212
Womack, Brantly, 3, 199, 207, 210,
Woodcock, Leonard, 52–53
World War II, 13, 27, 64, 132, 178, 191
Wuhan Military Region, 56, 72, 75, 94, 229 (n. 96)
Wu Zhong, 94

Xi'an Music College, 183
Xinjiang Military Region, 224 (n. 95)
Xisha (Paracel) Islands, 34, 225 (n. 101)
Xu Liang, 183, 184
Xu Shiyou, 11, 44, 56, 57, 71–72, 73, 74, 77, 83, 94, 96, 105, 106, 112, 113, 114, 137
Xu Xiangqian, 57, 59, 229 (n. 104)

Yang Shangkun, 176, 182
Yang Yong, 58, 59, 229 (n. 104)
Ye Jianying, 44, 53, 139, 177, 229 (n. 98)
Yen Minh, 105, 152, 153
Youyi (Friendship) Pass, 41, 97
Yunnan, 10, 11, 42, 56, 59, 64, 75, 76, 80, 84, 85, 143, 169, 175, 181, 186, 192, 201, 231 (n. 28); mobilization of civilian support in, 85–86, 87, 88, 118, 173, 174, 232 (n. 74); PLA operation from, 74, 99, 103, 104, 119; and Sino-Vietnamese border conflict (1980s), 146–47, 149, 158; and war contributions, 170, 171–73, 191, 218
Yunnan Provincial Military District, 159, 206

Zhang Aiping, 57
Zhang Dewei, 203–4
Zhang Sheng, 57, 247 (nn. 46, 53)
Zhang Wannian, 126–27
Zhang Wenjin, 46, 60
Zhang Youxia, 145–46, 165
Zhang Zhen, 11, 43, 59, 78, 79, 86, 177, 178, 180
Zhenbao Island, 30
Zheyinshan, 150, 151, 152, 153, 160, 173
Zhou Deli, 42, 71, 72, 74, 75, 87, 131, 222 (n. 22), 223 (n. 35), 225 (n. 81)
Zhou Enlai, 17, 18, 34, 36, 57, 202, 223 (n. 35), 225 (nn. 76, 81)
Zhu De, 54
Zhu Qizhen, 51